Taxation in a Low-Income Economy

This volume contains a stimulating collection of analytical studies focusing on taxation in Mozambique. It tells a compelling story about tax systems in a low-income economy increasingly integrated into the world trading system, but very much dependent on foreign trade taxes and international development assistance.

Key issues covered include:

- A better understanding of the historical background of tax reforms in a representative African economy (Mozambique) along with an assessment of taxation performance in a comparative perspective.
- Insights into the practice and implications of tax policy, both from the perspective of the consumer and the firm level.
- Discussion of the existing institutional set up in which tax policy and its enforcement operate and analyses of current tax practices.
- Taxation themes at the border and at domestic level, which are typical for low-income economies, characterized by a high degree of reliance on foreign trade taxes.

This volume is meant as a guide for developing country government officials and professional aid practitioners as well as academics, researchers and tax policy analysts working in the development field. It will also be of interest to students of development with a special interest in public finance issues in poor countries and how to improve policy-effectiveness, including tax policy, in a developing country setting.

Channing Arndt is Professor of Economics at the University of Copenhagen in Denmark.

Finn Tarp is Professor of Development Economics at the University of Copenhagen in Denmark.

Routledge Studies in Development Economics

Taxation in a Low-Income Economy

The Case of Mozambique

Edited by
Channing Arndt and Finn Tarp

Routledge
Taylor & Francis Group

LONDON AND NEW YORK

First published 2009
by Routledge
2 Park Square, Milton Park, Abingdon, Oxon OX14 4RN

Simultaneously published in the USA and Canada
by Routledge
711 Third Avenue, New York, NY 10017

Routledge is an imprint of the Taylor & Francis Group, an informa business

Typeset in Times New Roman by
Taylor & Francis Books

First issued in paperback in 2013

British Library Cataloguing in Publication Data
A catalogue record for this book is available from the British Library

Library of Congress Cataloging in Publication Data
Arndt, Channing.
    Taxation in a low-income economy : the case of Mozambique /
Channing Arndt & Finn Tarp.
    p. cm.
    Simultaneously published in the USA and Canada.
    1. Tax administration and procedure–Mozambique. 2. Taxation–
Econometric models. 3. Tax evasion–Mozambique. 4. Value-added tax–
Law and legislation–Mozambique. 5. Fiscal policy–Mozambique. 6.
Taxation–Law and legislation–Developing countries. I. Tarp, Finn, 1951-
II. Title.
    KSX3550.A76 2009
    343.67904–dc22   2008035910

ISBN: 978-0-415-74652-6 (pbk)
ISBN: 978-0-415-48053-6 (hbk)
ISBN: 978-0-203-88197-2 (ebk)

Contents

List of illustrations

List of tables

Contributors

Andrea Alfieri is a development economist currently working as an independent consultant in Mozambique. His areas of interest include trade, regional integration and rural development. At the time of writing, he was working as trade policy advisor at the Ministry of Trade of Mozambique and previously as ODI fellow at the Ministry of Agriculture.

Channing Arndt is Professor at the Department of Economics at the University of Copenhagen. His publications cover a range of topics, including poverty measurement, the macroeconomic implications of the HIV/AIDS pandemic, efficient sampling, validation and parameterization of computable general equilibrium models, agricultural productivity growth and demand systems estimation. Channing Arndt was resident in Mozambique from 2003–8, where from 2005 he coordinated the institutional capacity building support project in the National Directorate for Studies and Policy Analysis within the Ministry of Planning and Development. He also has substantial field experience from Morocco and South Africa and various other developing countries.

Aurélio J. Bucuane is a Mozambican economist. In 2006 he obtained the *licenciatura* degree in economics (with distinction) from the Eduardo Mondlane University in Maputo. From 2006 to 2007 he worked as a research economist in the Ministry of Planning and Development.

Bruce Byiers is a development economist currently working towards a PhD at the University of Sussex, UK. His research interests are in private sector development and its relation to the business environment, in particular in terms of enterprise behaviour and performance, informality and tax policy and its implementation. He previously worked as an ODI fellow in the Mozambican Ministry of Planning and Finance and as a consultant in the same ministry.

Xavier Cirera is currently a Research Fellow at the Institute of Development Studies, University of Sussex. He was an advisor on trade research issues at the National Directorate of Studies and Policy Analysis, Ministry of Planning and Development, Mozambique. He also worked as an ODI fellow at the Ministry of Industry and Trade in Mozambique and obtained his PhD in Economics from the University of Sussex.

Shakill Hassan is a researcher and advisor in the technical assistance project for the National Directorate of Studies and Policy Analysis in the Ministry of Planning and Development, Mozambique. He is a graduate of the University of Cape Town, the London School of Economics and the University of Cambridge, and he holds a PhD from the School of Economics, University of Cape Town (South Africa), where he is currently a Senior Lecturer.

Sam Jones is an economist currently working at the University of Copenhagen, Development Economics Research Group. Previously he spent four years in the Ministry of Planning and Development in Mozambique, working in the research unit as well as the Macroeconomic Projections Department. Areas of current work include the relationship between aid and growth, the natural resources curse and labour markets.

Alice Kuegler currently works in the Chief Economist's Office at the World Bank. Previously, she was working for the Central Revenue Authority (Ministry of Finance) of Mozambique as an ODI fellow. She has been involved in projects on microfinance for Oxford Policy Management and was a research assistant at the Centre for the Study of African Economies at the University of Oxford.

Christen McCool is a former employee of the International Food Policy Research Institute. She graduated from Swarthmore College with a degree in Economics in 2002 and from Sussex University with a Master's in International Economics in 2004.

Simon McCoy worked as an ODI fellow Economist in the General Directorate of Taxation of Mozambique (Ministry of Finance) from 2004 to 2006. Previously, he worked as a financial analyst and equity fund manager for an American investment bank. He currently works as Senior Economist in Vietnam for the University of Copenhagen.

Peter Mulder is an assistant professor at the Department of Spatial Economics at VU University Amsterdam, the Netherlands. From 2005 to 2007 he worked in Mozambique as a research economist in the Ministry of Planning and Development and the Ministry of Energy.

Virgulino Nhate is a Mozambican economist working in the Ministry of Planning and Development of Mozambique. His interests include poverty and inequality analysis as well as intra-household resource allocation. He holds a teaching position at the Eduardo Mondlane University of Mozambique.

Dieter Orlowski is an economist and public finance specialist, currently advising the Mozambican Ministries of Finance and of Planning and Development on improving the links between planning and budgeting in a medium-term perspective. His interest in tax issues arose from the observed difficulties in fitting donor-funded projects into the budget.

Eugenio Maria Paulo is a Mozambican economist. After spending some years working at the National Directorate of Studies and Policy Analysis at the Ministry of Planning and Development, he recently joined the newly created research unit within the Ministry of Finance. Previously he worked at the National Directorate of Treasury, Ministry of Finance.

Sherman Robinson is Professor of Economics at the University of Sussex and has a joint appointment as a research fellow at the Institute of Development Studies (IDS). He is an internationally recognized specialist in international trade, macroeconomic policy, income distribution, poverty, and policy-oriented general equilibrium modelling. He worked at the International Food Policy Research Institute (IFPRI) from 1993 to 2004 as Director of the Trade and Macroeconomics Division (1993–2003) and Institute Fellow (2003–4). Before joining IFPRI, he was a Professor in the Department of Agricultural and Resource Economics at the University of California, Berkeley.

Christoffer Sonne-Schmidt has been a research assistant at the Development Economics Research Group at the University of Copenhagen since 2005. Within this period he has been assigned to research projects in the Ministry of Planning and Development in Mozambique. His research is focused on applied microeconometrics in developing countries, especially related to economic behaviour of individuals and households in Mozambique.

Finn Tarp is Professor of Development Economics at the Department of Economics at the University of Copenhagen. He is also the Coordinator of the Copenhagen-based Development Economics Research Group (DERG). He has some 30 years of experience in academic and applied development economics research and teaching. His field experience covers numerous countries across Africa and the developing world more generally, including longer-term assignments in Swaziland, Mozambique and Vietnam.

James Thurlow is a research fellow at the University of Copenhagen and at the International Food Policy Research Institute in Washington, DC. His work focuses on understanding the role of agriculture and rural/urban linkages in the development process, and more specifically on identifying strategies for growth and poverty reduction in Sub-Saharan Africa.

João E. Van Dunem is an Angolan economist. He has worked as a research assistant in the Development Economics Research Group at the University of Copenhagen. Before that, he held positions in the Ministry of Finance of Mozambique, where he served from 2002 to 2004 as ODI fellow in the Customs General Directorate and later in the Ministry of Planning and Development, working as a research economist.

Preface

This volume was developed as an integral part of the activities of an institutional capacity building project funded by the Danish Ministry of Foreign Affairs (Danida), which supported the National Directorate of Economic Studies and Policy Analysis (DNEAP) in the Ministry of Planning and Development (MPD) of Mozambique. The group of 19 authors aspire to tell a compelling story about taxation in a low-income economy increasingly integrated into the world trading system. We provide an overview of past and ongoing experiences with tax reforms; give a frank assessment of the practice of tax policy; and point to a host of promising (but not mutually exclusive) avenues for further improvement in the Mozambican tax system. We believe these insights have wide applicability in other African countries; and throughout we demonstrate how existing economic analytical tools can help the academic and practitioner generate policy relevant insights that can help improve economic policy making.

Tax policy in less-developed countries merits the utmost interest. As governments seek to mobilize the needed resources to finance basic public expenditures, maintain macroeconomic stability and promote economic and social development, the ability to design effective tax systems becomes indispensable. Effectiveness, in conjunction with efficiency and equity, are desirable criteria for the tax system; but fulfilling these goals while pursuing macroeconomic stabilization, economic transformation and poverty alleviation is far from easy. Many trade-offs are inherent and critical, and in most developing countries tax policy options are invariably constrained by the structure of the economy, existing administrative capacity, and the complexity of the economic and political environment more generally. Consequently, actual tax systems in low-income economies regularly find themselves disconnected from guidelines emerging from optimal taxation theory.

In the absence of clear-cut links between reality and prescriptions from theory, country-specific studies are indispensable to the accumulation of knowledge for practical improvement of tax systems in developing country contexts. The present volume was written with this overall aim in mind, focusing on the characteristics and challenges of Mozambique, a representative poor African country where about 50 per cent of government revenue comes from taxes (tariffs, value added and assorted consumption taxes) levied at the border. Moreover, Mozambique is heavily dependent on the influx of foreign aid, so development of the domestic tax system will be of critical importance in the years to come.

We hope that this book will serve as a useful guide and reference for developing country government officials and professional aid practitioners as well as academics, researchers and tax policy analysts working in the development field.

Acknowledgements

Our intention of putting this book together developed during the first half of 2004 when the so-called fiscal policy and tax incidence project funded by Danida in Mozambique got underway. The project was originally set up in the National Directorate of Planning and Budget (DNPO) of the Ministry of Planning and Finance (MPF); and the Development Economics Research Group (DERG) of the University of Copenhagen (coordinated by Professor Finn Tarp) was requested to provide technical assistance together with the University of Sussex and international staff in the MPF, including in particular Professor Channing Arndt (then Purdue University).

Institutional reorganization of the Government of Mozambique (GoM) was begun after the new President took office in early 2005, and the project became located in the Direcção Nacional de Estudos e Análise de Políticas (National Directorate of Economic Studies and Policy Analysis) (DNEAP) of the Ministério de Planificação e Desenvolvimento (Ministry of Planning and Development) (MPD) alongside Swiss and Swedish institutional capacity building support.

The National Directors of the project, initially Dr José Sulemane, subsequently Mr Adriano Ubisse and finally Dr Antonio Sousa Cruz, have throughout supported our efforts in an effective manner, and without their expert guidance and friendly advice this book would never have come into existence. We hope that this book bears witness that we did listen to their questions and concerns and have tried to respond to them.

The group of 19 authors is truly international, and numerous meetings and seminars were part of preparing the 17 chapters of this book. Our work has benefited from being presented on countless occasions across the developing and developed world alike. We are grateful to the many participants in seminars in Mozambique, elsewhere in Africa, in the Nordic countries and in the UK and the USA for advice and suggestions.

Special thanks are also due to the following Danida staff: Thomas Thomsen, Lis Rosenholm, Niels Richter, Peter Engbo Rasmussen and Johnny Flentø. We appreciate their keen interest and encouragement and the financial support from Danida. We hope that this output of our joint efforts meets their expectations.

The original submission of our manuscript to Routledge was handled by Senior Commissioning Editor Terry Clague and his Senior Assistant Sarah Hastings. When they left for other duties Thomas Sutton and Beth Lewis took over their respective roles in expert fashion. For this we are most thankful, and the same goes for their consistent encouragement and support in producing this volume.

Finally, we would like to acknowledge the first rate work of Production Editor Paola Celli and the excellent assistance provided by Anna Folke Larsen. They helped put what was at one point a rather wieldy set of papers together in a coherent, stimulating and appealing book.

It is, finally, our hope that all of those mentioned will understand how grateful we are for their continued support. We trust they will agree that the quality of this volume improved due to their advice and interest. However, responsibility for any remaining errors of fact or judgement lies with the individual chapter authors and the editors.

Channing Arndt and Finn Tarp
Copenhagen, August 2008

Acronyms and abbreviations

AGOA	African Growth and Opportunity Act
ATM	Central Revenue Authority (Autoridade Tributária de Moçambique)
BLNS	Botswana, Lesotho, Namibia and Swaziland
CEPII	Centre d'Etudes Prospectives et d'Informations Internationales
CES	Constant Elasticity of Substitution
CET	Constant Elasticity of Transformation
CGE	Computable General Equilibrium
CI	Confidence Intervals
CIF	Cost Insurance Freight
COMESA	Common Market for Eastern and Southern Africa
CPI	Consumer Price Index
CRA	Central Revenue Authority
CTA	Confederação das Associações Económicas de Moçambique
CUT	Conta Única de Tesouro
CV	Compensating Variation
CVRD	Companhia Vale do Rio Doce
DANIDA	Danish International Development Assistance (Denmark)
DERG	Development Economics Research Group
DfID	Department for International Development (British)
DGA	Direcção Geral das Alfândegas
DGI	Direcção Geral da Administração Tributária dos Impostos
DNCP	Direcção Nacional de Contabilidade Pública
DNEAP	National Directorate of Economic Studies and Policy Analysis
DNIA	Direcção Nacional de Impostos e Auditoria
DNPO	National Directorate of Planning and Budget
DU	Documento Único
EAC	East Africa Community
ECA	Economic Commission for Africa
EdM	Electricidade de Moçambique
EGFE	Estatuto Geral dos Funcionarios do Estado
EPA	Economic Partnership Agreement
ERPT	Exchange Rate Pass-through
ESAF	Enhanced Structural Adjustment Facility

EU	European Union
FAO	Food and Agricultural Organization of the United Nations
FDI	Foreign Direct Investment
FE	Fixed Effects
FIAS	Foreign Investment Advisory Service
FOB	Free On Border
FP	Financial Programming
FTA	Free Trade Area
GATT	General Agreement on Tariffs and Trade
GDP	Gross Domestic Product
GEST	Gabinete de Estudos
GLS	Generalized Least Square
GNI	Gross National Income
GoM	Government of Mozambique
GTAP	Global Trade Analysis Project
HCB	Cahora Bassa Hydro Dam
HDI	Human Development Index
HIPC	Highly Indebted Poor Countries
HS	Harmonized System
IAF	National Household Survey (Inquérito aos Agregados Familiares)
ICA	Investment Climate Assessment
IEA	International Energy Agency
IFC	International Finance Corporation
IFPRI	International Food Policy Research Institute
IMF	International Monetary Fund
INE	National Institute of Statistics (Instituto Nacional de Estatística)
IPC	Investment Promotion Centre (Centro de Promoção de Investimentos)
IRPC	Corporate Income Tax (Imposto sobre o Rendimento das Pessoas Colectivas)
IRPS	Individual Income Tax (Imposto sobre o Rendimento de Pessoas Singulares)
IVA	Value Added Tax (Imposto sobre o Valor Acrescentado)
KISS	Keep It Sophisticatedly Simple
KU	University of Copenhagen
LDC	Least Developed Country
LEAP	Long-range Energy Alternatives Planning System
LM	Lagrangian Multiplier
LOP	The Law of One Price
LSDV	Least Squares Dummy Variables
LTU	Large Taxpayer Unit
METR	Marginal Effective Tax Rate
MFN	Most-Favoured Nation
MIGA	Multilateral Investment Guarantee Agency

MPD	Ministry of Planning and Development
MPF	Ministry of Planning and Finance
MTEF	Medium Term Expenditure Framework (Cenário de Despesas de Médio Prazo)
Mts	Meticais
MW	Megawatt
NER	National Electricity Regulator
NUIT	Individual Taxpayer Identification Number (Número Único de Identificação Tributária)
OECD	Organization for Economic Cooperation and Development
OLS	Ordinary Least Squares
PARPA	Poverty Reduction Strategy Paper (Plano de Acção para a Redução da Pobreza Absoluta), also abbreviated as PRSP
PCSE	Prais–Winsten Panel-corrected Standard Errors
PRE	Economic Rehabilitation Programme (Programa de Reabilitação Económica)
PRGF	Poverty Reduction and Growth Facilities
PRSP	Poverty Reduction Strategy Paper
PSI	Pre-shipment Inspection
PTM	Pricing to Market
RE	Random Effects
RENA	Rede Electrónica Nacional das Alfândegas
ROW	Rest of the World
SACU	Southern African Customs Union
SADC	Southern African Development Community
SAM	Social Accounting Matrix
SAP	Structural Adjustment Programme
SECO	State Secretariat for Economic Affairs (Switzerland)
SICR	Solução Informática para Gestão da Cobrança das Receitas
SIMA	Agricultural Market Information System (Sistema Integrado de Monitoria Agrícola)
SISTAFE	Sistema de Administração Financeira do Estado
SUR	Seemingly Unrelated Regression
TDCA	Trade, Development and Cooperation Agreement
TIMS	Trade Information Management System
TRQ	Tariff Rate Quotas
TSCS	Time-series and Cross-section
UNDP	United Nations Development Programme
UTRA	Unit for Restructuring Customs (Unidade Técnica de Reestruturação das Alfândegas)
VAT	Value Added Tax
VSAT	Very Small Aperture Terminal
WCO	World Customs Organization
WTO	World Trade Organization
ZFI	Industrial Processing Zone (Zonas Francas Industriais)

1 Introduction and overview

Channing Arndt, Sam Jones, Finn Tarp and João E. Van Dunem

1 Tax policy matters for development

Tax policy in less-developed countries merits utmost interest. As governments seek to mobilize requisite resources to finance basic public expenditures and promote economic and social development, the ability to design effective tax systems becomes indispensable. Effectiveness, in conjunction with efficiency and equity, is perceived as a desirable criterion. But fulfilling these goals is far from easy. Many trade-offs are inherent and critical, and in most developing countries tax policy options are invariably constrained by the structure of the economy and administrative capacity. Wealthier taxpayers are likely to try to avert tax reforms seen as prejudicial to them. On top of this, tax systems in developing countries are often unduly complicated, attempting to meet too many objectives, let alone riddled with exceptions and hence often beyond the capabilities of tax authorities to administer. All combined, these factors pose a potentially serious risk to the government's capacity to broaden the tax base and, ultimately, generate much-needed revenue.

A rather different reason why tax policy in less-developed economies deserves consideration concerns the pursuit of macroeconomic stabilization. Unless reasonably stable macroeconomic conditions are put in place, developing countries will have a hard time finding their way onto a path of sustained economic progress. In recent times, many of these countries have been confronted with growing fiscal deficits, as a corollary of unexpected negative external shocks blended with over-ambitious development programmes. In the face of rising debt burdens, declining commodity prices and ever-increasing trade imbalances, commitment to fiscal austerity appeared as a fundamental priority of macroeconomic policy. Sadly, in a very large number of cases, fiscal retrenchment to obtain budgetary balance entailed substantial cuts in government expenditure, often with adversely severe implications for social services offered to a vulnerable segment of the population. Strengthening tax systems can help not only to reduce the savings gap but also to alleviate the inherent costs of the adjustment process in developing countries.

Pursuing macro-stability is meant to create a more predictable basis for making decisions. It would be a mistake, nonetheless, to overlook the fact that in most developing countries the scope for economic stabilization via monetary and exchange rate policies is severely hampered by local circumstances. Well-organized and locally controlled money markets are frequently lacking, thus constraining the ability of governments to control monetary policy instruments. To give just one example, many financial institutions in less-developed countries happen to be simply overseas branches of private banks in developed countries. In addition, one must be mindful of exacerbating problems of currency substitution (cases where the local currency can be replaced by a foreign currency), openness of the economy (e.g. pegging of local currency against a foreign one) and an absence of transparency in credit markets with regard to, say, the disclosure of the quality of loan portfolios. The joint contribution of these aspects circumscribes the use of monetary and exchange rate policies, while making fiscal policy a very appealing and unique developmental policy instrument.

Tax policy in less-developed countries has also, in a large number of cases, incorporated fiscal concessions and incentives to attract foreign investment. Most governments in those countries tend to offer all sorts of favourable terms to foreign enterprises (very often large transnational corporations), including long periods of tax exemption, generous investment depreciation allowances, special tax write-offs, tax credits and so forth. Under such circumstances, the capacity of governments to collect revenue from these large foreign enterprises is thwarted. Given some discomfort about its real benefits, it is hardly surprising that the use of this particular policy has in some ways produced an ongoing controversial debate concerning the desirability of special tax treatments for foreign firms. When dealing with poor countries, accordingly, there is very little doubt that the formulation of a sound tax policy can make a huge difference in several important respects. It is intimately connected to their macroeconomic setting and so can be a powerful tool to influence their economic development.

2   Rationale for a tailored tax policy: the case of Mozambique

Mozambique is one of the poorest and most aid-dependent countries in the world. In 2004, this Sub-Saharan African country located in the south eastern part of the continent achieved an overall ranking of tenth from bottom in the Human Development Index (HDI), marginally outperformed by the conflict-afflicted Democratic Republic of Congo. Incidentally, none of its neighbours, including Zimbabwe, finished the year with a lower human development rank (UNDP 2006). Despite some recent progress, official estimates of poverty are high. On the basis of a 2002–3 national household survey, indicators suggest that 54.1 per cent of the population is not able to satisfy basic physical needs (including food, clothing and shelter).[1] Meanwhile, if we merely restrict our attention to the rural areas, where approximately 70 per cent of the population live, the picture becomes gloomier, with 55.3 per cent of the population believed to live below the poverty line.

The challenge to provide essential social services, primarily to the poor, is tremendous. Most basic social services, such as health care and education, are paid out of public funds. The country is currently highly dependent on foreign aid inflows, with approximately half of the national state budget being financed externally by means of grants and concession loans. To overcome both underdevelopment and dependency, a clear definition of long-term and interim objectives of various policies to be framed, including tax policy, is of critical importance. To be sure, reconciling the objectives of stabilization with high levels of public spending on essential services will require a strengthened effort from taxation in the coming decade. Also, local circumstances tell us that, to a considerable extent, the policy constraints discussed in the preceding section are prominent. For these reasons, tax policy in Mozambique must be viewed as a way to ease those constraints and enhance the government capacity to both finance the expansion of social services and redress internal and external imbalances.

Mozambique is not exempt from the tax policy challenges seen previously. These are standard among less-developed economies. But, like any low-income country, it too has special characteristics. It varies from other poor countries in several features such as size, history, natural resource endowments and even in the exact economic structure or capacity to administer taxes. Given the idiosyncratic nature and complexity of the economic and political environment, the tax policy space will tend to be dictated with a view to integrating country-specific circumstances. In more general terms, thus, it may well be the case that actual tax systems in low-income economies find themselves systematically disconnected from guides emerging from optimal taxation theory. In the absence of a clear-cut prescription from optimal taxation theory, country-specific studies turn out to be indispensable. They can serve the purpose of providing practical answers to questions where taxation theory cannot provide definitive advice. This book was put together with this intention in mind.

With tax data becoming more and more accessible, the formulation of the best feasible tax policy can benefit from in-depth country approaches that are able to evaluate taxation choices and the potential impact of changes to the statutory tax system. Headway in accessibility to reliable data has been made in Mozambique over the last few years and this development has made possible the variety of studies available in this book. The book contains four core parts. Part I begins by providing a better understanding of the historical background of tax reforms in Mozambique and offers insights into the practice and implications of tax policy, at the level of both the consumer and the enterprise. Part I also takes seriously the issue of taxation performance in Mozambique from a comparative perspective, attempting to draw some lessons from the taxation effort on the basis of international evidence. In Part II, selected issues related to the institutional set-up where tax policy operates are brought to the forefront. Finally, Parts III and IV address selective taxation themes at the border and at the internal level, respectively, and we document in the Annex an up-to-date Social Accounting Matrix (SAM) dataset for Mozambique.

3 Background and context

The first step in the analysis of tax policy in Mozambique is to provide a retrospective overview of the successive rounds of tax reform. Chapter 2 (Byiers) takes a brief look at the principal tax reforms in Mozambique since independence in 1975. It gives a preliminary analysis by drawing lessons from the tax reform experience and revenue behaviour over the past 30 years or so. In particular, Byiers considers the fiscal impact of recent tax reforms and arrives at the conclusion that those were insufficient by themselves to encourage sustained increases in public revenue, in spite of sporadic gains over time in revenue-to-GDP ratios.

As noted earlier, the principle of equity is traditionally viewed as a central criterion when attempting to design or evaluate tax systems. In developing countries, actual tax systems are often far from progressive. This necessarily motivates a reasonable amount of concern and demands appropriate consideration on a country-by-country basis. The purpose of Chapter 3 (Sonne-Schmidt) is to explicitly address incidence analysis in the Mozambican context. By making use of a countrywide household survey, the author employs a standard non-behavioural tax incidence methodology to investigate the progressivity of taxes. The author is able to demonstrate that there is scope in Mozambique for the tax system to be reformed in ways that would improve the welfare of poor households.

Household survey evidence is complemented, in Chapter 4 (Byiers), by a formal assessment of the application of tax policy and its impact at the firm level. Based on manufacturing enterprise survey evidence from 2002 and 2006, Byiers reports an inverted-U relationship between the size of a firm and its tax ratio, with firms at opposite ends of the firm-size spectrum experiencing a relatively low tax burden when compared to the ones located in the middle. What the analysis shows is that there is both revenue concentration and marked administrative pressure on mid-size firms, which also creates room for possible disincentive effects for firm growth. At the origin of this is tax policy action. This study is able to identify, nonetheless, other factors deemed important in explaining firm tax ratios. The empirical findings show, finally, that bribery and corruption play a more significant role than firm-size in explaining the practice of under-declaration of sales.

From policy at a micro level, the analysis evolves in Chapter 5 (Jones) with an evaluation of a cross-cutting issue. Standard optimal tax theory has very little to say with respect to the ideal overall tax level for an economy. So, Part I ends with an appraisal of the aggregate performance of the Mozambican tax system, judged against the international experiences of other developing countries. It is widely established that the taxation potential of a country depends, to a large extent, on factors like the income-per-capita level, the social, political and institutional setting, the importance of various types of economic activity and the industrial structure of the economy. The study in Chapter 5 builds upon an approach widely used in the 1960s and 1970s to establish the *appropriateness* of aggregate tax levels.[2] Specifically, Jones develops a cross-country panel dataset to investigate the hypothesis that taxation receipts in developing countries are constrained by relatively slow-moving institutional and structural factors. In line with previous scholarship, the author shows empirically the importance of these constraints for the volume of tax revenue governments are able to raise. Calibrated with Mozambican data, the model suggests that Mozambican taxation performance has not deviated significantly from its predicted levels.

4 Institutional framework and current practices

Against this background, Part II considers the institutional setting in which tax policy and its implementation take place. Tax administrations in developing countries are notoriously weak. Chapter 6 (McCoy and Van Dunem) discusses the institutional design of the tax-gathering branches of government and its ongoing transformation process. For reasons that mainly lie with their individual stage of reform process, there is an obvious need to proceed analytically, making a clear distinction between the customs authority (*Alfândegas*), being the department responsible for the collection of border taxes, and the department administrating internal taxes. At a time when a semi-autonomous revenue authority is being made fully operational, the authors present key insights with regard to fiscal administration, by using the 10-year-long experience with reform in customs as their basis of assessment. The chapter underscores the fundamental role of factors such as the political commitment and the institutional setting (notably in the area of internal incentives), if efficiency gains are ever to materialize.

The subsequent chapter, Chapter 7 (Orlowski), focuses on the current institutional relationship between donors and the Mozambican government in the sphere of donor-funded projects and their resulting fiscal obligations. There is a pattern in many low-income economies in which payment of indirect taxes resulting from donor-funded public works is guaranteed by the recipient governments, since most donors decline the payment imposed under normal conditions. Orlowski addresses this question, certainly of great relevance within the Mozambican context. Usually, to avoid the introduction of further exemptions, governments pay the tax levies from their own domestic resources. In principle, from the fiscal point of view, the adoption of this type of practice should be equivalent to the outcome with exemptions in place. The chapter shows that this model of government as taxpayer on one side and tax collector on the other leads, in practice, to under-budgeting of tax votes and growing arrears with contractors. Beyond diagnosis of the dilemma, the chapter proposes a solution that opens the way for donors to reconsider their 'no tax' rule.

Chapter 8 (Jones and Paulo) takes a detailed look at the fiscal modelling tools used in Mozambique. It argues that while there is substantial theoretical debate regarding different approaches, there is little concrete guidance for the policy-maker in low-income countries. As a result, the chapter presents a general evaluation framework for macro-fiscal models which is then applied to the specific case of interest. The authors document that the model used in Mozambique – essentially a financial programming tool with additional budgetary detail – has seen considerable improvements over recent years. Even so, one of the more fundamental challenges regards the management of the model and its effective input into policy-making. A broad conclusion is that the character and adequacy of quantitative models reflect deeper political economy influences on the management of macroeconomic and fiscal policy. Over the short to medium term there is scope for reasonable enhancements to the modelling approach, incorporating further attention to the behaviour of major tax lines.

The search for improved revenue forecasts is certainly an important element of the institutional framework. In Mozambique, some limitations to the fiscal forecast process exist, including uncertainties partly related to the national income accounts forecasts, considered to be a vital ingredient in the overall forecast process. Chapter 9 (Jones) suggests an analysis about the quality of public macroeconomic and revenue forecasts. Based on a unique dataset of outcome and forecast variables for Mozambique (1995–2005), this chapter shows that forecasts are persistently optimistic and have deteriorated for major variables over the period to date. In turn, Jones also shows that forecasts have not outperformed a relatively simple and naïve forecasting rule.

5 Taxation at the border

Chapters 10–13, corresponding to Part III, focus explicitly on tax policy issues at the border. Over the past two decades, Mozambique has proceeded with significant trade liberalization, seeking to deepen integration of its economy at regional and global levels. Under certain circumstances, economic integration may lead to a better allocation of resources and deliver welfare gains. An important dimension of economic integration is the extent to which price signals are transmitted correctly from one country to another. Chapter 10 (Cirera and Nhate) is an attempt to quantify the degree of price transmission from border to retail prices in Mozambique. The analysis uses data from the Customs authority to provide evidence at the micro or product-specific level on the determinants of consumer price changes. The principal finding here is that the exchange rate pass-through is high and symmetric (similar for appreciation and depreciation episodes). The results exposed in this chapter also demonstrate that other transmission elasticity estimates, resulting from changes in import unit values or trade taxes, tend to be small or statistically insignificant. Implicit in these results is the idea that distribution margins may be used to offset changes in import unit values and trade taxes.

Chapter 11 (Arndt and Van Dunem) is a study of a different, but no less pertinent, relationship. It examines the causal relationship between border tax rates and tax evasion, employing a methodology that aligns and compares (at the product level) bilateral trade flow data between Mozambique and its largest trade partner, South Africa. The results here show that high levels of taxation are associated with high levels of underreporting of import values and that tax rates have a strong and positive effect on tax evasion. The approach enables, at the same time, the detection of fraudulent classification of merchandise into lower-taxed product categories. Estimates of evasion point to slightly more than one unit of imports smuggled for every three units that enter the country officially. Moreover, simulations conducted in the same study suggest that formalization of trade, resulting from trade liberalization, softens but does not reverse the negative revenue impact. In light of previous examination of public services spending requirements, the policy implication of these results is that there is a need for a careful appraisal of alternative sources of taxation (i.e. domestic), along with sustained efforts to improve the efficiency of the tax administration. Major political and institutional responses to address the latter are provided in Chapter 6.

From a trade policy perspective, the government of Mozambique faces key strategic options. The question, today, is one of choosing among a spectrum of trade regimes, rather than a binary choice between autarky and free trade. More concretely, the problem at hand is whether to continue with the Southern Africa Development Community (SADC) trade protocol, leading to a free trade area in the region, move towards a customs union through Southern Africa Customs Union (SACU) or deepen the process of unilateral liberalization on a most-favoured nation basis for all trading partners. Chapter 12 (Alfieri and Cirera) addresses this fundamental issue by considering the likely impact of these alternative trade policy regimes on imports, prices, tax revenue and welfare. The empirical findings reveal that the Most-Favoured Nations (MFN) and SACU liberalization scenarios are welfare enhancing, as long as suitable adjustments are made to the revenue calculations to account for exemptions, fraud and revenue redistribution from the SACU revenue pool. Finally, Chapter 13 (Arndt and Tarp) seeks to pursue examination of the implications of trade policy reform by making use of a detailed computable general equilibrium (CGE) model applied to Mozambique. A special feature of the model is that it explicitly considers exemptions and evasion. Simulation results point to outcomes consistent with results in the previous chapter, with broad welfare gains resulting from trade reform (with the exception only of those agents who, at the very outset, enjoyed duty free importation).

6 Domestic taxation

In Part IV, attention is shifted to a wide range of issues related to domestic taxation. Chapter 14 (Hassan) draws on fundamentals of corporate finance to illustrate the effect of taxes on the cost of capital for Mozambican firms. More precisely, the chapter shows how Mozambican income taxes favour lending relative to equity investment by applying double taxation in the case of the latter. Removing the fiscal bias against equity investment would require either that dividend payments qualify as expenses when the firm computes its tax liability or, alternatively, that the dividends received are exempted from personal income tax.

So far, as in other parts of the world where they have been put in place, tax concessions and incentives have been largely designed to attract private business. The competition among developing countries for preferential tax treatment of foreign investment has seemingly triggered substantial benefits for large multinational firms. But quite often, in contrast, countries suffer large fiscal losses without commensurate gains in their domestic economy. Chapter 15 (Kuegler) undertakes a review of the trade-offs involved and provides an overview of the fiscal incentives granted by the Mozambican government (in particular to investments of large dimension), with a view to approximate the magnitude of foregone revenues. Her findings merit attention as potential gains from effective action are significant.

Building on the preceding assessment of special tax treatment of foreign firms, Chapter 16 (Bucuane and Mulder) explores in further detail the arguments in favour of a tax on electricity consumption by projects of large dimension, commonly known as mega-projects, and a tax on electricity production. The argument developed by Bucuane and Mulder starts from the presumption that mega-projects provide a good opportunity to extend the tax base in Mozambique, with beneficial consequences for public revenues and, in addition, compensation for deleterious effects caused by environmental and social externalities. The authors make a strong case for a tax on electricity production, showing that the burden of a tax on electricity production will mainly fall on neighbouring countries due to the large share of electricity generation earmarked for export. In any case, the regional electricity market provides ample space to increase electricity prices without compromising Mozambique's current comparative-advantage position in electricity production.

The wave of fiscal reforms seen lately in low-income economies has brought with it the introduction of value added tax (VAT). One particular feature of this type of tax concerns its broad-based nature, seeking to maximize revenue with relatively low distorting costs. There are many country-level questions concerning VAT, though, that are worthy of attention. Unfortunately, in most developing countries attempts to improve understanding of the potential benefits and costs associated with the adoption of this type of tax have been scarce. Chapter 17 (Arndt, Byiers, Robinson and Tarp), the final chapter of the domestic taxation section and, indeed, of this volume, addresses this frequently encountered gap. After reviewing the literature on VAT in less-developed countries and discussing its specific characteristics in Mozambique, the chapter applies a CGE model to the Mozambican economy to explore a set of VAT scenarios and to consider natural issues as diverse as incidence, the appropriate design, the interaction with other taxes and the ability to counterbalance adverse effects resulting from trade liberalization. Empirically, the VAT performs favourably relative to trade taxes on both equity and efficiency criteria.

7 The way ahead: challenges and opportunities

Mozambique has come a long way in carrying out reforms in its tax systems. As a rule, activation of tax reforms aims to achieve long-term (rather than short-term) objectives. One interesting analytical contribution made in this study has been to inform the reader about the relative merits of initiatives in taxation reform introduced over recent times. In spite of acknowledged advances in many respects, the story of Mozambican taxation reforms is marked by a systematic failure to deliver on one of its most central objectives: enhanced revenue as a share of GDP. Evidence of tax reform experiences in other low-income economies, reported elsewhere, corroborates results documented here.[3]

Evidence from Mozambique and internationally suggests that success in engaging in difficult internal reform lies mostly in the hands of the governments of low-income economies. This is, in no small measure, a result of the need to be sensitive to national circumstances in the formulation of a sound and effective tax system in low-income economies. Instead of a *one-size fits all* approach, tax policy must be tailored to economic, political and institutional factors. So, there can be no single model that meets the requirements of any given country and this is what inevitably provides motivation for in-depth country studies such as those included in this volume. By considering a case study of Mozambique, an important lesson is that there is significant scope for the Mozambican tax system to be reformed in ways that would enhance fairness and encourage higher responsiveness in tax revenues.

By identifying a range of policy opportunities that potentially can be seized, this volume aims to stimulate a more informed policy debate. One way to improve the effectiveness and equity of the tax system consists in eradicating the fiscal biases that seem to persist in the current system. For clarifying purposes, evidence documented in this volume indicates that the structure of corporate tax systems imposes a disproportionate tax burden on firms of mid-size, while benefiting small and large enterprises. They are either small enough to evade taxation, in the case of the former, or benefit from special tax incentive schemes, in the case of the latter. The bias in the tax system occurs in spite of nominal rate progressivity.

For the sake of augmenting tax revenue, it is important to encourage an expansion of tax bases so as to make them more inclusive, i.e. cover both small firms and firms of large dimension. The overall benefits of special treatment to large multinational corporations are by no means self-evident and remain the subject of controversy. Further, tax incentives appear to play only a marginal role in influencing investment decisions. In conformity with widely accepted principles of a good tax system, policy-makers in low-income economies should thus recognize here the potential for enlarging considerably the public purse. This scenario would demand, if chosen, greater improvements in tax administration and sensitive amendments to the prevailing fiscal benefits law.

Enlarging the sources from which tax is collected is feasible as well as desirable. To take just one other example, a simple policy proposal likely to further extend the tax base is the introduction of taxation in energy consumption by mega-projects or taxation in electricity production. In both instances, there seems to be a very strong case. At a somewhat different level, there are a few tax measures suggested in the volume for progressive tax reform, basically aiming at a change in the present tax structure of consumer items. The advantage of this possible avenue for reform is that it paves the way for a welfare-enhancing condition among lower-income households.

Lastly, taxes on international trade make up a non-negligible proportion of total government revenue. Due to this reliance on trade taxes, the country must cope with the fiscal challenge posed by trade liberalization. Evidence presented in this volume points to significant unfavourable effects on trade revenues as a result of continuing trade liberalization. In order to reduce exposure to volatility or shortfalls in revenue, diversification of taxation sources seems a correct policy strategy to follow. For that, as shown, Mozambique is not, by any means, devoid of options. In sum, capitalizing on many of the tax policy opportunities available could make a great deal of difference to the potency of the social contract and, ultimately, to improvements in public policy and development planning. It is our hope that some of the policy routes presented in this book may inspire and renew Mozambican efforts to shape future policy outcomes and inspire reforms that strike a proper balance between equity, efficiency and the need for revenue.

Notes

1 See government official figures in MPF *et al.* (2005).
2 For a very short description of the method, see, for instance, Tanzi and Zee (2000), who also provide references to previous studies.
3 See, for instance, Fjeldstad and Rakner (2003).

Part I
Background and context

2 Taxation in retrospect

Bruce Byiers

1 Introduction

This chapter provides a review of tax policy reforms in Mozambique since national independence and an analysis of their revenue impacts. Despite a long history of tax reforms and the recent introduction of a number of significant new taxes in Mozambique, analysis in this area has been limited. This chapter attempts to address this with a view to increasing understanding of the tax system and providing a basis for discussion of future domestic tax policy options.

The importance of understanding tax policy and revenue issues in a resource-scarce country such as Mozambique is clear. At seventh from last in the Human Development Index (UNDP 2004), Mozambique is one of the poorest countries in the world, requiring continued high levels of expenditure on public goods such as health, education and infrastructure to help reduce poverty levels in the medium to long term. With approximately half of its state budget currently financed externally through grants or preferential loans (MPD 2005), any medium- to long-term vision of reducing Mozambican aid dependence requires that domestic resources be raised through taxation, a point which is explicitly acknowledged in the government's Poverty Reduction Strategy Paper (the Plano de Acção para a Redução da Pobreza Absoluta – PARPA), the latest version of which foresees revenues at 15.1 per cent of GDP in 2009 (GoM 2005a).

The problem of insufficient domestic resources is potentially further exacerbated by the current climate of proliferating regional and multilateral trade liberalization agreements which remove, or at best reduce, a major source of revenues for most developing countries. Mozambican participation in the Southern African Development Community (SADC) Trade Protocol has already brought a reduction in customs revenues, while ongoing discussions with the European Union regarding an Economic Partnership Agreement (EPA) and the possibility of joining the Southern African Customs Union (SACU) have the potential to further reduce trade revenues.

Nonetheless, the government's Five-Year Programme for 2005–9 highlights the importance of private-sector development and the need to create a favourable environment for investment and national enterprise (GoM 2005b). Raising domestic revenues whilst remaining faithful to this objective will therefore require a broader understanding of and capacity for analysis of the impact of tax reforms and the tax system in general.

The remainder of the chapter is organized as follows. Section 2 provides an overview of revenue performance from 1975 to 2005. Section 3 discusses the main tax reforms and their impacts in three periods: the immediate post-colonial independence period from 1975 to 1986; the structural adjustment period from 1987 to 1998; and the period covering the most recent wave of tax reforms from 1999 to 2005. Section 4 concludes the chapter by drawing some general lessons from the whole tax reform experience and from the analyses carried out.[1]

2 Overview of post-independence tax reforms and their impacts

2.1 Background

Since national independence, Mozambique has experienced a number of major economic and social upheavals. These resulted from independence itself, the subsequent adoption of a socialist agenda and centrally planned economy soon after, a debilitating 17-year internecine war and an economic crisis in the early 1980s. This was followed by membership of the Bretton Woods institutions and accompanying increased tolerance and eventual encouragement of private-sector activity, with the government abandoning the earlier socialist rhetoric to embrace the market economy and large-scale privatization in the late 1980s and early 1990s. The peace accords in 1992 also led to a massive in-flow of foreign aid money which continues to flow today. In addition to these 'man-made' events, instability was also brought by periodic flooding and droughts, most recently the massive flooding in 2000 and 2001. All of the above inevitably impacted on the economy, placing high and variable demands on public finances, requiring accompanying reforms to the fiscal system at each stage. As government preferences and priorities altered, tax policy was adapted to the times, with three major policy reforms occurring in the period between 1975 and 2005.

The first major post-independence tax reform took place in 1978 with the objective of altering the inherited colonial tax system to better reflect the aims of the newly independent socialist state and to finance ambitious public expenditures. After the socialist experiment met with severe difficulties, cul-minating in economic crisis in the early 1980s, moves towards a market economy were accompanied by another major set of tax policy reforms in 1987, once again reflecting a change in the demands made of the fiscal system and the beginning of an extended period of structural adjustment. Finally, after the resumption of peace and several years of high economic growth rates, the most recent wave of tax reforms were introduced in the period from 1999 to 2003, ostensibly to consolidate previous reforms and establish a public finance system with the potential to develop into a sustainable and efficient system (IMF 2004a).

2.2 1975–2005 revenue overview

Given the turbulence of recent Mozambican history, it is little surprise that government tax revenues experienced a high level of volatility over the period from 1975 to 2005, as illustrated in Figure 2.1. Starting from a low 7.4 per cent of GDP at independence in 1975, total revenues reached 14.1 per cent of GDP in 1983, their highest level since independence. Other peaks were reached at 13.6 per cent of GDP in 1993 and 12.9 per cent in 2000. These were interspersed with drops to just 8.0 per cent of GDP in 1985, 10.5 per cent in 1996 and 11.7 per cent in 2002. Such revenue fluctuations reflect a variety of factors, including sweeping tax reforms in 1978, 1987 and 1999, but also variations in compliance control, administration and alterations in tax rates and exemptions between major reforms. In recent years revenues have tended to stagnate, remaining between 11.7 and 12.9 per cent of GDP from 1999 to 2005, and attaining 12.6 per cent of GDP in 2005.

As Figure 2.1 illustrates, revenues from expenditure taxes dominate overall revenues and drive the volatility of overall revenues. Of particular note, and further discussed below, is the dramatic fall in expenditure tax revenues (and to a lesser extent other revenues) after 1983, when a combination of the intensifying internal conflict, expansive government programmes and

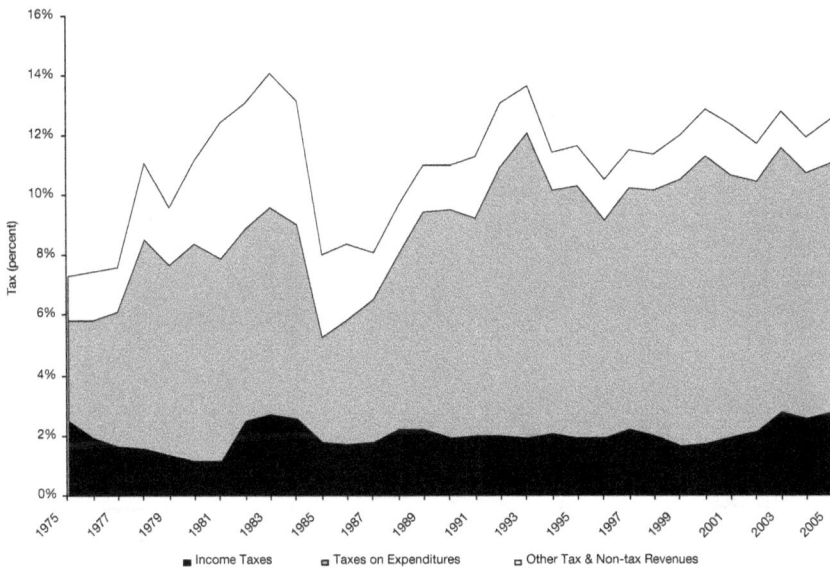

Figure 2.1 Nominal tax revenues 1975–2005 (% of GDP)
Source: MPD (2005), MPF (2004) and Sulemane (2001), author's calculations.

inappropriate macroeconomic polices led to economic crisis and a resultant steep decline in purchasing power. Figure 2.2 shows that GDP growth also fluctuated considerably during the period from 1975 to 2005, real GDP remaining below its 1975 level for every year but one (1981) until 1996. Although GDP growth was markedly less volatile than growth in total revenue, Figure 2.2 also illustrates that continuous economic growth only really began after 1992 and the resumption of peace.

Although Figure 2.2 suggests that revenues are pro-cyclical in relation to GDP, it also shows that, despite economic growth from 1992, sustained real revenue growth only began after 1997. Until 2000, revenue growth was considerably faster than GDP growth, implying beneficial revenue effects from a widening tax base, the impact of new tax policies and/or improved tax administration. However, since 2000 revenue growth has been weaker, raising questions regarding the sustainability of the previous growth.

Underlying total revenue growth, expenditure tax revenues have increased almost continuously since 1986, reaching more than five times their initial 1975 level in real terms in 2003 and well above total revenue or GDP growth. In contrast, revenues from income taxes were consistently lower than in 1975 until the late 1990s, when they began to increase and experienced a positive break in 2003 with the introduction of new income taxes. Despite

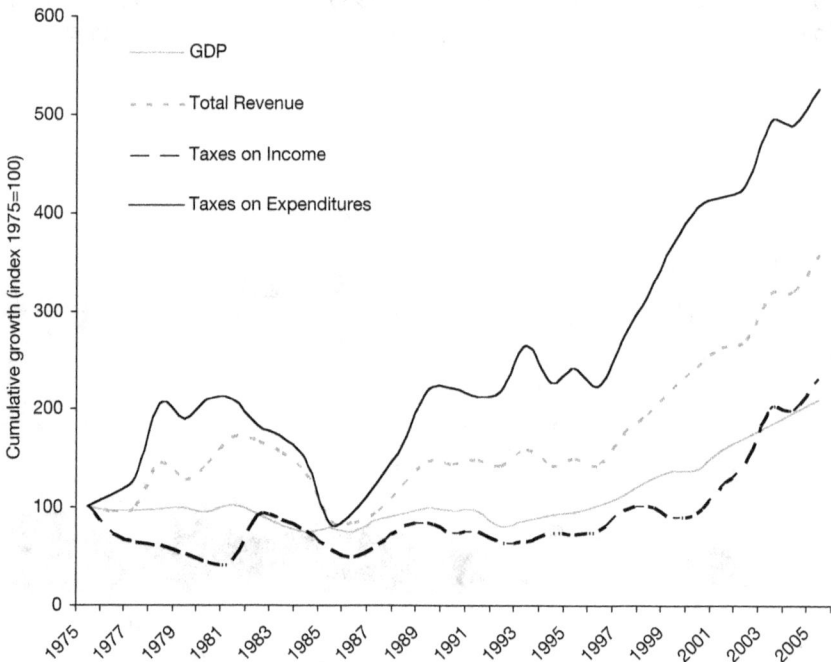

Figure 2.2 Cumulative growth of revenue and GDP 1975–2004 (1975=100)
Source: MPD (2005), MPF (2004) and Sulemane (2001), author's calculations.

this late growth, income tax revenues as a share of overall revenues have continuously decreased in the period from 1975 to 2003 as a reflection of the growing dominance of expenditure taxes. Figure 2.3 illustrates the behaviour of both personal and company income tax revenues over the period from 1975 to 2005. This traces the declining contribution of company income tax revenues as a percentage of GDP since 1988 despite the general stagnation and subsequent growth of total revenue seen above. Personal income tax revenues provided a higher but declining proportion of GDP up to 1982, when the introduction of progressive company income tax rates in 1982 brought a sudden increase in those revenues. Personal income taxes then grew from 1987 and overtook business income tax revenues after 1995. The reasons behind this contradictory behaviour of personal and business income taxes from 1988 onwards merit further investigation. Figure 2.4 presents data on expenditure tax revenues, comparing domestic expenditure taxes with those on import expenditure.[2] Notably, revenues from taxes on imports are generally increasing over the period and overtook those on domestic expenditures in 1999. This was despite measures to liberalize trade, as discussed below, and was due to the introduction of a value added tax (VAT) in 1999.

Finally, Figure 2.5 compares the contributions of revenues from taxes on imports with overall domestic revenues. Although import tax revenues fell less than domestic tax revenues in the crisis of the early 1980s, since 1987 these have increased in importance, in particular with the introduction of VAT, as highlighted above. As such, taxes on imports represented 4.7 per

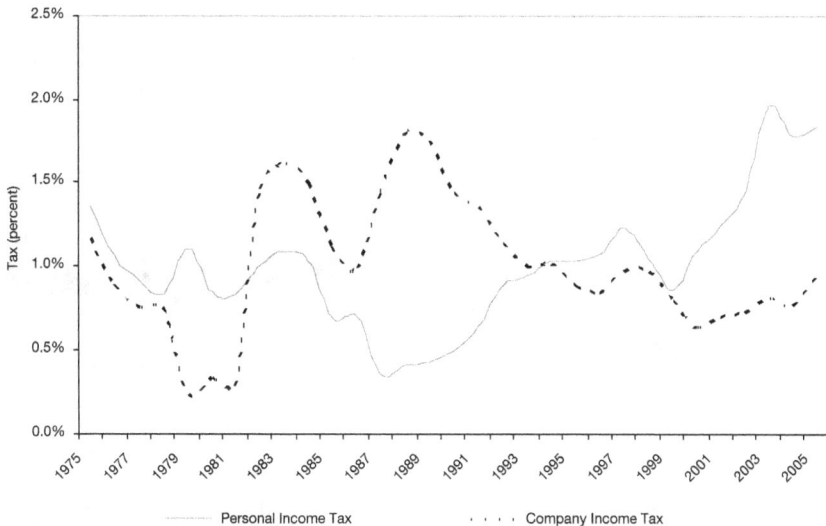

Figure 2.3 Taxes on personal and company income 1975–2005 (% of GDP)
Source: MPD (2005), MPF (2004) and Sulemane (2001), author's calculations.

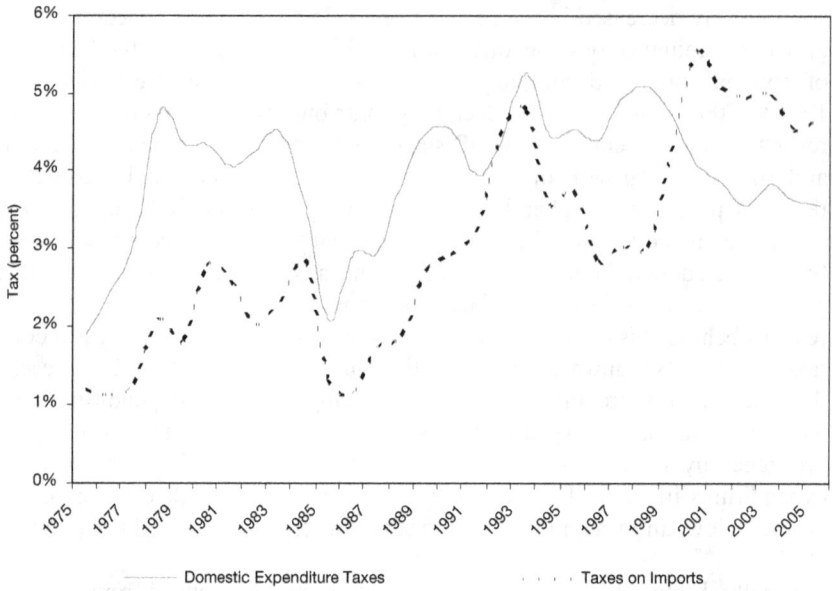

Figure 2.4 Domestic and import expenditure taxes (% of GDP)
Source: MPD (2005), MPF (2004) and Sulemane (2001), author's calculations.

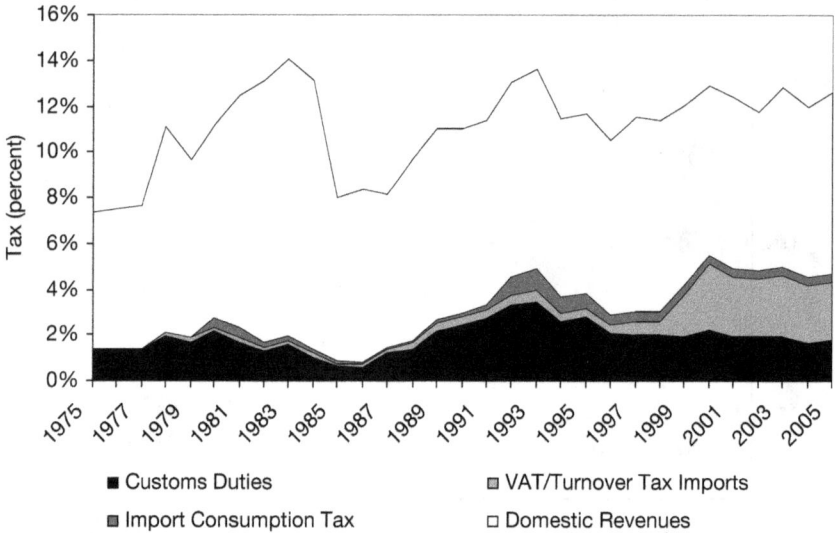

Figure 2.5 Domestic and import taxes (% of GDP)
Source: MPD (2005), MPF (2004) and Sulemane (2001), author's calculations.

cent of GDP in 2005, equivalent to 37.1 per cent of total revenues, compared with only 1.5 per cent of GDP in 1987 and 1.4 per cent in 1975.

These results and those in Figure 2.4 are in apparent contradiction to the generalized result that countries switch from dependence on revenues from cross-border trade to revenues from domestic taxes as the economy grows and administration and control improve, thus highlighting the potential importance for revenues of further trade liberalization.

3 Tax reforms and their impacts by period

3.1 1975–1986: post-independence socialism

3.1.1 Post-independence tax reforms

The first post-independence tax reforms of 1978 are best understood by considering the atmosphere of revolutionary socialist fervour in which they took place. The nationalization of many private properties and services and ambitious programmes of universal free education and health services which epitomize this period (Chabal 2001: 197) were accompanied by an escalation of the internal armed conflict, thus creating a need for large quantities of new resources. According to tax legislation, a principal objective of the 1978 tax reforms was to alter the perception of taxes from

> [a] colonial instrument of domination [to] ... the duty of each citizen to contribute ... to the costs of the programmes of the Popular State in order to create the conditions for the introduction of socialism.
>
> (GoM 1978a: 12)

Legislation stated that the new tax system was to reduce complexity and counteract the disappearance of certain revenues due to the 'new economic reality' (GoM 1978b).

Reforms included the introduction of a 'National Reconstruction Tax' (Imposto de Reconstrução Nacional), a single progressive income tax to simplify the array of colonial-era taxes on income (GoM 1978a), the 'Circulation Tax' (Imposto de Circulação), a 3 per cent uniform rate turnover tax on consumption, and reforms to the Consumption Tax (GoM 1978c), while rents from nationalized housing also provided a new additional source of non-tax revenue. The introduction of two new taxes, in particular the National Reconstruction Tax, led to the need to revise the Income Tax Code in order to transform the relatively insignificant Complementary Tax (0.3 per cent of GDP in 1978) into a tax on capital incomes, private property and non-salary incomes (with exemptions for the state and the ruling party FRELIMO).

Following this initial reform, some further smaller reforms were carried out in 1982 with adjustments to the Complementary Tax (Imposto Complementar 'B') and the Capital Tax (Imposto de Capitais), which then became covered by the Industrial Contribution (Contribuição Industrial) on company profits. This period also saw the introduction of progressivity into the Industrial Contribution, which had been a fixed rate proportional tax since its introduction in 1968 (GoM 1982).

3.1.2 Post-independence revenue impacts

As illustrated in Figure 2.6, the initial impact of the reforms was an immediate boost to revenues, which leapt from 7.6 per cent of GDP in 1977 to 11.1 per cent in 1978. Although 1979 saw faltering revenues, in particular with respect to Customs Duties, which fell by 1.1 per cent of GDP, the increase was resumed the following year, with overall revenues eventually reaching 14.1 per cent of GDP in 1983.

The new National Reconstruction Tax had a limited impact on overall income tax as revenues from taxes on incomes, particularly business incomes, continued their pre-1978 decline. The introduction of the Circulation Tax widened the expenditure tax base from its pre-1978 reliance on consumption tax revenues (from alcohol and tobacco) and import duties, thus increasing the dominance of revenues from expenditure taxes, although this may also reflect the high rates of inflation experienced after 1981 and an inelastic demand for certain consumption goods. Other Tax and Non-tax Revenues also increased, from 1.5 per cent of GDP in 1977 to a peak of 5.5 per cent of GDP in 1981, mostly due to the inclusion of public housing rents, which in 1978 constituted a new revenue source worth 0.6 per cent of GDP.

Despite the general increase in revenues after 1978, this was short lived. Further intensification of the armed conflict after 1980 destroyed key infrastructure and severely restricted mobility, while continued expensive social programmes, low export levels and inefficient socialist planning finally led to severe economic decline in the early 1980s and collapse in 1986. This was preceded by a severe decline in tax revenues from 1983 to 1985, shown in Figure 2.6, particularly for the Consumption Tax and Customs Duties, which fell from 3.1 per cent to 1.3 per cent of GDP and 1.5 per cent to 0.3 per cent, respectively, reflecting a sharp drop in consumption due to shortages.

3.2 1987–1998: structural adjustment

3.2.1 Structural adjustment tax reforms

Mozambique's first Structural Adjustment Programme (SAP) was implemented from 1987 to 1989 in support of the government's Economic Rehabilitation Programme (Programa de Reabilitação Económica, or PRE), a programme of fiscal adjustment, price liberalization, monetary restraint and adjustments to the official exchange rate, designed in conjunction with the IMF in an attempt to reverse the economic decline seen in the first half of the 1980s when GDP fell by almost a quarter (IMF 2004a). For the second

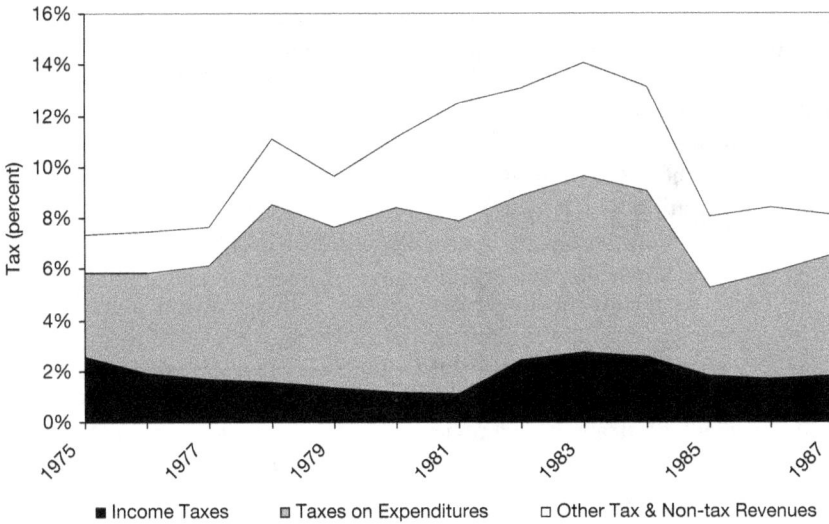

Figure 2.6 Revenue categories 1975–87 (% of GDP)
Source: MPD (2005), MPF (2004) and Sulemane (2001), author's calculations.

time in 10 years, the new economic and political environment thus brought a major revision of the tax code, which was redesigned in collaboration with the IMF and World Bank, although these 'exerted massive influence on the policymaking process' (Tarp *et al.* 2002), re-establishing the foundations of the tax system as a whole. This was followed by an Enhanced Structural Adjustment Facility (ESAF) running from 1989 to 1995 and a second ESAF from 1996 to 1999 which continued to liberalize the trade regime whilst attempting to further reduce the role of the state in the economy and reduce fiscal imbalances (IMF 2004a).

While the previous 1978 tax code had 'consecrated the principles of social justice' and permitted 'the concentration of increasing amounts of resources in the State Budget', by 1987 'huge legal and illegal profits [were] accumulating in the economy', due to a 'strong focus on direct taxation of incomes' (GoM 1987a: 16, 17).

Despite the evidence in Figure 2.5 that direct taxes on incomes accounted for only 20 per cent of total revenues in 1986, whilst indirect taxes accounted for 42 per cent (MPD 2005), the 1987 tax law provided the legal framework to 'revitalize and reinforce indirect taxes' and 'perfect the direct taxes on incomes in order to more effectively personalize the tax and reach higher incomes and in particular those from capital' (GoM 1987a: 16, 24).

Specific reforms included returning the Industrial Contribution (Contribuição Industrial) to a flat rate of 50 per cent on profits and extending it to state companies. A new proportional personal income tax was introduced in the guise of the Labour Income Tax (Imposto sobre Rendimentos de Trabalho), while the National Reconstruction Tax was turned into a form of poll tax. At the same time, Decree No. 1/87 increased the Circulation Tax rate from 3 per cent to 5 per cent for wholesalers and 10 per cent for retailers, both on domestic transactions and imports (GoM 1987b), thus increasing the cascade effect characteristic of this kind of tax, although exemptions were granted for small traders.

Following the PRE, reforms under the ESAF included the introduction of the Compensation Tax (Imposto de Compensação) on motor vehicle ownership in 1989 and the Special Fuel Tax (Imposto Especial sobre Combustíveis) in 1990, levied as fixed amounts per litre of fuel (depending on fuel type) on domestically consumed fuels, with the proceeds transferred to the Road and Bridge Maintenance Fund. In addition, it included tariff reforms which eliminated specific import duties and simplified the tariff schedule as of 1991, establishing a maximum tariff rate of 35 per cent.

An element of strategic tax policy was also introduced in 1993, with a number of different sectoral rates for the Industrial Contribution. Further, the Investment Law was approved, with specific sectoral incentives, aiming to promote investment in infrastructures, human capital, technology and improving the balance of payments through both exports and substitution of imports[3] (GoM 1993a; GoM 1995). This established a legal framework for foreign and national investments, guaranteeing security and protection of property rights, and remittance of funds abroad whilst providing fiscal incentives in the form of tax and customs benefits.[4]

Customs reforms also began in 1993 with the rationalization of taxes and tariffs on imports, reducing the number of different tariff rates from 12 to 5, whilst ad-hoc tariff exemptions were eliminated and customs control strengthened (IMF 2004a). However, as customs revenues continued to fall, the Unit for Restructuring Customs (UTRA) was formed in 1996 and a private company, Crown Agents, contracted to take over its management in order to improve administrative efficiency and capacity (see Chapter 6, Section 2 for more details).[5]

3.2.2 Structural adjustment revenue impacts

As the economy emerged from the crisis period of the early 1980s, tax revenues began to increase even prior to implementation of the 1987 tax reforms (see Figure 2.6). This trend continued following reforms, with total revenues climbing from 8.2 per cent to 13.6 per cent of GDP between 1987 and 1993. However, thereafter revenues fell once again, reaching a low of 10.5 per cent of GDP in 1996 and recovering only slightly in 1997 and 1998, to 11.5 per cent (see Figure 2.7).

The increase in revenues up to 1993 was again mostly due to taxes on expenditure, whose revenues rose from 3.8 per cent to 6.7 per cent of GDP, whilst taxes on income contributed around 2.0 per cent over the period from 1987 to 1997. As Figure 2.8 illustrates, the increase in revenue from expenditure taxes was principally down to the Circulation Tax, which more than

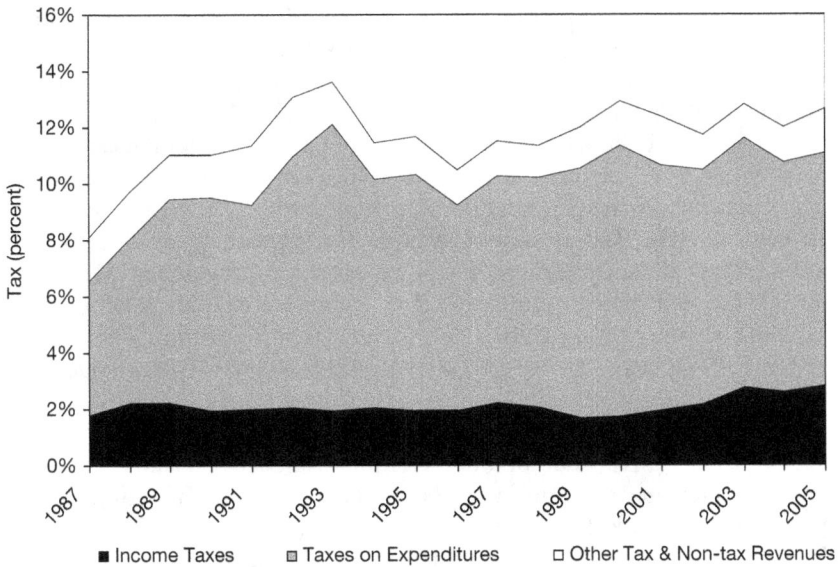

Figure 2.7 Revenue categories 1987–8 (% of GDP)
Source: MPD (2005), MPF (2004) and Sulemane (2001), author's calculations.

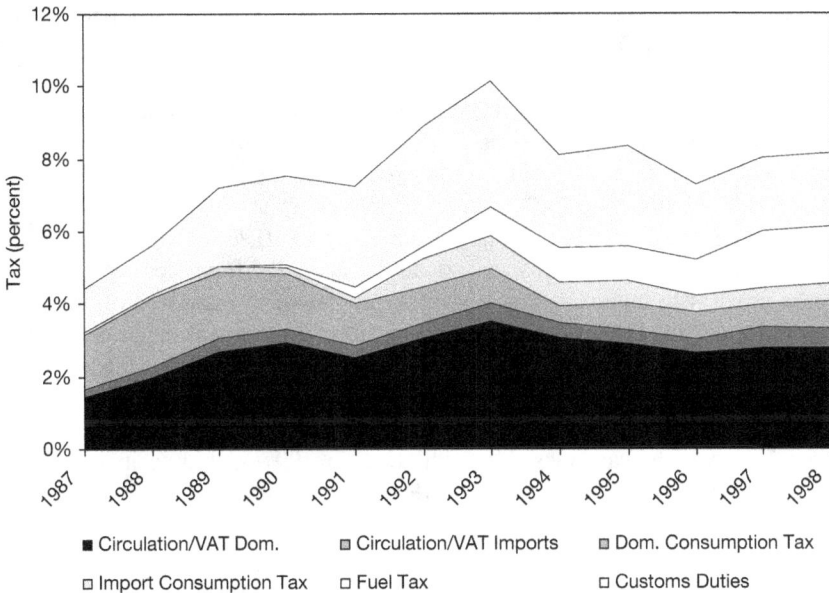

Figure 2.8 Taxes on expenditure 1987–8 (% of GDP)
Source: MPD (2005), MPF (2004) and Sulemane (2001), author's calculations.

doubled as a proportion of GDP from 1987 to 1993, from 1.7 per cent to 4.0 per cent. This large jump presumably reflects both the increased rates and the resultant cascade effect as the tax was applied all the way down the value chain and the low initial base following the crisis.

Figure 2.8 also shows a surge in Customs Duties (including customs services fee) from 1.2 per cent of GDP to 3.5 per cent between 1987 and 1993, and revenues from the Consumption Tax on Imports from 0.1 per cent to 0.9 per cent of GDP. This is surprising given the increase in tariff exemptions and Customs administration problems experienced at this time (IMF 2001a) but may instead reflect rising levels of consumption as a result of increased economic stability brought about by the reduction in inflation from 160 per cent in 1987 to below 35 per cent in 1991 (IMF 2004a). Mozambique's high level of dependency on imports and the resulting strong link between consumption and import levels add credence to this hypothesis. However, it is also potentially a reflection of a depreciation of the real exchange rate which may have increased the import tax base relative to GDP. In addition, GDP growth in the period from 1987 to 1992 was very low, with GDP actually decreasing in real terms, as illustrated in Figure 2.2. Thus the increase in revenues was also in conjunction with poor GDP growth, something which may have had additional long-term constraining effects.

Despite the resumption of peace, relative stability and the beginning of continued economic growth after 1992, total tax revenues fell as a percentage of GDP from 1993 to 1997 (see Figure 2.7), again mostly attributable to a fall in Circulation Tax receipts, from 4.0 per cent to 3.0 per cent of GDP from 1993 to 1996. Customs Duties also fell from 3.5 per cent to 2.1 per cent of GDP. Circulation Tax revenues on imports are directly related to the levels of Customs Duties, thus indicating that the decline of revenue from both these sources may have been due to the weak customs control and ad-hoc exemptions experienced in this period (this is discussed in Chapter 6, Section 2). In addition, there is a possibility that exemptions resulted from the implementation or abuse of the 'specific incentives' granted by the Investment Law, ostensibly implemented to promote investment. Taxes on incomes once again had little impact, remaining steady at around 2.0 per cent of GDP.

As previously mentioned, overall revenue began to increase continuously only after 1996. However, whilst the customs administration reforms may have influenced the 0.3 per cent of GDP increase in Circulation Tax receipts on imports, they merely stemmed the decline of revenues from Customs Duties. In fact, the main influence on reversing the decline in revenues is the Fuel Tax, which was revised for inflation in 1997 and thus increased its contribution from 1.0 per cent of GDP to 1.6 per cent.

3.3 1999–2005: Post-structural adjustment consolidation

The period from 1999 to 2003 corresponds to the first of Mozambique's IMF Poverty Reduction and Growth Facilities (PRGF), the objectives of which were to sustain the GDP growth levels and low inflation achieved in the previous programmes but with a greater emphasis on combating poverty through the government's Poverty Reduction Strategy Paper (Plano de Acção para a Redução da Pobreza Absoluta, or PARPA). The PRGF also had a specific emphasis on strengthening government revenue (IMF 2004a) and reversing the recent poor revenue performance, reflected in the array of new tax reforms implemented in this period. The signing of a second PRGF (2004–6) with the IMF in July 2004 was also accompanied by statements referring to the need to improve revenue performance.

3.3.1 Post-structural adjustment tax reforms

Tax reforms in this period include the introduction of Value Added Tax (VAT) (Imposto sobre o Valor Acrescentado, or IVA), the Specific Consumption Tax (Imposto sobre o Consumo Específico) and the Special Fuel Tax (Imposto Especial sobre Combustíveis) in 1999, followed in 2003 by the introduction of the Individual Income Tax (Imposto sobre o Rendimento de Pessoas Singulares, or IRPS) and the Companies Income Tax on company incomes (Imposto sobre o Rendimento de Pessoas Colectivas, or IRPC). These reforms were also accompanied by implementation of trade reforms and continued assistance to improve customs capacity and efficiency.

Law 3/98 simultaneously approved VAT, the Specific Consumption Tax and the Special Fuel Tax with the goal of creating a 'more efficient and neutral system' (GoM 1998a) which would eliminate the cascade effect of the Circulation Tax and the Consumption Tax. Implementation of the new indirect taxes began on 1 April 1999 with VAT set at 17 per cent, payable on both domestic transactions and imports of goods and services, including Customs Duties and other import taxes. Whilst following the basic logic of a standard destination VAT, with amounts payable by firms calculated as VAT received on enterprise sales minus that paid on inputs, the VAT Code also establishes 'special regimes' within the overall framework as well as exemptions for certain products and activities considered of major importance (GoM 1998b).

The special regimes include the 'Exemption Regime' for small enterprises with an annual turnover of less than Mts100m (approximately US$4,000) and the 'Simplified Regime', applicable to those non-import/exporting enterprises with annual turnover between Mts100m and Mts250m (i.e. approximately US$4,000 and US$10,500), for whom VAT is payable at a rate of 5 per cent on final sales but not deductible for inputs from the amount paid to the government, thus equating this regime to a 5 per cent turnover tax on these firms.

In addition there is an array of exemptions on goods and services. These include basic products such as corn flour, rice, bread and medicines as well as agricultural inputs, goods relating to health and education services, financial services and exports. VAT exemption is also granted in the case of exemption from Customs Duties and goods destined for international organizations, Special Economic Zones and Export Free Zones.[6] Finally, some basic goods, such as corn flour, rice and bread, are eligible for reimbursement by government of VAT paid on inputs (GoM 1998b).

VAT implementation is very important and illustrates how the introduction of a fairly complex tax system can increase the burden on the tax administration and, as a consequence, the private sector. Problems relate to the special regimes and in particular to the length of delays in reimbursements, which prejudice the operations of companies, for whom the amount to be reimbursed can often be sizeable. Thus administrative problems are equivalent to an additional tax on certain activities, in particular exports, and continue to be the bugbear of the private sector.

Following implementation of VAT, 2001 brought implementation of the SADC Trade Protocol, signed in 1996 and ratified in 2000, with the longterm aim of forming a free-trade area following a period of adjustment (Khandelwal 2004). The maximum import tariff was reduced from 35 per cent to 30 per cent, to 25 per cent in 2003 and to 20 per cent in 2006.

In a more limited alteration in 2003, a Ministerial Diploma was published, providing a specific customs regime for the manufacturing industry (GoM 2003a). This regime, most likely a response to the VAT reimbursement delays experienced by large manufacturing firms, gave exemptions on Customs Duties (and therefore automatically VAT) on imported inputs to enterprises in the industrial sector (comprising agro-industry, food, textiles and footwear, metal, machinery, chemical, plastic and rubber), where these have an annual income of not less than Mts6bn (approximately US$250,000) and a value-added of at least 20 per cent.

Although not part of a wider strategy to promote large-scale industrial firms, this measure deprives the government of further revenue while effectively transferring funds to large enterprises, increasing their effective protection and the relative costs of small and medium-sized enterprises, whilst simultaneously undermining the philosophy of unifying fiscal incentives under the Fiscal Incentives Code.

An important administrative step was taken in 2003 with the introduction of the Individual Taxpayer Identification Number (Número Único de Identificação Tributária or NUIT), attributed to both individuals and companies and used in the payment of all taxes, both direct and indirect (GoM 2003b). The potential implications of change are great in terms of improving tax authority control and simplifying administration in the long run. However, its benefit will rely on continued administrative support before its introduction can be made widespread and the full benefits achieved.

One of the first applications of the NUIT was in the implementation in 2003 of the new Personal and Corporate Income Taxes (GoM 2002a). Although this was ostensibly to replace 'a complex system of five taxes on income whose base had been eroded by generous exemptions and deductions' (IMF 2004a: 12), such replacement was also complex in nature.

The Personal Income Tax (IRPS) is a progressive tax on all household incomes earned by residents in Mozambique, with rates ranging from 10 to 32 per cent. Annual income of less than Mts24m (US$1,000) is not taxed, while agricultural income is taxed at a maximum of 10 per cent. Where possible, tax is retained at source at a rate of 20 per cent for all incomes except those from capital (at 10 per cent), with total household income taxed according to the progressive rates given in Table 2.1, calculated at the end of each year and paid net of that retained at source. Various deductions apply to the calculated tax, depending on the marital status of the individual and the number of dependants.

A simplified accounting regime (Regime Simplificado) was also established for firms with an annual turnover of less than Mts1,500m (approximately US $62,500). As these firms are not required to keep detailed financial accounts, indicators based on 'technical-scientific indicators' are used to determine taxable income where these are approved by the Ministry of Finance, or, if not, this is determined as 20 per cent of sales income and 30 per cent of all other incomes.

Whilst stemming from admirable intentions, the new income tax raises many issues regarding administrative capacity, particularly in a country where this is already stretched. Detailed information on household incomes and number of dependents appears unsuited to the Mozambican reality of large extended family links.[7]

Accompanying the introduction of the IRPS was the Companies Income Tax (IRPC), which replaced the Industrial Contribution (Contribuição Industrial) on company profits, part of the Labour Income Tax, the Complementary Tax and the Urban Building Contribution (Contribuição Predial Urbana). The IRPC is applied on profits from commercial, cooperative and public enterprises (and on incomes not liable to IRPS) at a rate of 32 per cent (10 per cent on agricultural activities until 2010). Once again, incomes taxed at source are taxed at 20 per cent (10 per cent for telecommunications and international transport). Although a simplified regime also exists for IRPC, there are no benefits, the company simply being permitted to keep

Table 2.1 Individual Income Tax Rates (IRPS)

Annual Income	Rate	Subtract from Calculated Tax
Up to Mts28m (US$1.166)	10%	–
From Mts28m to Mts112m (US$1.166-US$4.666)	15%	Mts1,4m (US$58)
From Mts112m to Mts336m (US$4.666-US$14.000)	20%	Mts7m (US$292)
From Mts336m to Mts1.008m (US$14.000-US$42.000)	25%	Mts23,8m (US$992)
Over Mts1.008m (US$42.000)	32%	Mts94,36m (US$3931)

Sources: GoM (2002a)

accounts in a simpler format, something which may remain overly burden-some for many small and medium-sized enterprises.

Simultaneously with the new income taxes, the Fuel Tariff (Taxa de Combustíveis) was also introduced to replace the Special Fuel Tax (Imposto Especial sobre Combustíveis), in operation since 1990 (GoM 2002a), payable per litre or kilogram and updated (at a maximum of 5 per cent) on a quarterly basis according to inflation. The introduction of the Fuel Tariff and its updating mechanism resulted in an initial 63 per cent rate increase after having remained at a constant level since 1997, so that the tax on normal automobile fuel currently represents approximately 30 per cent of the total consumer price (equivalent to an ad-valorem rate of over 40 per cent), and a slightly lower percentage than this for diesel and lead-free petrol.

As the above tax reforms were taking place, the government also approved the Fiscal Benefits Code (GoM 2002b). Despite the Investment Law and first Fiscal Benefits Code of 1993, a proliferation of special tax regimes had arisen in the intervening period, resulting in a disparate collection of 30 laws, decrees and decisions on benefits, sometimes overlapping. The Fiscal Benefits Code, following the IMF recommendations, unified all fiscal benefits under one code, to be applicable to investments previously realized under the Investment Law (3/93), the Mining Law (14/2002) and the Petroleum Law (3/2001), with an array of fiscal incentives in the form of deductions from taxable income, accelerated depreciation, tax credits, reduction of tax rates, import regimes and deduction of the amount of tax assessed (GoM 2002b).

3.3.2 Impacts of post-structural adjustment reforms

Although less volatile than in the previous periods, the impact of the package of tax reforms on revenues over the period 1999 to 2005 was once again mixed, with revenues increasing up to 2000, before stalling, as illustrated in Figure 2.9. Over the period as a whole, total revenue increased from 12.0 per cent of GDP in 1999 to only 12.6 per cent in 2005, having reached 12.9 per cent in 2000 and 12.8 per cent in 2003. Despite the apparently disappointing revenue performance, the period was also characterized by high GDP growth rates, with real growth of 13.1 per cent in 2001 and rates of around 8 per cent from then on (MPD 2005). This implies a relatively inelastic revenue response to GDP growth overall.

As Figure 2.9 illustrates, the ambiguous behaviour of total revenues is an aggregation of mixed revenue behaviour in all tax categories. After increasing markedly for most of the period, Income Tax revenues as a proportion of GDP stagnate at around 2.8 per cent from 2003 to 2005, after a surge of 0.6 per cent of GDP with the introduction of the IRPS and IRPC in 2003. The increase in IRPS revenues is partially explained by the inclusion of civil servants in 2003, which contributed around 10 per cent of total IRPS.

The contribution of IRPC to this growth is more difficult to explain given the lower rates than the Industrial Contribution it replaced and considerable

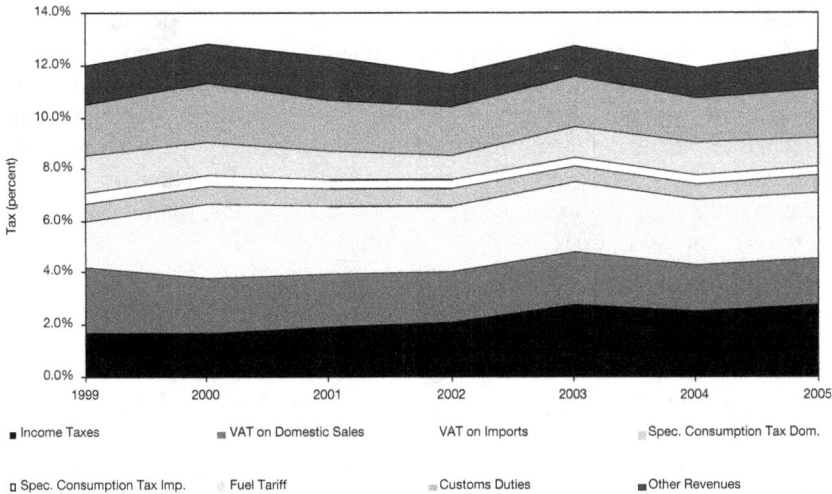

Figure 2.9 Revenue breakdown 1999–2005 (% of GDP)
   Source: MPD (2005), MPF (2004) and Sulemane (2001), author's calculations.

exemptions through the Fiscal Benefits Code. Thus it may indicate an improvement in administration and possible widening of the tax base with the introduction of the new tax or, if not, faster growth of profits than GDP.

VAT on both domestic sales and imports also displays mixed behaviour, with VAT on imports increasing markedly to 2.9 per cent in 2000 from 1.8 per cent in 1999 before declining to 2.5 per cent of GDP in 2004 and 2005, whilst VAT on domestic sales declined from 2.6 per cent of GDP in 1999 to 1.9 per cent in 2002 and 1.8 per cent in 2004 and 2005. The notable dominance of revenues from VAT on imports over domestic transactions is important and has implications for the future, when import tariffs are reduced as an element of regional trade agreements.

Thus, although VAT receipts reduced the negative effect of import tariff reductions on overall revenues, Customs Duty revenues declined from 2.2 per cent of GDP in 2000 to 1.8 per cent in 2005, partly due to the reduction in the top rate of Customs Duties in both 2001 and 2003 and despite the large amount of these which are paid by the government itself for imported goods for public expenditure projects. Their value has fluctuated markedly in recent years, from 25 per cent of total Duties in 1999 (approx. US$21m) to 34 per cent in 2002 (US$27m) and 10 per cent (US$9m) in 2003 (MPF 2004). Also stemming the decline in revenues from Customs Duties was the reduction in exemptions. Data for the years 2001–2 indicate that the value decreased dramatically, from 50 per cent of collected revenue (Mts777,000m) to 10 per cent (Mts171,000m). One of the reasons for the drop is a reduction in 'Special Authorizations' from Mts434,000m in 2001 to Mts84,000m in 2002, although this still continued as the greatest category of exemption.

The impact of the Investment Law and Fiscal Benefits Code, introduced in 1993 and 2002, respectively, is more complicated to calculate given the need for hypothetical calculations of forgone revenues and large amounts of firm-specific information. Similarly, with regards to Industrial Free Zones, the information available is limited. Only 25 companies operate under the Industrial Free Zone regime (Centro de Promoção de Investimento 2004), so that, excluding Mozal and the two heavy sands projects, the revenue effects of these exemptions are relatively small. Anecdotally, those which have set up are mostly capital intensive industries supporting the Mozal aluminium smelter, indicating that the job-creating aspect of the innovation has been minimal.

Overall the tax reforms implemented in the period 1999–2005 have had a mixed impact on revenues, although the level was maintained above the levels experienced in the prior period from 1993 to 1999. However, as was also mentioned, these reforms have also brought some additional complexities, the exact consequences of which remain unclear and which may be felt in the medium to long term.

4 Concluding remarks

Despite the introduction of several major tax reforms in Mozambique since national independence and the recent wave of new taxes, analysis of tax policy and revenue impacts has been limited, something which this chapter attempts to address.

As this chapter has illustrated, each set of major reforms, most of which accompanied major changes in the economic system, was in general instigated following a period of revenue stagnation and resulted in initial positive revenue impacts. However, in each case, as the above analysis showed, initial gains were often followed by declines due to a constantly changing economic environment. Although this was partly due to government policy, outside factors such as the civil war and the vulnerability of Mozambique to natural disasters may also have played a role in affecting economic activity and thus tax revenues.

Given the various major economic and social changes, it is perhaps little surprise that Mozambican tax revenues appear not to fit in with the patterns predicted by tax theories based on the experience of other countries. In particular, the introduction of VAT has led to an *increase* in reliance on trade tax revenues as the economy has grown, rather than a fall. In addition, almost all revenue growth, when this has occurred, has been due to growth in revenues from regressive indirect taxes rather than from more progressive direct taxes.

Efforts to improve administration are going ahead with the creation of the Central Revenue Authority (ATM). However, real benefits from these new institutional arrangements will clearly take some time to be felt, and continuing efforts to improve tax administration and widen the tax base must continue. In the context of continuing trade liberalization and the reduction of aid dependency, it is of the utmost importance that tax policies be coordinated to ensure that the competing demands on public finances are met whilst also remaining faithful to the objective of promoting economic growth.

Notes

1 The main source of data used for this work is that provided by DNIA as their 'final version' submitted to the National Directorate of Public Accounts of the Ministry of Finance (Direcção Nacional de Contabilidade Pública, DNCP), which is based on information from all tax offices around the country on amounts collected. However, there are discrepancies between this data and those which appear in the Conta Geral do Estado (State General Accounts, CGE) (due to Treasury information) regarding the amounts actually received. Two time-series were provided by DNIA, covering 1975–92 and 1987–2003. Marginal differences exist in overlapping years which were overcome by using the most recent data. Tax data by their very nature are always open to some irregularities. Nonetheless, it is assumed that the data collected capture the most important elements of revenue behaviour and, given the caveats, are still of value for analytical purposes. The tax authorities are currently working to improve the quality of data, with relatively new databases in operation for VAT, company income taxes and import taxes which, over time, will help to improve the coverage, consistency and accuracy of tax records both for analytical and for administrative purposes. However, at present these remain problematic in terms of usage data for analysis. Official government data as presented in the CGE were published only as of 1998 and provide very little detail. Similarly, the Anuário Estatístico (Statistics Annual) only provides tax data at a very aggregate level.
2 Note that taxes on imports include Customs Duties, the Import Consumption Tax and VAT on imports.
3 Strategic areas, such as electricity and water provision, were reserved for the public sector, with or without private participation by the Investment Law Regulations.
4 This built on earlier legislation from 1984 and 1987 relating to foreign direct investment. To benefit from this, domestic investments had to have at least US $5,000 of capital, whilst Foreign Direct Investments (FDI) required a minimum value of US$50,000 (FOB). The decision to approve investments depended on the amounts involved, with provincial governors able to approve projects with a value between US$5,000 and US$100,000, the Minister of Finance those with a value up to US$100m, whilst those worth more than US$100m had to be approved by the Council of Ministers.
5 This was carried out with the collaboration of DfID, SECO and DANIDA.
6 The Minister of Planning and Finance can also grant an exemption for the acquisition of goods and services destined for 'national institutions of public interest and relevant social purposes' (GoM, 1998b), although as of 2004 the position of the Minister of Planning and Finance no longer exists, with responsibilities being divided between the Ministry of Planning and Development and the Ministry of Finance. In addition, 'the importation of goods benefiting from import duty exemption' is also exempt under the terms of the following: Article 15 of Law 7/94, Article 7 of Law 4/94, Article 2 of Law 3/83, Article 18 of Law 2/95, Articles 40, 44, 45 of Law 41/96 (GoM, 1998b).
7 Indicative of these complications, the public administration itself was unable to correctly implement the IRPS on civil servants in its first year of implementation, instead estimating the overall amount due at the end of the year.

3 Household survey evidence

Christoffer Sonne-Schmidt

1 Introduction

The government of Mozambique has over the last 15 years relied on a range of policy instruments to regulate the prices of essential and strategic goods. Price controls in fuels and sugar are some of the most important, but other goods, specifically flour, tomato, tobacco, alcohol and soft drinks have also been directly subjected to fiscal policy instruments. Relatively little is known about who actually bears the burden of these taxes. This chapter aims at filling the gap using a countrywide household survey (IAF 2002–3) to trace the incidence of import tariffs, value added taxes (VAT) and excises (special consumption tax).

Government expenditure is close to 26 per cent of GDP, 56 per cent of which is self-financed by taxes and non-taxes on residents. The remaining 44 per cent is financed by external sources through grants and loan disbursements. Tax revenue is a key income source for the government. It is close to 12 per cent of GDP, and within that category it collects 57 per cent, or 3 per cent of GDP, from taxes on goods and services.[1] The size and volatility of external funds threatens fiscal stability, and therefore redistribution of income by public spending. To avoid ineffective cuts in government expenditure with undesirable effects on equity, Mozambique, like many African countries, needs to stabilize its tax revenue either by enlarging the tax base or by increasing taxes on the current base. The history and political economy of government interventions since independence is described in Chapter 2 by Byiers, who also reviews government revenue. Arndt *et al.* (2007) give an overview of aid flows and their volatility.

The fact that most people are employed in subsistence agriculture, and that merchants typically try to avoid the public eye, makes the formal economy quite narrow. Thus the scope for levying taxes is very restricted, generally limited to product taxes at international borders or on the largest firms. This need not be a problem for anti-poverty tax reforms. To the extent that rich and poor households purchase different consumption bundles, it is possible that some product taxes can be made strongly progressive or regressive. The potential for levying taxes to promote equity therefore needs careful examination (given information on consumption patterns). The analyst needs to know not only the relative importance of taxed goods in the consumption bundles of different households, but also whether the goods are actually likely to be subject to tax (e.g. purchases from a supermarket or petrol station will in general be taxed, but purchases of cassava from a market stall or street vendor will not).

A tax transfers real purchasing power from individuals to the state, and the incidence of taxes refers to whose real purchasing power is transferred to the state. In general, taxes are said to be progressive if individuals with a low living standard pay a proportionately smaller share of the tax than do people with a high living standard. For example, consumption taxes are generally assumed progressive if there are exemptions or low tax rates on goods heavily consumed by the poor, for example zero VAT on necessities, and higher rates on luxury items.

This chapter has two objectives, one substantive and one methodological. The substantive aim is to examine the effects of price interventions on the distribution of real incomes across different households. I do this by describing formal expenditure patterns for households in relation to their living standards. As a first approximation, a price increase hurts households in proportion to the amount of goods they purchase, so in order to know the distributional effects of a tax reform I depict who consumes taxed items and where consumers are situated in the overall welfare distribution. Such descriptions are important because they provide a first approximation of the immediate effects of a price change. Although such approximations contain a good deal less than we would ideally like to know, they are based on good data, and provide perhaps the only firm information we possess about the effects of change in pricing policy. Moreover, '[it] has been found to be a reasonably satisfactory shortcut for the study of a policy's distributional impact' (Sahn and Younger 2003: 29). The method, though, is not an appropriate tool for analysing the impact of composite tax categories, such as increasing or decreasing combined VAT or trade taxes. In such reforms there are many indirect effects. For such analysis computable general equilibrium (CGE) modelling is a more promising approach. Accordingly, this chapter focuses on single commodity taxes.

The second, methodological, objective is to add a new dimension to the graphical illustrations that have dominated the non-behavioural tax incidence literature. Lorenz-curves have been widely used in the literature to describe distributional inequality. Similarly, in the incidence literature (surveyed in Gemmell and Morrissey 2003) Lorenz-'type' curves for different goods are used to compare inequality in welfare loss of different taxes. The intuition is straightforward. If, for example, poorer households tend to consume less of a particular good, say diesel, and more of, say, flour, then reducing taxes on flour and raising taxes on diesel will improve the distribution of welfare. To determine if two curves are different, one can visually inspect whether one curve lies above another, or use a statistical test developed by Davidson and Duclos (1997) using a finite number of coordinates, to test if the vertical difference between two curves is statistically different from zero. My second, methodological objective is to combine these examination methods by creating confidence intervals for each curve. That done, one can visually inspect whether one curve is statistically different from another. I will do this by bootstrapping the calculations of curves (resampling observations from the data), which provides a way of estimating standard errors, and thus confidence intervals, for an infinite set of points on each curve. Bootstrapping provides a way of replacing analytic standard errors with computed standard errors. A non-technical description of the bootstrap procedure is given in Geweke *et al.* (2006).

The organization of the chapter is as follows. I begin in Section 2 with the assumptions and limitations of non-behavioural equity analysis. Section 3 provides the theoretical outline that motivates the empirical work, and in Section 4 I present the methodology of both the graphical illustration of tax concentration curves and their bootstrapped confidence intervals. Section 5 presents the data and in Section 6 the results of the substantive analysis are explained. Section 7 concludes.

2 Assessing the impact of taxes

This chapter adopts a partial equilibrium setup. That is, a group of final consumption goods is singled out and interaction with the rest of the economy is ignored. Doing this requires assumptions on how much of the tax burden is lifted by 'the rest of the economy' and how much is shifted onto the consumers in the partial model. I will follow the practice in most studies of incidence and assume that the burden of taxes on goods is shifted entirely onto consumers.

Merchants are usually legally liable to pay tax, but are often able to raise prices (or reduce supply) to recover some of their loss, so consumers of the final product pay all or part of the tax. A standard result in the theoretical incidence literature is that the distribution of the tax burden depends on the relative demand and supply elasticities. The relative inelastic (least adjustable) side of the market will bear most of the burden (Salanié 2003: ch. 1). In seeking to determine how much tax each consumer pays it is important to determine how much of the tax payment is successfully shifted forward to the final product, and thus to households. For example, the Mozambican state collects most of its taxes from import firms and local producers. Changing prices shifts taxes either to firm owners, to their suppliers or to consumers of the goods. In studies of the impact of taxes it is typically assumed that a product tax will be passed on to consumers through a price increase equal to the tax rate. This is the standard result if markets are competitive and taxes only apply to final sales or value added (see Gemmell and Morrissey 2003), and a plausible simplification, especially for goods with a high share of imports. For these goods, supply is infinitely elastic and so a tariff on imports will be entirely passed on to consumers.

The three most problematic elements neglected in this common practice are: (1) the impact of tax evasion and avoidance through the shadow economy; (2) the welfare effect on local producers; and (3) the cascading of taxes through the economy's production structure. For example, in the first case, if the cigarette taxes get too high merchants will evade custom taxes by increasing smuggling, and if taxes on kerosene for cooking get too high households will avoid the kerosene tax by substituting untaxed firewood for kerosene.[2] In the second case, if the import tax on flour goes up, local farmers can claim a higher price for their produce. So to the extent that they supply more flour than they consume, they will benefit from the import tax. In the third case it is clear that diesel taxes will have a direct effect on the consumers of diesel, but an increase in diesel prices gives rise to increases in other prices, especially transport. Thus there is an indirect effect of increased diesel prices on the consumers of public transport, as was most vividly expressed during the February 2008 transport riots. Here, as described in the next section, I will account for some of this latter effect by assuming constant relative prices. The main idea is that if the price of diesel goes up, then the price of public transport will follow, proportionately, so that the diesel tax falls on both direct consumers of diesel and consumers of public transport (indirect consumers of diesel).

Much of the tax incidence literature attempts to correct for some of these neglects. Examples can be found in Chen *et al.* (2001), who examine both household and business taxation in Uganda, and Deaton (1989), who models the effect on welfare of rice consumers and producers in Thailand using a household income and expenditure survey. Haughton *et al.* (2006), Rajemison *et al.* (2003) and Muñoz and Cho (2003), all account for the cascading effect of taxes using input–output matrices.

Another standard assumption often adopted in public economics is the separability of fiscal policy in taxes, on the one hand, and government expenditure, on the other. This is clearly a useful analytical device, but in practice the revenue and expenditure decisions are interdependent in determining the complete distribution of welfare. That is, public expenditure may affect decision making of households. This happens either directly, as a public good that interacts in the welfare of households (for example water supply or garbage removal), or indirectly, as a productive input that lowers the price of private goods (for example infrastructure). Levying of taxes depends in general upon how the revenue is spent.[3] Public policy should aim at striking a balance between lowering taxes on goods heavily consumed by the poor (a progressive tax system) and increasing revenue to finance poverty reducing expenditures. Following this important observation, it is socially acceptable to use non-progressive taxes, as long as the revenue thus created is well targeted at poverty reducing expenditure so fiscal policy as a whole is redistributive in favour of the poor. The argument is especially true if the administrative cost of the tax authority or firm compliance costs related to a complex progressive tax system are very high (a main reason for using uniform taxes). That is, even a tax system based on simple uniform taxation can redistribute resources in favour of the poor as long as public expenditure is well targeted.[4]

3 Economic theory

This section uses simple utility theory to construct an economic frame that can be used with the survey data to provide simple and appealing graphics that both are easy to interpret and illustrate who benefits and who loses from a policy change. Later, I will add to the utility model information on constant relative prices, which will allow some shifting of intermediate goods taxes.

Two steps are involved. The first step pictures the basic principles of the model, while the second step will cover various technical complications. For readers interested only in the empirical results, only the first subsection with graphical derivations needs to be read.

Consider a single household which is maximizing a fixed budget over two goods, for example bread and a composite of all other goods, respectively x and y. If the price of the composite good y is set equal to unity, then units on the y-axis are equivalent to money units.

In the top panel of Figure 3.1, the budget line before the tax reform with a slope equal to the relative price of x to y is illustrated as VT. The optimal choice is E_1, where the initial indifference curve, U_1, is at a tangent to the budget line. Suppose a selective tax is levied on bread, causing the price of bread to increase. This relative price change turns the budget line inward around V. At the new budget line, VR, the optimal choice is E_2 at indifference curve U_2. This tax increase causes a reduction in household welfare, as indicated by the drop in the indifference curve from U_1 to U_2.

To satisfactorily answer questions about how the tax burden (on bread) is shared among all households we should, ideally, compare all households' utility losses arising from the tax change. However, comparing the magnitudes of household utility loss does not provide a useful measure of the change in the distribution of welfare – utility is an ordinal concept. It is, for example, not possible to conclude that a household which has lost 100 utility units suffers more under the imposed tax than a household that has lost only 10 utility units. With ordinal utilities we can only assess whether a household gains or loses compared with its initial situation, but that is not enough to evaluate who bears the larger burden of a tax levy.

Assume instead that after the tax reform we asked the household to report the amount of money it would have to receive to return to its initial indifference curve, U_1, that is, the amount of money that would wipe out the welfare loss of taxes, putting the household back to its original living standard. This amount can be outlined as the distance CV by noting that the household is indifferent between point E_1 – consumption before the tax – and point E_3 – consumption at new prices plus a compensating variation in the budget. In the welfare economics literature the distance CV has been

Good y

C

V

E_3

E_2

E_1

U_1

U_2

R   S

Good x

Price of x

p^2 B   D

Compensating
variation (CV)

A

p^1

Quantity of x

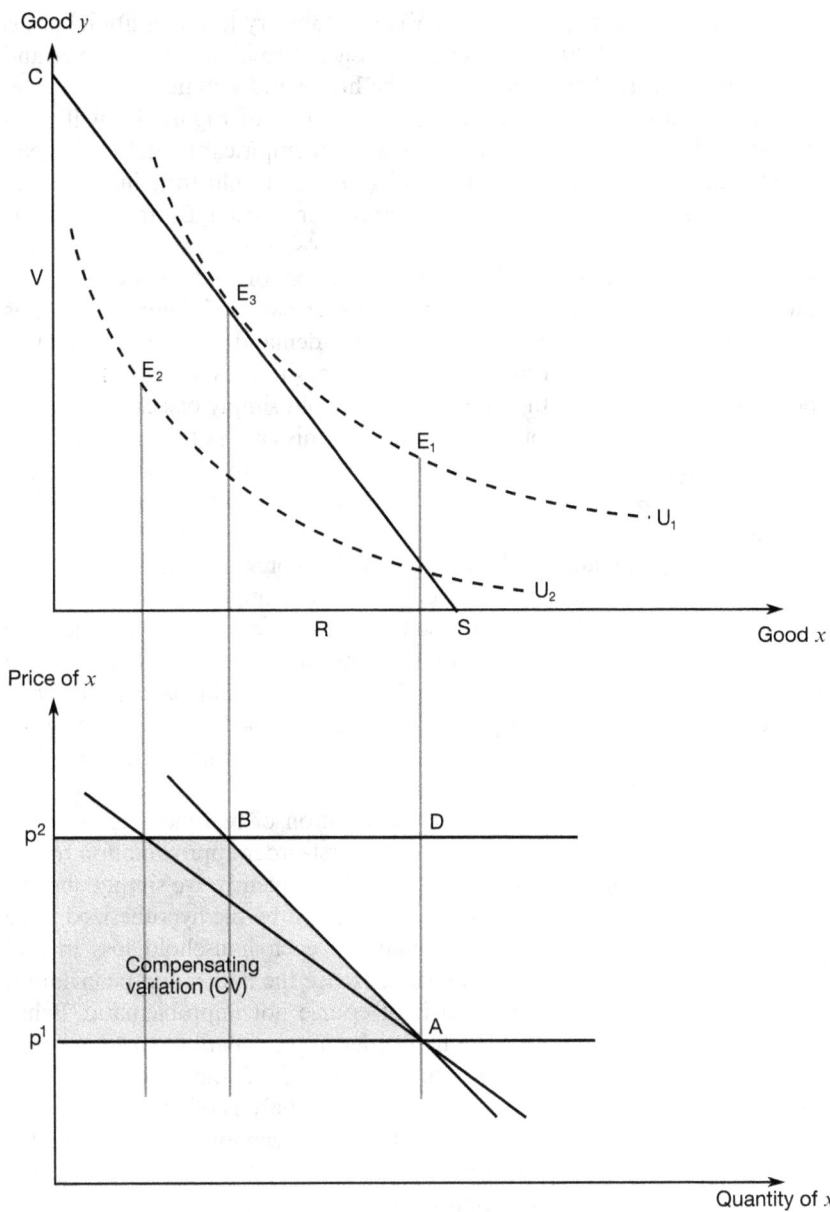

Figure 3.1 Compensating variation for a tax on good x

termed the compensating variation (CV) and, contrary to the utility loss, it is not affected by the arbitrary utility value assigned to indifference curves and can, therefore, be used as a measure of the household welfare loss.

Tracing out a demand curve from the top panel of Figure 3.1 will illustrate the final link between utility theory and an empirical model, which can be used with survey data such as the IAF (2002–3) to illustrate inequality in taxes. Moving along the initial indifference curve from E_1 to E_3 (as the relative price changes from pre bread tax to post bread tax) and mapping associated changes in demand reveals a fraction of a demand curve for bread. This demand curve is plotted in the lower panel of Figure 3.1, in this case a Hicksian (compensated) demand curve: demand changes as the price varies, keeping utility constant. This decomposition is of course only a hypothetical construction. In reality the household simply observes a change in price and chooses a new bundle of goods (in this case at E_2), in contrast to the Marshallian demand curve, which relates to the actual movement between E_1 and E_2 (fractions of both curves are drawn in the lower panel of Figure 3.1).

As a first approximation, the area Ap_1p_2D represents each household's loss in real income, which is observed bread consumption multiplied by a price change in bread. But, in response to the increase in the bread price, the household may choose to lower its consumption of bread, as illustrated in the movement from point A to point B, and thus avoid paying the price increase on withdrawn consumption. The area obtained after correcting for behavioural changes in consumption is the compensating variation (CV), given by area Ap_1p_2B.[5]

To predict how taxes impact on the distribution of real income, most tax incidence analysis uses information from the first-order approximation to CV so only the approximation Ap_1p_2D is used. Consequently, we simply observe the existing pattern of consumption and multiply it by the hypothesized price change, and use the result as an estimate of each household loss in real income, while ignoring behavioural effects. Hence the name: non-behavioural tax incidence analysis. This shortcut is of course not unproblematic. Behavioural responses may mitigate the first-order approximation, so to appreciate empirical results requires an understanding of the limitations this simplification imposes on analysis. First, for the analysis of small (marginal) price changes the model is fully consistent with economic theory but for large price changes we would expect changes in consumption to have some impact on utility. Second, the analysis is less accurate for elastic goods, as demand responses following a price change are more profound for such goods. And third, if we wish to say something about who pays a tax that falls on many goods, such as VAT, the current approach is less likely to be accurate. Composite taxes involve a multiple of behavioural changes compared with 'simple' tax reforms on individual goods.[6]

Alternatively, one may justify these tax incidence models by noting that, at worst, the household could simply continue with its current practices, so that the price change multiplied by the current demand is an upper bound on the reduction in real income.[7]

As mentioned in Section 2, there are several goods where it is obvious that taxes on inputs will cascade through the production onto the final good: for instance diesel and transport but also flour and bread. Accounting for cascading requires a bit more information, which can be obtained from assumptions on relative prices. I discuss this in the next subsection, where relative prices are defined more precisely, and then model compensating variation in a way that is specific enough to circumvent problems of cascading. The basic idea is that for simple production structures the relative price of the input to the price of the output good is approximately constant. Thus, changing the price of the input good will simply mark up the price of the output good and lower welfare from consumption of the output good proportionately. If so, we can more or less ignore cascading and treat the aggregate goods as one good:

$$v(p_i, p_j(p_i), m) \equiv \max u_h(q_i, q_j)$$

Consult the Annex of this chapter to see the necessary technical derivations.

4 Methodology

Pictures often speak more than words, and in the context of measuring the impact of tax reforms there is a nice diagrammatic way of depicting the distribution of taxes. These graphs are so-called concentration curves based on the principle of Lorenz-curves. Suppose we sort households in the data in increasing order of income and, on the horizontal axis, depict cumulative percentages of the households arranged from the poorest to the richest.[8] The vertical axis should measure the cumulative percentage of compensating variation (CV). But, from equation (4) or Figure 3.1, that is just the cumulative percentage of tax expenditure by any particular fraction of the population. Any point on these concentration curves is interpreted as the poorest x per cent of families paying y per cent of taxes. The graphics will also include a standard Lorenz-curve depicting the distribution of living standards, here measured as the distribution of expenditure (per adult equivalent). As the living standard Lorenz-curve, the concentration curve begins and ends on the 45° line: the poorest 0 per cent pay 0 per cent of taxes by definition, and the whole population must pay all taxes. The further the curve lies below the 45° line, the greater is the redistributive power of taxes for the good under consideration.

In addition to the 45° line, it is insightful to compare the tax concentration curves to the Lorenz-curve. A tax whose concentration curve is below the Lorenz-curve is progressive, and a tax concentration curve above the Lorenz-curve is regressive. That is, if a tax levy is regressive so its concentration curve lies wholly inside the Lorenz-curve of expenditures, the poor pay proportionately more of this tax than their share of living standards. Then increasing that tax marginally and refunding the proceeds in proportion to expenditure will decrease social welfare for all standard social welfare functions.

In the same way, it is possible to compare tax concentration curves for different goods. If the concentration curve of one tax is everywhere below that of another tax, then a revenue neutral tax reform (which increases the tax on the former and lowers the tax on the latter) will improve social welfare for any social welfare function that favours a more equitable distribution of income. This is also referred to as welfare dominance, meaning that one distribution of taxes' welfare dominates another (see Sahn and Younger [2003: 30] for a complete list of references to the literature on welfare dominance). A rule of thumb in remembering dominance is to note that the tax concentration curve smiles for the poor – the bigger the smile the happier are the poor. For subsidies, a negative tax, it is of course the other way around.

Concentration curves are based on cumulative shares, and thus are not sensitive to identical household errors. These cancel out in the numerator and denominator. So, as a practical matter, we may depict the value of consumption of a particular good or the value of taxes, as long as all households pay taxes and face the same tax rate.

4.1 Confidence intervals

As mentioned in the introduction (Section 1), one can determine if two curves are different either visually, by inspecting whether one curve lies above another, or statistically, using a finite number of coordinates to test if the vertical difference between the two curves is statistically different from zero. In the rest of this section I will describe the method used here to create confidence intervals (CI) for concentration and Lorenz-curves, which allows visual inspection of statistically different curves. I will do this by bootstrapping the calculations of curves. By resampling observations from the data, the bootstrap provides a way of computing standard errors and thus confidence intervals for an infinite set of points on each curve. This method is similar to Monte Carlo procedures (Geweke *et al.* 2006), just using the existing data to compute the population distributions.

Under the assumption that the sample distribution from the household survey is a good estimate of the underlying population distribution, bootstrapping provides a way of computing standard errors and CI. To illustrate how a CI for a concentration curve is calculated, imagine you have a dataset, say the IAF (2002–3) household survey, containing $N = 8,700$ households or observations. Then draw, with replacement, N observations from this N-observation dataset. In this random drawing, some of the original households will appear once, some more than once and some not at all. Using the new or resampled dataset, calculate the concentration curve and collect the cumulative value for each of the N observations. This is repeated many times, where each time a new random sample is drawn and the cumulative values collected.

Remember that any point on the concentration curve is interpreted as the poorest x per cent of families paying y per cent of taxes, so this procedure builds a dataset of replicated (cumulative tax shares) y-variables ordered from the poorest to the richest observation in the random draw. From this dataset, I calculate the standard error for each observation. This standard error is then added and subtracted from the original y-variable to create a 95 per cent confidence interval. Note that the graphed concentration curve is estimated from the original data, not the mean of replicated observations. That is, the concentration curve computed uses the original N households.[9]

5 Data

To estimate each household's 'loss in welfare', meaning taxes paid as described in (4), data are needed on the value of consumption, and to the extent that one wishes to calculate a composite of taxes and these cannot be described by proportionality in prices, the tax rate is also needed.

In this section, data from the IAF (2002–3) expenditure survey are used to describe patterns of demand. I shall be particularly concerned with how demand and living standards are related, and how the relationship varies geographically. I begin with a brief description of the survey design and collection method, and continue with a description of the relevant parts of the survey data and finally present general estimates of taxes.

The survey was designed to be representative at the national level covering all provinces and households living in urban and rural residence, excluding homeless, diplomats and people living in collective residential institutions (such as hotels, hospital or military barracks, etc.). The survey was collected, in three stages, as a stratified random sample based on the results of the 1997 population census. In the first stage, the country was divided into 858 UPAs (primary sampling units), from each of which one AE (enumeration area or statistical region) was randomly selected in the second stage. In the third stage households were chosen within the AE. For the AEs included, an updated listing of households was undertaken one month prior to the interview. From this list, 15 households were randomly selected if the AE was urban and 12 for rural AEs. Of the selected households, three were kept in reserve for non-respondents, giving a total of 12 urban and 9 rural households to be interviewed in each AE. The size of the initial sample was 8,727 households, of which 4,020 were urban and 4,707 rural. Of the 8,727 households, 8,700 were successfully interviewed, giving a response rate of 99.7 per cent. Of these, 91.8 per cent correspond to the initial sample, 7.6 per cent were substitutes for the absentees and only 0.6 per cent substitutes for refusals.

Households were visited three times within a seven-day period. During the first interview, recall data on the preceding day's and month's purchases was obtained.[10] At the second interview, three days later, expenditure data since the first interview were collected and in the third interview, another three days later, the outlays of the previous three days were again asked. The weekly diary also included receipts in kind and consumption out of own production (auto-consumption). Some goods are reported both as monthly and weekly purchases. To get an estimate of average daily consumption of these goods I took a simple average of (the daily averages of) monthly and (daily averages of) weekly purchases.

5.1 Consumption and welfare

Table 3.1 presents sample means for the main variables of interest. Total household consumption per adult equivalent (*caq*) is the preferred measure of welfare or living standards. It is measured here as the value of total household (weekly and monthly) consumption on non-durables per day divided by the number of adult equivalents in the household. Note first that in the numerator I use household consumption rather than income as my preferred measure of living standards. Households tend to report consumption more accurately than income – they have less incentive to hide consumption than income (from the interviewer or from other family members). Second, the life-cycle/permanent-income hypothesis suggests that consumption is a more stable representation of long-term household welfare than income. Households try to smooth their consumption over time. As a result, consumption patterns reflect households' own estimates of their permanent income over time and are thus a better proxy for long-term welfare. Third, adult equivalent measures are used.[11]

If we ignore price differences in the estimates in the top panel of Table 3.1, then, judging by the consumption per adult equivalent (*caq*) criterion of living standards, households in urban areas have in general higher living standards than those in rural areas. There are some regional inequalities in these means. For the average household in Mozambique consumption per adult equivalent in 2002–3 was just above Mts15,000 per day, or approximately US$0.64.[12] Divided by rural and urban households this measure is, respectively, Mts11,000 and Mts21,000. The regional inequality is primarily related to the southern region, with the capital Maputo. Here the average *caq* of urban households is close to three times the average of rural households. The inequality is the highest between the southern province of Inhambane and Maputo City. The average Maputo household enjoys more than five times the living standard of an average household in Inhambane (not reported).

Another way of describing consumption, with an eye to taxes, is to look at all consumption that potentially could be taxed or latent formal expenditure, measured here as expenditure minus auto-consumption. In what follows, this will be referred to as formal expenditure. For the average household the share of formal expenditure to total value of household consumption (*fxaq/ caq*) is 60 per cent. This means that the average household acquires three-fifths of its total consumption from formal expenditure. There are obvious regional differences in *fxaq/caq*, which on average is higher in non-rural households. Households in the rural north and central part of the country on

Table 3.1 Summary data

		North		Center		South	
	Total	*Rural*	*Urban*	*Rural*	*Urban*	*Rural*	*Urban*
Characteristics							
Adult equivalent	3.9	3.1	3.9	3.8	4.2	3.6	4.4
Family size	5.1	4.1	5.1	5.1	5.4	4.8	5.6
Share of fem. heads	0.3	0.2	0.2	0.2	0.2	0.5	0.4
Consumption / adult eq	15,196	9,851	13,222	11,020	12,863	10,566	28,255
Share of formal exp.	0.6	0.3	0.6	0.3	0.7	0.5	0.9
Total population	18.3	4.0	1.9	6.0	1.6	2.4	2.3
Consumption in Mt per day							
Total	7,627	1,309	6,387	2,249	8,824	5,162	18,822
Flour products	2,279	498	2,807	668	2,842	1,361	5,180
Flour	663	398	1,647	458	967	490	589
Bread	1,616	100	1,160	209	1,874	870	4,592
Tomato	671	60	732	131	1,064	335	1,599
Sugar	651	149	943	276	1,004	568	1,108
Soft drink	401	3	288	67	351	166	1,237
Beverages, restaurants	229	34	373	201	560	65	253
Kerosine	467	202	431	227	532	548	819
Gas	189	0	0	0	52	26	768
Transport	1,940	46	277	184	1,649	1,254	6,303
Car-fuel	948	36	247	80	1,016	896	2,730
Chapa	992	11	29	103	633	358	3,573
Alcohol	822	156	428	393	631	757	2,037
Beer	414	0	332	124	515	278	1,060
Wine	256	45	51	87	18	293	772
Spirits	152	111	46	183	98	187	205
Tobacco	168	160	107	102	193	108	284
Budget share in percent							
Total	14.02	4.81	15.34	6.27	20.78	11.16	25.57
Flour products	5.15	2.06	7.66	2.22	7.45	3.58	8.87
Flour	2.14	1.72	5.12	1.75	3.21	1.63	1.34
Bread	3	0.34	2.54	0.47	4.24	1.96	7.53
Tomato	1.59	0.23	1.83	0.43	3.23	0.89	3.08
Sugar	1.57	0.44	2.38	0.7	2.73	1.48	2.31
Soft drink	0.38	0.01	0.31	0.1	0.55	0.17	0.97
Beverages, restaurants	0.36	0.13	0.33	0.44	1.01	0.16	0.21
Kerosine	1.51	0.74	1.73	0.71	1.98	2.05	2.15
Gas	0.11	0	0	0	0.04	0.04	0.43
Transport	2.01	0.06	0.22	0.39	2.07	1.26	6.16
Car-fuel	0.38	0.03	0.16	0.13	0.63	0.41	0.82
Chapa	1.62	0.03	0.06	0.26	1.44	0.85	5.33
Alcohol	1	0.47	0.56	0.95	1.15	1.24	1.39
Beer	0.35	0	0.37	0.14	0.79	0.14	0.68
Wine	0.3	0.15	0.09	0.3	0.05	0.49	0.53
Spirits	0.35	0.32	0.1	0.51	0.31	0.61	0.19
Tobacco	0.45	0.67	0.32	0.33	0.61	0.33	0.42

(table continued on next page)

Table 3.1 (continued)

	Total	North		Center		South	
		Rural	*Urban*	*Rural*	*Urban*	*Rural*	*Urban*
Share of buyers							
Total	0.82	0.62	0.94	0.66	0.97	0.84	0.98
Flour products	0.49	0.22	0.62	0.2	0.68	0.42	0.87
Flour	0.17	0.14	0.34	0.09	0.2	0.13	0.2
Bread	0.42	0.11	0.46	0.13	0.61	0.33	0.84
Tomato	0.48	0.13	0.58	0.23	0.82	0.27	0.86
Sugar	0.31	0.12	0.46	0.2	0.62	0.21	0.4
Soft drink	0.06	0.01	0.05	0.03	0.11	0.02	0.15
Beverages, restaurants	0.04	0.02	0.03	0.07	0.1	0.02	0.02
Kerosine	0.48	0.35	0.65	0.28	0.6	0.65	0.51
Gas	0.02				0.01	0	0.1
Transport	0.18	0.01	0.03	0.06	0.23	0.1	0.5
Car-fuel	0.03	0	0.02	0.04	0.06	0.02	0.06
Chapa	0.15	0	0.01	0.03	0.18	0.09	0.47
Alcohol	0.1	0.05	0.05	0.14	0.11	0.13	0.1
Beer	0.03		0.02	0.01	0.06	0.01	0.06
Wine	0.04	0.03	0.01	0.05	0.02	0.06	0.05
Spirits	0.05	0.03	0.02	0.09	0.05	0.07	0.02
Tobacco	0.12	0.19	0.08	0.16	0.13	0.06	0.07

Note: Consumption per adult equivalent is value of total household consumption (in Mt) on non-durable goods per day, including auto-consumption and receipts in kind, divided by the number of adult equivalents in the household. Consumption (in the lower panel) is also in Mt per day (not per adult equivalent). Total population is in millions. Budget shares are percentages of total household consumption. Share of buyers is the share of households that have strictly positive consumption. Beverages are drinks, with or without alcohol bought in restaurants
Source: IAF 2002-3, author's calculations

average derive 30 per cent of their living standards from formal consumption. These households mainly live off their plots of land. For the average household in the area around Maputo, almost all expenditure is formal. In Maputo Province the average formal expenditure share is 80 per cent and in Maputo City the average is very close to 100 per cent.

Note also that both rural households and households in the north are slightly smaller with respect to both number of persons and adult equivalent, and in the south there is a higher average share of female-headed households. The average share of female-headed households is more than twice that of northern and central regions.

The lower panel of Table 3.1 shows the regional consumption patterns of commodities in the analysis. For each good, I show the value of the average household's consumption, the budget share and the share of households who buy the good in that region. The latter may by thought of as a political economy parameter. It indicates how many households will be affected by a price change.

There is a great deal of variation in the importance of goods in the budget, and thus the extent to which households are affected by taxes. The average household in Mozambique derives one-seventh of its living standards from the goods considered here, but for the average urban household in the south this share is as high as 26 per cent. The most important goods in the budget are flour and bread, with marked regional differences. The average rural household in the north devotes 2 per cent of its budget to bread and flour, whereas, at the other extreme, the average urban household in the south spends almost 9 per cent of a three times larger budget on flour products. Notice also the difference in flour and bread purchases. Some households buy flour (to bake bread), whereas other households buy the bread. This demonstrates the consequence of not including both bread and flour in the incidence of flour taxes. In the analysis, I will examine both the incidence of a price change on flour alone and the incidence of a price change in flour on aggregated flour products. The aggregate analysis will include not only the direct taxes on flour, but also the indirect cascading of flour taxes on bread consumption. To do this, I am effectively assuming that the prices of the two products move in parallel, following derivations in the Annex of this chapter.

Beverages bought in restaurants, with or without alcohol, are on all three measures more important in central regions and, understandably so, in the urban areas. Both the share of central households drinking beverages in restaurants and the budget share of the average central household are more than three times as high as that of northern and southern households (figures not reported). Soft drinks and beer are more essential in urban areas both with respect to the mean share of households buying these refreshments and with respect to the average household budget share. The average urban household share of income used on soft drinks and beer is seven to eight times higher than for an average rural household. In the average rural household, consumption of aguardente and other liquors is, on the other hand, more than twice as important as in the average urban household.

Chapas (small semi-public buses) drive almost exclusively in urban areas and in 2002–3 were mostly an urban-south phenomenon. Some 32 per cent of the southern households use chapas compared with only 9 per cent and 1 per cent of central and northern households, respectively. The discrepancy in budget shares between an average urban household in the south and an average rural household in the north is close to 188:1. Fuel for cars, bottled gas, and kerosene for illumination and cooking are also used more intensively by urban households, and the share increases the further south the average household is located.

Notice that 82 per cent of households consume the goods considered here, and in the urban areas it is almost 100 per cent of the households who will be affected by price changes relating to these goods.

5.2 *Taxes*

The principal tax on goods and services in Mozambique is VAT, which is levied at a standard rate of 17 per cent but with a zero rate on exports and, for example, on inputs into agricultural production and medical supply. The VAT is complemented by several excise taxes, notably on tobacco, alcohol sugar, and fuel (such as diesel and kerosene for illumination and cooking), as described on p. 50.

Import prices are affected by four non-zero tax brackets. Raw materials are taxed at 2.5 per cent, and capital goods and intermediates are as a rule in the 5 per cent and 7.5 per cent import tax brackets. The 20 per cent bracket is reserved for luxuries and processed goods, but, notably, many agricultural products, including meat, dairy and fruit and vegetable products, are also charged the high duty rate.[13]

To identify the distributional incidence of taxes on combined goods I must rely on extra assumptions (used in the next section to calculate the taxes on flour, alcohol and tobacco). The survey does not report taxes paid by the household so I calculate the share of taxes from the reported value of each purchase using the statutory tax rates, though some goods may have been bought at the untaxed informal market.[14] For import taxes, I additionally assume that in areas (the southern regions) for which import is a large share of the market, the price of goods goes up by the amount of the import duty. Thus those who pay the tax are consumers of the good in high import areas, whether it is imported or produced domestically. In the last case, the full payment does not go to the government; some of the benefits from the import duty go to protected local producers, who can charge a higher price for their output. Thus the cost to consumers is not equal to the government revenue.

6 Results

Averages such as those in Table 3.1 conceal a great deal. The broad inter-regional patterns of consumption tell us which areas benefit and which lose from different price strategies. But there are rich and poor households in all of these regions, and consumption patterns are far from independent of household income. If it is true that urban households are better off and poor households live in rural areas, then the direct effect of higher prices on, for example, kerosene (which we have just seen is consumed predominantly by urban households) might well be to improve the distribution of real income. In the following section, the concentration-curve methodology is used to present comparisons based on individual households rather than regional groups of households.

6.1 Flour and tomato

Flour and tomato fall in the high import tax bracket of 20 per cent, but are exempt from VAT. Recall that households which consume the taxed commodity are assumed to pay the associated taxes. Now, due to poorly integrated markets, especially connecting northern and southern regions, and since the southern regions, in contrast to the northern and central regions, are net importers of agricultural products, I assume that import taxes are only paid in the southern provinces (Gaza, Inhambane, Maputo Province and Maputo City). Thus the prices of flour and tomato in the southern provinces are assumed to go up by the amount of import tariffs. Likewise, in the southern provinces there are fewer farmers selling flour and tomato. Consequently, few households will benefit from custom taxes, and it would rarely be useful to include flour and tomato producers in the analysis. Currently, South African imports dominate the southern region, especially the Maputo market.

Figure 3.2a shows concentration curves for taxes on direct consumption of flour and tomato. These are both regressive, and significantly so. To the extent that the administrative costs of exempting these goods from VAT are not too high, this is a good argument for keeping a low tax on flour and tomato.

Since much flour is consumed as an intermediate into other goods, most noticeably as bread, bread prices will indirectly be affected by an increase in flour prices. I have tried to model this indirect effect, in Figure 3.2b, by assuming that the relative price of flour and bread will remain constant. This assumption is, as described in Section 3, similar to saying that if we tax flour, then the price of bread will change proportionately. The results of this

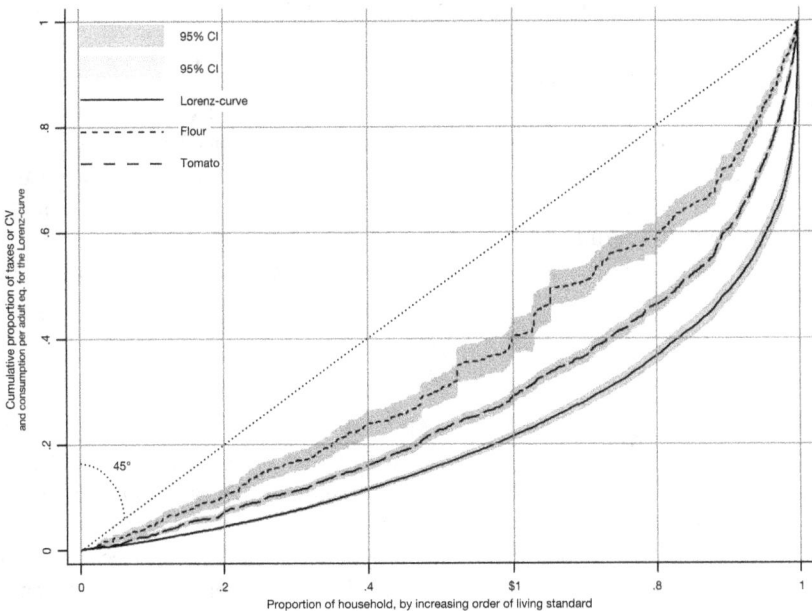

Figure 3.2a Concentration curves of family living standards and tax payments
Note: CV is compensating variance of price changes and $1 is the cut-off point for households with expenditure per adult equivalent below US$1.
Source: IAF (2002–3), author's calculations.

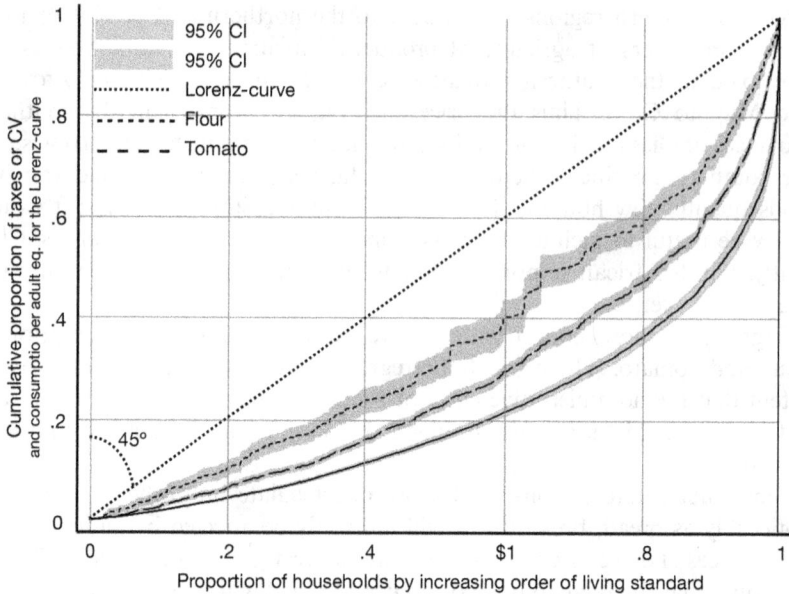

Figure 3.2b Concentration curves of family living standards and tax payments
Note: CV is compensating variance of price changes and $1 is the cut-off point for households with expenditure per adult equivalent below US$1.
Source: IAF (2002–3), author's calculations.

exercise do not change the view that VAT exemption of flour favours the poor. Surely, the same distributional and revenue impact could be obtained in a simpler tax system, where the import tariff is replaced with VAT.[15] As the economy progresses and becomes more formal, there is the additional advantage of charging VAT on flour and tomato, and more of the local horticulture and milling industry would contribute to government revenue. It is, politically, much easier to introduce VAT on these products now than later, when the industry is formal.

6.2 Sugar and beverages

Sugar falls in the import tax bracket of 7.5 per cent, but it is subject to VAT and a variable import surcharge ranging from 90 per cent to 100 per cent, rationalized by the authorities as infant industry protection. Most of Mozambique's sugar is consumed by the domestic market but some is exported. Currently Mozambique is enjoying a preferential price under a quota system on markets in the European Union, but in the coming years this price will gradually be adjusted to a competitive market price (although under a compensation scheme allowing local sugar producers to adapt to the new liberalized environment). Also Brazil, which is by far the largest producer of sugar, is expected to switch to ethanol production, consequently increasing the world market price. Both occurrences could potentially affect the variable surcharge and the domestic price of sugar.

Figure 3.3, shows that any increase in the domestic sugar price will be highly regressive, so on equity grounds this calls for a reduction in sugar duties. The two lower concentration curves are for soft drinks, such as juice and soda, and for alcoholic and non-alcoholic beverages bought in restaurants. The former is in contrast to the very progressive sugar tax, while the latter is not significantly different from a neutral tax. That is, both poor and rich take a drink in restaurants, but mostly rich households buy soft drinks in shops and markets.

The big consumers of sugar are the local branch of Coca-Cola and the breweries. Thus there is an indirect sugar tax on consumption of these products. The interesting question remains how much of the sugar tax is shifted onto consumers of soft drinks and beverages. I could assume constant relative prices, but in this case this is not very useful. Coca-Cola and the breweries are major buyers of local sugar so they can pressure (and have) the four functioning sugar mills for preferential prices by opting to import sugar from South Africa. Given the complexity of such negotiations the price of sugar and the price of beverages may not even move together. So, to answer the question of how much of the sugar tax is shifted onto consumers of sugar-containing products would require more information, for example

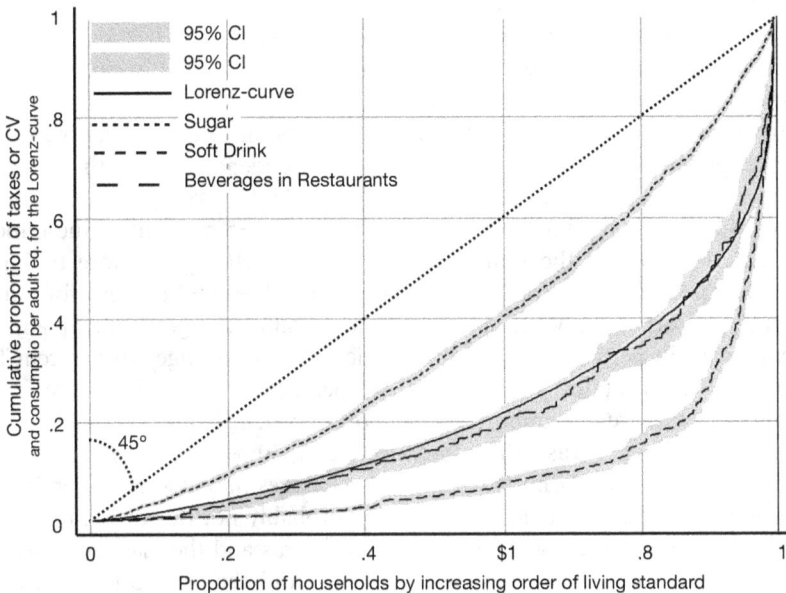

Figure 3.3 Concentration curves of family living standards and tax payments
Note: CV is compensating variance of price changes and $1 is the cut-off point for households with expenditure per adult equivalent below US$1.
Source: IAF (2002–3), author's calculations.

knowledge of the sugar cost in these goods.[16] Nevertheless, assuming that an increase in the sugar price will at least not lower the price of drinks, we can say that sugar taxes are less regressive than the sugar tax curve shown in Figure 3.3. However, whether the tax becomes neutral or even progressive cannot be seen.

6.3 Fuel and transport

In the household survey there is information on three types of fuel; kerosene used for illumination and cooking, bottled (butane) gas used for cooking and car-fuel for transport, where most of the car-fuel is diesel but there is also a little petrol. The following focuses on taxes on these three fuel types. Fuel prices are administered prices given by three variables: (1) the import price of fuel; (2) taxes; and (3) a margin for fuel contractors (distributors, for transport, and retailers). Fuel falls in the import tax bracket of 5 per cent and is also subject to VAT and a specific (unit) tax (Taxa Sobre Combustível), levied as a flat sum per litre or kilo of fuel.[17] Government officials review fuel prices every month and adjust or stabilize them whenever the cost of importing fuel changes by more than 3 per cent, or whenever there is a variation in the specific fuel tax. Accordingly, every month new fixed public prices are set.

The margin or mark-up for fuel suppliers is based on a pre-negotiated margin (the base-margin), and calculated as a pre-weighted sum of the inflation corrected base-margin and the deflation corrected base-margin. That is, fuel contractors will not bear any burden of taxes, which was also one of the assumptions in the theoretical setup.

In general, there has been a reluctance to pass on to consumers the world market prices of fuel; instead, there has been a tendency to smooth fuel price fluctuations and to change relative prices. In 2005, the average specific tax on diesel was just above 3,300Mts/l, or approximately 35 per cent of the import price (CIF). For gas the same numbers were 500Mts/kg, or close to 7 per cent. Kerosene was exempt from the specific tax. The total tax levy for a litre of fuel (import duty, VAT, specific tax and stabilizing government adjustments) was, in per cent of the import price and on average, 70 per cent for diesel, –9 per cent for kerosene and 42 per cent for gas. The percentage increase in the average import price before it reached the public, including the supplier margin, was 110 per cent for diesel, 30 per cent for kerosene and 147 per cent for gas. Admittedly, these percentages may fluctuate, depending on the import price, but the examples are probably not out of the ordinary. That is, diesel has the highest tax, followed by gas and then kerosene, which in some months, as here, may be subsidized, and the total price difference between import and consumer price is the highest for gas, followed by diesel and kerosene.

From an administrative point of view, there are two immediate problems with the kerosene subsidy: First, it absorbs an important amount of scarce public resources and, second, it increases the risk of having kerosene smuggled out of the country to countries where kerosene is more expensive, for example Zimbabwe, in which case the Mozambican state is subsidizing kerosene consumption in other countries.

Figure 3.4a depicts concentration curves for direct and indirect fuel taxes. The direct taxes are those on car-fuel, gas and kerosene. Direct taxes on kerosene are highly regressive. However, as noted above, the monthly adjustment of fuel prices may subsidize kerosene, in which case the poorest households receive a higher share of these subsidies than their share of income. That is, kerosene *subsidies* are progressive. Direct taxes on car-fuel and gas are the most progressive of all the taxes analysed here. These curves follow each other quite closely and are not significantly different. However, in contrast to gas, most car-fuel is consumed as an intermediate good into other services, predominantly transport. I try to account for at least part of this indirect impact by assuming that the price of semi-public transport (chapas) moves in parallel with diesel prices. Under this assumption, a price increase in diesel will increase the price of chapa in a fixed proportion of the diesel price increase, so users of chapas would bear part of the burden of the tax. This may on average not be an unreasonable assumption, given that the fare is regulated by government.[18] Figure 3.4a also shows constructed concentration curves for direct chapa expenditure (or chapa VAT) and Figure

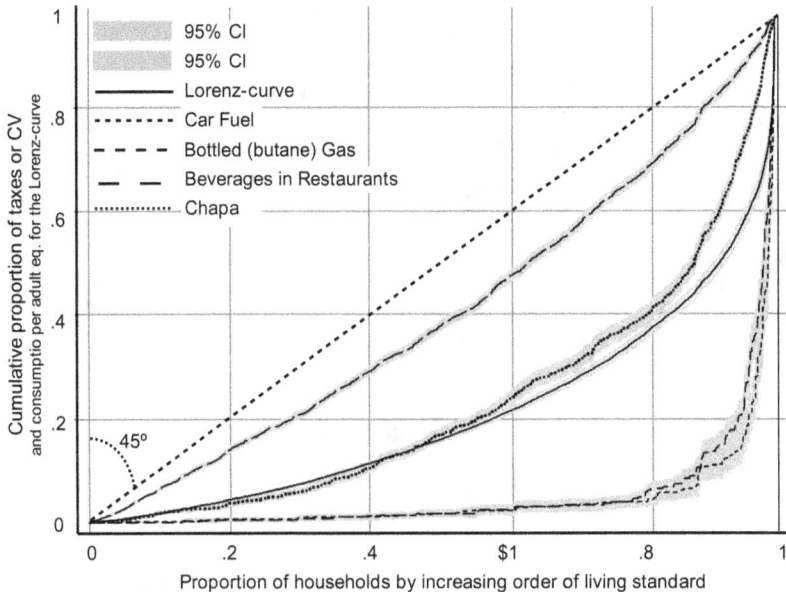

Figure 3.4a Concentration curves of family living standards and tax payments
Note: CV is compensating variance of price changes and $1 is the cut-off point for households with expenditure per adult equivalent below US$1.
Source: IAF (2002–3), author's calculations.

3.4b depicts the combined effect of direct purchases of diesel fuel and indirect purchases through chapa transport. The result shows that tax on diesel, including the indirect effect on chapa transport, is also progressive, mostly because it is concentrated among urban, better-off households, which is similar to results in Younger *et al.* (1999).

An administratively easy way of setting taxes on fuel would be to set a uniform ad valorem tax on all fuel products. This would not only simplify administration, but would also minimize the risk of corruption in the monthly negotiations and the real value of such a tax would not be eroded by inflation. In Figure 3.4b, I have simulated such a tax reform for the fuel products considered here. I do not know the average structure of taxes on fuel in 2002–3, the period of the survey, but, assuming that the expenditure pattern would have been the same if diesel was taxed 100 per cent, gas 60 per cent and kerosene untaxed, the administratively easy, uniform tax would produce a concentration curve that is not significantly different from a neutral tax.[19] Even if I include the indirect increase in chapa fares, this result is unchanged, which shows that a process of revoking the tax provoked relative prices changes in favour of a uniform tax that will not affect the poor disproportionately. This is so, in particular, if the revenue from these taxes is well targeted towards the poor.

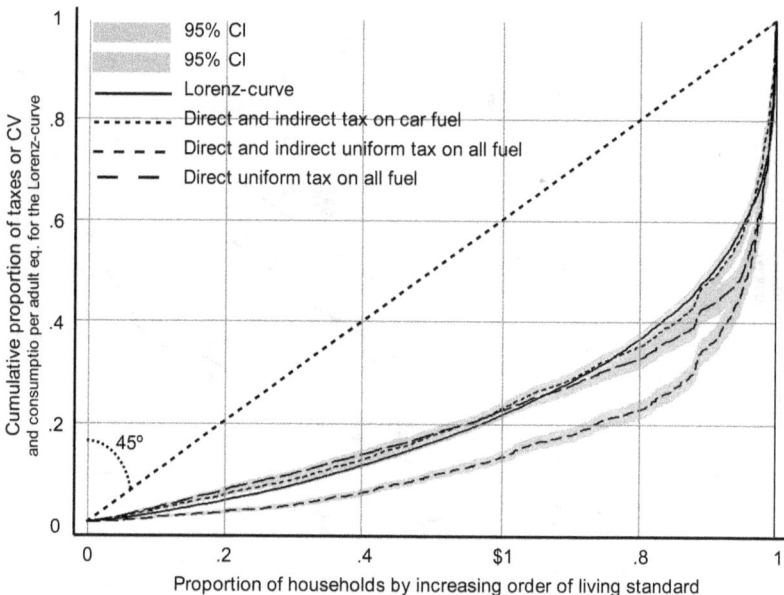

Figure 3.4b Concentration curves of family living standards and tax payments
Note: CV is compensating variance of price changes and $1 is the cut-off point for households with expenditure per adult equivalent below US$1.
Source: IAF (2002–3), author's calculations.

6.4 Vices

There are two excise tax brackets (Imposto de Consumo) for alcohol and tobacco, one low, at 40 per cent, and one high, at 65 per cent (see customs guideline, MPF 2002). The low bracket is used for beer and wine, while tobacco and spirits (such as aguardente and other liquors) fall in the high bracket. These are accompanied by a high import tax of 20 per cent and by VAT. Tobacco and alcohol are often viewed as vices, so households may misreport their consumption of these goods. If this measurement error is correlated with living standards, say rich households consume more alcohol than poorer households but they underreport their drinking, then the esti-mate of tax incidence will be too regressive.

The concentration curves in Figure 3.5a for tobacco and spirits are sig-nificantly different from and dominate those of beer and wine. Hence a revenue neutral tax reform, lowering the tax of spirits and tobacco by increasing taxes on beer and wine, would improve social welfare. Another way of looking at this is that a uniform tax on all alcohol and tobacco is easier to administer. In Figure 3.5b I have redrawn concentration curves for tobacco taxes, and drawn taxes for all alcohol combined and a concentration curve for a uniform tax on vices (tobacco and alcohol). Here I use the label 'sin-tax' because it often is seen as a way of discouraging consumption of objectionable

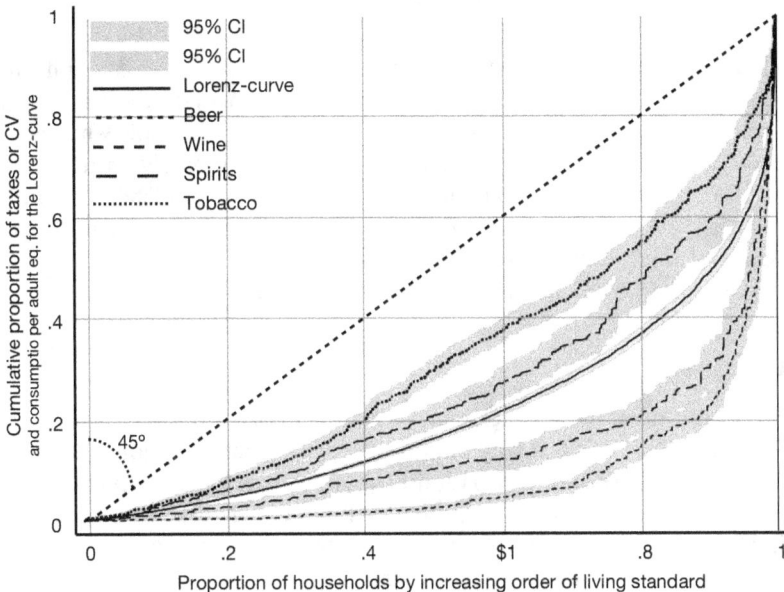

Figure 3.5a Concentration curves of family living standards and tax payments
Note: CV is compensating variance of price changes and $1 is the cut-off point for households with expenditure per adult equivalent below US$1.
Source: IAF (2002–3), author's calculations.

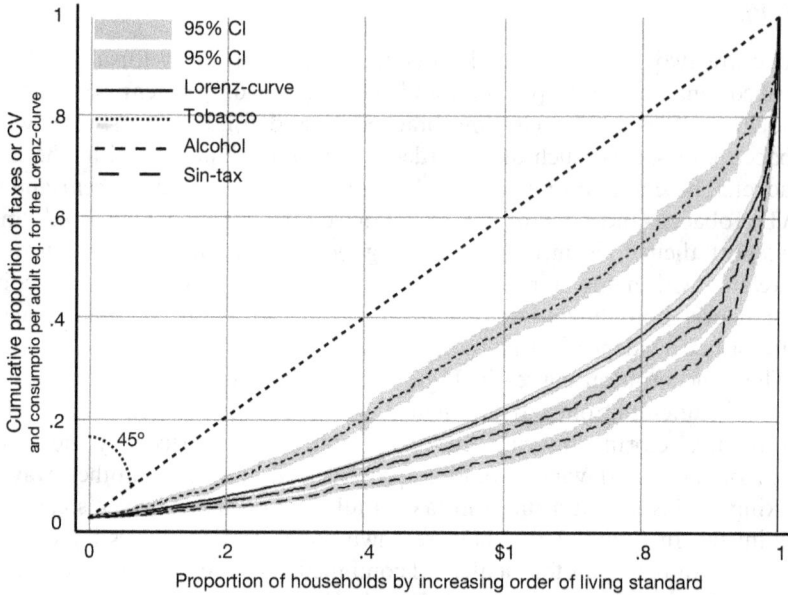

Figure 3.5b Concentration curves of family living standards and tax payments
   Note: CV is compensating variance of price changes and $1 is the cut-off
   point for households with expenditure per adult equivalent below US$1.
   Source: IAF (2002–3), author's calculations.

products. The results show that a uniform tax on alcohol is significantly progressive, and even the uniform sin-tax is progressive, though less significantly so.[20] Thus, given the usually low elasticity on vices, policy makers can rest assured that such taxes would not fall disproportionately on the poor.

Continuing the assumption that taxes are shifted completely forward to consumers, this means that if a beer now costs Mts50,000 it would increase Mts9,000 if the excise tax were raised from the current 40 per cent to match the high excise tax on spirits and tobacco of 65 per cent.

7 Conclusion

This chapter measured the incidence of taxes (import duties, VAT and excises) on several goods, using survey data on household consumption to construct estimates of compensating variation of a tax change (assuming that the full incidence falls on the final consumers). I presented these non-behavioural estimates of compensating variation or tax payments in concentration curves, together with their confidence intervals, which permitted examination of progressivity and dominance of the different tax levies.

Supplementing the standard tax incidence methodology with graphical estimates of uncertainty proved very powerful, both in visual inspections and in distinguishing dominance of one tax over another. Due to the richness of observations in household surveys, the confidence intervals are quite narrow, so it is possible with a high degree of statistical confidence to draw conclusions on the dominance of taxes.

The theoretical section of this chapter illustrated the limits of non-behavioural incidence analysis. Policy makers should be careful when using results on composite tax reforms, where heterogeneous behaviour may mitigate the welfare impact of taxes. That is, if taxes induce a large shift in the consumption of poor households compared to that of better-off households, then this type of analysis would overvalue the welfare loss on the poor. Consequently, I have taken a cautious attitude towards assumptions that may potentially misrepresent the distribution of taxes, and tested robustness of results using different assumptions. All tests confirmed robustness of qualitative results, so findings in this chapter and the methodology developed should be useful in deriving tax reforms.

Taxes in Mozambique are generally narrow in scope, placing a high burden on a small base. The taxes chosen here are usually considered to be good tax handles, in the sense that it is difficult to evade or avoid them either because they are target goods produced by a few formal, easy to control, local producers or because almost all consumption is imported so the goods cross international border control. Politicians can therefore affect short-term revenue by adjusting these taxes.

The main substantive finding is that special consumption taxes can be used to make the tax system very progressive. Increasing excise taxes on car-fuel, bottled gas, wine and beer while lowering taxes on kerosene, sugar and tobacco will have a significant effect on direct tax payments and thus the living standards of poorer households. Taxation of intermediate inputs raises the problem of knowing how the tax affects the final prices of goods consumed. Indirect effects need to be taken into account to get a complete picture of the distribution of taxes. In particular, sugar and fuel taxes may be shifted onto indirect consumers of these goods. Including indirect effects attenuates the incidence or inequality of these narrow-based taxes. For fuel taxes the distribution of direct and indirect tax payments is not significantly different from a neutral tax. Also, a combined tax on alcohol and tobacco, here labelled 'sin-tax', shows attenuation towards a neutral tax. To be exact, a uniform excise tax on alcohol and tobacco would only be slightly progressive.

Finally, this chapter showed that policy makers may beneficially replace the high import tariff on flour and tomato with VAT and a lower import tariff. The distribution of flour and tomato taxes would be unaffected by such a reform. Yet eliminating VAT exemptions would subsequently simplify (customs) tax administration and prepare the tax system for a formalization of the industries.

Annex: technical derivations

The reduction in household real income resulting from the imposition of a tax can most easily be seen by using an indirect utility function. Here, household utility (or real income) is written as a function of its income and prices. With many goods consumed in different shapes, for example flour and bread or diesel and public transport, it is important to use as well a model that recognizes the dual role of goods. That is, changing prices on flour will cascade through bakery production into changing prices of bread. There is a direct effect of flour taxes on the price of bread and, therefore, an indirect effect of flour taxes on the living standards of bread consumers.

Consider a simple representation of household living standards, given by the indirect utility function over two goods, where the first good, say good i, is both a final consumption good and an intermediate good into the production of the second good, good j. If good i is flour or diesel, then good j would be, respectively, bread or transport. The indirect utility function is then given by

$$v\left(p_i, p_j(p_i), m\right) \equiv \max u_h\left(q_i, q_j\right) \tag{1}$$

Here q is consumption and $p_j(p_i)$ is the price of q_j given directly as a function of p_i, the price of the input good. This function gives the maximum utility, uh, achievable for household h at a given price vector, (p_i, p_j), and income, m. Now imagine an increase in the flour price, p_i. This will both affect the living standards of flour consumers (directly) and the living standards of bread consumers (indirectly). Nevertheless, without further knowledge of how that increase in the cost of the input good transforms into a change in p_j, it is not possible to determine the household reduction in living standards from consumption of good j.[21]

In simple production structures it is possible, though, to account for the cascading effects of the price change. To do this we must be able to formulate assumptions on the relative prices. Proportionality in prices is not only a convenient tool to account for cascading but also suitable because it automatically allows for the possibility that goods can be consumed in a variety of qualities, as well as being in different stages of production.[22] Suppose the price p_j is always proportional to the input price p_i so that $p_j(p_i) = \lambda p_i$ where λ is a scalar. If the goods of interest are bread and flour, then this condition requires that the relative prices of bread and flour remain constant (they increase and decrease in the same proportion).

When implementing the model using household consumption data, I will use this assumption to group together incommensurate items, where the price of the output good is arguably a mark-up over the input good.

From (1) and under the assumption of proportional prices the effect of a (marginal) price change on household real income is straightforward to derive as follows,[23]

$$\frac{\partial v}{\partial p_i} = \div \frac{\partial v}{\partial m}\left(q_i + \lambda q_j\right) \tag{2}$$

where the equality comes from the use of Roy's identity (linking the indirect utility function to Marshallian demand; see, for example, Varian [1992:

106]). $\partial v/\partial m$ is the private marginal utility of money, and λq_j is consumption of good j adjusted to its 'effective' contents of good i.[24]

Since welfare of different households will in general weigh differently in the government objective function, we can go from the household level of welfare to social welfare by inserting (1) in an aggregated (Utilitarian) social welfare function, and rewrite (2) for social welfare W,

$$\frac{\partial W}{\partial p_i} = \div \sum_h \theta_h \left(q_{ih} + \lambda q_{jh} \right) \tag{3}$$

where

$$\theta_h = \frac{\partial W}{\partial m_h} = \frac{\partial W}{\partial v_h} \frac{\partial v_h}{\partial m_h}$$

θh is a weight that represents the social value of transferring one metical to household h – the social marginal utility of money in the hands of household h. Notice that (3) summarizes only the effect of the price change on household real income and social welfare. Producer welfare and government revenue will also change, but the social value of this is not included in (3) and has to be taken into account separately.

Representative values of consumption levels q in (3) can be obtained from a household survey such as the IAF (2002–3) but the θ parameters are subjective. In particular the θ's may vary for different observers. Outside agencies may, for example, value welfare of interest groups or segments of society differently than a ministry of finance. The typical example where these conflicting views find expression is in giving social weight to powerful lobby groups. In the empirical analysis I will, therefore, avoid making any value judgement on the distribution of welfare. Instead I will chart the way in which consumption varies with what is likely to be the most important factor determining these weights – household living standard. To do this, it is convenient to work with a slightly different form of equation (2).

For a *marginal* price change, dp_i, households would require a compensating variation in their budget, CV, equal to observed consumption multiplied by the price change. So from (2) it follows that

$$CV = \left(q_i + \lambda q_j \right) dp_i = p_i \left(q_i + \lambda q_j \right) d \ln p_i \tag{4}$$

The compensating variation of a *marginal* change in the price of good i is simply the change in the consumption budget that is necessary to keep the consumption basket constant. The proportionality assumption is very convenient. The burden of flour taxes of a bread consuming household depends on λp_i, while the flour consumer tax burden depends directly on p_i. If p_i changes with the bread price moving proportionately, the compensation CV in (4) is $(q_i + \lambda q_j)dp_i$. The bread consumer loss is proportional, not to q_j, but to λq_j. Using the fact that for small price changes $dp_i = p_i \, d\ln p_i$, CV, accounting for cascading of prices, can be written as $(p_i q_i + \lambda p_i q_j)d\ln p_i$, which, since $\lambda p_i q_j$ is just the value of purchases of good j, is the sum of purchases of good i and j multiplied by the relative change in p_i.

(4) ignores behavioural changes the price change might induce; for large tax reforms it is necessary to account for the demand responses.[25]

Notes

1 Rounded numbers in 2005 (see IMF 2006: 24).
2 It is worth mentioning that for very elastic goods the standard (own- and cross-price elasticities) behavioural effect of price changes may also be quite large.
3 Turnovsky (1996) provides a more elaborate model of simultaneous determination of optimal tax and expenditure, but such analysis is beyond the scope of this chapter.
4 Heltberg *et al.* (2001) assess the welfare distribution of government expenditure in Mozambique and find that expenditure is distributed disproportionately in favour of the poor.
5 For marginal price changes these two areas coincide. Elaborations on this will be given in the following, more technical subsections. The intuition is the following: for a utility maximizing household a price increase will have a direct effect on increased expenditure on that good. There will also be an indirect effect, in that the household will want to change the consumption bundle. But since the household consumes at an optimum (setting marginal gain of increased utility is equal to marginal cost of increased consumption) any such infinitesimal change must yield zero additional utility.
6 Consequently, I will make no attempt to judge the overall progressivity of VAT or trade taxes, not to say the entire tax system. For the larger part of the analysis I will instead stick to taxes on individual goods. On a practical matter, it has not been possible to retrieve tax rates relating to 2002–3, which I should preferably use to present aggregate taxes.
7 Under the assumption that the behavioural responses of the producer are negligible.
8 In the analysis I will use household weights from the survey data, thus points on the axis do in fact refer to the poorest x percent of the *population*, and not *sample households*. Dropping household weights has no impact on qualitative results.
9 Generally 50–200 replications are needed for estimates of standard errors. In the application, the confidence intervals are calculated from 100 bootstrap samples. I have tried using as few as 10 replications, but with the number of observations that I have this has visually little or no effect on computed standard errors.
10 The recall data on the previous month's expenditure relate to goods where dynamic effects could be important, for example for durable or storable products, whereas the weekly record lists, mostly, temporary consumption. The longer the recall period of expenditure estimates, the more likely it is that these estimates will be biased. People generally forget details of expenditures the further such purchases slip into the past and might also include in their response events that happened before the beginning of the recall period. Asked about expenditures during the previous month, respondents might include kerosene they bought 35 days ago, and incorrectly recall the value of the kerosene. On the other hand, a short recall period increases the risk of interviewing households in a low or high

purchasing cycle, and thus not observing the average consumption pattern of that household. The present survey design diminishes these problems because big purchases of (for example) storable goods are made less often but are clearer in people's memory.

11 Qualitative results on incidence are robust to using per capita and per adult equivalent measures. Equivalence scales are from FAO and are listed in Appendix II of an earlier version of this paper, available from the author's homepage: www.econ.ku.dk/css.

12 In 2002–3 the average exchange rate was 23,730 Mt per US dollar (World Bank 2005a).

13 Here I will assume that all trade is SADC trade, so no attempt is made to calculate import duties based on the country of origin.

14 From the standard formula used to calculate netvalues: revenue = expenditure × (tax rate/(1 + tax rate)).

15 Remember there are only a few local producers who are able to charge a higher price due to the high import tariff, and VAT would not provide the same protection to these producers (as long as these are formal, and accordingly pay VAT). If producers are informal they would gain the same protection and revenue would be unchanged.

16 This can, for example, be read off an input–output table.

17 I have tried to calculate concentration curves for specific taxes (Taxa Sobre Combustível) on fuel, kerosene and gas as well (using quantities instead of expenditure). These follow very closely the concentration curves shown, and are not significantly different from these. So in the following analysis taxes refer, equally, to unit taxes and ad valorem taxes.

18 I have also tried to assume that diesel accounts for 20 per cent of the cost of semi-public transport (as in Younger *et al.* 1999). This does not change results.

19 In most empirical work some kind of aggregation is necessary, and the tax rates chosen here are by no means obvious, though they have some relation to the described average tax rates in 2005. Within a reasonable distance from the chosen tax rates, results do not hinge on the assumed (weighted) tax rates.

20 Notice that these concentration curves do not include expenditure in restaurants and bars, though including indirect taxes from this expenditure is not likely to change results. Figure 3.3 shows that expenditure in restaurants and bars is also slightly progressive.

21 The formal proof of this is given in Appendix I in the first draft of this paper, available from the author's homepage: www.econ.ku.dk/css.

22 For a complete discussion of the quality choices in household demand, see Deaton (1997: ch. 5.3), who argues that the relative price of different quality is constant.

23 See again Appendix I, in the first draft of this paper, available from the author's homepage.

24 Roy's identity:

$$\frac{\partial v / \partial p_i}{\partial v / \partial m} = -(q_i + \lambda q_i)$$

where q is a weighted sum of directly related goods.

25 For larger price changes one could amend (4) with a set of price elasticities accounting for the change in demand as prices change, but that is beyond the scope of this chapter.

4 Enterprise survey evidence

Bruce Byiers

1 Introduction

Despite several major tax policy reforms since independence and implementation of a series of important new taxes in recent years, as documented in Chapter 2, tax policy in Mozambique has received only limited analytical treatment. Furthermore, where studies have taken place, these have tended strongly to focus on tax revenues from a government and therefore macroeconomic standpoint. As such, while government policy ostensibly seeks to simultaneously provide a sustainable source of revenues and promote economic growth, there is very little formal analysis of how tax policy is applied in practice or of its subsequent impact at the microeconomic level. This chapter addresses this lacuna by analysing enterprise data relating to tax burdens and undeclared output using results from two manufacturing enterprise surveys carried out in Mozambique in 2002 and 2006.

Government tax policy must find a balance between revenue, equity and efficiency by raising sufficient revenue, taxing individuals and firms in an equitable manner, minimizing the effects on incentives and administrative costs, and promoting stability and economic growth. Individuals and firms then weigh up the benefits of tax evasion against the costs of detection and punishment, behaving according to the outcome of that trade-off. As Burgess and Stern (1993) point out, developing country economies are generally characterized by a number of factors which hinder governments in the implementation of an effective tax policy, including a large primary sector, economic and social dualism, extreme income inequality, a concentration of economic activity in very small enterprises, extensive uses of permits, licences and rations, weak administrative capabilities and pervasive corruption. As such, the cost of non-compliance is often relatively low, resulting in higher levels of evasion.

In addition, a lack of productive investment often leads developing country governments to use tax incentives to encourage investments, thus further eroding the tax base. As a consequence, evidence suggests that in developing economies even broad-based taxes only manage to capture revenues from a small proportion of the statutory tax-base (Gordon and Li 2005), resulting in what can be termed revenue concentration. Gauthier and Gersowitz (1997) and Gauthier and Reinikka (2001) analyse tax-base erosion and concentration for Cameroon and Uganda, respectively, and find that this is strongly associated with firm size, defined by the number of employees. They find an inverted-U relationship between tax burden and firm size, with firms at the lower and upper ends of the firm-size distribution experiencing a relatively low tax burden compared to those in the middle of the size distribution. This is interpreted as a result of small firm tax evasion, large firm access to tax exemptions and a lack of means to escape for firms in the middle of the size distribution.

This revenue concentration violates principles of equity and efficiency, with potentially negative economic consequences. By creating an institutional environment which varies according to firm size and/or other firm characteristics, incentives for enterprise growth are potentially distorted, with negative consequences for economic growth, formal employment creation and ultimately poverty reduction. In addition, incentives to comply with tax laws are reduced by a perception that few others are doing so, such that tax revenues themselves are affected, potentially resulting in a vicious cycle of higher and more distortionary taxes and further rounds of revenue concentration on more visible firms to compensate for losses of government revenue from economic activity which goes unreported.[1]

Johnson *et al.* (2000) and Dabla-Norris *et al.* (2005) use firm-level data to uncover the principal determinants of unreported output. Using data on over 4,000 firms in 41 countries, Dabla-Norris *et al.* find that 'while firms are affected by financing, corruption, tax and regulatory and legal obstacles, the impact on [hidden output] clearly depends on firm size' (Dabla-Norris *et al.* 2005: 13). Johnson *et al.* (2000) carry out a similar analysis for five transition economies in Eastern Europe. They do not analyse firm size but find that hidden output is positively associated with bribery, although the direction of causality is unclear. Thus size may not be the only factor at work in determining firm behaviour with respect to taxation.

Survey evidence on firm growth and survival in Mozambique reveals some unusual patterns relating to firm size, potentially related to differing institutional treatment among firms, particularly with regards to taxation. Anecdotally, Mozambique is also characterized by the factors which hinder effective tax policy, as highlighted by Burgess and Stern (1993). The present chapter addresses the issue of tax-base erosion and concentration for Mozambique following two approaches: the first investigates the hypothesis that current Mozambican tax policy leads to an inverted-U relationship between tax-burden and firm size following Gauthier and Gersowitz (1997) and Gauthier and Reinikka (2001); the second analyses the determinants of firms' hidden output following Johnson *et al.* (2000) and Dabla-Norris *et al.* (2005).

The results of these analyses suggest that the tax burden indeed varies with firm size, although bribery and corruption are also important. In addition, evidence suggests that bribery and corruption have more influence than firm size on the under-declaration of sales, suggesting that a combination of these factors is at work in determining the overall outcome of tax policy. The remainder of this chapter takes the following form: Section 2 summarizes the principal tax laws to which firms are subject under the Mozambican commercial code. Section 3 provides a description of the survey sample on which the analysis is based. Section 4 provides the results of the regression analysis to explain the tax burden, while Section 5 provides the results of the analysis of hidden output. Section 6 provides the principal conclusions from the analyses.

2 Principal enterprise taxes

As highlighted in Chapter 2, the private sector in Mozambique has had to adapt to a number of major reforms to the principal taxes in recent years. Anecdotal evidence suggests that some of these reforms, the new income tax code in particular, have also increased the complexity of the tax system, resulting in relatively high compliance costs, in particular for an economy where 78.5 per cent of enterprises have only five employees or fewer (INE 2004).[2]

The principal tax paid by enterprises is the IRPC (Imposto sobre o Rendimento das Pessoas Colectivas – Collective Persons Income Tax) applied at a rate of 32 per cent on declared company profits. This applies to all firms except for those in agriculture, which have a rate of 10 per cent until 2011. In addition, cases where incomes are taxed at source are subject to a rate of 20 per cent, while agricultural, handicraft or cultural cooperatives are given a 50 per cent reduction (GoM 2002a). Enterprises also provide the principal collection mechanism for IVA (Imposto sobre o Valor Acrescentado – Value Added Tax [VAT]), which was introduced in 1999. Firms collect 17 per cent on the sale value of their output and deduct the tax paid on their intermediate inputs, transferring the net value to government. Being a destination VAT, enterprises pay IVA on domestic transactions and imports. IVA on the latter is calculated on the CIF price plus import duties plus consumption taxes where applicable (e.g. imported alcohol), while exports are not subject to IVA. Domestic producers of cigarettes, alcohol and a number of specific goods are also subject to excises on production.

The enterprise fiscal code incorporates an assortment of tax exemptions. Small enterprises with a turnover of up to Mts100m (US$5,000) are exempt from IVA, while those with a turnover of between Mts100m (US$5,000) and Mts250m (US$12,500) pay a simplified sales tax of 5 per cent with no right to deduct IVA paid on inputs (GoM 1998b).[3]

As already seen in Chapter 2, the Fiscal Benefits Code also provides a number of specific fiscal incentives for enterprises registered under the 1993 Investment Law.[4] These take the form of deductions from taxable income, accelerated depreciation, tax credits, reduction of tax rates, improved import regimes for capital goods and deduction of the amount of tax assessed (GoM 2002b), with specific IRPC and import duty exemptions for investments made in so-called 'Rapid Development Zones' and those carried out in Industrial Free Zones.[5]

Finally, large investments of over US$500m receive 'exceptional incentives' subject to a proposal by the Minister of Finance and approval by the Council of Ministers (GoM 2002b). Examples of this latter special treatment include the Mozal aluminium smelter, which pays a 1 per cent turnover tax on total sales, as do the heavy sands mines at Moma and Chibuto, all with renewable contracts of 50 years, as discussed in Chapter 15. While exemptions exist for very small firms and a large number of fiscal benefits are also available for larger firms, there is also anecdotal evidence of a high degree of tax evasion. One study by the IMF reports that, in 2002, 8.8 per cent of GDP was collected through income taxes, value added tax and trade taxes, compared with theoretical potential revenues of 20.9 per cent of GDP. In particular, they note a difference of 8.6 per cent of GDP between collected VAT and potential VAT (IMF 2005b: 35). Although some of this shortfall is due to the exemptions described, a substantial proportion is due to non-compliance.

3 The enterprise sample

Data for the present analysis comes from two enterprise surveys carried out on a sample of Mozambican manufacturing firms in 2002 and 2006, respectively. The first of these took place under the auspices of the World Bank's 2002 Pilot Investment Climate Assessment (ICA) programme, covering 192 manufacturing firms in five sectors in and around the main economic centres (IFC 2003). The 2006 survey had the objective of revisiting those same 192 firms to form a panel of data such that firm sampling was predetermined by the technique used in 2002 (DNEAP and KU 2006).[6]

Due to a combination of firm exits, reluctance to participate and difficulties in locating some enterprises, the 2006 survey interviewed a total of 158 firms, providing a panel of 137 firms with data from both 2002 and 2006.[7] Of the sample collected in 2006, 25 per cent of firms were from the food processing sector, 22 per cent from the wood and furniture sector, 15 per cent from the textiles and garments sector, 22 per cent from the metal-mechanics sector and 16 per cent from other manufacturing sectors. In terms of location, 65 per cent of the sample was based in Maputo, 13 per cent in Beira, 11 per cent in Nampula, 6 per cent in Chimoio, 5 per cent in Nacala and less than 1 per cent in Gurue. Finally, for the purposes of this study and following the classification used in Gauthier and Gersowitz (1997) and Gauthier and Reinikka (2001), 8 per cent of sampled firms are classed as micro ($\leq$ 5 workers), 30 per cent as small (6–25 workers), 32 per cent as medium (26–100 workers), 17 per cent as large (101–200 workers) and 9 per cent as very large (200+ workers).[8]

Although the original sample is not statistically representative at the national level, with a disproportionate concentration of small and medium firms compared to the national census in particular (INE 2004), it nonetheless comprises a selection of firms of all sizes in the main economic centres of the country and the principal manufacturing sectors, thereby allowing for analysis of empirically relevant patterns and providing a basis for future survey work with more representative datasets. Table 4.1 highlights some important results from the two surveys regarding firm growth and survival. It presents a growth transition probability matrix which gives the probability of a firm which was in a size category in 2002 (rows) either remaining in the same category, closing or being in a new size category in 2006 (columns). Thus, a firm which was considered micro in 2002 had a 0.87 probability of remaining micro, or 0.13 probability of entering the small category. From our sample, no micro firms exited or grew beyond the small category, thus showing high survival rates and low growth rates, contrary to a number of studies for developed economies (e.g. Evans 1987; Dunne *et al.* 1988; Rossi-Hansberg and Wright 2004), but in keeping with a small number of studies in developing countries (e.g. McPherson 1996).

In the larger size categories, based on our sample there is notably less probability of growth into the larger size categories than for micro to small firms, but a far higher probability of exit, with small firms in 2002 having a 0.29 probability of being only micro in 2006. Even large and very large firms have high probabilities of exiting, suggesting that something is occurring in the economy which halts the progress of these firms even once they are large, established producers. This is likely to be related to a number of factors, one of which may be the variable tax burden according to factors other than profit levels.

Following Gauthier and Gersowitz (1997) and Gauthier and Reinikka (2001), an enterprise's tax burden is summarized by the *tax ratio* variable, here defined as the ratio of the total taxes paid to total sales revenue as reported in the surveys.[9] Summary statistics on the tax ratio and a number of other variables of interest are provided in Table 4.2, which also provides a breakdown of the sample by firm-size category. As the table shows, firms face tax ratios ranging from near 0 to 65.0 per cent, with a mean of 10.3 per cent, close to the median of 7.6 per cent.[10] Also, within this range there is

Table 4.1 Growth Probability Transition Matrix

	Exit 06	Micro 06	Small 06	Medium 06	Large 06	V.Large 06
Micro 02	0.00	**0.88**	0.13	0.00	0.00	0.00
Small 02	0.29	0.04	**0.63**	0.02	0.00	0.02
Medium 02	0.11	0.00	0.09	**0.74**	0.04	0.02
Large 02	0.17	0.00	0.03	0.11	**0.60**	0.09
V.Large 02	0.22	0.06	0.06	0.00	0.17	**0.50**

Note: In 2002 one very large firm was in the process of sale and operating with administrative staff only in 2006, thus appearing as micro.
Source: IFC (2003) and DNEAP and KU (2006), author's calculations

Table 4.2 Enterprise Summary Statistics

Variable	Obs.	2002	2006	Mean	Std. Dev.	Median	Min	Max	Micro	Small	Medium	Large	V. Large	Size n/a
Tax ratio [a]	88	44	44	10.3	10.4	7.6	0.0	65.0	4.2	12.0	9.6	9.2	11.3	
Employment	339	187	152	88.9	150.2	42.0	1.0	1003.0	3.8	14.1	46.8	120.3	445.6	
Firm Age (Years)	333	186	147	26.4	16.8	23.0	3.0	92.0	33.4	21.8	24.9	29.7	30.5	44.5
Manager Educ. (Secondary+)	348	191	157	0.7	0.5	1.0	0.0	1.0	0.5	0.6	0.8	0.9	0.8	0.4
Exemptions (yes=1/no=0)	237	86	151	0.4	0.5	0.0	0.0	1.0	0.3	0.3	0.4	0.6	0.4	0.4
No. Tax Forms	292	142	150	1.8	1.7	2.0	0.0	8.0	1.4	1.4	1.9	2.2	2.4	2.2
Bureaucracy [b]	287	141	146	10.3	13.6	6.0	0.0	106.7	9.1	8.7	9.8	14.3	9.4	10.6
No. Inspections	343	191	152	3.0	2.9	2.0	0.0	17.0	2.5	2.6	3.2	3.6	2.6	2.4
Formal Accounts (Y/N)	301	161	140	0.8	0.4	1.0	0.0	1.0	0.3	0.5	0.9	0.9	0.9	1.0
Sales Declared [a]	220	117	103	74.3	34.9	100.0	0.0	100.0	86.2	73.6	73.0	78.9	72.6	48.3
Bribes [a]	185	100	85	4.6	6.7	2.0	0.0	50.0	1.6	4.9	4.6	5.2	4.5	3.3
Tax Rate Constraint (0-4)	338	183	155	2.3	1.6	3.0	0.0	4.0	1.2	2.2	2.5	2.6	2.5	1.4
Tax Admin. Constraint (0-4)	337	183	154	2.0	1.6	2.0	0.0	4.0	1.4	2.0	2.2	1.8	2.2	0.8
Costums Constraint (0-4)	308	167	141	1.9	1.6	2.0	0.0	4.0	0.6	1.6	2.2	2.3	2.3	1.3
Corruption Constraint (0-4)	314	179	135	2.5	1.6	3.0	0.0	4.0	1.2	2.2	2.9	2.7	2.6	1.7
Total Obs.									22	102	113	68	34	9
Obs. 2002									9	54	63	42	19	4
Obs. 2006									13	48	50	26	15	5

a: Percentage of sales revenue; b: percentage of management time
Source: World Bank (2003) and DNEAP (2006), author's calculations

considerable variation among firm-size categories, with micro firms having an apparently lower average tax ratio than all other size categories.

Using the pooled sample of firms with employment data from the 2002 and the 2006 surveys, the mean firm size for the whole sample is 100.5 employees, well above the manufacturing sector mean of 15.8 as calculated from the national enterprise census (INE 2004). This reflects the bias in the survey sample towards larger firms, although micro firms are not entirely unrepresented given the number of micro firms and employment figures as low as one worker.[11]

As a further indicator of the diversity of firms in the sample, Table 4.2 reports firm ages, which have a mean of 26.4 years and a median of 23 years (with a range of 3–92 years). Interestingly, micro firms have a mean age of 33.4 years, well above the average and above the mean ages of all other size categories. As micro enterprises are generally considered either to be successful and grow into larger firms or to be unsuccessful and exit (see Evans 1987, for example) this is an unusual result, potentially related to the higher survival rates of micro firms described above. A further firm characteristic reported in Table 4.2 is whether or not the general manager has secondary education or above. This is often used as a proxy variable for efficiency, assuming a more educated manager will employ more efficient and up-to-date management techniques in the workplace. Approximately 70 per cent of surveyed firms have a manager with this level of education, although again this varies with firm size, with micro firms representing the category with least educated managers. A dummy variable for *exemptions* from taxes is created which takes the value one for those firms reporting at least one tax exemption and zero for all others. As Table 4.2 and Figure 4.1 show, the

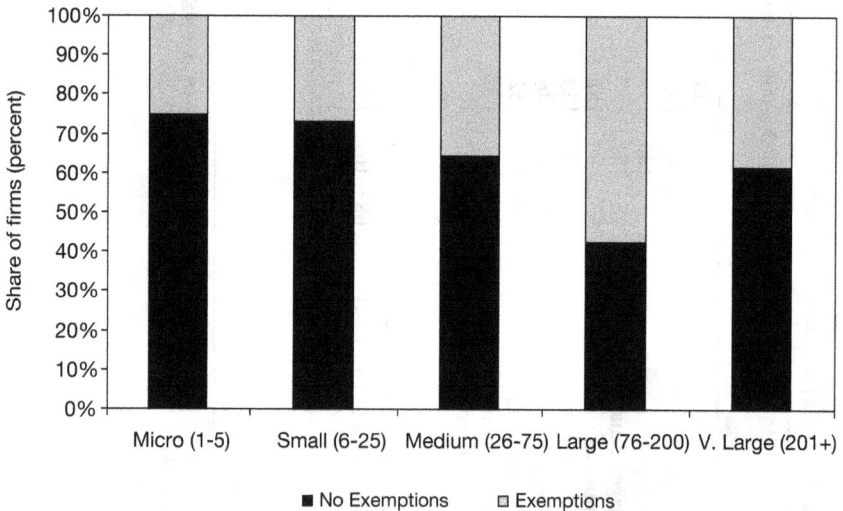

Figure 4.1 Reported tax exemptions by firm size category

share of firms reporting exemptions increases with size category, from 25 per cent of micro firms reporting having exemptions to 27 per cent of small firms, 36 per cent of medium firms and 57 per cent of large firms, although this unexpectedly drops to 38 per cent for very large firms.[12] Thus, despite the small sample and in particular the absence of the major very large Mozambican firms, there is an initial indication that access to tax exemption is related to firm size.

Table 4.2 also reports the average number of tax forms completed by firms on a monthly basis. This again varies with firm-size category, from an average of 1.4 forms for micro and small firms to 2.2 for large and 2.4 for very large firms. Despite this variation, the proportion of management time spent on bureaucracy in general, reported by *bureaucracy*, reflects potentially higher compliance costs for micro firms, with more time spent as a proportion of manager time than small firms, although medium and large firms have the highest levels of all size categories.

A firm's 'visibility' to the tax authorities might be measured by the number of *inspections* it receives from the authorities in a year, where these include tax, labour, health, environmental and other inspections. Again, micro and small firms have the lowest average number of inspections, 2.5 and 2.6, respectively, while medium and large firms have an average of 3.2 and 3.6, respectively. Interestingly, very large firms receive on average the same lower number of inspections as small firms, again suggesting increased visibility of medium and large firms in comparison with firms at either end of the firm-size distribution. The degree to which a firm can or could be forced to comply with taxation laws is also determined by whether or not it keeps *formal accounts*. Although the sample has a disproportionate number of large firms, the *accounts* variable suggests that only 80 per cent of interviewed firms keep formal accounts. As expected, given the legislation discussed above, a high share of micro firms have no formal accounts (73 per cent) compared with other size categories, although the fact that any medium, large or very large firm should not have formal accounts is important in itself.

Survey data also include responses relating to potential tax-evasion, as reported in Table 4.2 under *sales declared*. Assuming direct questioning on tax evasion would be fruitless, firms were asked what proportion of sales they believed the 'typical' firm of their size and sector declared for tax purposes. Although highly approximate, as in Dabla-Norris *et al.* (2005), this can be used as a rough proxy for the actual under-reporting of sales and thus a measure of the degree of a firm's tax evasion. Interestingly, sampled micro firms report the highest declaration of sales for tax purposes, at 86 per cent of total sales, compared with 74 per cent for small, 73 per cent for medium, 79 per cent for large and 73 per cent for very large firms. The determinants of the level of declared sales are given further treatment below.

A factor in developing economies commonly associated with tax evasion is the presence of corruption (e.g. Johnson *et al.* 2000). Given the sensitivity of the subject, this information is again approached indirectly, with firms asked what they estimate the typical firm pays in *bribes* per annum as a percentage of sales. This has a mean value of 4.6 per cent of sales and a median of 2 per cent, ranging from 0 to a very high 50 per cent, with 25.8 per cent of responding firms estimating that firms pay bribes of at least 10 per cent of sales per annum.[13] As Table 4.2 shows, this again appears to vary with firm size, so that micro firms estimate that only 1.6 per cent of sales revenues is paid in bribes, while all other size categories estimate an average of more than 4.5 per cent of sales.

The final four variables displayed in Table 4.2 report the level of constraint posed to firm growth and development by tax rates, tax administration, customs regulations and administration, and corruption, respectively. These ordinal responses range from a value of 0 for no constraint to 4 for a serious constraint, representing the subjective responses of managers regarding the business environment. By this measure, corruption and tax rates were identified as representing higher constraints to firms than tax administration or customs regulations and administration. Again, these vary across firm-size categories, with micro firms generally taking a less severe view of the constraints posed to their business than larger size categories. This may be due to a lower degree of contact with the authorities rather than ease of compliance or contentedness with the business environment in general.

4 Tax exemptions and evasion

To begin analysis of the relationship between the tax burden and firm size, Figures 4.2 and 4.3 map tax ratios against the log of the number of employees in a scatter-plot.[14] A fitted line is also included using fractional polynomial estimation of the log of employment and the tax ratio.[15] The resulting curve displayed in Figure 4.2 provides preliminary evidence that an (albeit shallow) inverted-U relationship does exist for the small sample of manufacturing firms in Mozambique. Figure 4.3 provides clearer evidence of this relationship by plotting the same graph excluding six firms from the alcoholic beverages sector, which is subject to a 65 per cent excise tax unlike other sectors in the sample.

As in Gauthier and Reinikka (2001), more concrete evidence of this inverted-U relationship and its determinants is modelled using regression analysis. Due to the lack of reported financial data and thus limited data on tax ratios, this is carried out using the pooled sample of data from 2002 and 2006, thus ignoring the panel aspect of the data, and using Ordinary Least Squares (OLS).[16] Table 4.3 provides the resultant estimated coefficients, all of which are estimated with Huber–White variance correction for heteroscedasticity.[17] The first column, OLS1, looks at the simple relationship between tax ratio and the number of employees, with a quadratic term to allow for the inverted-U seen above. It also includes a dummy variable for observations from 2006 to control for any change in macroeconomic

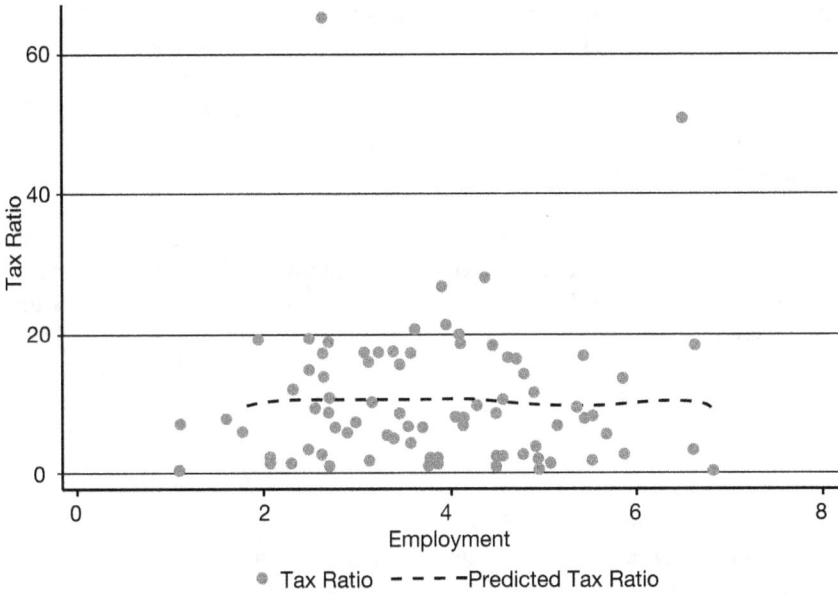

Figure 4.2 Tax ratio on employment with fractional polynomial fit
Source: IFC (2003) and DNEAP and KU (2006), author's estimates

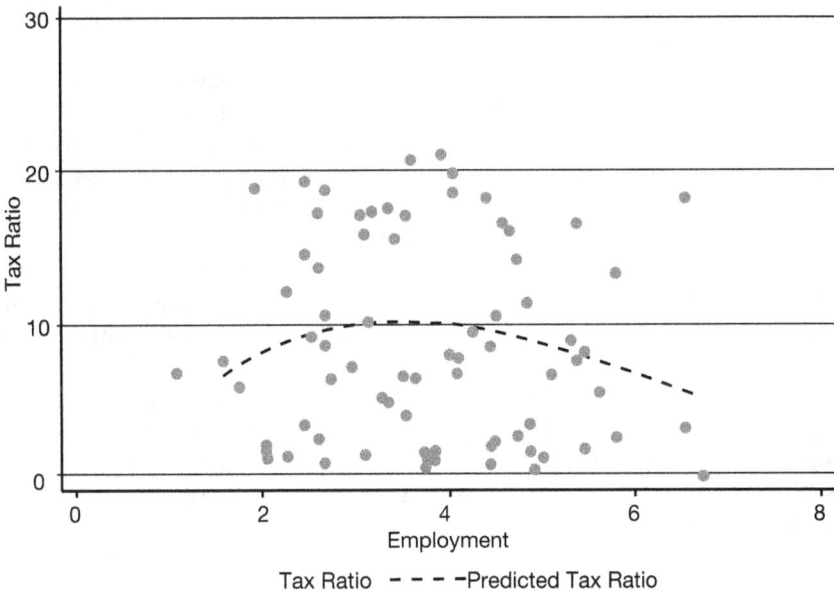

Figure 4.3 Tax ratio on employment with fractional polynomial fit excluding alcohol
Source: IFC (2003) and DNEAP and KU (2006), author's estimates

circumstances which may have an impact on the explanatory variable, and for firms which produce alcohol and therefore are subject to excises. Although not statistically significant, the signs of the coefficients on log employment and its quadratic indicate the likely presence of an inverted-U relationship between tax ratio and employee numbers. The dummy variable for firms producing alcohol is statistically significant at 10 per cent and implies an increase in the tax ratio for those firms of 23.6 percentage points.

OLS2 divides the firm-size distribution into the same five categories used above and in Gauthier and Reinikka (2001), allowing that separate segments of the size distribution be dealt with in a separate manner. The results here indicate that all firms with more than five employees have a higher tax ratio than those with five or less, the coefficients of almost all categories appearing as statistically significant once the year and alcohol sector are taken into account. Small firms in particular have the highest tax ratio relative to micro firms, significant at the 1 per cent level. Interestingly, the coefficients found for small and medium firms are considerably larger than those found in Uganda by Gauthier and Reinikka (2001), suggesting that the inverted-U relationship may be more pronounced in Mozambique.

OLS3 continues with the division of the firm-size distribution as an explanatory variable for the tax ratio but includes some additional variables which may impact on a firm's tax burden.[18] In particular the variables for *exemptions*, share of management time spent on *bureaucracy*, *manager education*, estimated *bribe* amount, those who found *tax administration* to be an obstacle and those who found *corruption* to be an obstacle are included in the regression OLS3.[19] As Table 4.3 shows, the inclusion of these additional explanatory variables alters the size coefficients such that medium and very large firms have the highest tax ratios relative to micro firms, where the medium-sized firm coefficient has increased statistical significance compared with OLS2. This suggests that size is at least in part a proxy for other firm characteristics. The coefficients for *bribe* and *exemptions* are negative, consistent with the definition of exemptions and also the hypothesis that willingness to bribe can reduce a firm's tax burden, a result found in a number of other studies on informality and corruption, such as Johnson *et al.* (2000), De Soto (1989) and Dreher and Schneider (2006). However, these coefficients are not found to be statistically significant for the small sample under analysis.

On the other hand, the coefficient for management time spent on *bureaucracy* is found to be positively associated with the tax ratio and statistically significant at the 1 per cent level, suggesting that, even controlling for firm size, higher tax ratios are also associated with higher compliance costs in terms of administration. On the other hand, *manager education* is found to be negatively related to tax ratio, with a relatively large and again statistically significant coefficient, suggesting that higher levels of manager education, commonly associated with a firm's efficiency, allow a firm to reduce its tax burden by 7.4 percentage points.

Table 4.3 OLS Results for Tax-Ratio

	OLS1	OLS2	OLS3	OLS4
ln(empl)	2.468			
	[3.336]			
ln(empl)^2	–0.312			
	[0.454]			
Small		6.347***	4.782**	
		[2.039]	[2.237]	
Medium		4.255*	6.626**	
		[2.240]	[2.587]	
Large		4.998**	4.640*	
		[2.388]	[2.507]	
Very Large		4.900*	5.524	
		[2.605]	[3.344]	
Exemptions			–1.207	–0.773
			[2.234]	[2.148]
Bureaucracy			0.098***	0.085**
			[0.035]	[0.036]
Manager Educ.			–7.374***	–6.532***
			[2.118]	[1.968]
Bribes			–0.230	–0.198
			[0.149]	[0.158]
Tax Admin. Constraint			5.006*	5.549*
			[2.777]	[2.810]
Corruption Constraint			4.664*	4.924**
			[2.513]	[2.370]
Year 2006	–0.989	–1.25	–0.884	–0.947
	[1.726]	[1.767]	[2.237]	[2.390]
Alcohol	23.614*	22.997*	19.134	19.176
	[13.516]	[13.260]	[14.689]	[14.133]
Constant	5.375	4.864***	4.605***	8.334***
	[5.751]	[1.512]	[1.672]	[2.244]
Observations	88	88	50	50
R-squared	0.22	0.24	0.46	0.44
F-test: all coeffs = 0	1.05	2.87	6.67	7.54
Prob. > F	0.39	0.01	0	0

Robust standard errors in brackets
* significant at 10%; ** significant at 5%; *** significant at 1%

Source: IFC (2003) and DNEAP and KU (2006), author's estimates

Finally, the variables for whether or not a firm finds *tax administration* and *corruption* to be an obstacle to the growth and operations of their business are both found to be positively related to the tax ratio and statistically significant. This raises issues with interpretation given the imprecise definition of what these variables represent. One possibility is that these represent unobserved heterogeneity in firm legal abidance, with a greater concern for tax administration and corruption correlating with the individual firm costs inherent in complying with taxes and not succumbing to corrupt officials.

Alternatively, they may simply reflect that a firm is more 'visible' to the tax administration in ways other than simply through firm size, and thus the subject of more attention with regards to their tax return or attempts to elicit bribes. Either way, there is an apparent association with the tax ratio which also affects the impact of firm size.

Finally OLS4 removes the size category variables in order to analyse non-size effects only. As Table 4.3 shows, this does little in terms of the statistical significance of the explanatory variables but does have some impact on their magnitude. The negative impact of *bribes* and *exemptions* on tax ratios is reduced, as it is for *manager education*, and time spent on *bureaucracy*. However, removal of the size dummies increases the impact of concern for *tax administration* and *corruption*, suggesting some collinearity with firm size.[20] Although the sample sizes are rather small, particularly when the additional explanatory variables are included in OLS3 and OLS4, the evidence appears consistent with tax ratios, which vary with firm size. The results also suggest that size and other firm characteristics may themselves be related and affect tax ratios through a combination of their effects.[21] That manager education is apparently associated with a firm's tax ratio is of interest given its potential connections with firm efficiency levels. Similarly, the firm characteristics represented by concern for corruption and tax administration (which increase a firm's tax burden) also suggest that some unobserved behavioural effects may be at work in determining a firm's tax ratio, while the positive association between bureaucratic burden and tax burden implies that a firm's 'visibility' to the authorities may be important and not just related to size.

5 Determinants of hidden output

As pointed out in Gauthier and Gersowitz (1997) and Gauthier and Reinikka (2001), these results raise questions relating to tax administration and the degree to which firms are forced to comply with tax laws. Although complete tax evasion is not identifiable from the present data, tax evasion through under-declaration of sales can be analysed by investigating the determinants of the levels of *sales declared*, as in Dabla-Norris *et al.* (2005) and Johnson *et al.* (2000).[22] As Table 4.2 showed, non-financial data have a higher response rate that therefore allows panel data techniques to be employed. Responses regarding the share of sales which a firm will typically declare for tax purposes are necessarily censored at 100 per cent of sales, representing what Wooldridge (2003) calls a corner solution outcome and thus recommending the use of a Tobit model.[23] Using the unbalanced panel of data and a random effects Tobit model, Table 4.4 reports the marginal effects for the probability of *sales declared* (y) being uncensored, $\Pr(y < 100 | x)$, and for the expected value of *sales declared* (y) conditional on being uncensored at 100, $E(y | x, y < 100)$ where x represents all independent variables.[24]

Table 4.4 Tobit Results for Proportion of Sales Declared for Tax Purposes

	TOBIT1		TOBIT2	
	Pr(y < 100)	E(y|x,y < 100)	Pr(y < 100)	E(y|x,y < 100)
Small (d)	0.108	–3.937		
	(0.196)	(7.434)		
Medium (d)	0.197	–7.338		
	(0.188)	(7.546)		
Large (d)	–0.078	2.674		
	(0.212)	(7.058)		
Very Large (d)	0.271	–11.793		
	(0.196)	(10.968)		
Exemptions (d)	0.118	–4.287	0.089	–3.319
	(0.094)	(3.520)	(0.088)	(3.335)
Bureaucracy	–0.003	0.097	-0.003	0.121
	(0.003)	(0.112)	(0.003)	(0.108)
Manager Educ. (d)	0.061	–2.1		
	(0.109)	(3.685)		
Bribes	0.015*	–0.534*	0.014*	–0.503*
	(0.006)	(0.212)	(0.006)	(0.206)
Tax admin. constraint (d)	0.023	–0.804		
	(0.104)	(3.615)		
Corruption Constraint (d)	0.400***	–13.261***	0.426***	–14.714***
	(0.105)	(3.651)	(0.089)	(3.294)
Alcohol (d)	–0.034	1.166		
	(0.255)	(8.622)		
Observations	118		119	
Expected Value	0.468	68.895	0.468	67.798
Chi-squared	27.287		22.358	
P-value	0.004		0.000	

Standard errors in brackets
(d): Marginal effect is for discrete change of dummy variable from 0 to 1
Estimated coefficients: * significant at 10%; ** significant at 5%; *** significant at 1%

Source: IFC (2003) and DNEAP and KU (2006), author's estimates

Tobit1 models the share of sales declared as a function of the size category of the firm and the explanatory variables used to explain *tax ratio* above. Under this specification, the average probability of a firm not reporting 100 per cent of sales is estimated to be 0.47. The results suggest that all size categories except large have a lower probability of declaring all sales than micro firms, although the estimated coefficients on the size variables are not well determined.

A preoccupation with the effects of *corruption* on a firm's growth and performance almost doubles the probability of under-declaring, while increments in the share of *bribes* estimated as being paid marginally increase this probability. Concern with *corruption* appears to be highly significant, as is *bribes*, although less so. Contrary to what might be expected, *exemptions* is positively related to the probability of under-declaring sales, as is *manager education* and concern about *tax administration*, although these coefficients are small in comparison with *corruption* and again are not well determined. Tobit1 also gives an expected value of 68.9 per cent of sales declared for tax purposes, conditional on sales declared being less than 100 per cent and estimated at the mean of the explanatory variables. The marginal effects imply that very large firms report approximately 11.8 percentage points less of their sales than micro firms, medium firms report 7.4 percentage points less than micro, small 3.9 per cent less, and only large firms report 2.7 per cent *more* of sales than micro firms. This would suggest that large firms have less room for manoeuvre in terms of avoiding taxation through hidden sales, although their tax burden was found to be less than medium firms in the previous analysis (potentially due to the higher incidence of exemptions in this category, as shown in Table 4.2) and again their coefficients are not well determined. The reported marginal effects also imply that a one percentage point higher share of sales paid in *bribes* is associated with a 0.5 percentage point lower level of declared sales, while corruption is associated with a reduction in declared sales of 13.3 percentage points. However, as Johnson *et al.* (2000) state, it is unclear whether bribes are paid in order to hide output or if output is hidden in order to avoid bribes.

Tobit2 reports the marginal effects from an estimated model which removes the size variables as explanatory variables. Their removal leaves the probability of a firm under-declaring sales for tax purposes unchanged, and only marginally reduces the conditional expected value of reported sales. The size and signs of the other coefficients remain broadly as before, again suggesting that the previously included variables had little effect in determining the estimated level of declared sales and, in particular, that size is not a strong determinant of the share of sales declared for tax purposes.

Although firm size is found not to be important for sales declarations in this subsequent analysis, this result may be related to a number of factors. Most importantly, it may result from the indirect manner in which the data on *sales declared* were collected. Although this provided more observations than directly determined data on *tax ratio*, the fact that it is based on manager perceptions of the 'typical' firm leaves it open to considerable ambiguity. The same can be said for the variable employed on *bribes*, which again collects an estimate of what the 'typical' firm pays but need not be an indicator of how the firm in question actually behaves.[25] This is an unfortunate consequence of the nature of the topic, which by definition does not invite easy collection of accurate data.

6 Conclusions

The Mozambican tax system has been subject to some major changes over recent years relating to rates, taxes and their administration. Although some analyses have been carried out regarding the revenue impact of these changes over time, until now little work has been carried out from the enterprise point of view. In particular, little attention has so far been paid to the potentially heterogeneous impact of tax policy and its administration according to firm size and other characteristics. For a country such as Mozambique with a highly skewed firm-size distribution, this has the potential to be of great importance.

The available evidence, based on a limited dataset of manufacturing firms, suggests that an inverted-U relationship exists between the size of a firm and its tax ratio. The level of education of the manager and the share of management time spent on bureaucracy also appear statistically significant in determining the tax ratio, as do concern with corruption and tax administration, though to a lesser extent. Although size is therefore not the only factor, the results are consistent with a situation of revenue concentration and administrative pressure on firms caught in the middle of the size distribution. These firms are assumed to be too large to hide but too small to benefit from exemptions.

Subsequent analysis of the determinants of tax evasion through hidden output suggests that size, manager education and bureaucratic burden are less important than factors relating to corruption and bribery. Although based on indirect evidence only, this would imply that the role of hidden sales in determining the tax ratio is only a small part of the story. The importance of these results lies in their potential negative effect on firm growth and more generally on economic growth and formal employment creation. If tax policy implementation is subject to the distortions suggested by the above results, circumstantial evidence suggests that it may also be creating disincentives to firm growth. This would be consistent with the observation that the majority of micro firms in our sample did not grow between the two surveys. As a consequence, changes to tax policy and its administration potentially have the power to radically alter how firms behave, with major effects for economic growth. To be avoided is a vicious circle whereby tax administration becomes more focused on easier targets, thus further increasing the tax burden on medium-sized firms.

Notes

1 Although not the subject of this study, simultaneous expenditure reforms to improve equity may also be required to reduce public resistance to paying taxes, a problem found, for example, in Ghana (Addison and Osei 2001). This also relates to issues such as 'the diverse psychological, moral and social influences on compliance behaviour' highlighted by Andreoni *et al.* (1998: 855), amongst others, which clearly also have a role to play in the compliance decision. Kaplow (2006: 71) also points out that, even for developed countries, 'on average, evasion tends to be worse as a percentage of income at the bottom of the income distribution whereas avoidance tends to be more significant at the upper end, in both cases on account of differential opportunities for tax reduction'.

2 According to firm census data (CEMPRE), 27.5 per cent of all enterprises have only one employee, 56.4 per cent have up to two employees and 68.7 per cent have up to three employees (author's calculations based on data from INE 2004).

3 Enterprises with annual turnover of up to Mts 1,500m (approximately US$62,500) are exempt from keeping formal accounts (GoM 2002a),

4 Details on how a firm can invest under the investment law are provided in Chapter 15. Enterprises carrying out wholesale and retail commerce are not eligible for fiscal benefits. Besides, see GoM (1993).

5 Rapid Development Zones include: the Zambeze Valley, Niassa Province, Nacala District, Mozambique Island and Ibo Island. 'Rapid Development Zones' benefit specifically from five years of IRPC tax credits of 20 per cent of the value of the investment and exemption from import duties on capital goods in the first three years. Investments in Industrial Free Zones benefit from a 60 per cent reduction in their IRPC bill for ten years and exemption from import duties, IVA and Consumption Tax on all goods except alcohol and tobacco (GoM 2002b).

6 The sample used in 2002 was in turn based on a sample used by the World Bank in 1998, prior to the firm census which took place in 2002, thus making it impossible to carry out random sampling.

7 Details of the 2006 survey and initial comparisons with 2002 can be found in DNEAP and KU (2006).

8 Three per cent of interviewed firms gave no details on worker numbers.

9 Gauthier and Gersowitz (1997) and Gauthier and Reinikka (2001) use data on specific taxes, whereas total taxes paid by the firm are used here due to inability or reluctance to provide a detailed breakdown.

10 Firms with non-responses were removed from the sample, while zeros had to be considered non-responses due to the difficulty inherent in distinguishing between this and overt admission of evasion. In addition, one firm was removed from the entire analysis as an outlier with a tax ratio of more than 65 per cent even though it came from the metal-mechanic sector. Tax ratios exist for only 88 firms due to widespread reluctance to report financial data, thus markedly reducing the size of the sample available for analysis, as seen in Tables 4.2 and 4.3.

11 Further, more detailed comparisons of the sample with national enterprise characteristics can be found in DNEAP and KU (2006).

12 The firm-size categories adopted correspond to those utilized by Gauthier and Gersowitz (1997) and Gauthier and Reinikka (2001) and are as follows: Micro (1–5 employees), Small (6–25), Medium (26–75), Large (76–200), Very Large (200+).

13 Three firms gave a response greater than 20 per cent of sales (of 25, 35 and 50 per cent of sales).

14 Limited reporting of financial data in both surveys means that the present analysis of tax burdens pools the data into one sample, therefore including firms which may have ceased to exist since 2002 and some which were introduced in 2006 (in existence but not interviewed in 2002). Although this implies the forfeiting of a certain amount of useful information, the results are nonetheless considered relevant and insightful, in particular given the relevance for Mozambican tax policy.

15 This is carried out using the 'fpfit' graph option in Stata, which produces twoway fractional-polynomial prediction plots. As Royston and Altman (1997) explain, fractional polynomial regressions provide a flexible, parametric approximating equation for a smooth relationship between two variables for which the exact mathematical form may be unknown or complicated. Fractional polynomials are like conventional polynomials but are allowed to include non-integer and negative powers of the explanatory variables as well as integer powers. The Stata default, employed here, is to use two power terms. The resultant line is selected according to likelihood criteria of goodness of fit.

16 Although the dependent variable of tax ratio is bounded by 0 and 100 and OLS potentially predicts values outside the [0,100] region, in practice this occurs only infrequently. Gauthier and Reinikka (2001) also use Ordinary Least Squares.

17 The results from an OLS regression without robust standard errors fails the Lagrange Multiplier test for multiplicative heteroscedasticity as implemented in Stata. In addition, it should be noted that sectoral dummies in addition to that for the alcohol firms did not alter the outcome of these results and their coefficients were statistically insignificant in any case.

18 Note that the sample size is greatly reduced with the introduction of these explanatory variables due to missing data which differ by variable and by firm. For 28 firms, this is due to no response to the question relating to estimated bribe payments as a share of sales. These firms are distributed as follows: 1 is micro, 9 are small, 8 are medium, 6 are large and 4 are very large, representing a minimum of one-quarter and a maximum of one-third of each size category. The potential implications of this are not given any specific treatment in the present study.

19 The constraint variables are employed in the regressions as 0/1 dummy variables, where 0 implies no constraint while 1 implies a slight to serious constraint.

20 Note that fitted values from all specifications are predicted within the [0,100] range.

21 Although the present analysis follows the estimation technique used by Gauthier and Gersowitz (1997) and Gauthier and Reinikka (2001), it is feasible that there is an endogenous relationship between the tax ratio and firm size which would imply dual causality, thus leading to self-selection of firm sizes as a function of tax ratio, with a potential bias for the coefficient estimates. Although it would require more data, this issue could be resolved using a two-step Heckman procedure, although the present chapter does not pursue this more complex path. In any case, more attention is paid here to the sign of the estimates rather than the precise estimates obtained.

22 As explained above, the *sales declared* variable is only a rough proxy for actual hidden sales given that the question asked referred to the sales declared by a 'typical' firm of their size and sector.

23 Value of sales declared is theoretically also censored at zero. There were 21 zero observations (mostly from 2002); however, these were removed due to ambiguity about whether they really represented zeros or non-responses. Comparison of the coefficients under both methods does not reveal dramatic size differences.

24 Random effects are employed due to the limited data, which would not allow fixed effects to be carried out. This assumes that unobserved heterogeneity is uncorrelated with the explanatory variables. In any case, the marginal effects are found to be similar to those from running a pooled Tobit model with a 2006 dummy variable.

25 The analysis is limited in this regard by the indirect nature of the questions asked in the 2002 survey.

5 Comparative perspective

Sam Jones

1 Introduction

The complaint that developing countries raise inadequate tax revenues and have poor administrative systems is not new. Reforms to 'strengthen tax administration' and bolster domestic revenues are characteristic of IMF programmes across the developing world, in part verified by the rapid uptake of VAT in Africa and Asia since the late 1980s to the present day (see Ebrill *et al.* 2001). These issues have been prominent in Mozambique since the pursuit of structural adjustment and stabilization in the mid-1980s. To date the country has undergone various rounds of taxation reform; however, since 1993 these have yet to translate into a sustained enhanced domestic revenue position. The level of the tax ratio, defined as total tax revenues divided by nominal GDP, was around 11 per cent as at 2005 and has been the object of substantial concern particularly in light of external financing (via foreign aid) of the budget at well over 10 per cent of GDP.

Despite these criticisms, it is helpful to recall the empirical phenomenon described by Wagner's Law. This tells us that the relative size of government in the economy tends to increase with average economic prosperity, which also means that the relative volume of domestic revenues in low income countries tends to be smaller than that raised in richer countries. It remains uncertain, however, to what extent and in what ways domestic taxation possibilities are constrained by empirical conditions in developing countries. This is an important policy issue as a robust analysis would provide an analytical foundation to assess the adequacy of observed tax ratios and/or the realism of fiscal policy goals.

The principal objective of this chapter is to evaluate the aggregate performance of Mozambique's tax system against experiences of other developing countries. In the first instance, the nature of constraints to tax revenue generation is investigated at the cross-country level. In turn, this framework is applied to the specific case of Mozambique. Given the explicit focus on aggregate revenue levels, it must be highlighted that the administration of taxes and the fine print of tax policy are not explored here. This is not to dismiss their importance, however, particularly as administration and policy choices are fundamental determinants of the equity and efficiency outcomes of a given taxation system.

By way of structure, Section 2 provides a brief summary of critical perspectives on the Mozambican tax system. This leads, in Section 3, to an analysis of the cross-country evidence for the relationship between developmental conditions and overall tax performance via elaboration of an econometric model. Consistent with previous research (e.g. Teera and Hudson 2004), tax ratios in developing countries are found to be strongly related to 'deep' economic and institutional variables. In Section 4 the model is applied to Mozambique, permitting calculation of the expected tax effort based on economic and institutional conditions. Section 5 concludes.

2 Current perspectives

The history of the reforms and performance of Mozambique's tax system is documented elsewhere and need not be repeated here (see Chapter 2; also IMF 2005b). Two important points may be highlighted, however. First, over the last 20 years Mozambique's tax system has undergone two periods of reform. With the dismantling of socialist central planning in favour of market-based reforms in the mid-1980s, a new taxation system was implemented from 1987 including a modified sales tax and various income taxes. According to an IMF report (Lopes and Sacerdoti 1991), these reforms were integral components of the Economic Recovery Programme (stabilization and structural adjustment) pursued under the ambit of World Bank and IMF support. From 1996, however, a further wave of reform was initiated which involved replacing many of the principal taxation instruments with 'improved' variants such as a VAT (instead of a cascading sales tax) and comprehensive income tax instruments. Wide-ranging reforms to customs duties and administrative procedures were also introduced, including the employment of external consultants as temporary administrators of the entire customs organization (for details, see Chapter 6). As before, this second period of reform was supported heavily by external actors, with IMF experts providing detailed advice on the content of new instruments. Towards the end of this phase the IMF was able to conclude that the country owns 'a comprehensive tax system that is broadly in line with best practice' (IMF 2005b: 20).

Second, and despite the above, it is evident that since the first phase of reforms tax revenues have remained relatively stable as a percentage of GDP. This is depicted in Figure 5.1, which plots total and tax revenue for the period 1980–2005. Although there is short-term volatility, the long-term trend in both total and tax revenues has been flat during the post-war period (since 1992), averaging 12.1 per cent and 11.0 per cent, respectively. One also notes that the increase in total revenues registered in 2005 was primarily a non-tax phenomenon, in part associated with the inclusion of certain sectoral revenues (user-fees) previously not captured at a central level. The post-civil war period simply shows that real revenues have grown *pari passu* with real income.

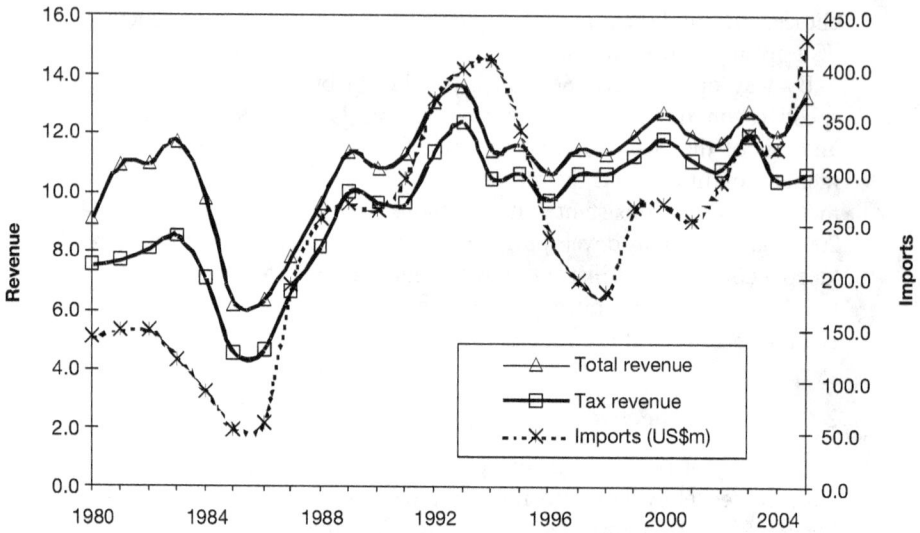

Figure 5.1 Historic total revenue and tax performance (% of GDP)
Source: Government of Mozambique.

With respect to criticisms of the current taxation system in Mozambique, two main perspectives stand out.[1] The first is motivated primarily by a concern that the tax ratio is insufficient and argues that increases in the ratio are necessary not only to enhance the sustainability of public finances but also to reduce the extent of fiscal non-compliance. The resulting recommendations focus on a combination of administrative improvements and a slight tightening of tax policy, the latter aiming to cut certain tax privileges and exemptions that have come to erode the tax base. This view is most prominent in two recent IMF studies for Mozambique (Varsano *et al.* 2006; IMF 2005b). Although these avoid defining concrete targets for overall revenues, they both suggest that the tax ratio potential of the country is around 20 per cent of GDP and that non-compliance and exemptions are the main causes of the observed ratio. Varsano *et al.* (2006), for example, cite Kenya as a suitable comparator due to its apparently similar economic structure and strong revenue effort of around 22 per cent. They assert that even a 'medium' tax effort by Mozambican authorities would be commensurate with a tax ratio of approximately 17 per cent of GDP. Importantly, underpinning this perspective is the opinion that the current set of tax instruments generally is adequate and tax rates should not be adjusted, at least before consolidation of the current system. Tax administration is considered the priority, to be supported by a stable tax policy environment.

An alternative viewpoint is advocated by analysts who emphasize private sector development. In common with the first view, this perspective places substantial weight on the need for comprehensive administrative upgrading as well as simplification of the tax system to support compliance among smaller firms. In particular, improvements in the processing of VAT reimbursements and an increase in minimum taxation thresholds to reduce the tax burden for smaller tax operators are recommended (e.g. Bolnick 2004a; Ernst and Young 2004). This perspective goes further, however, contending that the structure of incentives in the tax system is distorted in favour of larger, import- and capital-intensive firms who also are comparatively well-resourced in terms of their administrative capacity. These studies suggest that over the medium term Mozambique should move towards a system with a set of lower tax rates applied more equitably. This is in contrast to the current system, described as consisting of high effective tax rates by regional standards (Bolnick 2004b), which only are softened if a company is able to gain access to fiscal benefits and/or tax exemptions. FIAS (2006) estimates, for example, that small businesses operating in full compliance with the normal tax system face a marginal effective tax rate (METR) of over 70 per cent, against 11 per cent for a manufacturing firm operating under the investment incentives regime. Furthermore, as the fiscal benefits regime raises high bureaucratic transaction costs and directs significant reductions or exemptions towards capital items and/or intermediate imports, the regime effectively operates in favour of larger companies and capital-intensive investment. This argument asserts, therefore, that administrative improvements must be accompanied by deeper measures to reduce sector- and size-based distortions via a reallocation of the effective tax burden. Evidently, and at least in the medium term, such a reorientation of the tax system would not be compatible with measures designed to achieve significant increases in the tax ratio.

3 Tax revenue performance

3.1 Background

A fundamental difference between the above viewpoints turns on the appropriate medium-term revenue target for Mozambique. While this invokes a broad range of issues, taxation theory and experience inform us that in the pursuit of taxation goals there exist inherent trade-offs between equity, economic efficiency, revenue generation and simplicity concerns (for elaboration, see Slemrod 1991 and also Bolnick 2004a). For developing countries in particular, it is recognized that the government's scope to achieve specific objectives in any of these four dimensions often is limited by administrative capabilities as well as deep structural factors (Burgess and Stern 1993; Heady 2001).

With respect to the relative level of revenue that may be considered appropriate or desirable for a given country, the theoretical (optimal taxation) literature fails to provide clear guidance (Tanzi and Zee 2000; Slemrod 1991). However, empirical insights are plentiful and point in two analytical directions. First are Musgrave's (1969) famous 'tax handles', which refer to the extent of economic diversification as well as the nature of economic activities which may be inherently more or less difficult to tax. For example, low income countries dependent on a small number of (low return) agricultural activities are expected to raise less tax revenue than countries where economic activity is highly diversified and concentrated in the formal sector. Empirical scholarship which seeks to identify the structural determinants of tax performance is well established and need not be appraised here.[2] Suffice to say that real per capita income and trade openness are frequently found to be highly significant positive correlates of tax ratios across countries, while dependence on agriculture is a negative correlate. It is trivial to illustrate the existence of a positive relationship between average per capita income and the relative size of government revenues in GDP, as described by Wagner's Law. This is shown in Figure 5.2 for low and middle income countries, based on the dataset employed in this study.

A second analytical direction comes out of the extensive literature on the underlying determinants of economic growth (see Rodrik *et al.* 2004 for an overview). Taking the argument that exogenous factors such as institutions are deep determinants of growth, it is a short step to contend that they may also have a strong influence on taxation performance. This derives from recognition that taxation is inherently contested (Slemrod 1991). As such,

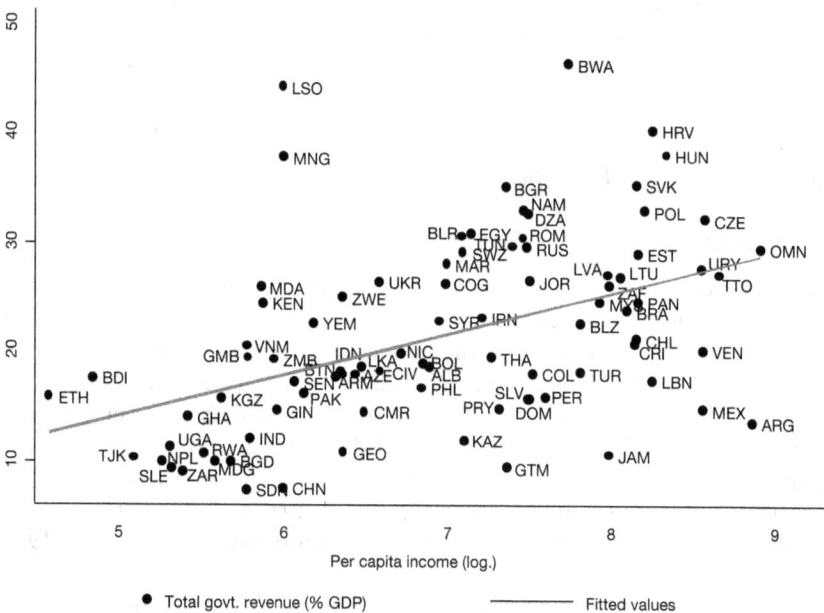

Figure 5.2 Comparison of (total) government revenues with per capita income (averages for low and middle income countries for the period 1990–2004) Source: World Bank (2005a), author's calculations.

the nature and effectiveness of taxation are dependent on the political relationship between tax payers (society) and tax raisers (state), which itself is closely associated with the quality of governance institutions. This line of argument, given prominence in the institutional economics literature, is supported by a considerable weight of historical evidence for both developed and developing countries, as detailed in Moss *et al.* (2006) (also see Bird *et al.* 2004). A related line of scholarship argues that the institutional and political features of developing countries have deep roots in exogenous geographic characteristics as well as former colonial experiences (Acemoglu *et al.* 2000; Ylönen 2005). Institutional factors related to colonial heritage are particularly relevant in the case of taxation. First, tax legislation in most developing countries, as well as the structure of the judicial system, was directly inherited from colonial administrations. Second, the political acceptance of both the level and certain forms of taxation may have deep colonial roots. As such, these factors are likely to represent slow-moving constraints on the economic possibilities and/or interests of the state to achieve rapid, sustainable increments in the tax ratio.

3.2 Analytical framework

The above insights can be used to develop a general framework to inform analysis of taxation performance. The contested nature of taxation indicates that the observed level of taxation may deviate from the level envisaged by government in accordance with fiscal policy. Rather, the actual level reveals the preference of economic actors to pay. Assuming that taxation enforcement is both costly and limited, the decision of a given actor to fully comply with his legal requirement to pay therefore will depend on a range of factors. Critical among these will be the perceived enforcement capacity of the government vis-à-vis the supposed difficulty of enforcement in light of the structure of economic activity. Furthermore, assuming that economic actors are imperfectly informed, it follows that past trends in aggregate economic performance and taxation compliance are likely to guide current tax payment decisions.

Following from the above, and without developing a formal model from first principles, the observed nominal level of taxation R at time t can be defined as:

$$R_t = a_t Y_t \tag{1}$$

$$a_t = f(a_t^*, r_{t-1}, Z_{t-1}) \tag{2}$$

where Y is the nominal level of income, a is the effective average rate of taxation (or the revealed preference to pay), a^* the desired average rate of taxation as set by government policy, r the tax ratio ($r = a = R/Y$), and Z a vector of variables capturing economic structure, such as per capita GDP, and government enforcement capacity. In other words, Z refers to the demand and supply-side factors referred to in the previous subsection.

An important theoretical and empirical issue to address is the influence of the taxation system on growth and the structure of economic activity more generally, i.e. that the vector Z may not be strictly exogenous to a.[3] Economic theory certainly indicates that fiscal policy can have an effect on output growth. However, the channels by which it can do so are considered to be numerous, with the final outcome being dependent on the combined effect of all forms of government financing and expenditure allocations on economic incentives (Gemmell 2004).[4] In this sense, analysis of the relationship between growth and individual aggregate fiscal variables, such as the tax ratio, is unlikely to give robust results in the absence of more detailed fiscal policy measures. This is confirmed by empirical studies which fail to show a consistent or unambiguous partial impact of the aggregate taxation burden on output growth (Gemmell 2004; Easterly and Rebelo 1994; Gerson 1998). Furthermore, given the existence of numerous non-fiscal (deep) determinants of growth, as well as the proposition in equation (2) that economic structure influences taxation performance with a lag, it is reasonable to agree with Tanzi and Zee (2000) that the *primary* direction of causation runs from these structural variables to taxation performance. Even so, one must not dismiss the point that the effective tax burden may be a material variable in a given country's growth function. As such, possible simultaneity between equations (1) and (2) must be considered in any empirical estimation; this point is discussed further below.

An immediate contribution of this framework is the clear suggestion of path-dependency in taxation performance, in turn giving an explanation for the frequently observed phenomenon of 'fiscal inertia' (World Bank 1988; Bird and Zolt 2005). The existence of fiscal inertia, which refers to the relative stability of the tax ratio over time within countries, is demonstrated in the available data. Figure 5.3 plots the cumulative distribution of the median rate of growth in taxation ratios (the rate of growth of the weight of taxation in GDP) over the period 1990–2003 for each country in the dataset (see Section 3.4). It reveals that the distribution is tightly packed around zero, with over 75 per cent of countries achieving a growth rate of under 3 per cent per annum. As Burgess and Stern (1993) remark, without political will and the support of the private sector, attempts at revenue expansion are often systematically frustrated. This is exemplified by the 'Mexico paradox', discussed in Bird and Zolt (2005), where the tax ratio has remained stable for over 25 years despite marked enhancements in both tax administration and fiscal policy. This leads the authors to conclude that long-term changes in the tax ratio for Mexico will be possible only when an explicit consensus is reached between the private and public sectors as to both the level and suitability of higher revenues. Referring to equation (2), this implies that the credibility of both government taxation policy and desired revenue targets may be key determinants of effective taxation performance.

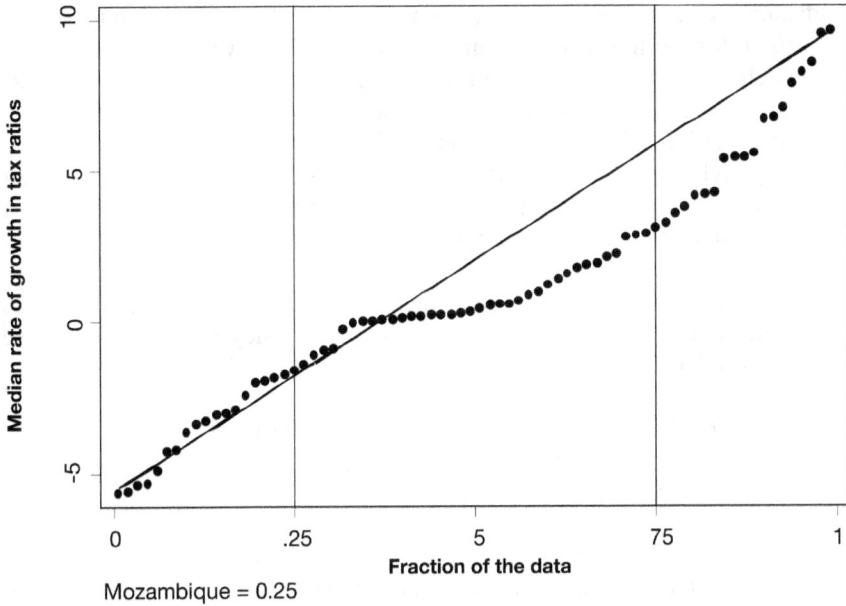

Figure 5.3 Cumulative distribution of median annual rates of growth in the taxation
　　　　ratio for 1990–2004 (low and middle income countries only)
　　　　Source: World Bank (2005a), author's calculations.

3.3 Regression model

The analytical framework suggests that Mozambique's revenue performance
may be constrained by slowly changing structural features of the economy. If
this is the case, and especially given current concerns, it follows that estimates of the magnitude of these structural constraints would represent valuable inputs into policy and planning processes. To put it another way, the
optimal choice for the revenue target (a^*) can only be made in light of other
elements of equation (2). With this motivation in mind, the hypothesis for
empirical investigation is that differences in economic structure and institutional quality explain a considerable share of the observed long-term differences in tax ratios. Remaining unexplained variation could then be attributed
to differences in tax policy and administration, as well as to idiosyncratic
country-specific effects of either a long- or short-term nature.

To test the hypothesis, a regression model of equation (2) must be constructed. Although this could be stated in either static (levels) or dynamic
terms, the former is preferred given our interest in slowly-changing structural
factors, including time invariant effects. Moreover, given the proposed form
of equation (2), a robust dynamic specification would be problematic given
the complex lag structure and endogeneity issues involved. To avoid these

difficulties, a static specification is chosen in which four-year period averages are used for both the dependent and independent variables. Given this approach, and assuming values for *a* are highly correlated with the vector *Z*, it is unnecessary to include a lagged value of the tax ratio as a regressor in this specification. Thus the model simply focuses on the relationship between average levels of the observed tax ratio and *Z* for a given period. Note that comparative, cross-country analysis is valuable precisely because there is not sufficient time series data or counterfactual evidence to analyse the relationships of interest at the individual country level.

The demand-side structural factors included in the model represent variables encountered frequently in the relevant literature. They are used to capture the key 'tax handles' available to the government. Specifically they are:

- real per capita GDP (measured in constant 2000 US$);
- the share of industry in total value added;
- exports as a percentage of GDP;
- imports as a percentage of GDP.

Institutional factors are notoriously difficult to measure, a particular problem being that of how to deal with the endogeneity of policies and institutions to current economic conditions. This is relevant with regard to taxation performance as adequate public revenues are required to finance a sound tax administration system. Thus weak public institutions may be endogenous to low tax revenues, setting in motion a vicious circle. In order to minimize the theoretical and econometric problems associated with institutional endogeneity, however, the model does not include (either directly or via instrumentation) measures of *current* institutional quality. Rather, a set of 'deep' variables are selected that are evidently both prior to taxation performance and frequently associated with institutional quality in the research literature. As their values are time invariant, these variables represent a set of background factors or fixed effects on cross-country taxation performance. The chosen variables are:

- the percentage of the country's territory located in the tropics or sub-tropics based on the Koeppen–Geiger climate zones dataset;[5]
- dummy variables representing the primary, long-term colonial power which historically governed the country (if any), based on the CEPII geodesic distances dataset;[6]
- a dummy variable to indicate whether the country is landlocked, also taken from the CEPII dataset;
- dummy variables representing the major continent in which the country is found.

According to the framework set out in Frankel (2002), the tropics variable captures the influence of tropical geography on both institutional evolution and economic performance more generally. Use of this specific variable follows Dalgaard *et al.* (2004), who find it to be a robust predictor of economic performance. The colonial variables refer to the impact of colonial systems on current taxation performance. In contrast to the 'standard' employment of settler mortality rates to instrument for the overall quality of institutions in developing countries (see Acemoglu *et al.* 2000), only colonial dummy variables are included in the model. This strategy reflects the specific interest of this chapter in taxation institutions, which in the cases of colonized countries were directly inherited from the colonial power. Both the landlocked and continental dummy variables are used to reflect aspects of trade openness as well as broader neighbourhood effects. Finally, the time trend variable is included in order to capture global shifts in taxation policy or ideology, such as international movements toward multilateral trade liberalization.

At this juncture, discussion of the nature of the dependent variable is pertinent given the important distinction between taxation and total government revenues. The former set of revenues is relatively well defined, referring principally to the direct and indirect taxation of economic activity. The latter is considerably wider in scope, capturing all revenues raised by the government, including both tax revenue and a broad range of non-tax revenues such as fees, service charges and (natural resource) rents.[7] As shown by the summary statistics given in Table 5.1, referring to the dataset constructed for this study, the size of the gap between taxation and total revenues is neither insignificant nor homogenous across countries or regions.[8] A host of explanatory factors for variations in this gap across countries could be cited, including differences in policies (e.g. the application of user-charges) and the extent of natural resource extraction. However, the position adopted here is that the possibilities for raising such financing are both highly country

Table 5.1 Total Revenue and Tax Revenue Ratios (% of GDP, low and middle income countries)

	N	*1990–1997*		*1998–2003*		*1990–2003*		
		Total	*Tax*	*Total*	*Tax*	*Total*	*Tax*	*Diff.*
Africa	44	25.0	18.8	25.3	19.5	25.1	19.2	6.0
America	23	18.1	14.1	18.7	13.2	18.4	13.7	4.7
Asia	31	20.0	13.6	17.4	11.9	18.7	12.8	5.9
Europe	15	30.1	18.5	30.4	17.0	30.2	17.7	12.5
All	113	22.5	16.2	21.8	14.8	22.2	15.5	6.7
Low income	59	18.9	15.2	17.9	13.2	18.4	14.2	4.2
Resource poor	19	21.4	17.1	19.5	15.0	20.5	16.0	4.4
Mozambique	1	11.8	10.6	12.2	11.3	12.0	11.0	1.1

Notes: 'N' refers to the number of countries in each group; 'Low income' refers to countries with real average GDP per capita below US$1000; countries included correspond to the sample used for empirical estimation.
Source: World Bank (2005a) and Government of Mozambique

specific and poorly documented. As such, it is more appropriate to restrict cross-country comparison of revenue performance to the more circumscribed concept of tax revenue performance.

Even so, it would be simplistic to dismiss the possibility that the level of tax revenues may be endogenous to the availability of non-tax income sources. Assuming this effect will be greatest where natural resources are under extraction, it follows that the availability of substantial natural resource rents may diminish the government's financial dependence on domestic taxation and thus reduce incentives for the government to develop a constructive (growth-conducive) relationship with the private sector via fiscal policy. Practical measurement of such an effect clearly is not straightforward, particularly as mineral wealth is not homogenous and natural resource access rights can be allocated in numerous ways, in turn influencing government taxation instruments. However, an alternative is to focus on a less ambiguous set of resource-poor countries. The corollary argument is that these countries may face comparatively greater incentives to raise revenue via taxation alone. Such countries can be identified by the wealth estimates in World Bank (2006b), defining a resource-poor country as one which falls in the bottom quartile of the distribution of per capita subsoil and timber resource assets under exploitation.[9] Thus the final regressor, added to the set of structural (supply-side) variables, is a dummy variable taking the value of one for resource-poor countries.

3.4 Dataset and regression estimators

Unless otherwise indicated, the World Bank's World Development Indicators (2005a) are used to construct the dataset, providing the most extensive coverage of taxation data for developing countries in a standardized format. Although originally not included, aggregate tax revenue information is inserted for Mozambique based on the standard IMF classification. As noted above, the time series dimension of the dataset consists of non-overlapping four-year averages for the chosen variables, a standard practice of the empirical (cross-country growth) literature. In terms of the cross-section dimension, only low and middle income countries are included so as to avoid contamination from higher income countries which arguably face greater flexibility in their choice of revenue target.[10] The resulting sample covers 113 countries for the period 1990–2003, composed of African (39 per cent), Latin and Central American (20 per cent), Asian (27 per cent) and East and Central European (13 per cent) states. Table 5.1 includes summary statistics, showing the average tax and total revenue ratios for the period covered.

With respect to the model estimator, a fixed effects (within) panel estimator is not suitable primarily because the research hypothesis focuses on the static influence of observed structural variables, including time invariant effects, rather than changes over time *within* each country. On the assumption of moderate fiscal inertia, the effects of our explanatory variables are expected to be most clearly discernible across (between) countries for the relatively short time period observed. However, in the absence of theoretical guidance as to the correct (panel) estimator to apply, results are presented from a range of estimators regularly employed in the literature. These include a standard OLS estimator with robust standard errors, a GLS random effects (RE) estimator, and a Prais–Winsten panel-corrected standard errors (PCSE) estimator which adjusts for the effects of autocorrelation and heteroscedasticity in the residuals (see Beck 2001).[11] In order to explore the merit of including the demand-side variables, a restricted model representing only the supply-side regressors plus time is examined first, followed by the full specification.

3.5 General results

From the regression results given in Table 5.2, two findings are immediately apparent. First, the estimated coefficients are extremely consistent across estimators. Second, the coefficients for the supply-side variables are stable to the introduction of the demand-side variables, in terms of their size, direction and significance. For model validation, a Hausman (1978) test is used to distinguish between the suitability of a fixed versus random effects estimator. The results indicate that while the random effects estimates are not consistent under the restricted model, they are both efficient and consistent when the institutional variables are added. In other words, country fixed effects become obsolete once the demand-side variables are entered. This is confirmed by the greater explanatory power of the full model – under the RE and OLS estimators the restricted model explains approximately 30 per cent of variation in tax ratios, rising to 65 per cent with the full specification.

A more detailed review of the regression data, however, suggests that despite the four-year panel structure, certain time series problems remain. Arellano-Bond (see Roodman 2004) tests for serial autocorrelation in the OLS specification, for example, indicate non-stationarity in the residuals. Consequently, the PCSE estimator is preferred due to the adjustments it makes for serial autocorrelation.[12] Moreover, for both the restricted and full specifications the PCSE estimator provides greater explanatory power, as indicated by the R-squared measure.

In general terms, the results confirm the hypothesis that *both* supply- and demand-side factors represent robust determinants of tax ratios across countries and over time. The direction and significance of the coefficients on the structural regressors are consistent with empirical results from previous studies (e.g. Teera and Hudson 2004). In particular, the strong result that the share of imports is positively related to tax ratios confirms the established argument that cross-border flows are a relatively easy 'tax handle' for developing countries to grasp. However, neither the share of industry in total value added nor the share of exports in GDP is significant in any of the models/estimators (thus they are omitted from Table 5.2). This may be the case as these variables provide little independent information once per capita

Table 5.2 Regression Results, 4 year panels

Dependent variable: Natural logarithms of average tax revenue as % GDP

	RE		OLS		PCSE	
	Restricted	*Full*	*Restricted*	*Full*	*Restricted*	*Full*
Variables:	A	B	C	D	E	F
Constant	11.88***	11.07**	21.17**	12.29	14.57**	10.39*
	(2.67)	(2.52)	(2.12)	(1.56)	(2.13)	(1.81)
GDP per capita	0.14***	0.16***	0.12***	0.10***	0.12***	0.12***
	(4.17)	(3.84)	(5.22)	(3.11)	(4.72)	(3.36)
Imports % GDP	0.30***	0.28***	0.34***	0.26***	0.33***	0.28***
	(4.09)	(3.89)	(4.27)	(5.03)	(4.41)	(4.70)
Resource poor	0.17**	0.29***	0.20***	0.27***	0.18***	0.28***
	(2.00)	(3.68)	(4.46)	(6.13)	(3.18)	(5.27)
Time trend	–0.01**	–0.01**	–0.01**	–0.01	–0.01**	–0.01*
	(–2.53)	(–2.45)	(–2.11)	(–1.52)	(–2.05)	(–1.75)
% Land tropics		–0.17*		–0.26***		–0.22***
		(–1.83)		(–4.18)		(–3.37)
Landlocked		0.14*		0.09		0.12**
		(1.83)		(1.61)		(2.00)
Belgium		0.21		0.28**		0.23**
		(1.06)		(2.46)		(2.06)
China		0.83***		0.80***		0.79***
		(2.82)		(8.35)		(7.87)
Germany		0.53***		0.53***		0.56***
		(2.66)		(5.09)		(3.97)
France		0.41***		0.38***		0.42***
		(3.03)		(4.04)		(3.64)
Great Britain		0.38***		0.39***		0.40***
		(3.30)		(5.16)		(4.24)
Netherlands		0.51*		0.49***		0.52***
		(1.89)		(4.75)		(4.05)
Portugal		0.24		0.27**		0.26*
		(1.08)		(2.45)		(1.83)
Asia		–0.32***		–0.32***		–0.30***
		(–3.43)		(–5.01)		(–4.53)
N	235	235	235	235	235	235
R squared	0.30	0.64	0.31	0.66	0.90	0.93
Chi squared	55.6	151.1	...	...	107.6	1116.8

* p<.1, ** p<.05, *** p<.01; t-statistics given in parentheses

Notes: variables are as described in the text – specific countries and continents are specified as (0 / 1) dummies; variables which are not significant in any specification are excluded; RE, OLS and PCSE refer to the different regression estimators, also described in the text.

Source: World Bank (2005a) and Government of Mozambique, author's estimates

GDP and the share of imports are included. The strong positive result for the resource-poor dummy supports our hypothesis that these countries face relatively stronger incentives to raise revenue via taxation. While this does not shed specific light on any 'resource curse' argument, it does confirm the broad argument that observed taxation (revenue) choices are endogenous to economic structure, including the availability of resource rents. Finally, the negative time trend found for all estimators indicates there has been a moderate decline in tax ratios once the effect of other variables has been taken into account. Again, although the processes behind this result are somewhat opaque, trade liberalization effects and/or reforms to improve conditions for business investment by reducing tax burdens may be at play here.

Results for the supply-side variables also are consistent with previous research. The robust negative effect of the fraction of land in the tropics affirms the general finding that this factor is associated with weaker economic and institutional performance (Dalgaard *et al.* 2004). The partial effect of colonial legacy is also significant in certain cases. For the major colonial powers, the strongest and most significant influence is found for countries formerly colonized by Great Britain or France. The model suggests, *ceteris paribus,* that these countries achieve an average tax ratio of up to 1.5 percentage points higher than countries not colonized for any long period (e.g. Turkey).[13] This effect may derive from inherited colonial administrative procedures and/or a legacy of formal sector taxation compliance. The significant result for the landlocked dummy, which tells us to expect a higher tax ratio for landlocked countries (*ceteris paribus*), appears counter-intuitive given arguments that landlocked countries face a more constrained set of economic growth opportunities (e.g. MacKellar *et al.* 2000). Possible factors behind this result, however, are differences in the nature of the 'tax handles' and corresponding institutions in landlocked countries. For example, one can speculate that sea borders create greater opportunities for smuggling and tax evasion than are possible over land. In any case, the overriding message is that in addition to structural economic features, exogenous determinants of institutional performance also explain a large portion of the observed variance in tax ratios across countries over time.

4 Application to Mozambique

Turning to the specific case of Mozambique, Table 5.3 states the predicted tax ratios for each of the four-year periods in the panel using the PSCE estimator. For illustrative purposes only, Figure 5.4 plots the predicted (and actual) tax ratios calculated by applying the same (panel) coefficients to annual data. In both cases the results are highly informative. First, and in support of the regression results, movements in the predicted tax ratio for Mozambique closely correspond to actual changes both within *and* outside the model's sample period (1990–2003). The model correctly determines the direction of all major changes in Mozambique's tax ratio over the last 25 years, including the drop in tax revenue in the early 1980s, its rise from 1986 to 1993, as well as the subsequent decline from 1993 to 1996. Recall that the model is based on cross-country data, contains no (direct) information regarding either tax administration or tax policy and includes no country 'fixed effects'. Given the explanatory power of the model, it is therefore

Table 5.3 Observed and Predicted Values for Mozambique's Tax Ratio

		1990–93	*1994–97*	*1998–01*	*2002–03*	*Average*
Restricted	Tax ratio	10.4	11.6	11.1	10.9	11.0
	s.e.	1.1	1.1	1.1	1.1	1.1
	Tax effort	103.0	89.4	101.2	104.5	99.3
Full	Tax ratio	9.3	10.3	10.0	10.2	10.0
	s.e.	1.1	1.1	1.1	1.1	1.1
	Tax effort	115.2	100.5	111.3	111.8	109.5
Observed	Tax ratio	10.8	10.4	11.2	11.4	10.9

Source: Government of Mozambique, author's regressions

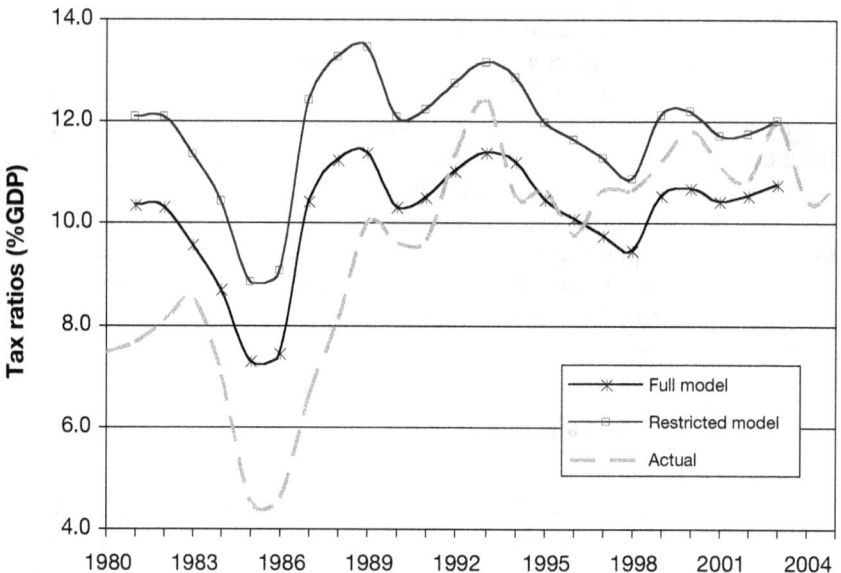

Figure 5.4 Actual versus predicted tax ratio
Notes: Calculations based on coefficients from PCSE panel model applied to annual data.
Source: Government of Mozambique, author's regressions.

reasonable to conclude that observed shifts in the tax ratio in Mozambique have been strongly driven by movements in underlying economic structure ('tax handles') despite changes in policy or administrative efficiency. Moreover, as can be ascertained from Figure 5.1, changes in the import share appear to have been a critical factor behind short-term movements in the ratio, particularly during the period 1988–94, which witnessed large humanitarian inflows as well as a significant UN peacekeeping operation (see Arndt *et al.* 2007) charged with overseeing the peace agreement reached in 1992.[14]

Second, although Mozambique's observed tax ratio is relatively low by regional and international standards (see Table 5.1), averaging 11.1 per cent for the period 2000–5, its historical performance has been extremely faithful to its predicted level according to either the full or restricted models (see Figure 5.4; also Table 5.3). Once one takes into account the expected effect of exogenous influences on Mozambique's institutional performance, which act to reduce the predicted tax ratio, actual tax collections appear to have been marginally higher than the model's predictions. Accordingly, cross-country evidence suggests we should not expect Mozambique's current tax ratio to be equal to the regional or international average for (low income) developing countries. To put it another way, Mozambique's past performance is not an outlier in comparative terms once the effects of structural and institutional conditions are taken into account.

Following from the above, the model allows us to evaluate Mozambique's tax effort over time. Tax effort is defined as the observed tax ratio divided by the ratio predicted by the model, in this case based on the results from the PCSE estimator(s). The results of this calculation are presented in Table 5.3 for the sample period. They suggest that since achieving robust improvements during the mid-to late-1980s, broadly coinciding with the initiation of structural adjustment reforms (and thus improved access to foreign exchange and taxation reforms), the tax effort has remained relatively stable. According to the results from the full specification, Mozambique has sustained an average tax effort within the expected 95 per cent confidence interval predicted by the model since 1990.

Notwithstanding these results, it is important to assess the validity of applying the framework to the case of Mozambique. In other words, are there specific factors germane to Mozambique's tax performance (or potential) which are not adequately reflected in the model? On the one hand, the country's close proximity to South Africa and the strong economic links they share may have a positive influence on taxation via higher levels of trade and investment. However, in principle these factors should be captured by the model, not least by the income per capita variable which reflects the overall level of economic activity. Furthermore, Mozambique is not a member of the Southern African Customs Union (SACU), which operates a revenue sharing mechanism. As discussed further in Chapter 12, revenue sharing with South Africa goes a long way to explain the comparatively high tax ratios recorded in Swaziland, Lesotho and other SACU member countries.

A second potential critique is that the model is of limited relevance to cases of rapid and sustained real output growth, such as in Mozambique.[15] This would have force if the effect of rapid/sustained growth on the tax ratio was not captured by movements in the structural explanatory variables, i.e. there are omitted variables. Alternatively, the coefficients may be biased if the association between growth, structural change and taxation performance did not correspond to the four-year periods employed to estimate the model. For example, a slow dynamic lag running from income growth and other structural changes to the tax ratio (see equation 2), could mean that the model in fact over-estimates the impact of *recent* structural change on the tax ratio. This comes from the fact that the main sources of variation in the dataset derive from differences between, rather than within, countries. For Mozambique, however, neither of these two concerns appears to be highly relevant. First, analyses of the drivers of post-war growth highlight strong post-conflict recovery effects as opposed to more fundamental structural changes (World Bank 2005b; Arndt *et al.* 2007). Second, despite ongoing tax reforms in Mozambique, the strong predictive performance of the model when applied to annual data would seem to reject the argument that there are important factors omitted from the model. This is confirmed by a comparison of the prediction errors (regression residuals) for 'high growth' countries versus the rest.[16] A (non-parametric) Wilcoxon rank-sum test indicates there is no significant difference in the size of these errors between the two groups. Moreover, when the model is estimated only for the same group of 'high growth' countries, the tax ratio for Mozambique for the period 2002–3 is predicted as 10.9 per cent, falling inside the 95 per cent confidence interval estimated from both the restricted and unrestricted specifications on the full dataset.

Finally, the role of non-tax revenues merits comment. In overall terms the country's non-tax revenues have been comparatively low at around 10 per cent of tax revenue or 1 percentage point of GDP (see Table 5.1). This compares to an average contribution from non-tax revenues of over 4 percentage points of GDP in both resource-poor and low income countries. In part, the low contribution in Mozambique is attributable to the existence of substantial, but unrecorded (off-budget), non-tax revenues raised by individual government sectors, typically as user fees. As shown in Figure 5.1 for 2005, these revenues are slowly being included in official government figures, namely the budget, a trend which continued into 2006.[17] As such, one aspect of improving Mozambique's 'official' revenue position must embrace enhancements to the transparency of public financial management at all levels.

Also, (non-tax) revenues pertaining to natural resource extraction are recognized to be extremely low at under 5 per cent of revenues (World Bank 2005b). However, this is not for an absence of available natural resources. Rather, according to the resource definition used in the dataset used for this study, Mozambique falls in the second quartile of the distribution of countries, ranking alongside Ghana and Namibia in terms of estimated *per capita* wealth of non-renewable subsoil (energy and mineral) and timber resources. However, this estimate is based on figures for reserves under production as of 2000, rather than unexploited deposits. Indeed, a number of large mineral extraction operations are currently under construction or proposed in Mozambique, including one of the largest unexplored coal deposits in the world,[18] not to mention the recent establishment of operations by SASOL (a South African energy conglomerate) to pipe extensive natural gas deposits into South Africa. From this perspective, while the question of the exact level of natural resource taxation cannot be considered, a substantial upward shift in total government revenues should be expected once production from these projects comes on-line. In a general survey, the World Bank (2005b) estimates that natural resource rents raised by the government could double in size relatively easily in the short term to around 11 per cent of tax revenue, expanding over the medium term to around 3 percentage points of GDP.

The necessity of ensuring domestic revenue gains from (future) natural resource extraction in Mozambique has been emphasized by the IMF, particularly in light of generous fiscal benefits conceded in the early post-war period to attract first-mover foreign investors. Not only are the total costs of these benefits unclear, but the *same* fiscal benefits have been given to internationally mobile investors, who can use taxation as a core lever in any negotiations, as to geographically fixed natural resource operations (see Chapters 15 and 16for elaboration). Thus, while the empirical analysis of this study suggests that Mozambique's past tax effort has not been below expectations by international standards, future revenue plans must account for gains from natural resource activities.

5 Conclusions

The principal argument of this study is that governments face limitations on the volume of tax revenue they can raise. Analysis has shown that institutional and structural variables explain many of the differences in tax revenue levels across countries over time. In other words, and in line with previous scholarship, deep slow-moving economic characteristics, including the diversity and size of potential 'tax handles', act to fix plausible parameters for the tax ratio. It should be underscored, however, that this argument specifically refers to one of various taxation goals, namely the level of taxation revenues, and therefore should not be taken to undermine the importance of tax policy or administration concerns. Indeed, these dimensions are crucial determinants of the efficiency and equity of the taxation system, which have not been in focus.

Even so, it stands to reason that tax policy and administrative design must be sensitive to revenue constraints and be guided by a realistic aggregate target. Inflated revenue targets risk encouraging tax policies and/or administrative measures that are at best ineffective and at worst distort long-term private sector development. These points are germane to Mozambique given underlying disagreement as regards an appropriate medium-term tax ratio. When applied to Mozambique the cross-country model provides a remarkably robust prediction of movements in actual tax revenues over a 25 year period to the present day. On this basis alone, the results indicate that institutional and structural constraints have been sizeable and that Mozambique's recent taxation performance has not deviated significantly from its predicted levels. Cross-country evidence does not indicate that the current tax ratio of approximately 11 per cent in Mozambique is a (poor performance) outlier; nor does it suggest that the relative inertia in taxation performance is unusual despite the broad range of tax policy and administration reforms undertaken.

What, then, might be a realistic medium-term tax ratio target for Mozambique? Excluding considerable expected gains associated with natural resource extraction, the analysis suggests that large increases in tax revenues are unlikely to be achieved in the near term despite ongoing reforms. Thus a realistic medium-term target for Mozambique may be in the region of 13 per cent of GDP for tax revenues only, assuming continued economic growth and access to foreign exchange via the support of external aid. Of course, natural resource production growth should lead to substantial additional revenues; however, this will depend on specific policy changes regarding the treatment of natural resource operations and the regime of fiscal benefits more generally. An important advance in this regard, to support policy development, will be efforts to estimate the aggregate opportunity costs of these fiscal benefits.

Finally, it is evident that this conclusion runs counter to IMF analysis for Mozambique. However, returning to the analytical framework developed in this study, revenue outcomes can be understood as revealed preferences to pay on the part of economic agents. Thus, revenue targets should not be chosen in isolation from contextual factors such as the economic structure and the overall credibility of fiscal policy. Adopting more moderate and realistic revenue expectations in Mozambique would reduce pressure on collection authorities. In turn this would provide greater policy space to consider equity and efficiency reforms. It is exactly these reforms that are emphasized by the private sector on which taxation ultimately must depend.

Notes

1 What follows is a characterization of two divergent perspectives and, thus, deliberately ignores more nuanced positions.
2 For a general review of the literature, see Bird *et al.* (2004); for sub-Saharan Africa, see Ghura (1998) and Stotsky and WoldeMariam (1997).
3 For a general discussion of endogeneity in econometric modelling, see Engle *et al.* (1983).
4 Even the direction of the relationship between growth and taxation is not obvious a priori. For example, where coordination problems or other externalities mean

that public investment is more productive than that of the private sector, a higher tax ratio may be consistent with a higher rate of growth (*ceteris paribus*).

5 Available from the collection found at: www.ksg.harvard.edu/CID/ciddata/geographydata.htm.

6 Available from the Centre d'Etudes Prospectives et d'Informations Internationales (CEPII): www.cepii.fr/anglaisgraph/bdd/distances.htm.

7 Note, 'below the line' financial resources such as external grants, loans or internal debt-financing, are not included in these measures and are not in focus here.

8 The standard error of the mean gap between taxation and total revenues by country is 5.96 percentage points of GDP.

9 While the World Bank (2006b) data is extensive, a small number of countries for which taxation data are available are not covered; thus, in order to maximize the size of our dataset we define such missing countries as being non-resource poor.

10 The classification follows that of the World Bank (2005a). As a result, the sample contains countries with real GDP per capita ranging from under US$100 (for Ethiopia and the Democratic Republic of the Congo) to a maximum of US$8,210 (in the case of Oman).

11 All estimations are run in Stata. The PCSE estimator is applied via the xtpcse command using options for autocorrelation (not panel specific) and heteroscedasticity. This is preferred to a (panel) Feasible Generalized Least Squares estimator due to the more conservative disposition of the results.

12 The AR(1) autocorrelation parameter for the full PCSE model is estimated to be 0.642, confirming the need for this adjustment. If nothing else, this finding may be interpreted as evidence of substantial 'fiscal inertia' in the observed tax ratios. Dynamic panel specifications, such as inclusion of a lag of the dependent variable among the regressors, can be employed to adjust for the problem of serial autocorrelation. However, given the interest of this study in long-term effects from relatively static variables, such techniques are not deemed appropriate in this case.

13 Results for Chinese and Dutch colonization are somewhat stronger; however, these refer to a very small number of countries and therefore are not of general interest.

14 The regression results reveal that tax revenues in developing countries have a high effective import share; thus a 10 per cent increase in imports is associated with a 3 per cent increase in the tax ratio.

15 For the period 1994–2003, Mozambique is one of only eight countries in the dataset that achieved an annual average rate of per capita income growth in excess of 5 per cent.

16 High growth countries are defined as those achieving a median level of per capita growth in excess of 3.5 per cent per annum over the full period.

17 For example, preliminary figures for 2006 suggest that user fees raised in the health sector were twice their budgeted amount.

18 These are found in the District of Moatize (Tete Province); exploration rights have been granted to the Brazilian multinational CVRD (Companhia Vale do Rio Doce).

Part II

Institutional framework and current practices

6 Institutional design

Simon McCoy and João E. Van Dunem

1 Introduction

Over the last few decades, a number of distinct arguments have flowered in the public finance literature to make a cogent case for the need for vigorous state intervention and taxation in less developed economies.[1] Some of those arguments, to a certain degree inspired by concomitant developments in moral philosophy, include prevalent market failures, vulnerability due to extreme deprivation and inequality (for a classic discussion, see, for example, Burgess and Stern 1993). Still, even if public finance theory seems increasingly to suggest some role for taxation to play in promoting development, on the practical side developing countries face extremely complex challenges.

Notwithstanding the increasing attention that taxation merits in their economic policy agenda, an overwhelming majority of developing countries generally tend to be affected by weak tax administration capabilities. In this chapter, we consider the institutional design of tax administration in Mozambique, a country often cited as a typical case of successful economic reform in Africa. The chapter reflects some real preoccupations concerning particular problems in fiscal administration in Mozambique. It is recognized throughout that a robust, efficient and corruption-free tax administration has the potential to make a crucial contribution to resource mobilization and consequently to the lives of the Mozambican population. It is also recognized that increasing self-reliance, and thus reducing dependency on outside sources of financing, is critical to the development process.

At the time of writing, the fiscal administration in Mozambique is undergoing significant and far-reaching reform. The responsibility for the administration of internal taxes belongs to the Direcção Geral da Administração Tributária dos Impostos (DGI), while the Direcção Geral das Alfândegas (DGA) manages the collection and control of customs taxes at the national border.[2] Both directorates form part of the Ministry of Finance, with each respective General Director reporting directly to the Minister. These two agencies are going through distinct stages of their respective reform processes but are eventually expected to merge into a single central revenue authority from early 2007, with dual responsibility for the administration of internal and customs taxes.

Broadly speaking, in the years since 1997 both fiscal bureaucracies have registered considerable reform. Importantly, however, while the DGA has undergone a sweeping restructuring of its administration and today is able to enjoy a certain degree of autonomy regarding recruitment, human resource development and budget, the DGI is only now embarking on its own phase of internal reorganization. With this context in mind, the present chapter will also seek to outline some of the primary institutional challenges facing these tax agencies and emphasize the extent to which current (proposed and actual) reforms appear to address those. The authors of this chapter both served as economist fellows in each of the fiscal directorates over a two-year period, and the analysis below draws a great deal on their firsthand experiences.

The chapter will be split into three broad sections. We begin by reviewing the current institutional architecture of the Mozambican Customs Administration, locally known as Alfândegas. We approach the institutional design of Alfândegas from the perspective of the recent customs reform, by focusing on the main pillars of the institutional reform programme launched nearly 10 years ago. The discussion is then supplemented by an appreciation of their impact in conjunction with some persistent challenges that the customs authorities continue to face. We will then outline the primary features of the institutional design of the DGI and, through three representative case studies, consider some of the challenges confronting the authorities. The third and concluding section will focus on the central revenue authority and its design, with particular reference to the establishment of fiscal policy.

2 Customs administration: a view through the lens of reform

2.1 Background and promises of customs reform

This section takes on the background and chronological events that preceded the customs reform in Mozambique. In a fundamental sense, the reform of the customs institutions is inseparable from the World Bank and IMF adjustment-oriented conditionality,[3] which, typically, reduced the government's economic policy space. In Sub-Saharan Africa, early versions of this model of reform culminating in the creation of a central revenue authority were endorsed at first by Ghana as early as 1985, followed by Uganda in 1991. Perhaps of greatest concern, it has been reported in recent times that while those early tax administration reforms were accompanied by short-term revenue improvements, in the long run sustainability of such success has proved to be more elusive (Fjeldstad and Rakner 2003). Even so, modest improvements in these countries' administrations were not sufficient to prevent replication of the experiment in a large number of African countries or, at least, to encourage an open debate about the overall reform strategy. Among some of the countries affected by reform in the continent can be found Zambia, Tanzania, Malawi and South Africa – all part of the club of Mozambique's neighbouring countries – and, of course, Mozambique itself.

In August 1995, the World Bank issued a report entitled 'Mozambique: impediments to industrial sector recovery' (World Bank 1995). There, the Bank pointed to a wide array of factors behind poor industrial performance, including the inability of the customs administration to enforce payments of duties and taxes on competing imports. In particular, significant focus was put on the high levels of *negative* effective rate of protection faced by domestic producers, which, according to the Bank, required a 'radical reform ... to address the serious weaknesses encountered in Mozambique's Customs administration' (World Bank 1995: 28). This view mirrored widespread dissatisfaction within the domestic industry, severely hurt by rampant smuggling activity, especially from South Africa. The report also justified, in a rather explicit way, the existence of weak and inefficient mechanisms in the administration. More to the point, it asserted that the customs service faced a 'lack of appropriate standard operating procedures, weak enforcement mechanisms, lack of computerized information and management systems, and poor human and infrastructure resources' (World Bank 1995: 21). By that time, the Bank was already unveiling a reasonably good approximation of substantive dimensions to be tackled by an imminent customs reform. Launched approximately one year later, the reform was perceived as vital if the stabilization programme was ever to be deemed to accomplish any real success.

Similarly, from 1991, there was indisputable evidence that industrial activity had plunged, coinciding, especially in 1994, with declining customs tax revenues. Such circumstances were aggravated by large-scale exemption schemes applied under new special legal decrees. Only the first half of the 1990s saw the introduction of an ample legislative package exempting customs taxes merchandise destined for deputies and political parties. Likewise, goods intended to respond to natural disasters, imports by the Cotton Institute or merchandise meant for cultural purposes (scientific, sports and arts)[4] were all included as part of the new exemption package. With this background in mind, the reform of the Mozambican customs service appeared as a crucial opportunity to recover forgone revenue caused not just by inefficiencies and corruption but also by the adverse revenue effects connected to the new exemption laws. In that way, by enhancing tax revenue collections and contributing to restoring existing fiscal imbalances, the transformation of customs would inevitably be able to serve the objective of fiscal stringency embodied in the stabilization programme.

A different but no less significant motivation to trigger a radical change of customs was the acknowledgement of the necessity of curbing systematic corruption. The beginning of the 1990s witnessed a heavy backlash aimed at the Mozambican government for lack of transparency and political will to eradicate corruption. Faced with continuous accusations from virtually all segments of society, the government felt it had to come up with an appropriate response. Anyhow, to discharge its developmental functions effectively, a clear belief developed too that modernization of the state was required, including a fundamental contribution coming from the fight against corruption. At the time, Alfândegas was considered a public administration department that could perform reasonably well the function of catalyst for other departments of government. For that to happen, though, it was judged necessary to appoint a foreign company for the complete management of the customs service since, all too often, smuggling networks operated with Mozambican nationals from different spheres of public and private life.

To sum up: by the end of 1996, a highly delicate state of affairs in the Mozambican customs prompted remedial action. With the global reform cost mainly covered by World Bank and DFID assistance, the appointment of Crown Agents as a private contractor to assume the reorganization of the customs service was expected to yield a multiplicity of objectives. Broadly, these could be summarized in the following way: (1) modernize the overall customs services; (2) boost tax revenues; (3) bolster facilitation of legitimate trade while combating deep-rooted smuggling and corruption; (4) streamline customs legislation and simplify administrative and procedural requirements; (5) invest, develop and strengthen human resources capacity; (6) create and implement a strategy to improve and expand infrastructure and the communication systems; (7) computerize the administrative and customs services; and, finally, (8) ensure the overall sustainability of the reform process.

2.2 Overview of strategy and phases of reform

As we saw earlier, the contract for the implementation of the Customs Service reform was awarded to Crown Agents, a British private company, through international tender. Under the auspices of the Mozambican government and the Bretton Woods institutions, Crown Agents took over the operational management of Customs in 1997 for a three-year period, in what was clearly a very *sui generis* initiative, taking into account previous international experiences in customs reform. Crown Agents brought in around 60 customs staff formerly employed by HM Customs and Excise (UK), with a view to filling in phased sequence senior management and key operational positions at Alfândegas. The Crown Agents team was to accomplish the internal reorganization of Customs in the space of three years, before handing over management to a skilled and competent local staff, then operating in an evolved environment with new computerized information systems and simplified procedures (Hubbard *et al.* 1999).

Within this context of reform, the government established a special unit commonly known as UTRA (Unidade Técnica de Reestruturação das Alfândegas) to be in charge of the supervision of the overall customs reform process. UTRA equally had responsibilities in the formulation and proposal of legislation conforming to a modern customs administration. It would surely be inaccurate, in our judgement, to view UTRA's scope of action as limited to the reform *per se* since the range of its intervention extended to a few other important areas; in this respect, one should be aware that UTRA was actively involved in matters connected to the delivery of pre-shipment inspection such as carrying out regular monitoring of the quality of pre-shipment service. The government also appointed a company, Intertek, to provide pre-shipment inspection (PSI) services, with local verification of import consignments. At the time of engagement, some adjustment in the course of PSI was envisaged, with future action by Intertek expected to focus exclusively on precise tariff headings of the tariff nomenclature. This shift has already occurred and the PSI contract was renewed until June 2007.

The process of customs transformation is typically divided into three phases. The first phase, as seen above, is marked by the effective management control of the organization by Crown Agents. Alfândegas is submitted to broad modernization, as the organization undergoes a vast recruitment process and provides intensive training to new staff; staff retrenchment gets under-way; the capacity of management systems is enhanced through computer-ization; the control mechanisms are rationalized; and so forth. This phase is subsequently followed by a period where efforts are turned to deepening and consolidating the reform process (2000–3). In this new phase, Crown Agents' management is brought to a halt as Alfândegas progressively takes back executive authority; Crown Agents switches instead to a mentoring role; the rehabilitation of infrastructure is pursued and, in the meantime, the computer and communications networks are considerably expanded. Finally, at the time of writing, a transition phase (2003–6) was ongoing which it was hoped would strongly promote the transition to a Central Revenue Authority. During the whole reform programme, a Steering Committee joining together UTRA, Alfândegas, DFID, the World Bank and the IMF was engaged in a period-ical assessment of the project execution. Interestingly, these discussions also tended to allow an opportunity for donors and other agencies involved in the project to address their pressing concerns and voice their particular interests.

2.3 Simplification of the legal and procedural framework

To an increasing extent, tax policy specialists are convinced that aligning tax policy with administrative capacity in developing countries is necessary. Bird describes well this requirement when he argues that 'an essential precondi-tion for the reform of tax administration is to simplify the tax system in order to ensure that it can be applied effectively in the generally low-compliance contexts of developing countries' (Bird 2004: 135). A substantial bulk of evidence suggests that a comprehensive simplification in the tax system has led in fact to improvements in administration performance for many developing countries.[5]

During the process of trade liberalization, Mozambique has substantially deepened the internationalization of its economy.[6] Of course, coping with rising demands for their services depends upon the ability to enact an effec-tive and clear legal framework to improve the customs modus operandi. In that context, striking progress has been accomplished in the modernization of customs legislation and tax procedures throughout the reform process.

Previously outdated legislation and procedures have been updated and made more transparent. Most of the obsolete legislation had been in place since the 1940s, having lost considerable ground with regard to current internationally accepted standards. The new legal framework, introduced following periodic consultation with the private sector, covers widespread issues related to the customs administrative role, and includes: the regulation of transit goods and customs warehouses (covering fuel products); the licensing of import operators; the adoption of what is commonly called the Harmonized System (HS), making concordance of systems of tariff nomenclature easier (2002 version); the regulation on the implementation of the SADC trade protocol and other bilateral trade agreements signed with neighbouring countries (Zimbabwe and Malawi); and the creation of a Code of Conduct and Ethics applying to all customs staff. In what follows in this section, discussion is strictly consigned to a presentation of the major legal devices set up as part of efforts to promote trade facilitation.

In the past, soaring rates of tax evasion in customs were partly a response to sluggish and cumbersome customs procedures. One of the important advances attained by the reform has been the continuing removal of administrative barriers in trade operations, i.e. reducing both the cost of compliance for taxpayers and the cost of collection for the customs administration. Very significant is the introduction of a legal *customs declaration form* for customs trade operations, a so-called Documento Único (DU), a form which can be used either for import of for export operations. By contrast, the pre-declaration, a form submitted to customs authorities to prematurely announce imported merchandise, has been eliminated – and with it the *ex-ante* payment of a corresponding deposit equivalent to 15 per cent of the value of duties payable.

Furthermore, a major shift in PSI has taken place: 100 per cent PSI of goods has been replaced, on a preliminary basis, by a risk-profiled wind-down of selections. This, in turn, has been followed by inspection of only specific tariff headings[7] (while a complete phase-out of PSI is now due). Intertek conducts verification of import consignments in the country of export and in so doing issues to the importer a Documento Único Certificado from one of its offices in the country. This form is then used to clear the goods in customs. PSI physical inspections are, however, targeted at particular shipments through the use of risk assessment and profiling software. This risk-based operational strategy was designed to enable optimization in the use of resources by promoting a fast-track programme in which traders with good compliance records are able to benefit from the release of cargo with some degree of celerity.

An additional area of paramount importance for the enhancement of trade facilitation concerns the implementation of the WTO valuation agreement, formally known as the Agreement on Implementation of Article VII of GATT. The agreement forms part of the WTO agreements and its effective implementation should be complemented by the growing application of audit-based customs control. But in order to be beneficial the latter ought to take into consideration a number of characteristics of the Mozambican import sector: (1) by making use of a newly created intelligence service, attention should be focused towards risk assessment and profiling based on country of origin or product type, for example the fact that there are export countries more prone to underreporting practices, like Zimbabwe and Dubai; (2) close follow-up of products subject to a heavy tax burden or contributing significantly to tax revenue; (3) the number of trade operators in Mozambique is relatively small, so this should lighten up a bit the post-audit task. In this context, pending occasions where the price cannot be taken as a basis and five methods are sequentially adopted as preferred alternatives, the customs value is to be based primarily on the transaction value, i.e. the invoice declared by the importer. This sharply contrasts with the previous system where the customs value consisted of a predetermined reference price as established by the Brussels Value definition. Unequivocally, compared to the old system, customs valuation now favours the promotion of competition in international markets.

In addition, since the aim of the agreement on Customs Valuation is to expedite clearance of legitimate shipment, levels of smuggling could be reduced by inducing more import traders to opt for the legal importation. This argument can be justified on the following grounds. First, while the need for the pre-declaration is eliminated, the agreement secures also the immediate release of the product in case the customs authorities need to probe deeper into the value of the good. Second, implementation of the agreement has the potential to limit smuggling through reductions in the margins obtained by its operators. The spirits and alcoholic drinks sector provides a good example here. Reportedly, the sector was expected to achieve an average fall in customs value in the order of 25–30 per cent following application of the agreement.

2.4 Human resources and computerization: two central pillars of reform

2.4.1 Human resources

Jointly with computerization and IT, human resources policy is believed to be a centrepiece of the Mozambican customs reform. Transformation of the human factor is possibly the most testing component of a customs reform as chances of failure are not negligible. Nonetheless, if successful, the rewards of reform can be extremely high. The purpose of tackling the human resources component of customs organizations in less developed countries is of course commendable: to encourage higher levels of professionalism and improve their performance. In Mozambique, prior to the reform, only 2 per cent of nearly one thousand customs officers had higher education, while a considerable proportion had very modest levels of education. Problems in the shortage of well-qualified staff were compounded by the presence of internal networks of corruption and smuggling involving personnel from all ranks. This all contributed to a general distrust facing the organization.

The human resources reform programme aimed at improving the ethical stance and giving customs staff incentives to upgrade their professional capabilities in administration. With that in mind, the enactment of career paths requiring paramilitary training constituted a central spotlight. A policy of intensified and systematic training to expand the range of skills to successive new waves of recruited staff has also been pursued. In the first four years of reform, for example, more than one thousand newly recruited officials underwent training courses. While during the probation period (corresponding to the first two years of the assignment), performance for the new staff has been gauged on a quarterly basis, appraisal evolved afterwards to an audit-based system that hinged on systems and procedures. A retrenchment programme has also been introduced. All staff from the pre-reform era were subject to basic customs training, competence tests and assessments. In total, as many as 770 customs personnel took part, of which 534 were in the end eligible to be reintegrated in the new career path. The remaining 236 staff with unsatisfactory performance were either transferred to other government departments or agreed to quit upon a compensation payment.[8] In theory, then, assignment to postings is nowadays determined as a function of needs and prerequisites to fill the task at hand, although the multifunctional profile of staff enables the lawful transfer of every single customs official. These days, staff numbers in Alfândegas approach a total of 1,700 customs officers.

As mentioned earlier, a new Code of Conduct has been introduced. This served to ensure that customs staff are aware of their duties and rights, but also to help foster an ethic underscoring service to the citizenry. Staff rotations, at a national level, have been established following the recommendations of the World Customs Organization. A new General Directorate for Internal Control has been established to focus, primarily, on investigating cases of internal fraud and corruption.[9] Recruitment and promotion systems have evolved, at least formally, to a merit-based system where salaries have been lifted on average, being at the moment tied to individual performance and assessed every semester in accordance with publicized criteria. The meritocratic system, if operated properly, can engender a variation in income of 25 per cent according to the level of performance of the individual. Some emphasis has been placed too on the question of HIV/AIDS, due to its devastating border impact (allegedly, on average 60 per cent of the population in the Mozambican border regions are HIV positive). A prevention programme is therefore ongoing, seeking mainly to raise awareness among potentially at-risk customs officials.

2.4.2 Computerization and IT

The significant improvements made in computerization and information technology merit at least as much special mention. During the customs pre-reform period, computers were virtually lacking. It is widely believed, in fact, that only two computers were available in Alfândegas, with perhaps one or two staff members able to use them. Today, the number of computers in use has risen beyond 350, according to the latest Alfândegas figures. It remains essential, even so, not to circumvent the important feature of sequencing for the successful computerization-enhancing in Alfândegas. Mechanisms were judiciously built in from the start, like rehabilitation and re-equipment of certain areas of customs, to safeguard against problems of inadequacy in most of the customs infrastructure, because of degradation or destruction after the war. Hence, a large preliminary investment in infrastructure has been made, facilitated by the assistance of donors in addressing this concern.

Another key aspect of computerization relates to the introduction of an electronic declaration-processing system, consonant with policies and procedures as required by law. The TIMS software (the name given to the computerized system developed by Crown Agents to support commercial processing of goods by customs) has been developed for a flexible functional usage, i.e. for a variety of trade regimes (e.g. definitive, temporary, transit or export). At another level, the recruitment of approximately 30 highly motivated computer technicians has made a significant impact in terms of the capacity for IT development and implementation. Prior to redeployment across the country, this team has been offered exceptional training opportunities and, after that, on-the-job training to deal adequately with the management of the TIMS system. The important point to note here is that, in practical terms, this well-functioning system grants the possibility these days of running a fully operational central statistics data warehouse, intended to provide statistical data upon request for either internal or external consumers. The application of Direct Trader Input, whereby the *trader* has the capability to complete remotely the full customs formalities, alleviates costs for customs and has seemingly contributed to an increasing speed in declaration processing.

Several other factors have contributed to advances in customs computerization. Let us take here just a few examples. A system to register and control exemptions has been designed. It enables, especially for customs data analysts, the identification and analysis of the fiscal cost of exemptions as well as implicit duty rates. Detailed analysis is likely to be constrained, however, by human errors in the introduction of trade data in the system, resulting too often from officials' lax behaviour coupled by high levels of indulgence from senior managers. In any case, such mistakes are more likely to occur in operations that fail to offer an effective 'safety net' (Van Dunem 2005b). Computerization and information technology are being applied also to internal procedures in managerial tasks of customs administration as diverse as human resources, finance or logistics. But equally important, at a later stage of the reform process customs communication infrastructure has been bolstered by the establishment of RENA (Rede Electrónica Nacional das Alfândegas), a modern VSAT system of communications that permits, for the very first time, voice and data communication between 20 customs clearance posts – as well as access to internet and email for 40 per cent of the personnel. In the case of South Africa, a trade partner with considerable weight for Mozambique, electronic exchange of information is foreseen in the near future between Alfândegas and the South African Revenue Service, a welcome move that should help curb corruption while improving the speed of declaration processing.

2.5 Evidence from Alfândegas performance during reform: some facts

2.5.1 Customs revenue

Perhaps a useful way to think about the idea of success of the Mozambican customs reform is in terms of revenue enhancement. The small number of evaluations addressing this aspect make a very compelling case for the spectacular surge in revenue collections with the onset of reform. An OECD report (OECD 2005) about trade facilitation in developing countries, for instance, documents a surge in Mozambican customs revenue of 38.4 per cent during the first two years of the programme, in spite of reductions in duty rates. The same report throws up the conclusion that whilst costs of customs increased dramatically during the early, very demanding stages of the reform programme (as new staff were recruited and trained, and the customs administration's infrastructure developed) these extra costs have been compensated for by subsequent rises in overall collection levels. More recently, Crown Agents has formally portrayed the outcome achieved for one of its main product offerings as 'impressive', claiming that the 350 per cent increase in collections throughout the entire reform period is merely symptomatic of it (Crown Agents 2006). To be fair, there is some truth in both of these arguments and few would doubt that the reform programme has been successful in its most basic task: raising revenues. What there is possibly not so much of a consensus about is the degree of sustainability in results.

Let us now, for a moment, take a cautious look at some *facts* from Alfândegas. During the opening phase of reform, from 1997 to 2000, the overall picture provided by collection indicators from Alfândegas fits nicely with the above descriptions. Customs revenues in real terms more than doubled in the space of three years. Indeed, Alfândegas increased its revenues (in US $) by nearly 120 per cent, while total customs tax revenues rose from 3.6 per cent of GDP in 1997 to 6.3 per cent in 2000.[10] The corollary of advances in administrative competence and efficiency came in 1999, coinciding with an amendment of customs tax policy inspired by a 'keep it simple' rule. To be more exact, this shift in tax policy materialized through a rationalization of the tariff structure (a reduction in the number of tariff rates from 12 to 5), the introduction of VAT (a rate of 17 per cent and a broader tax base by comparison with the previous imposto de circulação [5 per cent]), coupled with a reduction in top-tariff rates (from 35 to 30 per cent) and excises on trade. Simplification in tax policy, *in tandem with* improvements in administration, contributed to boosting customs revenues (e.g. in 1999, revenues in real terms increased by a staggering 36 per cent). As part of a new autonomy-enhancing design, the level of available resources for Alfândegas' yearly budget has been proportionally tied to efficiency in collecting customs revenue so that higher levels of revenue soon became tangled with enlarged budgets as well.

Oddly enough, analysis of implications of reform for customs revenue tend to skip the second phase and leap to more general conclusions, leaving thereby the second period of reform (2000–3) without appropriate independent scrutiny. There is no question that consideration of performance during the course of that particular period should draw an important level of interest mainly because it marks the transfer of management control and power into the hands of Mozambican nationals. If we adopt a similar logic, what the same Alfândegas data show is that revenues in real terms have increased by a mere 4 per cent from 2000 to 2003, with real collections actually dropping in 2001 by nearly 9 per cent, hinting thus at a possible decline in administration efficiency. As a percentage of GDP, total customs revenues have, conversely, remained relatively stable around the 6.2–6.5 per cent range.[11] In more general terms, notwithstanding a low annual rate of growth in real revenues, it appears that revenues as a percentage of GDP tended to stagnate until recent times by virtue of action from several other factors (e.g. exchange rate fluctuations) that are supposed to influence nominal revenue. The renewal of Crown Agents' contract for a supplementary three years (i.e. until 2006) maybe should come as no surprise then, when one takes into consideration veiled symptoms of administrative malaise like the one just described. Of course, revenue collections are only partly determined by tax administrations, hence we are aware that they might be a crude measure of performance. They are, nevertheless, an easily available indicator which, whenever used, must be used with both alertness and objectivity.

Having said this, marked improvements in trade facilitation constitute more authentic symptoms of the positive effects of reform. The introduction of computerization, boosted by Direct Trader Input and other customs procedures, and the phasing out of PSI have together helped a remarkable decline, in average terms, in processing times for declarations. The quality of the customs service is also widely regarded as having benefited from more courteous and friendly customs personnel. These tangible symptoms of trade facilitation may have played a fairly important role in lessening tax compliance costs after the start of reform, i.e. playing a role in the observed short-term revenue increases.

2.5.2 Corruption levels

Jointly with customs revenues, relatively moderate (but not sustained) headway has been made in the area of corruption, if we set as the basis of assessment a dismal pre-reform state.[12] The pattern of corruption, in a way, sheds light on developments for revenue. It is quite clear that the modest progress in reducing fraud and corruption levels in the Mozambican customs can be, to some extent, attributed to the introduction of automated systems. The TIMS software relies heavily on a standard process in which the amounts of discretion enjoyed by officials in the past have been seriously curtailed. A quick glance at a few simple cases may facilitate a better understanding of the argument.

First, with a well-functioning computerized TIMS system, the levels of control have improved considerably since many functions are *automatically* undertaken by the computer system rather than being done manually (e.g. calculation of taxes payable, straight connection between the tariff book position and theoretical taxes). Second, clearing declarations – i.e. the omission of the requirement to fill in a notice of release, the so-called *nota de saída* – before actual payment has taken place is now forbidden. Third, the system permits detailed recording of actions taken by officials involved in the clearance of goods (e.g. date, time, name of officer and so on) which is not likely to stop malpractice but at least introduces a deterrent by suggesting that officers can be challenged at any time, culprits can be questioned and – when necessary – disciplined on the basis of evidence made available by the system. Fourth, the possibility of visualizing the time taken to carry out certain phases of the declaration process should allow senior managers the opportunity to put pressure on station managers to clean up the 'delay factor', an additional cause of corruption. Fifth, the system allows a database of importers and exporters to be set up as a by-product of the declaration process, thereby enabling a more systematic investigation of trends and repeated behaviour (e.g. one can conduct historical searches on the types of products imported by any given importer over time). Sixth, certain functions have been centralized, taking some activity away from the local *estancias* (clearance posts) and restricting the opportunities for collusion among staff. Finally, with computerization the customs agency is currently in a much better position to track cheques and alternative methods used for payment; it can also confirm these against bank deposits and other forms of financial information, i.e. making it possible to reduce compliance costs.

Introducing a secure computer system has the simple virtue of massively reducing the discretionary interface between customs and private operators. But, as Bird cleverly puts it, 'even the best computerized system will not produce useful results unless there are real incentives for tax administrators to utilize the system properly' (Bird 2004:138). Unfortunately, with the benefit of hindsight, there are *de facto* a number of arguments that one can currently use to call the actual structure of incentives to collect customs tax revenue into question. One needs to recognize, most importantly, that this structure of incentives is really *endogenous and independent* of the realm of reform *per se*. Overcoming this thorny problem and moving towards a more encouraging path where the potential of the tax administration is realized, in line with its own capacity constraints, is a responsibility that only the Mozambican government can take. Today, the potential of the administration is still far from being met.

Next we shift attention to a few plausible causes of the failure of reform to impact the performance in terms of customs revenue and corruption *in a sustained way*.

2.6 *Understanding the core factors behind unsustainable outcomes*

2.6.1 *Weaknesses in professionalizing staff*

Less discretion in Mozambican customs procedures nowadays does not mean, still, that the computer system cannot be ignored on occasion or even abused. There is no question that when good incentives are not in place, administrative efficiency can easily be undermined. To illustrate this argument, imagine an automated system like TIMS that offers the opportunity for senior managers to exert countervailing checks and balances over customs stations. If a particular station takes too long to carry out final verification after payment and things get especially aggravated due to an unprofessional station head and operational superiors who choose to shut their eyes to the delay, the computer is obviously powerless to hasten completion of the procedure: the computer cannot, for instance, refuse to accept declarations pending satisfactory treatment of those already processed. In the same line of reasoning, the system has to 'believe' consistently the information introduced by customs officers and has no means of knowing that the brand new BMW is worth more than the recorded $10,000 value or that the country of origin picked for the imported product circumvents fraudulently the tracking down of the risk-profiled system (e.g. Sweden instead of United Arab Emirates). Nonetheless, the system allows recording of the names of 'actors' involved during the clearance procedure, such that managers are able to know ex-post *who keyed in the value* or *who verified it*, i.e. they are able not only to identify malpractice and culprits but also to take suitable action accordingly.

The cases presented above suggest that computerization is a necessary but not sufficient condition to improve the standards of tax administration. The professionalism and ethics of personnel are critical requirements. The mechanisms of control and good management by superiors (complemented by a newly operating anti-corruption unit) should not be, therefore, mutually exclusive. Of course, the shift in human resources policy was meant to address issues of the professionalism and ethics of staff. A newly designed semi-autonomous regime allowed a new system of rewards for personnel whereby: (1) remuneration levels, unlike those for the rest of the civil service, were raised in an attempt to reduce the temptation towards corruption; (2) the system of merit, if operated correctly, could lead to a variation in income of 25 per cent according to the level of performance of the individual; (3) from time to time, certificates of honour would be awarded to customs officers with exceptional performance.

Thus far, even though there has been some progress in technical competence, the new rewards system has clearly left expectations unfulfilled as corruption remains a serious entrenched constraint. Salaries and awards appear ineffective – and in fact symbolic – when compared with the value of bribes and other advantages derived from fraudulent activity. Experience from the merit-based system seems to suggest that the majority of personnel end up receiving the highest classification, so eventually the incentive becomes eroded. In spite of replication in a few other state agencies, an urgent need to review this system has already been acknowledged and called for. In a context of thriving corruption, one might have valid reasons for admitting that the merit-based system of incentives could actually be counter-productive by penalizing honest officials who decline to infringe the law.

Further, counter-productivity in the incentive mechanisms can be fuelled by staff rotation systems, a very legitimate source of concern in the Mozambican context. The underlying problem is best described by Fjeldstad and Rakner (2003), who suggest that rotation systems create a danger of 'increased corruption as collectors may use the opportunity to try enriching themselves while they are stationed in the most "lucrative" posts' (Fjeldstad and Rakner 2003: 19). This complex problem paves the way for other inherent complications as postings swiftly acquire a transaction value. The Namaacha and Ressano Garcia border posts (corresponding, respectively, to the borders with Swaziland and South Africa) are often cited as very attractive and always in very high demand. One has to take note that these systemic contributions to inefficiency in administration can augment the risk of generating further distortions in the economy as new taxes are sometimes created or tax rates increased in an attempt to make up for the resulting revenue loss.

Enacting a customs reform process does not, by itself, represent a success. Externally driven reform can assist the promotion of tax laws, logistics, competence or even skills, as the Mozambican reform has shown. Regrettably, it is harder to buy commitment, honesty and ethics from public servants. A fundamental lesson from this case study is that the Mozambican government has not succeeded, much in the same manner as other Sub-Saharan African countries, in building up a cadre of civil servants imbued with a spirit of public service for the demanding tasks of administration. Overturning this trend and fostering higher standards of integrity in public life is a task which will require nothing less than strong and credible political engagement.

2.6.2 Need for enhanced political commitment

In a sense, the reform of Alfândegas – and that of DGI too – has had the positive additional effect of increasing public awareness about the need for improvements in administration.[13] Such a development is indeed welcome. It appears that, even so, some non-compliance could result from a widely held belief that the current tax system suffers from internal inefficiencies along with severe inequities in tax compliance: the tax law seems to apply fully to the 'weak and poor', while the Mozambican elite tends to receive favourable treatment.[14]

The problem for the customs tax administration of how to improve compliance levels would substantially decrease if the present wave of fraudulent and lethargic practices could be effectively beaten back. Put differently, a change in the way the tax administration is widely viewed by most taxpayers could carry positive benefits resulting from a change of norms and social attitudes, i.e. incentives towards tax compliance. As taxpayers realize they are treated more fairly by the administration, they should be more willing to follow the law. Some non-compliance could be, furthermore, explained by an inadequate connection between taxes and social benefits, even though altering this gloomy situation might realistically be a trickier mission.

The government has the responsibility to renew its efforts and give due prominence to reorienting the strategy and purpose of a tax administration tailored to serving the objective of self-reliant development. In our own view, the muscle to radically transform internal incentives into a path of integrity must emanate from the political administration. This could be achieved by relying on a more comprehensive and gradual approach to reform, involving primarily an independent judiciary sector and the backing of a free press. Interestingly, evidence from other developing countries' latest experiences in customs reform (e.g. the Philippines) seems to point out that the involvement and engagement of the President and Ministry of Finance is decisive for the outcome of reform (Hors 2001).[15] We believe that establishing and intensifying greater international co-operation with successful tax reform countries with some identical characteristics and problems could also prove to be extremely valuable. By learning the practical lessons which could be drawn from developing countries' past experience, Mozambique could then take the necessary steps to endorse fruitful strategies adopted elsewhere and, as a result, surmount internal problems with less difficulty. In that perspective, to effect change an expansion of South–South cooperation is recommended.

Within a more longstanding perspective, priority should be given to boosting the *human capacities* of the Mozambican people. It will be up to the government to work out the tactics needed and also to determine its own timetable. But if the government is to signal real commitment to reform, this must presuppose preventive public action through conceding a growing prominence to education and health policies for human capital development. As a matter of fact, fomenting specific educative and pedagogical programmes aimed at judiciously appointed public servants could be, in our view, justifiable as well. The argument in favour of the application of this measure is that it may inculcate more positive values and cultivate a commitment for change. This last option is finely tuned with recommendations from landmark documents such as the Arusha Declaration drafted by the WCO and the IMF Integrity Paper.

2.6.3 Country-specific challenges

A meaningful point worth noting is that the capacity to attract high calibre professionals to work in the public sector has been generally strained by low educational standards in the country, let alone the brain drain to either private or international institutions justified frequently by higher financial rewards. Accelerating the expansion of the educational capabilities of the Mozambican people would necessarily contribute to improvements in the quality of the workforce available for employment, not only in the tax administration service but elsewhere too.

A further point that must be taken into account is that it is not trivial to measure the degree of honesty of job market candidates. Despite the promises of autonomy and its ensuing meritocratic recruitment method, Alfândegas should be expecting beforehand to attract a large proportion of individuals who see enrolment primarily as an opportunity for a lucrative venture, not a personal contribution to Mozambican public service. But more significantly, getting credit for attracting and retaining technically capable staff would also be very misleading because of systemic incentives. In this respect, insufficient attention has been given to the dilemma of honest and highly talented university graduates who, as corruption-averse individuals, tend to give preference to more technocratic job postings where the extent and the external *reputation* of fraudulent activity does not loom so large. There are currently a few signs that might point towards the existence of such apprehension among young job seekers.

By the same token, the causation behind the limited effectiveness of computerization is probably not simple. We believe that it must be understood in terms of the interaction of numerous factors like the complete lack of prior experience of Mozambican staff with computers, aggravated by the lack of existing professionals with IT competence for immediate recruitment. It seems of the utmost importance, on the other hand, to acknowledge that the robust and extensive infrastructure critically necessary to ensure good service provision by the TIMS network backbone was missing. The early days of the reform project, for example, witnessed the transportation of customs data on floppy disks. Even nowadays, service provision is extremely variable. Further, consideration of theft and frequent damage (by world standards) of equipment due to electrical storms, flooding and power surges is an additional source likely to reinforce the difficulties faced by a promising new automated system. One needs to recognize, moreover, the presence of a trading community with an ingrained tradition of corrupt habits and actively seeking ways in which to make contact with customs officers and distort the proper use of the system. And in most African countries cultural idiosyncrasies can simply make this kind of human interaction very easy.

2.6.4 Discretion in administering customs tax systems

A semi-autonomous Alfândegas has not, fundamentally, prevented widespread systemic corruption. In the last couple of years, although the widespread practice of corruption has remained a subject prompting high levels of concern, Alfândegas figures seem to show, surprisingly, that the total number of expulsions corresponds to less than 2 per cent of the total work-force. The reality is that establishing a semi-autonomous customs service has not been conducive to formulating a new disciplinary procedure system for customs staff. The Estatuto Geral dos Funcionários do Estado (EGFE), applying to civil servants, still remains the leading disciplinary system, even with the endorsement of a new Code of Conduct. The rules in EGFE are excessively intricate and, in any event, require a level of proof almost equivalent to that for murder. This weak repressive mechanism is aggravated by a lack of will to enforce the law as these internal discipline mechanisms have a tendency to exhibit purely decorative functions.

The granting of tax exemptions as an incentive to promote investment is frequent in the tax policy agenda of developing countries, including for imported merchandise. Evidence suggests, even so, that its effectiveness in attracting incremental investment is doubtful and the revenue cost could well be high. In Mozambique, it has been documented by Van Dunem (2005b) that the cost of fiscal exemptions in customs has soared in recent years (between 2002 and 2004) due to discretionary exemptions approved by the Minister of Finance, subsequent to proposal by the Alfândegas General Director. Currently, the levels of discretionary exemptions are not negligible and end up having a direct impact on fiscal revenues.

The adoption of Article VII of GATT should have been complemented by rising post-import audits. Until now, progress in this direction has been flawed since the administration has failed to demonstrate real dynamism in taking on post-import and VAT audits. The principle of post-clearance audits is that Alfândegas must release without delay the goods subject to valuation problems while conducting and shortly afterwards conduct valuation audits. This requires appropriately trained personnel in post-clearance audit and increased staff and resources to do the follow-up, which, at the moment, customs still does not have. Those two factors are often cited to explain the stalled process (Makanza and Munyaradzi 2004).

3 The General Directorate of Taxation (DGI): institutional design and challenges

3.1 Institutional design and overview

In this section we will outline the primary features of the institutional design of the DGI, and with this context in mind will consider, through the three windows of the payments system, the process of VAT refunds and, finally, the audit and control of corporate taxpayers, some of the challenges faced by the authorities of the DGI as they look to increase revenue collection.[16]

As Bird (2004) notes, the simplification of the fiscal regime represents an essential precondition for the reform of the tax administration. With literally hundreds of disparate fiscal laws, it is widely acknowledged that Mozambique was lacking a common thread providing some cohesion to incumbent legislature, and guidelines establishing broad and clear fiscal rules. In response to this, a general tax law was written, and approved in December 2005.[17] Whilst a detailed description of the intricacies of the new legislation, with some 219 articles, is perhaps unnecessary here, broadly speaking, the objective was to adopt mechanisms simplifying and modernizing existing fiscal procedures, guaranteeing, it is hoped, the increased efficiency of the fiscal administration and thus facilitating voluntary compliance by taxpayers. In brief, the law will provide a single point of reference, for the taxpayer and the tax authorities, for the primary fiscal principles and norms.

Turning now specifically to the management of internal taxes, the DGI is structured into organs at the central and local level. Centrally, the DGI is comprised of eight directorates organized into three broad areas: (1) *General Administration*, including the directorates of human resources and training; (2) *Inspection and Technical Support*, overseeing the directorates of inspection, 'studies, planning and technical help' and statistics; and (3) *Technical Operations*, overseeing the directorates of 'fiscal management, collections and reimbursement', 'audit and control' and 'fiscal justice'. Whilst it is perhaps beyond the scope of this chapter to provide a full consideration of the duties of all the directorates,[18] we would highlight the directorate of 'fiscal management, collections and reimbursement', to give some flavour of the new structure of the tax administration. Activities within this directorate are wide ranging, but are organized neatly into various smaller departments, including one dedicated to the management of fiscal benefits and incentives. Whilst the analysis of fiscal benefits was of course conducted before the reforms, the creation of a specific department comprising around 10 people dedicated to the management and administration of such an important component of the Mozambican fiscal profile represents a significant step forward.[19]

In general terms, it is interesting to note that the current mode of organization of the tax administration, as described above, is explicitly based on *functions*. Departments are organized along broad activities (for example registration and payment, tax refunds, analysis, audit and so on), enabling standardization of tasks and processes across taxes. Whilst this transition is still very much ongoing, the new directorates described above have nevertheless been constructed, detailed responsibilities defined, and work using the new structure has started.

In addition to these central organs, DGI comprises 30 local tax offices located around the country and organized into four groups (A–D) based broadly on an index of size measures, including the number of taxpayers serviced, the monetary amount of taxes collected and the geographical area covered. It is one of these offices that the taxpayer is registered at, receives his tax bill from and pays his obligations to the fiscal authorities through. It is also here that the majority of DGI staff are employed, and where perhaps the greatest challenges are faced. Relations between DGI central functions and these offices are managed through a series of circulars written as and when the need arises, though currently an effort is underway to centralize all of these to gain some clarity as to all the obligations that the tax offices must fulfil. Wages of all employees are paid centrally, however; for other expenses such as utility bills, stationery, fuel and other current operational obligations the offices receive a fixed monthly allocation, depending on their classification (A–D). The use of this money is audited carefully at the central level, with all receipts, invoices and bank statements sent to the head office every month.

This decentralized nature of DGI is emphasized time and time again, with the tax offices located far from the capital apparently following guidelines only very loosely. Again, efforts are underway to address this, with, for instance, a significant recent tightening of the control over their monthly budgets at the central level. However, resources in many of the offices remain at a very basic level, and this is often blamed by the head of such offices for any shortfall of revenue collections relative to programmed levels. Nevertheless, the top-heavy nature of Mozambique's fiscal structure, with over 80 per cent of total revenues in 2005 collected in the Maputo area, means that the long tail of local tax offices is, according to many, often overlooked. Collections originating in the northern zone of Mozambique, for example, comprising nine local tax offices in the provinces of Niassa, Cabo Delgado and Nampula, represented less than 6 per cent of total tax receipts in 2005.

In 2005 the DGI employed approximately 950 staff, of whom 270 work in the head office based in the capital of the country and 680 in local tax offices. Of those working centrally, over 30 per cent have high levels of education,[20] up from 18 per cent in 2002. Reflecting the lack of capacity outside the capital, just 4 per cent of staff working in the local tax office had high levels of education in 2005 – roughly one person per unit. Approximately 40 per cent of total staff are women. With the introduction of the ATM, a uniform and a significantly improved salary scale for workers (relative to normal civil servants), salary scales independent of government and incorporating a performance-based incentive designed to enhance productivity and morale are slowly being introduced. For many mid-range technical analysts in DGI, this has meant a near doubling of their net wages.

3.2 Large tax payer units

For many low income countries, one observes a marked skew in the distribution of tax revenue by size of the taxpayer. In direct response to this, the 1970s saw the introduction of large taxpayer units (LTUs) starting in South America, and then spreading to a number of African countries, under IMF guidance, during the early 1990s (Burkina Faso, 1995; Mali, 1994; Kenya, 1998). Mozambique is no exception, with a large proportion of total tax collection being accounted for by just a handful of taxpayers,[21] and it was somewhat inevitable, therefore, that the country followed suit with the creation of two LTUs in 2002 and one a couple of years later, located in the three principal cities of the country: Maputo, Beira and Nampula.

As Baer notes, the fundamental objective of an LTU lies both in facilitating the compliance of large taxpayers with their fiscal obligations and in acting as a 'pilot or incubation centre to test administrative reforms' (Baer 2002: 5). Official justification for the establishment of the three LTUs in Mozambique cites these aims. It is hoped that such units will provide some stability, influence and control over receipts from large taxpaying entities, and that in time some of the reforms implemented can become DGI-wide. The vision is of an independent unit located in key points around the country, offering a complete service – registration, declaration, payment and information – to the taxpayer. At the time of creation, the criteria used to define a 'large taxpayer' were fairly ad hoc and informal. Basic indices were constructed, with sales volume and the type of tax paid as the main inputs, but in reality companies were simply considered on a case-by-case basis. In addition, all financial taxpaying institutions (banks and insurance firms) were registered in the new units.

The lack of a clear and measurable counterfactual, as well as the difficulty associated with isolating cause and effect, means that evaluating the impact that the three LTUs have had on fiscal performance is tricky. Nevertheless, using basic metrics the news is mixed. Total tax collections in the LTU of Maputo, for example, rose by 93 per cent in the period 2002–5 (versus 87 per cent for the DGI as a whole). However, while the three LTUs taken as a whole accounted for a healthy 69 per cent of Fiscal Receipts[22] in 2003, this fell to just 57 per cent in 2005.

Such a centralization of tasks has, however, brought with it problems. The effective creation of a parallel fiscal administration has incited unhealthy competition for financial and human resources, with the 'normal' tax offices, in particular those located in the same area as a new unit, drained in order to feed the LTU. In a couple of cases, a specific tax office has seen a marked fall in its tax collections as a number of its most important contributors have been transferred. The shift in emphasis, at the central level, away from the other tax offices has also caused a marked fall in staff morale and effort. In part responding to this, in part in recognition of the lack of a written plan for LTUs going forward, work is underway drafting a more formal approach to the operations of an LTU and the criteria employed to define a large taxpayer.

3.3 The tax payments system

In 2002 a law was passed creating SISTAFE (Sistema de Administração Financeira do Estado), a new financial system for Mozambique (Lei 9/02), encompassing the entire budgetary cycle, from the first stage elaboration to final execution. In broad terms, the law aims to address many of the problems previously associated with the budget cycle – in particular, a live electronic budget system has been created, enabling, it is hoped, accurate transferral of approved budget allocations consistent with the pattern of revenue collections over the year. An important component of the system has been the aggregation of all National Treasury accounts into a single unified account (Conta Única de Tesouro, CUT), into which all public receipts, including those collected by the DGI, are deposited, and from which all expenditures are withdrawn.

While for many the design of SISTAFE has focused primarily on the expenditure side of the state budget, it is critical that all revenue deposited in the CUT is classified for the proper functioning of the system. Importantly, the execution of expenditure relies not only on the availability of funding, but on the availability of *classified* funding. The accurate and timely classification[23] of revenues represents a new set of challenges and hurdles for the DGI, to which we now turn. Such challenges are perhaps best explained in the context of the tax payments process.

How does the money travel from the taxpayer to the Treasury? First, the taxpayer presents himself at his local tax office, receives his tax assessment and pays, usually by means of a cheque, the amount due. At the end of the day, the tax office deposits the cheques in its bank account and finalizes its accounts, using the tax assessment forms as a base for the classification of the deposited revenues. Crucially, Mozambican law does not prohibit the payment of tax obligations by non-validated cheques – such cheques, then, need to be cleared by the bank of the respective tax office. In theory, the bank should clear such cheques within 72 hours; however, in reality the time taken can be anything up to two weeks. Moreover, the bank does not provide information detailing the clearance of cheques at the transaction level – which cheque has been cleared, which has not. The tax office will simply learn, on an aggregate basis, the total value of cheques cleared during the previous day.

As a result, the local tax offices are unable in many cases to identify the actual flow of revenue to their bank account, that is, to accurately classify taxes effectively paid. It can and does happen, for instance, that a tax office transfers funds to the CUT (via their bank), basing the classification on their tax assessment forms from that day, which do not accurately represent taxes collected.

In order to address this problem, the smaller tax offices around the country (groups C and D) have been granted some discretion as to when they transfer (and classify) funds from their bank accounts to the Treasury. Waiting a few days for all cheques to be cleared before transferring funds to the CUT will, it is hoped, permit the complete and accurate classification of revenues in the SISTAFE system. Unfortunately, perhaps in an over-eagerness to fulfil their responsibilities, perhaps to avoid an overly burdensome classification of many days of tax collection, many tax offices still prefer to transfer and classify revenues before they have full information regarding bounced cheques. For the larger tax offices, where the Treasury cannot afford to wait for the clearance of cheques, funds are transferred on a daily basis to the CUT, and the classification is based in part on an assessment that is subsequently revised. It is therefore guaranteed that funds will flow without delay, with classification being finalized ex post.

In conclusion, then, the transfer of revenues is not yet happening in a systematic and efficient way. Moreover, there exists no guarantee that the revenues transferred to the CUT are correctly classified. Classification of large numbers of tax receipts into a large number of tax classifiers, by a workforce not yet fully familiar with the new tax codes, lends itself to human error. Daily examples of the tendency to group taxes into the same tax code for ease of classification can be found.

Such problems are manifested most clearly when one considers the tax collection data, based on monthly communications from the individual tax offices, which the DGI used and continues to use for internal and external purposes. Approximately one week after the end of the month, tax offices will begin to send their tax collection numbers from the previous month to the DGI central office. These are sent by fax or communicated by telephone, and are then entered manually into a spreadsheet. The scope for error is large in this process: examples encountered on numerous occasions include human error in the re-keying of data, miscommunication due to the poor quality of a fax printout, and misclassification of revenues, often due to a lack of understanding regarding the precise definition of a revenue classifier. In theory, of course, such data should be equal to the amount of money actually entering the CUT described above. In reality, data from 2005 show large discrepancies. With an undertaking of such magnitude, teething problems are to be expected, though the degree of differences in some of the tax offices is surprising.

The introduction and gradual rollout of a computerized system of revenue classification (Solução Informática para Gestão da Cobrança das Receitas, SICR) means that the above situation should be ameliorated greatly, though a large number of the regional tax offices, in particular the smaller ones more prone to error, remain 'off-line'. Nevertheless, by the end of 2006 and moving into 2007, it was anticipated that the majority of revenue flows would be captured by SICR. One should, however, not get too excited about this system. For many, SICR really represents no more than a fairly primitive database, and while the basic data problems described immediately above should disappear as a result of the system, it suffers from one major weakness: that there exists no formal link to SISTAFE or the single treasury account (CUT), or any move to formalize. The discrepancies between taxes actually paid, the money entering CUT and the tax collections data the DGI continues to use for publication and analysis will therefore most likely persist.

3.4 Value added tax and its refunds

Following the establishment of a commission in 1996, the government of Mozambique introduced a Value Added Tax (VAT) three years later (GoM 1998b). VAT is levied on the invoice of goods and services minus the VAT paid on the invoice of inputs and imported goods, and is collected from suppliers, who generally pass the extra cost on to consumers. In that sense, the VAT effectively acts as a tax on domestic consumption. Three regimes characterize the current system. The first is the Normal Regime, in which 'large taxpayers' (minimum turnover of Mts250m per annum) are subject to 17 per cent VAT and are entitled to reimbursement of VAT paid on inputs. Second, 'small taxpayers' are classed in the Simplified Regime, contributing 5 per cent of VAT on sales volume, and are not entitled to any reimbursement.[24] Finally, there exists a long list of exempted items, upon which no VAT is paid. Of these, certain items are entitled to no refund, including medical supplies (Article 9), while others, including many common food-stuffs such as rice and flour, can claim reimbursement. Importantly, in addition, all exported produce do not attract VAT but is subject to a full refund of VAT paid on inputs.

As alluded to above, the amount of VAT due is the difference between the amount of tax collected from purchasers of goods and services (zero for the exempted items listed) and the tax previously paid on goods and services purchased for use in business. VAT is thus collected on the value added at each stage of the supply chain – as long as the transactions involve registered entities.[25] In cases where the amount due is negative, that is, the taxpayer is in a net credit position, a refund may be claimed from the government.

An evaluation of the efficacy of the administration of these refunds depends on who you speak to, with the process characterized by a distinct divergence of opinion between the private sector and DGI. In 2001, the target period of the government for reimbursement was 90 days. This was subsequently reduced to 60 days, and further reduced to 30 days more recently (GoM 2004). Within this context, the business community cites numerous examples of prolonged delays, sometimes extending to well over a year, and points to implicit and explicit deals to 'oil the wheels'. In contrast, the DGI claims that the majority of valid refunds are treated well within the 30-day period, with any delays due to improper documentation on the part of the claimant. Indeed, VAT refund forms (Pedido de Reembolso, Modelo A) do require a wealth of information, including, for example, that the past three VAT monthly declaration forms are attached. Such paperwork is often simply not attached, and, more generally, refund staff claim to be constantly faced with forms incorrectly filled in.

Importantly here, any failure to receive reimbursement within the deadline does give the taxpayer the right to claim penalty interest – though the interest will not be attributed unless the claimant makes a specific request for it to be calculated. The DGI for its part may, however, suspend the payment of reimbursement for six months whenever, 'because of circumstances attributable to the taxpayer, it is impossible to verify the legitimacy of the requested reimbursement' (Decree 29/2000). This clause was introduced with the direct intention of controlling more tightly the payment and calculation of reimbursement payments when the supplied documentation contains mistakes or is incomplete.

In acknowledgement of the animosity that exists between the authorities and the private sector in this area, a dialogue between the two parties has been established in the form of a monthly meeting of the department of VAT refunds and the CTA (Confederação das Associações Económicas de Moçambique), a society of private sector members and entrepreneurs. The agenda of such meetings follows certain specific cases that both actors wish discuss, and, by all accounts, the initiative is proving to be extremely constructive, with both sides softening their views considerably having seen the others' point of view.

In theory, of course, refunds for non-exporting companies should only arise in 'exceptional circumstances' (see www.iva.mz), such as a start-up company incurring large initial procurement costs and low sales. Somewhat surprisingly, therefore, the DGI receives a huge number of refund requests every month, from companies claiming to be in a net credit position vis-à-vis the tax authorities. To address this, in other countries many tax codes incorporate a carry-forward period of a few months, allowing the transient net credit position of such entities to self-extinguish, and thus reducing the administrative burden on authorities. While the period in Mozambique is currently a generous 12 months – seen by many as almost too long – this is offset to some extent by a very low limit over which refunds can be claimed immediately.[26] Though aggregate data detailing the reasons behind refund claims have not been compiled, tax officials do blame a plethora of low-value refund claims for clogging up the system – refund claims that in many cases would almost certainly 'work out' after a few months.

Further slowing the system is the fact that refund payments, once approved, are treated as expenditures, thus requiring approval from the National Treasury. The country budget simply does not include a line item specifically for VAT refunds, with revenue booked on a net basis. Such an arrangement is viewed by many private sector actors as unacceptable – approved refunds represent money rightfully belonging to the taxpayer, not the government.

As a result of the above system and associated complications, the ratio of VAT refunds as a percentage of VAT collections over the past five years has been between 5 and 10 per cent, though rising more recently. Unfortunately no organized and accurate data exist for the reasons behind reimbursement requests, though anecdotely a large proportion arises from exporters. Moreover, a significant number involve relatively low amounts, just above the aforementioned lower limit over which refunds can be claimed – giving further credence to the argument for raising the bar in this regard.

3.5 *Audit and control of corporate tax payers*

Like the majority of national fiscal systems, the collection of taxes in Mozambique relies largely on self-declaration and assessment. As McCarten notes, such a system is based on 'the presumption that it is possible to attain a reasonable level of taxation compliance by test-checking a small sample of

[tax] returns' (2004 :6). This observation can never be more true than in the case of Mozambique, where the audit department suffers from a very real lack of human resources.

As with the case of tax collections, taxpayer registration and so on, it is the local fiscal authorities who are responsible, at least initially, for conducting the audit and inspection of corporate taxpayers. At the start of the year, a plan is submitted detailing target sectors and individual companies to be audited, and inspections are conducted throughout the coming twelve months, with support from the central level. Above all, the process of audit is characterized by a marked lack of human capacity, and in many ways this is the primary influence on strategy. It is simply impossible to conduct audits of the same company on a regular basis. Therefore companies are often targeted according to their track record.[27] Moreover, large companies are prioritized, with the few highly qualified staff working on such cases. The process is also an interactive one – exploiting the fact that, in general, companies are willing to help the auditors and are not necessarily evading their tax obligations on purpose. Informative letters communicating the upcoming visit and its objectives are thus sent to the target company in advance, and following the inspection findings are communicated to the company, giving them a chance to react and implement recommendations before proceedings continue.

Due to the lack of capacity to conduct regular inspections, it is often the case that audited companies in one year are those that were not audited in the preceding year. It is difficult to know exactly what proportion of tax returns are audited, though it is a safe assumption that the number is very low. Currently, there are approximately 100 qualified auditors in DGI, trying to manage 20,000 corporate taxpayers. As a result, long periods of time can pass between audits, with the only certainty being that a company would expect to receive at least one visit every five years, given that that is the period over which debts to the tax authorities expire.

The complexity of the tax code also represents a significant hindrance. Taking corporate tax,[28] the tax levied on profits earned by a company, as an example, to arrive at the 'taxable profits' figure numerous additions to and deductions from gross profit are required. Checking the accuracy of the numbers provided by the corporations on their tax forms in this regard is by no means easy, with a large element of inbuilt trust on the part of the authorities – for instance, when a statement from the bank account of a taxpaying company is required for audit purposes, it is the company which solicits the information from its bank, not the tax authorities. The DGI, therefore, has no way of knowing whether the taxpayer is providing the complete picture of all of its bank accounts and, consequently, the totality of its earnings.

In 2006, the objective was to audit over 600 companies, with particular attention on the hotel, wholesaler and civil construction sectors. However, more broadly, the emphasis in the audit department is very much on training the existing workforce, as well as on the recruitment of an additional 50 qualified accountants. Education of the taxpayer is also a priority, with various initiatives underway to facilitate self-assessment and voluntary compliance. Common problems encountered during audits include the misclassification of expenditure, and in the case of VAT the lack of any issuance of invoices.

In this regard, the recent introduction of a 'tax shop' in Maputo should help. Located centrally, a 'one-stop shop' for all fiscal queries has been set up, offering help on all matters related to tax. The shop currently serves approximately 150 customers per week, primarily advising taxpayers on how to fill in their tax returns and clarifying fiscal legislation. The office also has a computer terminal where one can register formally for a personal tax identification number (NUIT). Pending the success of this initiative, other similar units are planned, to be installed in some of the other larger towns around the country over the coming years.

There is no doubt that the tax administration of Mozambique faces significant and fundamental challenges if it is to increase collections efficiently and equitably. However, what is clear, most notably in the recent past, is that many of these problems are acknowledged by the fiscal authorities themselves, and a number of steps have been taken in the right direction. In nominal terms, domestic tax revenue consistently rises by double-digit amounts year on year, most markedly in the key items of corporate tax, income tax and VAT. Importantly, given past high inflationary conditions, the same can be said when analysing collections growth in real terms. In relation to the taxable capacity of the economy, a crude measure of the ratio of tax receipts to GDP yields more mixed results, though the overall trend is a positive one. There remains, however, a long way to go if Mozambique is to reach levels in line with its peer group in Sub-Saharan Africa, who enjoy tax collection to GDP ratios in the high teens.[29]

4 The next step: a central revenue authority

In the same month as the general tax law of the DGI was approved, December 2005, the Assembly of the Republic approved a law creating the Autoridade Tributária de Moçambique (ATM).[30] The ATM is an organ of the state, under the tutelage of the Ministry of Finance but enjoying administrative autonomy. In effect, we see the creation of an authority with responsibility for the administration of *all* taxes, today collected by the fiscal authorities of both the DGI and DGA. The body will be gradually introduced through three broad phases, becoming fully operational, it is planned, by the end of 2010. The ATM, then, is basically a fusion of the DGA (responsible for the application of customs and excise duties and VAT on the border) and the DGI (responsible for the collection, control and audit of domestic taxes) into a central revenue authority. At its core, the broad administrative idea behind its creation is to promote a synergy between the different common functions of the collecting bodies.

The hope is to present the taxpayer with a unique fiscal representative body, improving relations between taxpayer and the state, and ensuring the efficient application of the fiscal law. Officially, given ATM's autonomy-enhancing mechanisms, justification for its creation cites many of the points one might expect: to improve the efficiency and equality of the application of internal and external fiscal policy; to obtain economies of scale in the use of public resources by rationalizing many of the costs of fiscal administration; to increase capacity to detect tax evasion; to take further action in the area of fiscal education and the public understanding of fiscal obligations; to further disseminate access by the public to all tax-related information; and to facilitate taxpayers to fulfil, voluntarily, their fiscal commitments.

All laudable objectives, certainly, and difficult in many cases to question. However, it remains unclear what is the true extent of integration between the two collecting bodies that is envisioned. At the moment, the two institutions, the DGI and DGA, have been very much kept separate, operating in their respective silos, and with only some cursory interaction in terms of day-to-day work. Given the different cultures and stages of reform, it may well be some time before one sees a true and complete merger. Moreover, once one moves away from some of the broad textbook rationales outlined above, it becomes difficult to identify many more tangible possible benefits. Working together in the area of audit and inspections, for example cross-checking data and so on, provides one example here.

Having said that, one can broadly identify two areas where the sharing of functions is legislated. First, in addition to the two legs of the DGA and DGI, a third is planned in the form of a Directorate of Common Services. It is potentially here that one will see many of the more tangible efficiencies being gained from the new structure, with common human resource, information technology, internal audit and budget functions. Second is the area of policy formulation, and it is to this that we now turn.

In this regard, two units are envisaged. Interestingly, neither lies within the DGI or the DGA. First is the Conselho Superior Tributário,[31] the highest organ of the central revenue authority. Comprised of the President and the General Directors of the ATM, and envisaged to convene once every three months, this unit is responsible for the proposal and preparation of fiscal and customs policy, the establishment of the general guidelines which will orientate the ATM, and the definition of the objectives and priorities of the ATM's principal activities. In addition, we see the Conselho da Fiscalidade,[32] a unit currently planned to report directly to the President of the ATM, and described as a consultative organ, with the objective of analysing and accompanying the evolution of the fiscal system and tax policy. Interestingly, the unit is legislated to incorporate a diverse range of actors, led by the President of the ATM, and not only including the General Directors of DGA and DGI and other sub-directors, but also three representatives from the private sector and any invited experts, external to the ATM.

Importantly, a special advisory unit reporting directly to the minister has also been proposed by a number of external actors looking at the tax administration. Such a unit would act to complement, not replace, the Directorate of Studies within the DGI, and would broadly look to advise the Minister on the formulation of tax policy and on any decisions in the area. The office is viewed as highly necessary by its advocates, who worry that tax officials generally will tend to assign a greater emphasis to the ease with which taxes can be collected and to the financial interests of the government than to the quality of the taxation and the economic implications of different fiscal policies. The unit would sit between the President of the ATM and the Minister of Finance. Given the apparent extensiveness of expertise to be involved in the formulation of fiscal policy within the ATM, and the existing Office of Studies of the Minister of Finance, one may well question the need for an additional policy unit.

5 Concluding remarks

This chapter had a simple purpose: to outline selective institutional features of the two tax agencies that make up the recently established ATM. This has been done from two different angles. In the case of Alfândegas, we focused on the institutional design and challenges from the perspective of the recent customs reform. In the process, we have also attempted to draw some basic preliminary lessons from autonomization based on comparisons of pre- and post-reform periods. We noted, at the same time, that customs administration-related outcomes are subject to a multitude of causal (exogenous) factors, so that measuring with precision the marginal effect of reform is often complicated, requiring more rigorous quantitative analysis (i.e. including availability of data). One key lesson from this case study of Alfândegas is that, more than anything else, getting internal incentives right (i.e. good top management and professionalization) really matters if the tax base is ever to be successfully expanded in a sustained fashion. In the case of the General Directorate for Taxation, on the other hand, we tackled the institutional design and challenges through the three windows of the payments system, the process of VAT refunds and the audit and control of corporate taxpayers.

We would like, finally, to highlight two important caveats that should be borne in mind having read the above account. First, the fiscal environment of Mozambique is an exceptionally complex one, with a huge diversity of taxpayers, tax legislation and initiatives being undertaken. As such we do not pretend to have produced an exhaustive account of all of the key issues. The hope is simply to give some *flavour* of the institutional design, the reforms and the challenges faced. Second, things are continuously changing as we speak: the exact organizational structure of the ATM continues to be tweaked, and reforms are answering certain problems, while new challenges are arising. The chapter is reporting on the fiscal status quo of Mozambique, and it is likely therefore that certain points written might become less relevant in the months and years to come.

Notes

1 This chapter draws on valuable insights from Adam and Bevan (2001), Enterplan (2004) and Nathan Associates (2004).
2 Internal taxes on soft and alcoholic drinks and cigarettes are the only exception as their control and collection is exercised by the DGA.
3 See Chapter 2 for further details.
4 We refer to laws no. 02/95, 07/91, 53/95, 04/94 and decree no. 0791.
5 The experience since the mid-1980s of Latin American countries such as Bolivia, Chile and Colombia is a good illustration of this argument.
6 For further details, see Chapter 12, Introduction.
7 From January 2003, PSI is mandatory for cereals, flour, sugar, vegetable oil, cement, chemical products, pigments, most medicines, dry cells, used clothes, paper, tyres and vehicles. In the cases of grain, flour, cement, paper, used clothes and vegetable oil, if the amount imported is small (less than 100 kilos or 20 litres) it is considered exempt from inspection.
8 Only a very limited number of staff opted, in the end, for retirement.
9 This Directorate has been sub-divided into four departments: (1) audit and technical inspection; (2) staff irregularities; (3) anti-corruption; and (4) order, discipline and security.
10 Calculations based on data from Alfândegas.
11 This trend in customs tax revenue ratios is confirmed by IMF staff data (IMF 2005b), as we might expect.
12 This important point is made based on prevalent perceptions. It should be noted that, even today, as in many customs administrations that have gone through reform in Africa (e.g. Kenya), corruption practices still remain quite common.
13 Interpretations in this sub-section focus on the DGA but are equally applicable to the DGI, discussion of which is reserved for the next section.
14 In 2006, the government commissioned a poll to survey public perceptions of governance and corruption. According to the results, the tax agencies were among those most affected by corruption.
15 The Philippines, a success story in customs reform, apparently benefited from a strong personal commitment from the President and Customs Commissioner, in contrast to Bolivia and Pakistan, where reform seems not to have replicated the same level of success.
16 Under the guidance of the International Monetary Fund, in 2007 the DGI will aim to increase tax collections as a percentage of GDP by 50 basis points, to 14.9 percent.
17 Lei Geral Tributária, Lei 2/06.
18 Specific responsibilities of the directorates are outlined, in some depth, by the Diploma Ministerial no. 265/2004.
19 See the Tax Benefits Code (GoM 2002b).
20 'High' here is defined as to university degree level.
21 In the LTU Maputo, for instance, the twenty largest taxpayers contributed in the region of Mts3,100m in 2006, representing a sizeable share of total collections.
22 Receitas Fiscais – collections of DGI, excluding non-fiscal receipts, earmarked revenues and Capital.
23 Unclassified funds in the CUT are granted until the end of the forthcoming month to be classified. If they are still not classified, the SISTAFE system automatically labels them as Fiscal Receipts.

24 This is seen by many as a very innovative component of the VAT regime, rarely seen in other countries.
25 In this respect, an initiative is underway attempting to assign a personal tax number, and therefore to effectively register, every taxpaying entity – individual or collective, in the case of a company paying corporate tax or VAT. In 2005 over 120,000 personal tax identification numbers were issued, taking the total current number to approximately 300,000.
26 Currently Mts50m.
27 For example VAT credit accumulations and year-on-year losses declared.
28 IRPC: Imposto Sobre o Rendimento das Pessoas Colectivas (Corporate Income Tax).
29 As mentioned in note 20, under the guidance of the IMF the DGI aimed to attain 14.7 per cent in 2007.
30 Lei 1/06.
31 Conselho Superior Tributário, Lei 1/2006, Artigo 7.
32 Conselho da Fiscalidade, Lei 1/2006, Artigo 10.

7 VAT and external aid

Dieter Orlowski

1 Introduction

Many donors that provide funds for infrastructure projects in developing countries do not accept the payment of fiscal charges which recipient governments would impose under normal circumstances. Since recipient governments are trying to limit exemptions in the fiscal regime in order to broaden the tax base and reduce the scope for fraud and tax avoidance, many countries apply the normal fiscal rules and regulations to donor-funded investment projects and pay these taxes out of general government funds in order to comply with the donors' rule. Mozambique has also adopted that approach.

In theory, and assuming that donors would not disburse and execute projects unless there was a sufficient provision for the payment of the tax-related part of contractors' invoices in the budget, the full amount of these indirect taxes paid by the state flows back to the revenue authorities swiftly as revenues, which would provide the funds for the payment of these project-related charges. Thus, the availability of funds for other areas of public expenditure would not be affected. In effect, from the fiscal point of view, it makes no difference whether the government spends more on taxes and thereby collects more revenues, or whether it exempts the respective projects and contracts from tax.

Due to the mechanisms and phasing of the budget process and widespread incomplete understanding of the VAT mechanism, however, provisions for the payment of taxes in the budget tend to be grossly inadequate. The shortfall is dramatic in Mozambique. Instead of scaling down project execution and disbursements, however, most donors continue to disburse. The projects go on, while the state is accumulating arrears. Various special rules and partial exemptions have been put into place in order to alleviate the effects on contractors' liquidity and profits. This temporary solution is not sustainable, but can actually go on for a considerable period of time.

A solution is actually not too difficult. If the administration paid fiscal charges on donor-funded public works swiftly and in full, most of the additional payments would flow back to the revenue authorities. If government exempted such projects from taxes (in the sense of zero-rating), similarly to how exports are treated, the revenue loss would be small. It is important to assess the potential revenue loss, which has not been done so far. The author's best guess is that the net effect on the availability of funds for other purposes will be quite small.

This chapter, after an analysis of mechanisms and scenarios, argues that most of the VAT which the state is not paying is also not received by the revenue office. The part that is received essentially stems from involuntary credits of contractors to government – and thus domestic financing – or is born by donors via inflated prices.

The chapter looks at alternative solutions, such as zero-rating of contracts and invoices of which donors finance the non-tax part, or an improvement of the budget process, which would ensure that the state's obligations to pay the VAT and import charges receive the funding that it reserves.

In the final section, the wisdom of the current practice of many donors under which they insist on not paying taxes is questioned. After all, the principles and rules were instituted at a time when public finance in recipient countries was generally not transparent and where the focus of aid organizations was on balance-of-payment gaps rather than budgetary constraints. It is proposed that in addition to government changing its budgeting procedures, donors start paying taxes for the infrastructure projects which they support. This would speed up implementation, avoid special rules and their potential for abuse, and probably also reduce the cost of public works in those cases where contractors make bids which include a safety margin to cover the event that payments of the tax part of their invoices to public sector clients may take a long time to materialize.

2 Background

In project-related financial aid, most donors and financial institutions decline payment of indirect fiscal charges, such as value-added tax and import duties, on public works which they finance.[1] The rationale is straightforward: donors fund the full resource cost of an investment. If they were to pay taxes on top, which do not constitute resource costs, they would be providing additional and non-earmarked funds to the Treasury, over and above the economic resource cost of the project. Consequently, project donors as well as staff in donor offices and beneficiary sectors would see such taxes as illegitimate fines on donations or soft loans.

As long as the donor bears the full resource cost of the project, domestic revenues and expenditures are indeed not negatively affected. If, for example, a donor pays the full CIF cost of an imported piece of machinery and also that of the transport and labour to bring it to its destination, but no taxes, all other activities would go on as before, and the tax revenue of the state would remain at the same level as before. Exempting donor-funded projects does not appear to be harmful.

However, the idea of exempting project-related activities from indirect taxes conflicts with governments' efforts to cut down on exemptions and limit the discretion of tax collectors. Since administrations tend to be weak and corruption endemic, this seems to be an adequate approach. Therefore, tax legislation in Mozambique, similar to that in many other countries, does not allow tax exemptions for donor-funded projects. Instead, indirect taxes and import duties are paid from general budgetary resources. As a result, donors' requirements are met.

From a theoretical point of view, this mechanism should not have negative effects on the availability of budgetary funds for other purposes because the additional taxes paid by the state would translate into additional revenue which the state collects. Other expenditures would not be squeezed out. Both solutions, the exemption path and the option where the state pays the taxes to itself and thereby increases revenues by an equal amount, are virtually equivalent with regard to the amount of revenue that is available for other purposes.

3 Underbudgeting for fiscal charges

In practice, however, budget allocations for payment of indirect taxes relating to donor-funded projects tend to be extremely inadequate in Mozambique. This is due to two factors.

First, many of the players (on both sides, donors as well as government) have an incomplete understanding of how the value-added tax works. A common yet false argument is that a contractor surrenders only part of the tax which is received from his government client because the contractor is allowed to deduct the VAT paid on his suppliers' invoices. The fact that the suppliers themselves and their own suppliers each surrender VAT on the basis of their respective value-added is often not taken into account. Therefore, the argument that the full amount of tax paid from budget resources would flow back to the revenue authorities is frequently questioned.

Second, the budget process disguises the impact which the failure to settle obligations relating to the payments of the VAT part of suppliers' invoices would have on revenues. Budget preparation starts with an estimate of domestic revenue and an assessment of general budget support to be expected. Expected yields of the various taxes are projected on the basis of historic results, adjusted for expected growth and the presumed impact of any planned policy change. Of course, growth rates of an industry's output and of its value-added depend in part on demand from donor-funded public works. However, the percentage of estimated tax yields that depends on such projects and works is not identified explicitly. Due to the cascaded nature of the value-added tax, it would indeed be difficult to assess the impact, since the industry that surrenders the tax to the revenue authority is often not the one where the change in final demand occurs.

At some point, the revenue estimate is closed, and the budget preparation process proceeds to the allocation of funds to spending units. As a first step, ceilings are issued for recurrent expenditure and, separately, for domestically funded investment expenditure which includes the payment of indirect taxes for donor-funded public works. In practice, the ceilings allocated for investment tend to be a residual after recurrent requirements have been taken into account. Quite frequently, the amounts that are 'left' for investment expenditures are already insufficient to cover the tax payments required for externally funded investment projects at this stage already.

When the spending units ('sectors' in Mozambican jargon) then prepare their respective detailed spending proposals within the allocated ceilings, tax payments related to externally funded projects appear to conflict with other investment expenditures, many of which are in fact current and even recurrent in nature. As a result, the overall amount allocated to payments of indirect fiscal charges relating to donor-funded projects tends to be insufficient. Long discussions often take place, but typically no consensus can be reached on either cancelling projects or allocating more funds to tax-related expenditure items. It is claimed that other internal investment expenditure and in particular the recurrent expenditure cannot be reduced. Since the overall expenditure ceilings have been fixed before, there appears to be a trade-off between the payment of taxes that relate to donor-funded projects and other expenditures.

Yet virtually no attention is paid to the fact that the allocation for tax payments has repercussions on the validity of the revenue estimate. If the revenue estimate implicitly assumed that taxes on donor-funded projects would be paid out of internal budget resources, that revenue will be less if the budget does not pay the taxes. This mechanism, however, is not considered. There is no feedback loop in the process.

In essence, the budget process suggests a trade-off which does not exist. Attempts to allocate expected revenues that depend on the state paying the tax in the first place to other uses is futile since that revenue would no longer be available if it is to be spent on something else.

4 Reactions and work-arounds

In principle, donors should stop disbursing when the provision for tax payments from domestic, general budget resources is insufficient. Furthermore, the Ministry of Finance should even insist on a reduction in donor spending when it thinks, rightly or wrongly, that it is unable to provide internal funds for the payment of project-related fiscal charges. In practice, neither of these reactions occurs. No ministry wants to lose external funds, and a consensus about which project to eliminate can generally not be reached. Ministries and ministers want the job done and results achieved. Donors want to see the funds which they have made available actually spent. And contractors want to stay in business and are not inclined to walk away just because the tax part of their invoices is not being paid. Thus there is an unholy alliance to 'muddle through'.

Under a normal VAT regime, the obligation to surrender value-added tax to the revenue authorities sets in when the company issues an invoice. It does not matter when payment is actually received. This general principle is also enshrined in Mozambican VAT law and regulations. If the rules were adhered to, contractors and their suppliers would be required to surrender the full amount of the VAT invoiced, irrespective of whether or not they have actually received the payment relating to that part of the invoice. Obviously, a huge drain on companies' financial resources and a severe reduction of profitability would result if payments were delayed or did not occur due to systematic underbudgeting for fiscal charges.

But since 'the show must go on', various special mechanisms have been put in place which mitigate the effects of systematic underbudgeting for tax payments. The first mechanism is a general budget line for the payment of import-related charges denominated '*encargos aduaneiros*'. This budget line, which is not attributed to specific spending units, can be used for the payment of customs duties and VAT levied at the border if the project is supported by external funds and inscribed in the budget. In order to utilize that budget line, the spending unit requests a payment order from the Ministry of Finance and deposits it with the customs administration *in lieu* of actual payments. Customs account for the payment order as revenue. No actual flow of funds is involved.

This facility is also available to suppliers that carry out work for government agencies. For example, if a contractor builds classrooms for the Ministry of Education on the basis of donor funds, the Ministry of Education can request the payment order against this budget line for import duties and taxes on behalf of the contractor. As a result, the construction company does not have to pay the import-related charges – duties as well as VAT – on, say, steel or cement.

A second work-around is a clause which exempts major pieces of equipment like construction equipment from import duties as well as VAT.[2] This is particularly important for local companies which need to import heavy earth-moving equipment.

Third, a decree was issued in 2000 which allows contractors for public works to request assessment of tax liability on the basis of payments received rather than invoices issued.[3] This facility can be extended to subcontractors, but not to normal suppliers. Although this facility mitigates the effects of late payments, it does not specifically address the fact that the pre-tax part of the invoices tends to get paid normally while the VAT-related part remains outstanding for a long period of time.

A creative interpretation of that decree, however, provides more relief. This interpretation allows contractors to defer the entire VAT payment to the revenue authorities as long as they haven't received the payment from government which relates to the tax portion of the invoice. Thus, when the contractor receives payment relating to the pre-VAT part of the invoice from the account which holds the external project funds, no VAT at all is surrendered to the revenue authorities. Only later, when the payment relating to the VAT element of the contractor's invoice is received, is the full amount of the VAT, minus the VAT paid on invoices of suppliers' and sub-contractors' invoices, due. The peculiarity of this decree is that it allows contractors to allocate payments to the tax and the non-tax part of the invoice. The normal rule would be that VAT is considered to be included proportionally in all payments.

Another work-around should also be mentioned. In Mozambique, a large portion of the fuel tax yield is earmarked for routine road maintenance. But since the allocated funds for payment of fiscal charges in the context of donor-funded road construction and rehabilitation are insufficient, the Road Fund uses part of the receipts from the fuel tax to pay VAT relating to donor-funded construction work. In essence, earmarked tax revenues are transformed into non-earmarked tax revenue, while spending on routine road maintenance remains lower than it should be.

As a result, the show can indeed go on in spite of inadequate budgets for tax payments on donor-funded public works. But the state keeps accumulating debts with construction companies, construction companies with their subcontractors, and the latter two with the revenue authorities.

5 Fiscal and other effects

Obviously, the state is collecting less revenue when it is accumulating arrears with its own tax payments and deferring tax liability. But is the amount that the state could collect equal or near-equal to the amount that it would have to budget and pay? This is actually difficult to assess without some empirical research. At the same time, it is amazing that this question does not appear to be addressed in ongoing studies.[4]

The difference between tax which the state pays and the resulting revenue which the state would collect depends on the following factors and mechanisms:

1 The amount of VAT which contractors and sub-contractors pay to *local* suppliers who are not subcontractors. There is no exemption or deferment for these transactions; the contractor has to support the VAT until it can be off-set against VAT received.
2 The incidence of the facility that fiscal charges on imports are paid for against the general allocation for import-related charges, with the effect that the contractor would not have VAT claims to off-set against VAT received.
3 The amount of work which these contractors and sub-contractors do for non-government clients. If the non-government portion is big enough, they are able to off-set the VAT paid to suppliers against the VAT received from non-government clients. But if the non-government portion is very low or non-existent, they would be sitting on large amounts of claimable VAT paid to suppliers which they cannot off-set because they have no VAT revenue.

4 The percentage of contractors to which the 2000 decree is applied. It appears that not all of them use that facility.
5 The number and amounts of donor-funded projects which are delayed or cancelled due to the fact that allocations for tax payments in the budget are insufficient.

Given the fact that VAT relating to big contracts is probably deferred and that the smaller contracts are being executed by companies which also have non-state clients, and that VAT on imports does not become a claimable item because it is paid for by a payment order on behalf of the importer, it could well be that the state would collect more than 90 per cent of additional VAT payments as revenues, with very little or even no delay. The part that would not flow back is composed of the following:

- VAT which contractors or subcontractors surrender in spite of not having been paid because the rules of the Decree 27/2000 do not apply;
- VAT paid to suppliers who are not subcontractors, to the extent that the contractor and subcontractor have so few other contracts that they cannot off-set the respective amounts against VAT received on these other contracts in their monthly tax declarations.

Although VAT transactions relating do donor-funded public works are effectively suspended, and although most of our contacts in the donor community think that the volume of externally funded investment is not affected, there are real repercussions. The discussion of the VAT issue consumes considerable time and effort of staff at donor offices, ministries and suppliers. Administration of the deferment scheme is cumbersome and prone to abuse. The state, and often enough the donors as well, end up paying considerable contractual penalties because of the delays which occur in the process of payment of VAT from budget resources; there is the suspicion that these penalties actually represent a windfall profit for the contractors because they do not pay fees, penalties or interest for the deferment of their obligation to pay to the revenue authorities.

It is also likely that contractors are bidding at higher prices because they know from experience that the VAT part of their invoices will be paid at best with long delays. Therefore, they might increase their pre-tax bid prices in such a way that this covers not only the real cost and profit, but also the VAT which they may have to surrender to the revenue authorities in spite of not having received the equivalent amount from the government client. The irony is that this would result in the donors effectively paying indirect taxes through inflated prices, even though they are formally refusing to do exactly that.

Thus a resolution of the issue is urgent, which is also reflected in repeated statements in IMF and joint donor-government reviews of general budget support.

6 Defining a lasting solution

Short of donors changing their policy, there are three alternative solutions to consider:

1   proper and adequate budgeting for payment of the VAT and import duty-related fiscal charges;
2   zero-rating of invoices;
3   full exemption of the contractors from the VAT regime.

For the *proper budgeting approach* to work, the budget process must become more sophisticated. Knowing that most of the additional tax which the budget would pay as counterpart financing would flow back as revenues at almost the same time, the budget lines relating to such payments have to be given the highest priority in the budget preparation process. In defining budget ceilings, it is necessary to specify the amount which is meant for tax payments and distinguish it clearly from ceilings for other types of expenditure. When sectors present their budget proposals, it has to be verified that they respect that split. No reallocation between the items must be allowed. But if a sector needs more funds for tax payment purposes, it should be possible to go beyond the initial ceilings.

In addition, a feedback loop to revenue estimates needs to be established. After the ceilings for tax payments are established, it needs to be checked whether this is compatible with the revenue estimate. Upward or downward adjustments of the revenue estimate must be made if this is necessary in order to achieve full compatibility. However, this calculation cannot be scientific since it is not evident from tax receipts and declarations to what extent the revenue relates to government-paid or other forms of tax. A trial-and-error approach is required, which might start with the assumption that maybe some 80 per cent of *additional* budget allocations for tax purposes would flow back as *additional* revenue.

Measures need to be taken which prevent spending units from reallocating funds from votes for taxes to other types of expenditure within the fiscal year. In the beginning, the best approach would probably be to create a centralized budget line for taxes related to donor-funded investment projects against which sectors can draw for this purpose. With this simple measure, it is evident that those funds cannot be reallocated to other uses because they are not part of a sector's budget allocation.

In order to prevent insufficient cash allocations to that budget line, spending units can be given the option to apply for a credit certificate in favour of the contractor which he, in turn, can present to the revenue authorities *in lieu* of VAT payment. At the same time, one has to be aware that the main contractor generally deducts VAT paid to his subcontractors and suppliers and will therefore not owe the full amount to the tax office. The amount of actual reimbursements of VAT from the tax authorities to the contractor will increase and prompt settlement is required.

The *zero-rating approach* is totally equivalent from a fiscal point of view. To implement it, the Budget Directorate or the Budget Execution Directorate of the Ministry of Finance must be authorized to allow specified contracts to receive the same treatment as exports. In practical terms, the contract would need to be approved and certified, and the contractors would need to keep a record of zero-rated invoices which they issue under each contract.

To the extent that the contractors have paid VAT on their suppliers' and subcontractors' invoices, they would have the right to claim the respective amounts back from the revenue authorities unless they have collected VAT through other work for private clients against which they can off-set the VAT which they paid to their suppliers. Still, the number of continuous refund cases will increase, particularly in the roads sector, where the government is the main or even exclusive client for most contractors.

Although all exemptions and waivers open the door to abuse, we assume that this can be controlled. The number of companies that execute infrastructure works for government is limited, and they can probably be inspected more closely. The procedures for approving tax-exempt works contracts must be watertight.

The zero-rating approach comes with two problems, though. First, it does not easily accommodate those cases where the donor refuses to pay import duties. This aspect needs to be handled either by way of a continuation of the existing budget line for import-related fiscal charges or through a budgetary allocation to cater for such charges if the contractor presents proof and a corresponding invoice. Second, the solution is difficult to implement in those cases where financing agreements with donors require a counterpart contribution from government which is defined as a percentage and where this percentage has been calculated to reflect the typical fiscal charge in different types of expenditure.

Third, government and in particular the Ministry of Finance need to be prepared to fend off requests from other spending units to be treated in the same manner, i.e. get a waiver on value-added tax, although the contracts and payments do not relate to projects for which a donor finances the full economic, non-fiscal cost. Very likely, spending units which do not fully understand the rationale for the tax waiver will point out the economic, social and political importance of what they are doing, refer to the severe funding constraints under which they are operating, and request relief through a waiver on value-added tax. If this request is made through the right channels, the waiver could easily be granted even against the opinion and recommendation of the Ministry of Finance. The danger of this type of abuse is fairly high.

The third option would consist in taking the contractor fully out of the tax regime. It would consist in the contractor neither charging VAT on the invoices nor being able to claim a refund for VAT paid to suppliers and subcontractors. This solution is sometimes brought into discussion because of alleged lower impact on revenues compared to full zero-rating.

However, we reject this solution. First of all, it would require the creation of virtual companies or subsidiaries in those industries where companies tend to work for private sector clients as well as for government. It would make it difficult to distinguish between normal work for government and those special cases of donor-funded projects where donors insist on not covering fiscal charges. The solution would also favour companies with a high degree of vertical integration against those who subcontract parts of their work and buy supplies locally. Finally, the partial tax exemption which this solution brings is not in line with the spirit of the donor policy, under which they do not accept to pay *any* fiscal charges, irrespective of whether they are direct or indirect.

One may also be tempted to propose a full VAT exemption (in the sense of zero-rating) of all public works contracts for public entities, irrespective of whether or not the project is funded by a donor. However, this approach would be difficult to control in practice and would result in high claims against the revenue authorities for refund of VAT paid to suppliers. Therefore, we do not consider this option further.

7 Managing the transition

As we have seen, tax revenues relating to donor-funded projects are currently low because the state is not paying the full amount of tax that it should. But the shortfall may be less than the amount not paid by the state. Although this is not a sustainable situation, it still implies that all suggested solutions could result in some reduction of the amount of funds that are currently available for other purposes.

Estimating the amount of revenue which the government would lose under a zero-rating approach or the (equivalent) amount of additional payments of taxes from budget resources that would *not* flow back would not be excessively difficult, though. One would essentially need to know the VAT amount due but not budgeted in one year in the main affected sectors (roads, water, education), and then look at a sample of contractors and their sub-contractors and assess how much *more* they would surrender to the revenue authorities if the public clients paid according to contractual obligations. Our guess is that some 80–90 per cent of additional payments would in fact become additional revenues as well, maybe even more. It would be useful to carry out a study about the likely percentage of additional VAT paid by the state which would not flow back as revenue. The study would take a sample of companies and assess the amount of pre-tax that these companies have been unable to off-set against tax liabilities. The potential shortfall of additional revenue compared to additional tax paid by the state depends critically on that amount.

The transition can even be managed gradually. The budget could give priority to tax payments relating to donor-funded public works, and the allocation of liquid resources for that purpose could get high priority. Then the effect on VAT yields can be monitored.

A practical solution might also include a provision whereby the state issues certificates which contractors can deposit at the revenue offices *in lieu* of payments which relate to that part of the arrears which the contractors would have to surrender directly, and a phased amortization of the remaining debt in actual payments.

To what extent interest and penalties on arrears have to be paid needs to be negotiated with each contractor. A fair compensation for the delays depends on whether the debt is denominated in local or foreign currency, whether the contractor has to pay penalties for late (and possibly also for deferred) payment to the revenue office and whether the contractor has actually surrendered the tax which was due but not paid by the government client.

8 The donor perspective

One conclusion from the previous discussion is that some indirect taxes on donor-funded investment projects are being received by the revenue authorities even when government does not live up to its obligation to settle the VAT-related part of contractors' invoices. Who is, in the end, supporting these revenues?

At first sight, it may look as if the contractors suffer a reduction of revenues and therefore see their financing requirements increase and their profits lower than expected. But since the situation has been ongoing for several years, it is probably safe to assume that this was already factored into the bid and contract prices. Since the donors pay for the lion's share of the contractors' invoices, it is the donors and financing agencies who, in the end, do not get the value for money which they would otherwise get. In effect, the donors probably bear the cost of those taxes that are being surrendered to the revenue office even though, officially, they refuse to cover fiscal charges. Maybe this should make donors rethink their policy.

There is another reason why donors might want to reconsider their stance. The 'no tax payment' rule originates from a period when governments in developing countries were not elected, public finance systems were not transparent and dialogue about spending policies and priorities was virtually inexistent. Under these circumstances, the donors' refusal to provide non-earmarked funds to governments made some sense.

The origins of the rules also go back to a period where most developing countries' currencies were severely overvalued and shortages of foreign exchange were addressed by administrative rather than market mechanisms. Consequently, the donors' and governments' main focus was on the balance of payment constraint. In this period, it was thought that the donors' main role should be to relieve foreign exchange constraints. Consequently, it was thought that not only indirect taxes but also other local costs such as clearing costs at harbours or domestic transport should be supported by recipient governments' own resources.

These days, however, many of the donors who insist on not paying taxes on project support also provide general budget support. Where market mechanisms are used to allocate foreign exchange, donors and governments look at budget constraints much more than balance-of-payment constraints. Donors nowadays analyse budgets and financial reports of recipient countries and have an ongoing and often fruitful dialogue on policy and spending patterns with the governments of the countries which they support. Wouldn't it therefore be appropriate to simply accept the payment of indirect taxes and consider them as indirect budget support?

Abandoning the no-tax clause would have several advantages:

- It would alleviate a considerable burden on the administration because it would make all these special rules and arrangements obsolete and lower the potential for abuse.
- It would lower the pre-tax price level for infrastructure work.
- It would do away with most of the time-consuming and therefore costly discussions about outstanding VAT-related invoices and allow donor and sector staff to move on to more productive uses of their time.
- Government budgeting and public finance management would become more straightforward. The impact of spending on tax for revenues does not have to be taken into account (which is difficult to do in the first place) and the issue of the impact of reallocations from tax to other purposes on revenues does not need to be considered. Reallocations across votes within a spending unit become less critical than they are at the moment.

On the negative side, two aspects should be mentioned, though. Such a shift in donor policy would require a renegotiation of the balance between project and programme aid between the various departments in the donor agency. When donors accept that they will pay taxes it is possible that fewer roads, boreholes and schools can be built with the current budget. Expected reductions in bid prices would compensate for part, but not for all of this. Thus sector departments may start claiming additional funds from the macro departments as compensation, arguing that the tax which they now have to pay represents budget support and reduces their impact. However, in a period when several donors are scaling up their aid to Africa and to Mozambique the rebalancing of the aid portfolio can probably be managed without too many controversies.

The other potentially problematic aspect relates to the reliability of governments' estimates of internal revenues. Donor funds spent on projects would now make a real and probably significant contribution to domestic revenues. Consequently, delays in project implementation would have a negative impact on government revenues. However, this being said, we would question whether this uncertainty is bigger than the current vagaries related to taxes paid from the expenditure side of the budget.

The World Bank has made a step in the suggested direction for new contracts recently. Common funds for sector support are becoming ever more popular. It is noteworthy that no one has insisted that construction work financed against the funds' resources should be exempted from tax. Apparently, and rightly so, donors have no problem with that. Peer pressure among donors to follow that example might be reinforced if the Mozambican government made a strong statement to the effect that it urges donors to abandon the no-tax policy and reserves the right to refuse funding with the non-tax principle in financial project aid in the medium term.

Donors who are engaged in policy dialogue with government would be well advised to make a strong point that a lasting solution, be it by way of proper budgeting or by way of zero-rating of relevant contracts, needs to be adopted quickly. The current muddle-through situation inflates prices for infrastructure work and absorbs too much managerial time. And donors who insist on tax exemption because they want their projects to get the same treatment as those of others might consider that most-favoured fiscal treatment might imply that their projects will become the most cumbersome to execute.

Notes

1 Actually, the rule applies to all financial aid and some aid-in-kind as well, but public works is the most visible practical case.
2 Decree no. 55/2004 (GoM 2004) changes the VAT code to the effect that equipment of class 'K' (heavy equipment) that is exempted from import duty on the basis of the Investment Law is also exempted from VAT.
3 See GoM (2000); this approves the 'Regime Especial de exigibilidade do imposto sobre o valor acrescentado nas empreitadas e subempreitadas de obras públicas'.
4 The European Union has recently financed a study on the problem of the non-payment of VAT and other indirect charges in the roads sector. The study tried to take stock of the arrears in VAT payment from the Roads Fund to contractors, but did not address the decisive question of how much would flow back to the revenue authorities if the state actually started paying taxes in full.

8 Macroeconomic modelling

Process and practice

Sam Jones and Eugenio Maria Paulo

1 Introduction

> One of the major challenges that face many African governments is the lack of well-trained professionals capable of preparing consistent short- to medium-term plans or a comprehensive long-term planning framework.
>
> (Economic Commission for Africa 2005: 1)

The critical role of macroeconomic and fiscal modelling is well established in both developed and developing countries. Where quantitative tools are inadequate, macroeconomic management may be undermined, in turn heightening the risk of economic imbalance. Weaknesses in this domain played an important part in the economic crises which beset much of Africa during the 1980s (Tarp 1993). Despite the known limitations of formal models, they are useful, if only to make core assumptions explicit and to help think through the inherent trade-offs with respect to stability, growth and development. Even when quantitative tools are simply absent, policy choices always refer to some form of implicit model – whether logically consistent or not. Quantitative tools typically also have a central place in budget management, providing the basis for identifying government financing needs and setting budget ceilings. In the current environment, robust tools to inform policy-making are growing in importance. The Economic Commission for Africa (2005), for example, notes that the forward-planning orientations of both MTEFs (Medium Term Expenditure Frameworks) and PRSPs (Poverty Reduction Strategy Papers) demand increasingly robust planning tools. The prospect of scaled-up aid flows represents a further source of pressure on macroeconomic policy-making.

Given the above, it is useful to assess the extent to which modelling approaches at the country level are adequate to economic management challenges. Although one might expect this to be a fairly routine activity, one notes a distinct lack of published material providing guidance on best practice in macroeconomic and fiscal modelling in developing countries. In other words, it is difficult to identify broadly accepted grounds on which country modelling practices may be assessed. In response to this gap, an initial objective of this chapter is to propose a general set of principles for the evaluation of macro-fiscal modelling at the country level. These themes are developed in Section 2, including a brief review of the relevant literature. Based on the authors' experiences in macro-fiscal modelling in Mozambique, Section 3 applies the framework to this specific case. We find that modelling practices have improved over recent years. They are, however, at an early stage of development and a number of weaknesses are obvious. In particular, we note the absence of tools to think through the relationship between investment (allocation), external resource flows and growth over the medium term. In addition, the informality of modelling practices tends to undermine their consistent use in the policy process. Our evaluation concludes with a consideration of the deeper factors that may determine improvements in modelling practices over the near term. Section 4 brings the chapter to a close.

At this point it is useful to clarify the position taken in this chapter. Our focus is on the practical side of modelling rather than its theoretical basis. This is not to say that theory is irrelevant. Theoretical positions are funda-mental to building and interpreting sound models. However, robust practical implementation is a prerequisite to inform policy-making. The point here is that models can be valid partners at the table in many key fiscal and mac-roeconomic policy processes (Don 2004). Modelling practices determine whether quantitative tools are adequate to policy challenges and/or have a clear 'voice' at the table. Our interest in macro-fiscal modelling practices thus concentrates specifically on models used within the government on a regular basis.

2 Towards an evaluation framework

2.1 Guidance from the literature

The vast literature that pertains to macroeconomic and fiscal modelling is dominated by theoretically oriented studies. Typically these focus on techni-cal matters, including variable selection and behavioural dynamics. While it is beyond the scope of this chapter to provide anything like a comprehensive review, three main categories of models can be distinguished. These are: (1) models concerned with short-term stabilization and the achievement of external and fiscal balance, as per IMF-type financial programming (e.g. Polak 1997); (2) models with a focus on the resources needed to finance sustainable growth over the medium and long term, exemplified by the World Bank's Revised Minimum Standard Model approach (see Tarp 1993); and (3) a broad category of economy-wide models, including macro-econometric and computable general equilibrium (CGE) models, which tend to focus on questions of sectoral allocation and income distribution.

This categorization makes apparent that a diverse array of plausible models exists, each with claims to validity. Moreover, models typically have relatively distinct and often quite specific domains of application. Simply put, different models have been developed to respond to different questions, implying that no individual model can respond comprehensively to the broad range of policy management issues faced by low income countries.[1] This point is well accepted, leading the IMF to recommend a multi-pronged approach:

> Since no single model is universally applicable, national authorities – and Fund country teams in advising them – must draw on a smorgasbord of small econometric models and single equation estimates ... as well as economic judgement for formulating macroeconomic and structural policies.
>
> (IMF 2004b: 6)

A second strand in the literature has a specific bearing on developing countries. This refers to discussion surrounding MTEFs, often described as 'best practice' public economic management tools required to ensure effective implementation of poverty reduction strategies (PRSPs). While there is no unique definition of what constitutes a desirable MTEF, there is agreement that the overriding objective of the process is to promote sound, forward-looking and coherent public financial management in order to secure a firm link between policies, resource allocation and outcome efficiency. Unsurprisingly, this literature is replete with calls to develop a coherent macroeconomic management framework both as a core input into the budget preparation process and to ensure aggregate fiscal discipline (Houerou and Taliercio 2002; Schiavo-Campo and Tommasi 1999). However, despite recognition of its importance, more detailed practical guidance on macroeconomic and fiscal modelling appears absent. In contrast, the literature tends to concentrate on either technical budgeting issues and/or the institutional framework required to support the MTEF.

This crude summary suggests that although various *specific* issues are treated in depth there remains relatively little research concerning the overall modelling framework. The latter refers to the selection, elaboration, organization and application of quantitative tools to inform public policy-making – described hereafter as modelling practices. This is especially the case for developing countries where guidance in critical areas remains lacking.[2] These ambiguities include: (1) which models or combination of models are best suited to current policy challenges; (2) what level of aggregation is desirable in different models; and (3) how models can best be used to inform policy debates.

This lacuna of advice on modelling practices has been noted elsewhere. With respect to the models associated with the World Bank, for example, Tarp (1993) comments that there is very little published guidance on how they should be implemented at the country level. Soludo's (2002) survey of modelling practices in Africa confirms that inconsistency and variety abound

(Houerou and Taliercio 2002). Not only do countries typically rely on *one* model alone, but also only the most basic reduced-form IMF and World Bank models tend to be used (Economic Commission for Afria 2005). Reliance on relatively simple models (compared to what is available in the academic literature) has a variety of motivations, among which data and technical capacity limitations are critical. Indeed, Soludo (2002) finds that in the majority of cases model elaboration has been dependent on (expatriate) consultants and there exists insufficient local capacity to modify existing tools. It is possible that this nascent state of (government) modelling in low income countries explains the paucity of the literature. However, this only reinforces the importance of evaluating modelling practices.

2.2 Evaluation principles

The above makes clear that there is neither a *de facto* standard approach to modelling in low income countries nor a clearly identifiable set of principles to inform 'best practice'. Of course, this does not mean that a uniform approach would be desirable – both country circumstances and political arrangements vary, implying that the practicality and relevance of different quantitative tools also will differ. Thus, rather than entering into detailed specifications, it is more helpful to suggest a set of broad principles against which modelling practices can be assessed.

As a point of departure we follow the IMF (2004b) and recognize that no single model is either theoretically or practically adequate to the task of providing comprehensive policy guidance. Different models and methods can be distinguished by their domain of policy relevance as well as their implementation feasibility given data and technical capacity limitations. Moreover, as these limitations are often large, more simple models that are both parsimonious and analytically tractable may be preferable. As argued in Zellner *et al.* (2001), many academics advocate that modelling should be guided by a type of KISS (keep it sophisticatedly simple) principle, and there is widespread evidence that larger complex models do not consistently outperform more simple specifications in (macro)economic forecasting (Vuchelen and Gutierrez 2005; Zellner *et al.* 2001).

Combining insights from both the theoretical and MTEF literatures at least three distinct policy domains can usefully be informed by quantitative tools in developing countries. First, we concur with Bolnick (1999) that some form of financial programming (FP) framework is necessary to support short-term macroeconomic management. Such a framework is advisable for countries under IMF programmes, not only to have a technical position from which to negotiate with the IMF but also to promote domestic ownership and technical capacity development in macroeconomic management.[3] In addition, these kinds of models provide a basis to make a clear statement of the macroeconomic targets and policy goals necessary to inform coherent planning by both the government and external partners (donors).

The above does not mean that an FP-type model is likely to be a sufficient basis for macro-fiscal management. These models lack a real side and therefore must take real output growth as exogenous. They are not suitable, therefore, to consider the long-term relationship between real growth, investment (allocation) and resource (financing) needs. Third, given the multi-sector and aggregate nature of FP models, it is likely to be useful to develop more detailed tools to assist in revenue and budget projections. The use of tools above and below an FP model also may assist in ensuring that the FP model is not over-stretched but rather remains focused on its specific policy domain of aggregate, nominal short-term sectoral balance. Needless to say, the consistency and coherency of the overall macro-fiscal policy framework will only be achieved via iterative cross-fertilization between these three policy areas and their associated model(s).

From these considerations, we are now in a position to suggest relevant benchmark criteria for an evaluation of a given macro-fiscal modelling framework. Most are reasonably self-explanatory, finding support in the above analysis as well as various insights for developing countries associated with budget (MTEF) preparation and economic forecasting more widely (e.g. Hendry and Clements 2001). We emphasize that the criteria are *deliberately* idealistic, creating a high standard which is unlikely to be reached in any situation. The general principles are:

1 *policy coverage*: the modelling framework should support policy making in at least three broad domains, namely long-term growth and resource-needs planning, macroeconomic stability and budget preparation;
2 *technical coherence*: modelling practices should be technically coherent;
3 *feasibility*: models should be adequate both to domestic technical capacity and data availability – the KISS principle (keep it sophisticatedly simple) may provide useful guidance in this regard;
4 *currency*: models should be current, in the sense of being updated with the latest historical data and estimates for behavioural parameters;
5 *formality*: modelling practices should be clearly defined and formalized (documented) – this refers not only to the objectives and outputs of each model, but also to the formal definition of the stages in the modelling process (from initiation through to finalization), modelling responsibilities and regular model evaluations;
6 *consistency*: outputs from the models should be employed consistently within the policy-making process.

Succinctly put, the modelling framework should be adequate to policy challenges, be sensitive to resource constraints and have a consistent voice at the policy-making table. Evidently, by dint of their generality the criteria demand further elaboration and interpretation. This can only be done at the country level. For example, the first criterion, referring to the sufficiency of model coverage, must be informed by the concrete features of an economy's structure and risk profile. The range of policy instruments available and feasible for government use always will be context specific. In this vein it can be noted that at the country level one must be sensitive to legislation which defines requirements or principles to which the macro-fiscal policy framework must submit. Finally, the above framework gives no sense of priority. Again, this can only be meaningful in specific circumstances; however, the very process of undertaking an evaluation can be valuable in weighing up short- and long-term concerns. With these points in mind, we can begin to examine the Mozambican approach.

3 The Mozambican approach

This section evaluates the macroeconomic and fiscal modelling practices currently found in Mozambique. We start with an overview of relevant features of the Mozambican models, followed by a brief description of the quantitative tools in place.

3.1 Background

As noted above, the evaluation criteria must be applied in a context-sensitive fashion. For Mozambique three relevant issues can be highlighted.[4] First, the government is heavily reliant on external aid, which on aggregate finances over 50 per cent of total public expenditures and is likely to continue to do so over the medium term and beyond. By virtue of its intensity, external financing brings substantial macro-fiscal management challenges. These embrace the volatility of aid flows, their impact on the real exchange rate (competitiveness), as well as its short-term nominal stability, the proliferation of aid flows outside official government accounting systems (off-budgets) and the impact of aid-financed investment on the long-term profile of recurrent expenditures. In addition, given its low income status the government does not have access to international capital markets and retains a close relationship with both the World Bank and IMF. The latter has played an influential role in Mozambique since the mid-1980s and is the lead donor on issues of macroeconomic management, undertaking regular assessments of government performance under Article 4 agreements. Second, the financial system is weakly developed and interbank markets are thin. As such, the instruments and scope for smooth government intervention in the monetary arena are relatively limited. Third, we should be aware of ongoing reforms of the public financial management system. In this context the approach and principles inscribed in the Government Financial Administration System Law and its associated Regulations are relevant.[5]

3.2 Modelling tools

The core agencies involved in macroeconomic management include an independent Central Bank, the Ministry of Finance and the Ministry of Planning and Development.[6] Two main quantitative tools are used to inform policy-making. Operated by separate departments within the Ministry of Planning and Development, they are: (1) a financial programming model, known as the Quadro Macro; and (2) a simple sectoral growth projections module.[7] The latter represents a set of relatively detailed production accounts, including both quantities and prices, which are aggregated to generate one-year-ahead growth forecasts. In turn these are inscribed in the government's annual Economic and Social Plan and are used as exogenous inputs into the Quadro Macro. Due to its more comprehensive coverage of macroeconomic aggregates and the government's aggregate fiscal stance, the Quadro Macro model plays a fundamental role in the planning cycle – it represents the basis for elaboration of the annual government budget and the medium-term expenditure framework (also prepared annually). In addition, the model is the focus for quantitative discussions as part of biannual meetings with the IMF, the lead donor on macroeconomic and fiscal matters.

The historical evolution of the growth model is somewhat murky. On the one hand it bears some relation to the era of 'scientific socialism' during which detailed production plans were elaborated at the sectoral (commodity) level by the National Planning Commission (Comissão Nacional do Plano). However, with the adoption of a market-based orientation from the mid-1980s, the roles of national planning and economic statistics were reconsidered. A National Institute of Statistics (Instituto Nacional de Estatística) was created in August 1996 and set about elaborating a more comprehensive set of national income accounts according to international standards. Part of this work involved a team of external consultants who developed a quantitative tool to estimate historical value-added (on the production side) based on available sectoral data from the National Planning Commission. Since then it seems that this (historical) model has been employed (unchanged) in a forecasting capacity, with annual projections added on an incremental basis. It is important to note that the model is only an accounting tool that aggregates information provided by individual government sectors. In other words, sectors are requested to provide annual estimates for production and prices which are plugged into the model to produce the GDP projections. No behavioural relationships are specified and the methods used to generate forecasts at the sector level are unknown.

In line with the above, structural reforms during the 1990s also embraced public financial management. Reforms were initiated (under a World Bank project) in 1997 with the objective of introducing a more rigorous and medium-term approach to planning. Expenditure projections undertaken by the health and roads sector as a part of their sectoral recovery plans had made clear that consistent forecasts of available financing resources were required. This was the motivation behind the elaboration of the first government-wide medium-term plan in 1998, at the time known as the Medium Term Expenditure Framework (MTEF, Cenário de Despesas de Médio Prazo). The underlying quantitative tool for this instrument was a CGE model developed by external consultants from Harvard University based in the Office of Studies (Gabinete de Estudos, GEST) within the Ministry of Planning and Finance (MPF). The MTEF thus represented Mozambique's first consistent planning framework providing an estimate of available resources and corresponding sectoral expenditures at a government-wide level.

From 1999 to 2000 modelling progressed, motivated by further attempts to develop a domestic MTEF (supported by donors) as well as the need to provide revenue and expenditure forecasts for the country's first PRSP.[8] During this period the same technical assistance team within the GEST elaborated a first version of the (current) Quadro Macro model. Departure from a CGE framework enabled both a more comprehensive treatment of the fiscal accounts (e.g. detailed revenue forecasts) and, owing to its relative technical simplicity, was more conducive to routine usage. Following its initial development, the model was transferred to the National Directorate for the Plan and Budget (within the MPF), where it remained until the creation of the Ministry of Planning and Development in early 2005. During this period the Quadro Macro emerged as the main quantitative tool for aggregate budget planning. Emphasis on its fiscal outputs (which were its original motivation), however, was accompanied by an increasing neglect of other sectors. This trend was reversed in 2005 with a substantial modification of the model, re-establishing its more comprehensive financial programming status. These enhancements also assured a much clearer distinction between endogenous and exogenous variables, as well as separating high-level targets from lower-level exogenous parameters to improve the clarity and usability of the model.

Looking more closely at the current model, the Quadro Macro captures the interrelationships between four main sectors – real production, external, monetary and fiscal accounts. Based on the output of the growth model, the real sector distinguishes between the contribution of large industrial investment projects (mega-projects) and the rest of the economy. Other key macroeconomic assumptions are also exogenous – inflation is chosen as a simple target from which the nominal exchange rate is derived once a target for movements in the real exchange rate is included. The external sector (balance of payments) separately identifies the contribution of mega-projects as well as detailed information on external aid resource flows which feed into the fiscal accounts. These external flows also are treated as exogenous, based on information from the main donors and/or past trends. The fiscal side of the model is the most detailed and follows the aggregate classification used by the Ministry of Finance. Domestic revenue forecasts are undertaken for each main instrument. In most cases the method is the same – revenue is derived from an exogenous assumption regarding tax effort as well as the elasticity of the revenue line to GDP calculated from past observations (see Chapter 9 for further details). On the expenditure side, recurrent expenditure projections are incremental, being based on simple target weights in GDP. Investment expenditure is the sum of external aid (minus budget support) and an internal investment component. The latter is a fiscal residual which comes from entering all other expenditure and revenue items into the government's budget constraint, holding fixed a target level for internal debt financing.

Finally, the monetary sector reflects movements in all other accounts, assuming the quantitative theory of money applies. In behavioural terms it is similar to the simple model outlined in Polak (1997). Changes in international reserves come directly from the external sector, while net credit to the government is taken from the fiscal accounts. Taken as a whole, the main outputs of the model include a set of core macroeconomic assumptions, a fiscal table covering the government budget, balance-of-payments projections (including international reserves) and forecasts for monetary aggregates.

3.3 Assessment

3.3.1 Coverage

With regard to the policy domains informed by quantitative tools in Mozambique, the Quadro Macro provides a consistent framework for agreeing targets for key macroeconomic aggregates (linked to the growth model) as well as more detailed fiscal projections on both the revenue and expenditure sides. Parts of the annual budget law are read off directly from the fiscal output of the model; also various medium-term planning exercises such as the government's MTEF and PRSP documents are based on the model. Even so, an evident gap in the framework is the treatment of medium-term growth, resource needs and investment allocations. This is particularly relevant in light of the government's reliance on external funding of public sector investment. Analysis of this kind would provide a useful high-level framework under which short- and medium-term applications of the Quadro Macro could be aligned; in addition, it would represent a more rigorous basis from which to consider the appropriate level and application of foreign aid.

Second, we note that the fiscal dimension of the Quadro Macro remains at a high level of aggregation. On the expenditure side, in particular, the salary bill is estimated at a government-wide level without detailed reference to the number of civil servants, their grading or distribution etc. There also is no quantification of the potential impact on recurrent costs of recent and planned new investments. Past experience has shown that failure to take these issues into account has come to generate fiscal management inefficiencies, such as in the roads sector (Arndt *et al.* 2007). However, formal attempts to develop quantitative tools, such as a more elaborate budget model, are, if anything, at a very early level of development.[9]

Finally, we can mention that the Quadro Macro does not facilitate evaluation of specific fiscal policies, such as tax rates. While these instruments are implicit in the behavioural specification of revenue lines, there is no simple means to simulate the impact of rate changes on outcome variables such as total revenues or the fiscal deficit. Their inclusion in a model would help focus attention on potential tax policy choices, an issue relevant to Mozambique given the widely commented need to increase domestic revenues (see Chapter 5 by Jones).

3.3.2 Technical coherence

Technical coherence covers various important modelling issues. First, there is the extent to which models conform to applicable theory – i.e. we should expect to find no fundamental specification errors given the theoretical approach adopted. Here the Mozambican models do not show major faults. The absence of behavioural relationships in the growth model essentially excludes the possibility of such errors (assuming the arithmetic is correct). The Quadro Macro, on the other hand, displays some confusion between instruments and targets in the closure mechanism. This recalls the Meade–Tinbergen rule, which states that for every independent target there must be at least one independent policy instrument. In the Polak FP model, for example, the standard targets are international reserves and prices which are fulfilled via changes in the exchange rate and domestic credit. This can be distilled down to an equality between the monetary and balance-of-payments accounts. In general form this can be expressed as:

$$f(p, e) = g(p, y) + h(c_p, c_g) \tag{1}$$

where p is changes in prices, e changes in the exchange rate, y real output growth and c_p and c_g changes in credit to the private and government sectors, respectively. The left-hand side derives from the balance-of-payments identity, indicating that where targets are fixed for prices and international reserves, an optimal level for the exchange rate is immediately implied. In turn, this requires a unique value for changes in total credit $h(.)$ to ensure the monetary account is consistent with the desired external balance. This can be achieved by fixing one of the credit components as a target, allowing the other to move to its optimum instrument value.

In contrast to the above, the current version of the Quadro Macro effectively treats international reserves as an instrument, permitting changes in the exchange rate to be the target. This is unusual as reserves are typically viewed as an outcome variable rather than a policy instrument. In addition, a modelling trick is used to allow targets to be set for both credit items. This is achieved via the inclusion of a 'hidden' residual in the monetary accounts, being an additional item on the right-hand side of equation (1). While this specification is not technically infeasible, it gives a false sense of certainty to economic policy and may generate misunderstanding as to the effective degree of freedom of government intervention in the economy. In particular, this approach does not clearly capture the potential impact of crowding out effects arising from increases in net credit to the government.

A second aspect of technical coherence refers to the technical articulation between models. Where more than one model is used, it is reasonable to expect that the models are linked (wherever feasible) in the sense that outputs from one model are treated as exogenous inputs in the others. In the Mozambican case this is not problematic – real output projections from the growth model are used as exogenous targets in the Quadro Macro. Also, the multi-sector nature of the latter ensures economic consistency across core accounts (income, fiscal, external, monetary, etc.) down to the elaboration of the budget.

A third dimension relates to the connection between the technical specification of the model and the real world. While modelling involves deliberate simplification, it may be the case that relevant aspects of reality are needlessly and incorrectly represented. This is pertinent to the modelling of tax revenue where the tax base is defined in law. In the Quadro Macro we can verify that forecasts for many tax lines make the implicit assumption that the full value of GDP (often including tax-exempt industrial projects as well as the large informal agricultural sector) is taken as the appropriate base. Whilst this is the most simplistic assumption, a more robust approach would be to attempt to approximate the sectoral incidence of each tax. Of course this would demand substantial technical work, including estimates of the size of formal and informal economic activity in each sector. Nonetheless, this could be undertaken gradually starting with the removal of obviously exempt (non-paying) sectors from the effective bases of a large number of revenue lines.

A final aspect of technical coherence refers to the calibration of behavioural parameters. While these cannot be evaluated according to given theory, one would expect rigorous estimation based on either past observations or a plausible (Bayesian) prior. Here some more substantial concerns can be identified. Throughout the Quadro Macro, core behavioural parameters (e.g. the elasticity of endogenous variables to changes in nominal GDP) are set exogenously without reference to econometric calibrations. In fact, in many cases values simply are chosen to generate a desired outcome. While econometric estimates are made difficult by a lack of stable time series data (among other factors), *ex post* model evaluation exercises could be used to identify plausible upper and lower bounds for many of these parameters.

3.3.3 Feasibility

The existence of severe capacity limitations in the Mozambican public sector is well recognized. Within the old Ministry of Planning and Finance, an evaluation of human resources (Hodges and Souto 2003) identified there were only 55 technical staff responsible for the elaboration and final production of all government-wide planning and budgeting instruments and their associated analytical support. The same report notes that only four of these staff had a master's degree or above and that there had been a significant drain of the most highly qualified, technically experienced personnel over recent years. Given this situation pertains to one of the more high-profile ministries, which has benefited from considerable external capacity building support, technical capacities in other ministries typically are even more severely limited.

In this context, the technical and local capacity feasibility of the existing models is generally good. The Quadro Macro model, developed initially through a technical assistance project, is no longer run by foreign experts. Recent improvements to the model combined with capacity building of local staff have enabled this transfer to take place. The model does not contain sophisticated theoretical extensions to a standard financial programming model and the underlying modelling techniques are relatively straightforward – relying on extrapolative rather than econometric methods. As such, a substantial level of economics training or experience is not a prerequisite for use or understanding of the model. In addition, the historical data necessary to update the model are produced on a regular basis, although at times they may be difficult to acquire. The growth model also is not reliant on external experts and is updated from information submitted by sectoral ministries.

Despite the above, four reservations can be stated about the overall feasibility of the models. First, only a very small number of technical staff have the experience and capacity to operate the existing models. This creates substantial vulnerability to staff absences or changes, particularly as the models are not documented. Second, outside the Ministry of Planning and Development – the *de facto* agency responsible for modelling – understanding and access to the FP model (or other multi-sector macroeconomic models) are extremely weak, limiting the possibility for technical debates concerning the outputs of the model as a whole as opposed to isolated sector-specific elements. Third, due to limited capacity and the fact that technical staff are not exclusively dedicated to modelling activities, the likelihood of realizing improvements or developing complementary models is extremely low. This suggests there is a real risk of model stagnation and, with time, deterioration. Finally, we note that the level of detail required to run the growth model – being at the product level and distinguished by sector of activity (household versus enterprise) – is such that the quality of the underlying data cannot even be guaranteed. The agencies providing the data do not have proven statistical capacities and, at the central level, the data are subject to neither quality controls nor basic coherency or consistency checks.

3.3.4 Currency

Keeping any model current is vital to secure its validity and efficiency. With respect to the Quadro Macro, we recall that when the technical assistance project under which the model was developed finished, certain aspects of the model fell into disuse and only the fiscal projections side was maintained. In part this was due to the unavailability of the necessary data. Recent revisions to the model, however, ensure it now can be updated on a regular basis based on official data. Although this generally takes place, it remains the case that due to weak capacity and poor verification processes (see Section 3.3.5) there is a risk that less visible parts of the model, particularly those without a direct impact on the budget, may not be updated regularly.

Updating the growth model is considerably more problematic. Since the model came to be used as a forecasting tool, it appears never to have been fully updated to include historical production data. In other words, projections for time t are extrapolated from a backward series of past projections rather than the observed figures produced by the statistics institute. The result is that the weights of each sector differ considerably between the official historical series and the forecast model. This generates obvious difficulties as regards the consistency and validity of the outputs.

Two further constraints can act against the full and timely updating of both the Quadro Macro and the growth model. First, government agencies can be slow to produce relevant data or, more confusingly, produce numerous versions of the same data over time. As there are only informal mechanisms to support such information transfers within the government, it is often the case that models include data which has been revised without the knowledge of the modelling agency. Second, data from different government agencies often are not harmonized and can differ significantly. This has been notably the case with figures for gross imports estimated by both the National Institute of Statistics (Instituto Nacional de Estatística, INE) and the Central Bank.

3.3.5 Formality

As might be expected in a low income country where formal modelling is at an early stage of development, the degree of formality in modelling practices is minimal. Perhaps most seriously, a clear definition does not exist of roles and responsibilities for the overall process of macro-fiscal management. It follows, therefore, that there are no clearly agreed (and hence documented) organizational processes which encompass the elaboration, use and finalization of outputs from quantitative models. Of course there is some informal delineation of responsibility, for example dividing budget and monetary policy issues between the Ministry of Finance and the Central Bank, respectively, but there is no formal clarity to this division and at best only weak mechanisms to ensure consistent dialogue and information flows between the various institutions, especially at the technical level.

An implication of the relatively *ad hoc* nature of macro-fiscal management, explored further in the next subsection, is that relevant government agencies are not formally allocated responsibility either to provide regular information to the *de facto* modelling agency or to participate in a review of possible scenarios before discussion with the IMF or presentation of final outputs at the ministerial level.[10] This situation has been aggravated since early 2005 by the splitting of the Ministry of Planning and Finance into two separate ministries, without an effective division of responsibilities for modelling activities. For example, while the Ministry of Finance is the main 'user' of the Quadro Macro in elaboration of the budget, the model itself remains housed in the Ministry of Planning and Development. Perhaps in response, the budget office of the Ministry of Finance recently established its own research unit, within which modelling activities are expected to take place.

In terms of model evaluation and revision, no formal processes have been put in place. This is particularly obvious in the case of the growth model, where, as mentioned, forecasts are extrapolated from earlier forecasts without the introduction of historical data. With respect to the Quadro Macro, Jones (Chapter 9) provides an initial contribution, undertaking a relatively comprehensive review of the quality of the forecasts of the model over an 11-year period to 2005. His analysis supports the need for regular model evaluation as well as efforts to deepen our technical understanding of the taxation base and the underlying dynamics of major tax revenue lines.

3.3.6 Use consistency

Finally, it is useful to consider how a given modelling framework is applied in the policy-making process. We have already noted that the Quadro Macro model directly informs elements of fiscal policy throughout the fiscal cycle. This includes setting indicative budget limits in the initial phase of the MTEF, as well as negotiation of the annual fiscal framework with the IMF. Consistent usage extends to implementation at lower (fiscal) levels; for example, the aggregate revenue targets stated in the Quadro Macro are dis-aggregated by the revenue collecting authorities to fix targets at the regional level. Finally, core macroeconomic variables from the same model, such as prices and growth, are inscribed in the government's annual Economic and Social Plan (Plano Económico e Social) as well as the various budget documents noted above.

Outside the fiscal arena, however, consistent usage of the modelling framework is less apparent, reflecting the informality noted above. For example, certain macroeconomic performance criteria are agreed with the IMF without reference to or alignment with the Quadro Macro model. This is most obvious in the case of the stock of international reserves, which, as noted above, is not specified as a target in the Quadro Macro but does appear as one of the key programme targets in the country's programme with the IMF. Indeed, the final output of the model resulting from the fiscal negotiations will often contain a forecast for international reserves which differs from the official target agreed between the Central Bank and the IMF.

The (aggregate) economic impact of proposed policy measures also frequently is not evaluated quantitatively. Moreover, due to weak intra-government communication, relevant new policy measures often are not reflected in the

Quadro Macro. By way of example one can refer to legislation passed in 2003 to provide import tax exemptions to large manufacturing firms.[11] The legislation was elaborated by the Ministry of Industry and Commerce and gives the same minister, as well as the Director of Customs, authority to give exemptions according to stipulated criteria. Prior to approval, we are not aware that any consistent analysis was undertaken of its potential fiscal or macroeconomic impact; to date no information or appropriate adjustment for revenue effects has been included in the fiscal projections Quadro Macro model. More recently, in 2006, the Customs authorities submitted different scenarios for import duty reductions for review by the Parliament. To the extent that any impact analysis was undertaken, the proposals were not elaborated with reference to the existing FP model or with support from the modelling agency. Furthermore, although changes to rates came into effect from 2007, the 2007 government budget proposal sent to Parliament at the same time made no adjustment for the effects of rate changes.

3.4 Reflections

The evaluation indicates an important distinction between the two models. The growth model cannot be seen as a policy tool in the sense that there are no targets and only weakly validated exogenous assumptions. In contrast, the Quadro Macro model has a stronger policy orientation with relatively clear applications and outputs, particularly on the fiscal side. At the same time, the weaknesses identified above undermine the policy effectiveness of the model. The shortcomings can be interpreted as symptoms of ambiguity concerning the objectives and policy use of the model, especially outside the fiscal sector. We recall that the model was developed primarily as a means to undertake fiscal projections and only recently has been enhanced to operate as a more complete multi-sector programming tool. However, these developments have not been accompanied by clarification or wider dissemination of the objectives and potential policy applicability of the revised model.

This evaluation should be put in perspective. Given the high benchmark suggested by the criteria, we have given more emphasis to negative aspects. As Tanzi (2004) remarks, however, it is not uncommon for economic policy-making to be only weakly informed by modelling tools in advanced countries. Thus, while there are evident weaknesses and gaps in the modelling framework, these should not obscure a recognition of valuable progress. Considerable strides have been made to improve macro-fiscal modelling in Mozambique and the government now boasts a functioning, broadly sound financial programming model (with additional tax detail) which is not dependent on foreign experts. In terms of immediate internal demand for modelling outputs, the model is 'fit for purpose'. Indeed, the technical staff of the IMF have been extremely positive towards and supportive of these improvements. These points suggests that in undertaking an evaluation it is necessary to place weights on the different assessment criteria in order to reflect local priorities. For Mozambique, model feasibility and technical consistency perhaps have been the most critical issues. This is likely to remain the case for the immediate future as basic model maintenance and capacity building must be assured.

Looking forward, three deeper factors may limit prospects for more substantial improvements in the modelling framework over the near term. First, general weaknesses in technical capacity at all levels of the government restrict both understanding and interest in quantitative models. Second, it can be argued that Mozambique's heavy reliance on external aid undermines both the political importance and *perceived* relevance of certain macro-fiscal management activities. While this is difficult to prove on aggregate, the continued existence of off-budget external funds as well as the absence of any coordinating aid strategy to inform the allocation of external funding certainly undermine the use-value of coordinating instruments. In this context the political necessity for sectors to fully engage in central negotiations is also weakened. Moreover, where external funding has a strong influence on policy changes, extended attempts at domestic policy formulation may be seen as futile. It follows that dispersed access to substantial external sources of funding can weaken the perceived need to coordinate policy-making and/ or undertake technical analysis via quantitative tools.

A third, related, issue is the fact that (short- and medium-term) targets for macro-fiscal indicators are agreed with the IMF.[12] These negotiations are relatively comprehensive, covering all sectors as well as the budget in detail. The scope and depth of the IMF's influence also may reduce the government's incentive to devote resources to developing a solid domestic policy stance as long as there is no reason to object to IMF-guided policies. On the contrary, there can be political benefits for the government to delegate key macro-fiscal decisions to the IMF, especially where such decisions involve sensitive trade-offs. It may be politically more attractive, for example, for the IMF to 'impose' a cap on government salary expenditure than for the government to negotiate an internal compromise. While further discussion of these complex political economy relationships goes beyond this chapter, we note that fiscal pressures connected to aid-financed expenditure are now generating challenging macro-fiscal management problems (for elaboration, see Arndt *et al.* 2007). We also observe that at the ministerial level there is limited negotiation of sectoral expenditure allocations, sector policy priorities or resource needs in a medium-term framework. In this sense there is some reliance on the IMF as a means to maintain a prudent macro-fiscal stance while avoiding political interference or potentially unmanageable internal debate. These factors suggest that weaknesses in macro-fiscal modelling practices are, at least in part, a reflection of deeper political economy dynamics. Thus changes in incentives at this deeper level will be critical to sustainable improvements in the modelling framework.

Over the medium term a number of modest improvements to the modelling framework should be possible. These follow from the above evaluation and might include: (1) simplification of the growth model; (2) development of a longer-term growth/resource needs analysis tool; (3) technical work to model major tax lines; and (4) enhanced consideration of recurrent cost implications of new investments. The latter suggestions indicate that more extensive modifications may necessitate the separation of the Quadro Macro model into an aggregate financial programming model and a more specific budget projections model. In any case, movements towards improved model definition and formalization can only be beneficial.

A final word can be said about prospects for developing a fully functional, detailed MTEF in Mozambique. We have shown that macro-fiscal management is informal, poorly coordinated and broadly reliant on IMF approval. As such, both incentives and formal mechanisms to agree coordinated domestic policies are weak. Quantitative budget estimation methods also remain rudimentary, being dependent on highly aggregate models and lacking details at the sector level. Combined with severe capacity limitations across government, it is difficult to envisage rapid sustainable progress towards a full MTEF involving extensive bottom-up budgeting and an iterative process of sectoral allocations. Rather, the analysis here would suggest modest goals are more appropriate, taking into account the feasibility of new instruments as well as the need to generate political space to negotiate expenditure trade-offs.

4 Conclusion

In response to a gap in the literature, this chapter has proposed a general framework for evaluating the strengths and weaknesses of practical macro-fiscal modelling approaches. Application to Mozambique has highlighted a range of strengths and weaknesses in local modelling practices, demonstrating the value of undertaking the exercise. The Mozambican approach consists, essentially, of a financial programming model with additional budget detail. This model is complemented by a simple production estimation tool based on detailed sectoral growth assumptions. Our assessment has highlighted important recent progress in improving the modelling framework from a low base. This has strengthened the feasibility, technical consistency and overall coherence of the financial programming model. At the same time, important shortcomings are evident in terms of the policy coverage and formal organization of modelling practices. In particular, the modelling framework lacks formal treatment of the interrelationships between growth, investment (allocation) and foreign aid. Definition of modelling responsibilities and its contribution to policy-making also remain weak.

More generally, however, we find that the state of modelling practices reflects deeper factors, including technical capacity limitations and the extent of political interest in technical, domestically owned policy formulation. This is not to say that attempts to improve models will be fruitless where political variables are unchanged. Rather, the message is that model development must be sensitive to the importance of simplicity, clarity, usability and long-term feasibility of our quantitative tools. Carefully designed simple models can play a part in enhancing policy awareness and stimulating policy debates. We believe efforts in this direction, opening space to think about policy trade-offs, would be beneficial for Mozambique.

Notes

1 One response to this problem has been a trend towards greater sophistication and complexity. This is evidenced by attempts to merge stabilization and growth frameworks into single integrated models (e.g. Khan *et al.* 1990); however, routine use of these models appears to be extremely limited (Tarp 1993).

2 For developed countries a number of studies describe the overall modelling framework employed (e.g. Pike and Savage 1998). Many fewer studies are available for developing countries, although model-specific studies are available (e.g. see the references in Economic Commission for Africa 2005; Oyugi 2005).

3 Uganda's development and use of a domestic FP model, for example, has enabled the government to shadow the IMF programme and, thereby, take a lead role in negotiations with the IMF (Houerou and Taliercio 2002).

4 For more general background on Mozambique, see Arndt *et al.* (2007).

5 These are known in Mozambique as the Lei de SISTAFE – Sistema de Administração Financeira do Estado – and its associated Regulamentos.

6 Note that the operations of the Central Bank do not feature in the discussion. This is mainly due to the extremely limited information available concerning its technical work.

7 As stated in the introduction (Section 1), we focus on models used regularly in policy-making rather than more irregular (one-off) modelling exercises undertaken to inform specific research questions.

8 Note that the development of PRSPs (or PARPAs) was one of the conditions for completion of the HIPC initiative.

9 For example, in recent years attempts have been made to quantify the salary impact of new recruits in the education and health sectors. However, these are *ad hoc* calculations and do not represent a comprehensive government salary model.

10 This problem was identified in 1998 by the technical assistance team supporting GEST and a proposal was made to institutionalize working groups (mainly in order to produce and finalize information prior to IMF negotiations). Evidently, however, these groups never became embedded.

11 This is via the Ministerial Diploma (Diploma Ministerial) 99/2003 of 13 August.

12 See Danninger (2005) for a broader discussion of the use of targets under IMF programmes.

9 Forecast quality

Sam Jones

1 Introduction

High quality fiscal projections can make a considerable contribution to public financial management and the achievement of social goals. Where budget forecasts are consistently misleading the overall efficiency and stability of government expenditures can be jeopardized and the credibility of public financial management systems may decline. Nevertheless, the practice of fiscal forecasting in low income developing countries has received relatively little research attention. This chapter breaks with this trend and reviews the quality of macroeconomic and revenue forecasts in Mozambique for the period 1995–2005. As such it provides an example of how forecast evaluations can be undertaken and illuminates some of the key factors which affect the forecasting environment in Mozambique.

Based on a unique dataset of forecasts and outcomes for both revenue and macroeconomic variables, the following questions are explored:

- What are the characteristics of the forecast errors?
- How have the forecast errors changed over time?
- How does the forecast model compare to a naive alternative forecast rule?
- What do the forecast errors tells us about the nature of the tax system?

The structure of this chapter is as follows. In Section 2 the relevant literature on fiscal forecasts in developing countries is reviewed. Section 3 presents the dataset and develops the analytical framework. Section 4 presents the results, including a simple description of the forecast errors (Section 4.1), their decomposition into component parts (Section 4.3), a formal review of their unbiasedness and efficiency (Section 4.2) and an analysis of their accuracy compared to a naive alternative forecasting model (Section 4.4). In Section 5 explanations of the observed trends in forecasts errors are explored, considering in particular the use of forecasts as normative targets. Section 6 concludes.

2 Background

The literature on forecast evaluation is extremely large and beyond the scope of this chapter. It is important to note, however, that the vast majority of

3.2 Forecast error definition

The evaluation of forecasts naturally focuses on the forecast error. For a given fiscal variable n_t, define the forecast error at time t as:

$$e_t = n_t^f - n_t^a \tag{1}$$

where superscript f denotes the forecast made at t-1 for the outcome at t, and a indicates the actual outcome value. As noted above, this is a simplified notation which ignores forecasts made over different horizons for the same period as these are not in focus here. With respect to the comparison of forecast errors both over time and across items, one must be sensitive to the choice of n. In the case of the macroeconomic variables (real GDP growth and inflation), the range of actual and forecast values in the data is relatively small and scale concerns are not an issue. Thus the relevant forecast errors refer to the difference in these rates expressed in percentage point terms. Revenue items are more problematic as in their nominal, local currency form they are non-stationary and not easily comparable across items. Moreover, nominal revenue forecasts often incorporate forecasts for other variables such as GDP and inflation.

Various responses to the above problem are encountered in the literature, such as the transformation of nominal revenue to a ratio of GDP (see, for example, Golosov and King 2002). For the purposes here, where different revenue lines are to be compared, none of these methods are unproblematic. As a result, it is useful to decompose the revenue variable into its component parts. Thus, define the observed nominal revenue at time t as:

$$n_t^a = n_{t-1}^a z_t^a p_t^a g_t^a \tag{2}$$

where p reflects the rate of inflation, g the real growth of output and z the overall elasticity of n to changes in nominal GDP, described here as the tax effort. The forecast for the same period is defined in exactly the same way, substituting the a superscripts for their forecast values for all variables other than the common base given by n_{t-1}^a. Second, taking natural logarithms and subtracting the forecast from the actual equations one gets:

$$e_t = (z_t^f - z_f^a) + (p_t^f - p_t^a) + (g_t^f - g_f^a) \tag{3}$$

where the parentheses on the right-hand side represent forecast errors in the tax effort, inflation and growth, respectively.

A number of aspects of this decomposition are of interest. First, from equation (2) it is trivial to calculate the individual tax effort measures (elasticities) for the forecast and actuals. This is useful as it permits a deeper analysis of collection behaviour; an effort (elasticity) equal to one (or 100 per cent) indicates nominal revenues adjust in line with nominal GDP, equivalent to an unchanged tax effort or a stable weight in GDP. Second, from (3) the tax effort error can be calculated, assuming it is the only unknown error component in the equation. This is the approach adopted for the analysis of revenue forecasts due to the desirable properties of the resulting errors – they are comparable across revenue lines, invariant to scale changes over time and cleansed of other observable errors. Third, the method emphasizes the extrapolative properties of revenue forecasts. Although this may not be appropriate in all countries, it is relevant for Mozambique as revenue forecasts employ a model of this form. Fourth, an assumption of the decomposition is that both the forecasts and actuals are extrapolated from the same base. In practice this does not always hold as forecasts are elaborated before the final value of n_{t-1}^a is known. As a result, the measure of the tax effort forecast error will incorporate any measurement noise. However, this unknown element can be treated as an integral part of the forecasters' problem and does not seriously undermine the validity of the approach. Finally, it should be stressed that z may be determined by a large number of intermediate variables, including tax policy instruments, the applicable tax base and administrative factors. Thus, any interpretation of movements in this measure must be undertaken with care.

3.3 Forecast evaluation

It is typical to review three distinct characteristics of forecast errors, namely their unbiasedness, efficiency and accuracy.[4] *Unbiasedness* holds when the expected value (mean) of the forecast error is equal to zero. Holden and Peel (1990) show that the preferred test for bias is a simple regression of the forecast error on a constant. Under the null of unbiasedness one expects to find the coefficient on the constant is equal to zero. For this test to be valid, however, the forecast errors should be approximately Gaussian. As this is by no means guaranteed, basic distributional tests on the forecast errors must be conducted in advance.

Efficiency refers to the full use of information available to the forecaster at the time of forecasting. This concept is discussed at length by Nordhaus (1987), who distinguishes between strong and weak forms of efficiency. While the former tends to focus on the full information set pertinent to the forecast, it is more typical to test for the latter via a simple regression of the current forecast error on its past values. For weak efficiency one expects to find no relationship between the dependent variable and the regressors:

$$e_t = \alpha + \beta_1 e_{t-1} \tag{4}$$

the point being that if a significant joint relationship is found, then, in principle, past forecasts could have been improved by an adjustment proportionate to β_1. Related to this test, two further issues can be highlighted. First, it is evident that equation (4) nests a test for unbiasedness, a main difference with a simple test being the reduction in statistical degrees of freedom due to an additional regressor. Second, the time series econometric literature distinguishes between different types of trend effects. Among these is a trend-stationary process, defined as a random walk around an underlying (linear) trend. This is relevant as there is no *a priori* reason to assume that any bias in the errors will be constant. Slow changes to the determinants of forecast quality, including political variables, may translate into forecast error trends. Thus, while equation (4) remains a sufficient test for weak efficiency, it does not distinguish between trended and non-trended inefficiency.

As a result, a general test for bias, trend effects and seriality in the forecast errors derives from a single regression of the form:

$$e_t = \alpha + \beta_1 e_{t-1} + \beta_2 t + \gamma Z_{t-1} \tag{5}$$

where Z_{t-1} is a vector of additional information available to the forecaster at time $t-1$ and therefore represents an expansion of the efficiency concept to information not contained in the lagged forecast errors. With regard to significance testing, simple parameter tests on the coefficients are appropriate to identify the source of any regularities in the forecast errors. Tests applied to the constant term, $\alpha = 0$, do not represent strict tests for bias (i.e. that $E(e_t) = 0$), but rather refer only to the bias remaining after adjusting for the effects of other variables.[5] Given that unbiasedness is a logically necessary condition for efficiency, an overall test for weak efficiency is given by the joint significance of the entire equation. Finally, although it is common in the literature to run tests for bias and weak efficiency via two separate regressions, a general specification is preferred for both analytical and econometric reasons. With respect to the latter, a 'complete' specification helps to reduce both omitted variable bias and the risk of spurious results arising from running a large number of regressions. Also, a general specification permits the analyst to distinguish between the separate (partial) influences of bias, serial correlation or trend effects that would not be evident from separate regressions.

Accuracy refers to the comparison of errors from two forecast models, namely the employed model and a naive alternative which only uses information from past observations. This evaluation is useful because the existence of bias and inefficiency does not necessarily imply that a simpler forecast model is to be preferred. A number of statistical measures have been proposed for this purpose and their properties have been reviewed extensively (for example see Hyndman and Koehler 2005). The approach employed here is based on Diebold and Mariano (1995) (hereafter DM). Their method is employed widely in the literature (e.g. Artis and Marcellino 2001), preferred for its focus on the statistical properties of the goodness-of-fit series generated by subtracting each naive forecast error from its non-naive (employed) counterpart according to a specified loss function. Thus, defining this loss function as $g(\cdot)$, the series of interest is calculated from $d_t = g(e_t^a) - g(e_t^b)$, where a and b respectively refer to the employed and naive forecast models. The formal DM measure is akin to a t-test applied to the series $\{d_t\}$, the main modification referring to the calculation of variance which adjusts for serial correlation in the series. However, as multiple forecast horizons are not in focus here, simple parametric t-tests can be used in place of the formal DM test, as long as $\{d_t\}$ is approximately Gaussian and free of other unwanted features. Even where this is not the case, other distribution-free approaches may be used, as discussed in Diebold and Mariano (1995).

For this study the above framework is applied for two loss functions: $g(e) = |e|$ and $g(e) = \ln(|e|)$. These are chosen as being most pertinent to the Mozambican context where our choice variables may exhibit substantial volatility arising from policy shifts, macroeconomic shocks or reliance on a poorly diversified tax base. As such, and in contrast to the more common use of a quadratic loss function, this does not give undue weight to large errors. The use of absolute error values indicates that it is only the size rather than the direction of the forecast errors that is of interest; while this may not be true for policy makers it represents our best prior in a Bayesian sense.

3.4 Time series cross-section considerations

Before moving to the presentation of results, it is necessary to reflect on the properties of the data from an econometric perspective. As the dataset contains both time series and cross-section (TSCS) elements one cannot assume all observations are identically and independently distributed either over time or contemporaneously. Rather, and for the revenue data in particular, it is reasonable to expect substantial contemporaneous correlation across the forecast errors given the common influence of macroeconomic variables as well as political pressures, notwithstanding the use of a common forecasting model. Our intended focus on the overall tax elasticity forecast error represents only a partial attempt to adjust for the contemporaneous impact of errors in the macroeconomic forecasts. Thus the meaningful application of any regression-based tests must not disregard TSCS econometric issues.[6]

Given the structure of the data it would not be appropriate or efficient to pool all observations, assuming common coefficients, or to run separate regressions for each of the choice variables. In contrast, in order to estimate equation (5) a full information approach, in the spirit of Zellner's (1962) Seemingly Unrelated Regression (SUR) technique, is necessary to provide unbiased and consistent estimates. For the macroeconomic variables and the revenue aggregates a standard SUR analysis is applied, incorporating different dependent and independent variables. For the disaggregated revenue items the same model applies to each line in cross-section; thus a general-to-specific approach is pursued. This involves, first, estimating a single general specification in which the slope and constant coefficients are permitted to vary for each line. On the basis of the results, groups of similarly behaved revenue lines can be identified and the model re-estimated employing these groups as pools. At each stage, Hansen tests for parameter stability (Hansen 1992) are used to verify the results. Finally, while there is some controversy regarding the best estimator for this kind of model, a Prais–Winsten panel-corrected estimator (PCSE) is used, which incorporates adjustments for the time series and cross-sectional properties of the data (e.g. see Blackwell 2005). This is preferred due to concerns that (alternative) feasible GLS estimators may underestimate the standard errors of the explanatory variables and thus over-play the significance of the results.[7]

4 Forecast error analysis

4.1 Description

To contextualize the analysis, Figure 9.1 shows trends in aggregate internal and external revenues as a percentage of GDP for the entire period. The rough equivalence of the two sources of income illustrates the weight of external financing in the government budget and, consequently, the importance of including these items in the analysis. Figures 9.2 and 9.3 plot the behaviour over time of the forecast errors for the aggregate variables, including both internal and external revenues. Three initial observations can be made. First, while external revenues as a percentage of GDP appear to have followed a relatively stable medium-term trend, changes in internal revenues can be divided into two periods – a period of consistent growth from 1996 to 2000, followed by an absence of any growth trend for 2000–5. Second, in both levels and forecast error terms, the dissimilar behaviour of internal and external revenues is noticeable, warning against a simplistic aggregation of these two revenue sources. Internal revenue forecast errors appear to follow a systematic trend; however, the errors for external revenues would seem to be a random walk. Finally, with respect to the two

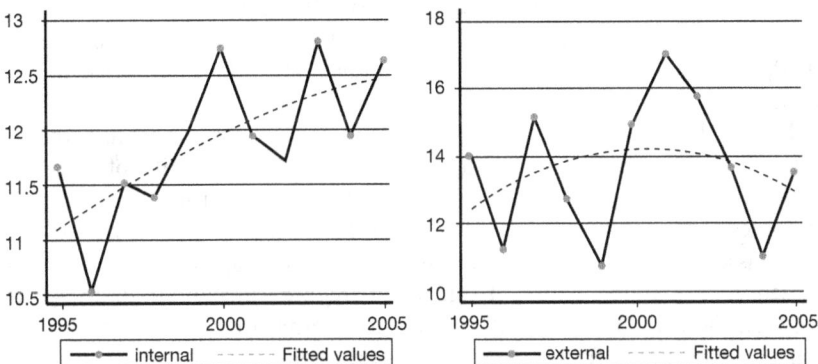

Figure 9.1 Total recorded revenues (% of GDP by internal and external sources)
Source: Government of Mozambique.

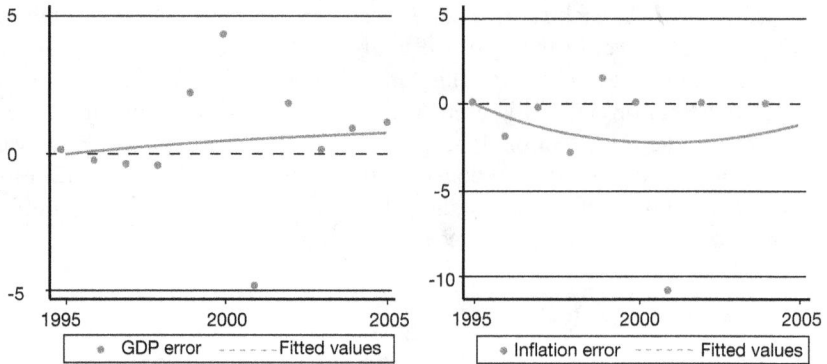

Figure 9.2 Scatter plots of real growth and inflation forecast errors (in percentage points)
Source: Government of Mozambique (various, see text), author's estimates.

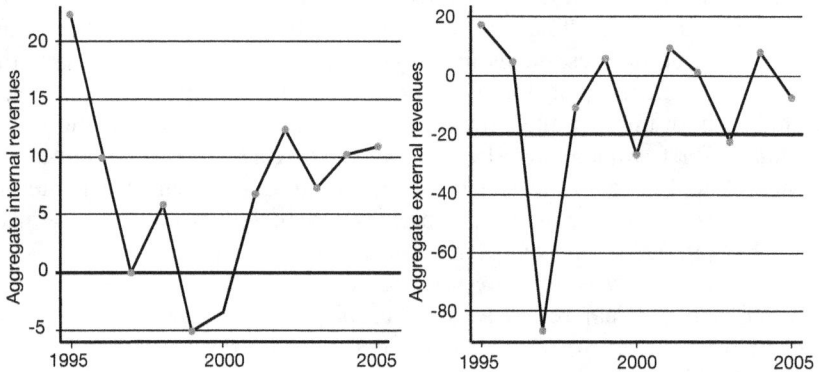

Figure 9.3 Tax ratio errors (total internal and external revenues)
Source: Government of Mozambique (various, see text), author's estimates.

macroeconomic variables the large error for 2001 can be explained (in part) by the unforeseen rapid economic recovery following catastrophic floods in 2000, the actual effect of which also is indicated in the GDP error for that year.

Table 9.1 provides a summary of the forecast errors, including the disaggregated external and internal revenue lines. The majority of errors are symmetric and approximately Gaussian. For those errors where the null hypothesis of normality can be rejected at the 5 per cent level or below this is often associated with a relatively large skewness measure, indicative of the presence of extreme values. Even so, there are substantial dissimilarities between the revenue lines. With respect to internal revenues, the mean error spans a wide range from a low of −4.71 per cent (income taxes) to a maximum of 24.53 per cent (other taxes). For external revenue lines the mean errors have opposite signs and their standard errors are comparatively large,

Table 9.1 Summary Forecast Errors

	N	Weight	Mean	SE	Skew	Kurtosis	P(norm)
GDP growth	11	–	0.40	0.68	–0.74	1.32	0.57
Inflation rate	11	–	–1.69	0.99	–2.13	3.76	0.00
Internal revenues	11	1.00	6.93	2.34	0.11	–0.25	0.57
VAT	11	0.34	6.49	2.16	–0.35	–1.19	0.15
income taxes	11	0.17	–4.71	3.44	–0.41	–0.68	0.74
luxury items tax	11	0.06	3.43	5.62	–0.44	–0.83	0.66
trade taxes	11	0.17	8.84	5.30	–0.12	–0.49	0.90
fuel taxes	11	0.10	7.82	4.99	1.24	0.91	0.06
excise taxes	11	0.04	15.08	7.29	0.71	–1.05	0.02
other taxes	11	0.04	24.53	14.50	–0.23	0.50	0.42
non-tax income	11	0.08	12.88	8.82	–0.05	–0.68	0.48
Pooled (unweighted)	88	1.00	9.30	2.66	0.72	3.68	0.00
External finance	11	1.00	–9.99	8.67	–1.84	2.68	0.00
grants	11	0.66	–14.90	9.09	–0.98	–0.26	0.08
credits	11	0.33	6.66	14.00	–1.10	1.54	0.17
Pooled (unweighted)	22	1.00	–4.12	8.48	–0.70	0.98	0.15

Note: N gives the number of observations; Weight is the average actual contribution of each revenue line to total revenues during the period; Mean is the forecast error (multiplied by 100); SE refers to the standard error of the mean; P(norm) gives the probability of falsely rejecting the null hypothesis that the variable is normally distributed based on the Shapiro-Wilks test.
Source: Government of Mozambique (various, see text), author's estimates

being greater than the mean in the case of credits. Thus, while it appears valid to apply the econometric methodology outlined above, one needs to be sensitive to the influence of extreme values and due care must be taken with regard to the cross-sectional nature of the data.

4.2 Bias and efficiency

Based on the techniques described in Sections 3.3 and 3.4, it is possible to formally analyse the characteristics of the forecast errors. Starting with the aggregate variables, a SUR of the form given by equation (5) is employed, adding a dummy variable to account for the effects of the shock recovery in 2001. The results, summarized in Table 9.2, confirm a number of the findings suggested above. First, after adjusting for the effects of the other regressors, the two macroeconomic variables are found to be biased in an optimistic direction – the average downward bias of the inflation forecasts being around 1.25 percentage points, while real growth forecasts are biased upwards by approximately 1 percentage point. In addition, the inflation forecast errors are serially correlated, the negative sign here reflecting the direction of bias. The overall explanatory power of the regressions for these variables is good

Table 9.2 Forecast Efficiency (aggregate variables, SUR results)

	Inflation	Growth	Internal	External
Constant	−1.23	0.96	2.02	−17.75
	(0.40)***	(0.46)**	(1.69)	(8.59)**
Lagged error	−0.21	−0.03	0.37	−0.15
	(0.07)***	(0.21)	(0.11)***	(0.26)
Trend	−0.02	0.12	1.01	3.17
	(0.13)	(0.15)	(0.47)**	(2.73)
Year 2001	−9.60	−5.85	4.99	19.90
	(1.20)***	(1.70)***	(4.67)	(26.39)
F	26.71	5.96	4.67	0.81
R^2	0.87	0.64	0.47	0.20
N	10	10	10	10

* p<.1, ** p<.05, *** p<.01; standard errors in parentheses
Note: columns refer to the results from the SUR in which the title variable is the regressand; model is as described in the text.
Source: Government of Mozambique (various, see text), author's estimates

($R^2 = 87.3\%$ for inflation; and $R^2 = 63.7\%$ for real growth), testifying to the systematic nature of these errors despite the small sample size.

The results of the SUR for the aggregate revenue variables are also insightful, but moderately less strong. For total external financing, there is some evidence of an underlying negative bias but this cannot be relied upon as the overall specification is not significant. For internal revenues on the other hand, and despite no evidence of a fixed level of bias throughout the period, the positive time trend on the errors indicates they have been increasing in size by an average of one unit (0.01) per year. These forecasts also are serially correlated and do not pass the overall test for weak efficiency; i.e. at the 5 per cent level the null hypothesis that all parameters are zero can be rejected. It follows that improved forecasts could have been made by better incorporating available information.

Turning to the component revenue lines, a full general specification, as described in Section 3.4, supports the contention that there are important dissimilarities across revenue lines such that pooling all internal and external revenues, either separately or jointly, is not advisable. Note the specification includes a dummy for 2001 as well as lagged forecast errors of the macro-economic variables to capture other information available to the forecaster. Due to the large number of regressors, however, these latter variables do not enter the respective SUR equation for each revenue line; rather they enter as separate regressions in the SUR system as a whole. Even so, the coefficients on these terms are allowed to vary according to the two-period division described above. Table 9.3 summarizes the results, showing for each variable only the values of those coefficients for the bias, trend and serial correlation terms of equation (5) which are significant at the 10 per cent level. The table

Table 9.3 Forecast Efficiency (forecast errors for disaggregated revenue lines, summary of unrestricted SUR)

	Bias	Trend	Seriality	Joint
VAT	19.27	4.43	–0.92	0.00
income taxes	–	5.30	–	0.00
luxury taxes	9.89	7.73	–0.48	0.00
trade taxes	13.88	–	–	0.00
fuel taxes	18.25	–	–	0.00
excise taxes	22.71	–4.17	–	0.00
other taxes	24.18	–	–	0.00
non-tax income	17.86	5.17	–	0.00
lag inflation error, '00-05	5.81	–	–	0.00
lag growth error, '95-99	26.38	–	–	0.04
lag growth error, '00-05	–12.24	–	–	0.00
Year 2001	40.9	–	–	0.00
R^2				0.55
N				94

Note: forecast error is the regressand; columns 'bias', 'trend' and 'seriality' give the coefficients on these regressors for each revenue line in the model; 'joint' gives the joint probability that all coefficients are equal to zero; model is as described in the text; only results significant at 10 per cent level shown.
Source: Government of Mozambique (various, see text), author's estimates.

also states the probability that these coefficients are jointly equal to zero, giving the overall test for weak efficiency.

Excluding the effects of the macro variables, the two external financing lines are absent from the table as no consistent pattern is found, meaning that the forecasts for these lines cannot be deemed to be inefficient. In contrast, all the internal revenue line forecast errors show some form of systematic, significant tendency and in no case can one accept the null hypothesis of weak forecast efficiency. A strong result is the significant positive bias across all revenue lines excluding income taxes (this is after adjusting for any trend and serial correlation effects)[8]. Bias ranges from approximately 10 per cent (luxury items) to over 20 per cent for excise taxes and the group of small unclassified taxes. Evidence for trend or serial correlation is not consistent across internal revenue lines; however, there is clear evidence of an upward linear time trend for three core domestic taxes which, together, represent well over one half of total internal revenues (VAT, income and luxury goods taxes). In contrast, excise taxes show a declining trend, perhaps evidence of a forecast-response to the large forecast errors of the early part of the period (depicted in Figure 9.4). There is no evidence for consistent serial correlation across the revenue lines, this being restricted only to VAT and luxury goods.

Table 9.3 also shows significant coefficients on the lagged macroeconomic variables. While this finding is explored further in Section 5, at this point it is

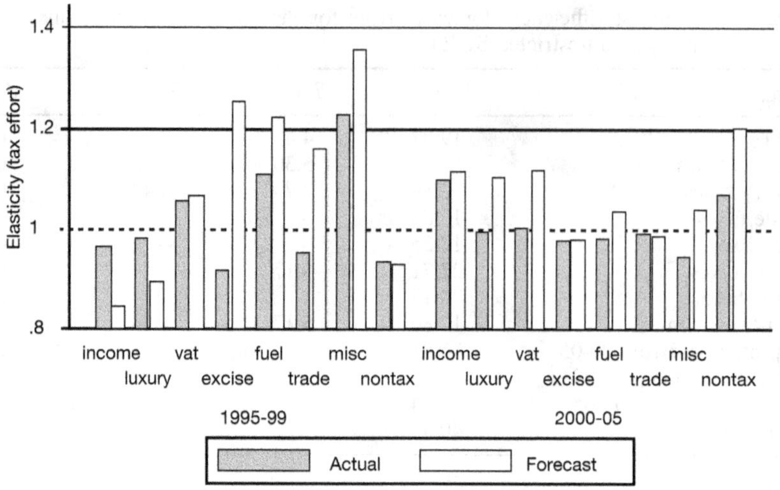

Figure 9.4 Actual and forecast tax elasticities (internal revenue line and period)
Source: Government of Mozambique (various, see text), author's estimates.

sufficient to note that the partial correlation of the tax elasticity with these lagged errors is particularly marked in the second period, running in the opposite direction to the mean error of the variables themselves. In other words, while the real growth forecast errors are positive on average, the coefficient in the SUR specification is negative – meaning that a one unit increase (improvement) in the growth error in the previous period is associated with an average 12.2 percentage point reduction in the predicted elasticity forecast error in the current period. Of course, one might question the assumption of a common coefficient across all revenue lines for these macroeconomic regressors. Hansen tests for parameter stability, however, indicate one cannot reject the null hypothesis that the results are stable across different sub-samples of the data. This finding also extends to all other variables as well the specification as a whole.[9]

Tests for parameter equality across the revenue lines suggest a more parsimonious, reduced-form specification can be used as compared to the general SUR. This is useful not only from the point of view of reducing the number of regressors, thus increasing the overall degrees of freedom, but also to identify common trends across groups of revenue lines. Tests identify four broad groups of similarly behaved revenues: (1) core domestic taxes (VAT, income and luxury goods taxes); (2) taxes at the border; (3) other taxes and non tax income; and (4) external financing items. Due to the weak findings as regards the serial correlation term, the reduced specification restricts the slope on this term to be equal across all revenue groups.[10] The results of this parsimonious specification are shown in Table 9.4; as expected, they do not present anything substantially new but rather summarize and affirm our previous results. Of note is the significant negative slope coefficient on the border-related group of taxes, suggesting that as a group these errors have followed a declining trend during the period. The overall strength of the regression ($R^2 = 47\%$) underlines the broad finding that forecast errors for the internal revenue lines are not efficient but rather contain persistent levels of bias, show time-trend effects and do not fully incorporate information available at the time of forecasting. Finally, the validity of this specification is

Table 9.4 Forecast Efficiency (revenues, restricted SUR model results)

	PCSE	FGLS
Lag forecast error	0.13	0.23
	(0.07)*	(0.04)***
Bias g1	8.43	11.72
	(2.93)***	(1.79)***
Bias g2	17.52	16.75
	(3.78)***	(1.81)***
Bias g3	14.78	15.04
	(4.68)***	(3.02)***
Bias g4	0.15	−1.23
	(6.00)	(2.64)
Trend g1	4.12	3.86
	(0.75)***	(0.42)***
Trend g2	−2.41	−2.30
	(0.92)***	(0.52)***
Trend g3	2.44	3.15
	(1.17)**	(0.96)***
Trend g4	1.88	3.70
	(1.82)	(0.86)***
Lag growth error, '95-99	10.12	−5.41
	(9.86)	(4.01)
Lag growth error, '00-05	−10.90	−10.06
	(2.53)***	(1.10)***
Lag inflation error, '95-99	2.91	8.92
	(1.68)*	(0.78)***
Lag inflation error, '00-05	5.02	4.93
	(1.48)***	(0.63)***
Year 2001	39.60	38.07
	(8.88)***	(3.85)***
R^2	0.47	−
Wald χ^2	153.53	1244.56
N	94	100

* p<.1, ** p<.05, *** p<.01; standard errors in parentheses
Notes: forecast error is the regressand; restricted SUR specification as described in the text; pools of revenue lines are denoted by: g1 (VAT, income and luxury taxes), g2 (border taxes), g3 (all other internal revenues), and g4 (external revenue items); PCSE and FGLS denote panel-corrected standard errors and feasible generalized least squares estimators respectively, both of which adjust for the time-series cross-sectional nature of the data; FGLS includes outliers.
Source: Government of Mozambique (various, see text), author's estimates

supported by Hansen tests – for none of the coefficients can the null of stability be rejected, either individually or jointly.

4.3 Decomposition

The error decomposition technique described in Section 4.3 can be used to further explore the forecast errors. Figure 9.4 compares the mean actual and forecast tax elasticities (efforts) for each internal revenue line across two sub-periods (1995–9 and 2000–5). Aside from the evident difference between the (mean) tax elasticity forecast versus the actual value, an important result is the reduction in variation across the lines between the two periods for both forecast and actual values. The plot for the second period has a flatter topography, suggesting that both the tax system and the forecast errors have come to behave in a more stable or regular fashion over time.

Further evidence for a stabilization effect is given by changes in the pooled distributions of the forecast and actual tax elasticities. As shown in Figure 9.5 both distributions show a general tightening (sharpening) between sub-periods, with a much more pronounced change in the distribution of forecast elasticities. In light of the persistence of forecast errors throughout the two periods, it follows that the more recent forecast errors derive from a more systematic error generating process than those of the first sub-period. It is also of interest that the actual tax elasticity measures are distributed around a mean (and median) of approximately one for both periods. For both aggregate and individual revenue lines, statistical tests reveal that one cannot reject the hypothesis that, on average, the tax elasticity is equal to one. This is indicative of long-term stability (inertia) in the actual tax system and confirms the point that measured forecast errors derive from the forecast component as compared to erratic actual behaviour.[11]

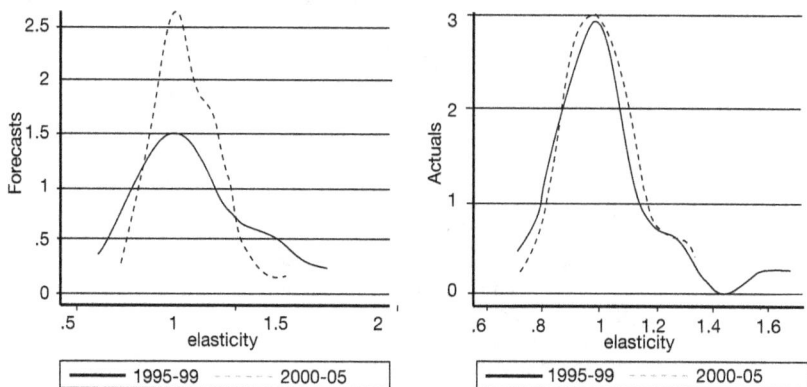

Figure 9.5 Kernel densities (pooled actual and forecast tax elasticities by period, internal revenues only)
Source: Government of Mozambique (various, see text), author's estimates.

4.4 Accuracy

The final analytical step refers to the accuracy of the forecasts, answering the question whether a naive forecast model could have outperformed the employed forecasts. As described in Section 4.4, the first step is to calculate and review the goodness-of-fit series based on a specified loss function. Note that while a large number of naive models might be used, for simplicity the naive forecast is defined as the value observed in the last period; for the revenue lines, therefore, this refers to the tax effort.

The goodness of fit calculated using the absolute loss function is analytically messy and unsuitable for parametric analysis. This derives from the existence of a small but not insignificant number of larger forecast errors. As a result, the non-parametric Wilcoxon (matched-pairs) signed-ranks test (see Siegel 1956) can be used to investigate whether the median difference between the employed and naive forecast errors is equal to zero. With respect to each of the variables in the dataset, the only significant result from this exercise is for real growth. This shows a significant negative mean difference, meaning that the employed forecast consistently outperforms the naive model; in other words, the employed growth forecasts have been more accurate than a martingale strategy. For all other variables, the performance of the employed and naive models is indistinguishable at the 5 per cent significance level (two tailed).

The logarithmic loss function generates a goodness-of-fit series which is approximately normal both across revenue lines and on a pooled basis. As a result, a standard t-test can be applied meaningfully, as discussed in Section 3.3. Figure 9.6 plots the pooled distribution of this series for all revenue items, distinguishing between the first and second sub-periods. The vertical lines represent the interval within which one can expect to find at least 75 per cent of all observations regardless of the distribution, based on Chebyshev's inequality (Abramowitz and Stegun 1972). This interval is also approximate to the 95 per cent confidence interval associated with a student's t-distribution. Whatever the benchmark adopted, the vast majority of observations fall within the confidence interval, suggesting there is no robust statistical difference between the employed and naive tax effort forecasts either between the two periods or across lines. In fact, the sharper distribution for the second period signifies that despite reduced variation of the mean actual tax elasticities across lines in the second period (see Figure 9.4), there has been no corresponding improvement in forecast accuracy vis-à-vis the naive model; rather, the tighter distribution indicates the very opposite is the case. This confirms the argument that despite reduced variation in tax effort (both forecast and actual), a corresponding improvement in forecast quality has not materialized.

Continuing with the same loss function, Figure 9.7 plots the relevant t-statistic (based on the logarithmic loss goodness-of-fit series) for each revenue line over the entire period. This provides no substantially new information compared to the tests for the absolute loss function, but at least confirms the consistency of the results. It can be pointed out, however, that the majority of the t-statistics for internal revenues are greater than zero, indicative of a marginally but not significantly better performance of the naive model in most cases. The significance of the t-statistics for the macroeconomic variables confirms the previous result for real growth; however, the statistic for inflation is now also found to be negative and significantly different from

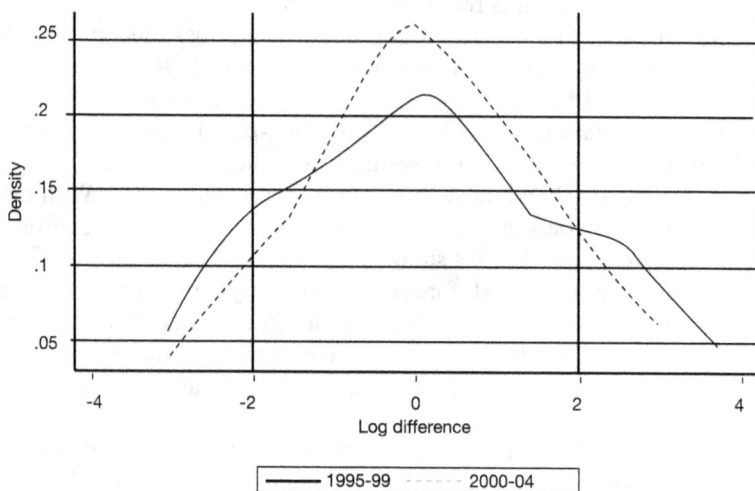

Figure 9.6 Distribution of logarithmic loss function (goodness-of-fit series by period)
Source: Government of Mozambique (various, see text), author's estimates.

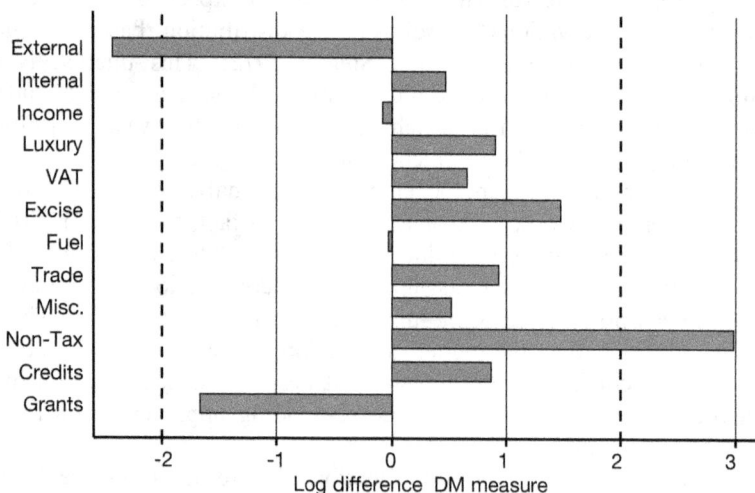

Figure 9.7 Individual t-statistics for logarithmic loss function (by revenue line)
Source: Government of Mozambique (various, see text), author's estimates.

zero at the 10 per cent confidence level (two tailed). The overall message, therefore, is that only forecasts for the macroeconomic variables appear to broadly outperform a simple martingale strategy. Of course this does not mean that our forecast model outperforms the hypothetical set of all naive models. For example, when real growth is volatile around a stable central tendency, an arguably better prior is not the last period's value, as tested here, but rather a long-term average. Indeed, it is simple to verify that an alternative naive forecast rule, which posits that real growth will always be 7 per cent, significantly outperforms the employed growth forecasts (based on the absolute loss function tested via the Wilcoxon signed-ranks test).

5 Explanations

The previous sections have analysed the characteristics of the forecast errors over time. While a comprehensive discussion of the underlying causes of the identified regularities is beyond the scope of this chapter, some important lines of argument can be sketched. Following the discussion in Section 2, the distinction between technical and normative influences on the forecasting process is important. From a technical perspective it is clear that instability in the economic environment, as well as structural changes or shocks, can undermine the quality of forecasts. Improvements in environmental factors of this kind certainly help to explain the reduced variation in tax elasticities over the period, as well as the observed trends in the tax effort errors for certain revenue lines. As described elsewhere (Arndt *et al.* 2007), the mid-1990s were characterized by substantial and strategic public sector reforms, including privatizations and the streamlining and eventual independence of the Central Bank. Since 1997 a programme of public financial management reforms has been implemented, focusing on the quality, coverage and transparency of the government budget. The enhanced predictability of the macroeconomic environment, rationalization of government intervention in the economy and the more prominent role given to fiscal planning during this period are likely to be valid explanations of the relative stabilization, including the reduction of extreme errors in revenue forecasts as shown in Figure 9.4. The enhanced predictability of the exchange rate, as well as an ongoing programme of customs reforms, including trade liberalization, also represents plausible explanations for the trend reduction in forecast errors of border-related taxes compared to other domestic revenues.

Working in the opposite direction, similar arguments can be employed to explain the trend increase in forecast errors for major internal taxes. During the period under analysis these tax instruments underwent substantial reform – namely, the replacement of a cascading sales tax by value-added taxation (VAT) in 1999 and the implementation of a radically revised income taxation code from 2002 (see Chapter 2).[12] Not only do major tax policy reforms often take time to 'bed in', but forecasters also may have difficulty in the absence of historical data on collections or knowledge of the effective (new) tax base. With respect to income taxes, for example, the reforms appear to have been broadly positive as estimates of the actual collection effort have risen to over one (see Figure 9.4), meaning that collections are now growing faster than real output. Even so, the forecast errors for these taxes have switched from being trend negative in the first period to being trend positive in the second, perhaps evidence that forecasters do not have a detailed understanding of these new taxes.

Although insightful, the latter arguments do not give a convincing explanation for the optimistic bias of the forecasts. Rather, they point towards the effect of expectations or normative influences. At least superficially, such normative forces would appear to be at work given the nature of the forecasting process. Projections incorporated in the government's annual budget cannot be considered *pure* technical estimates as they are the outcome of both internal political processes and discussions with the IMF. As such, forecasts are consistent with fulfilment of the applicable IMF programmes, which repeatedly have stressed the need for increases in domestic revenue as a percentage of GDP (e.g. IMF 2005b). Other government documents also manifest this conflation of normative targets and technical forecasts. For example, the macroeconomic position taken in the government's first poverty reduction strategy paper (GoM 2001) emphasizes the objective of reducing dependence on external revenues via growth in the tax ratio from 12.4 per cent in 2000 to 15.4 per cent by the end of 2005, or an average annual increment of 0.6 percentage points. As shown in Figure 9.1, since 2000 the domestic revenue ratio has oscillated around a mean of 12.3 per cent of GDP with no robust growth trend. However, this has not engendered any major revision of expectations – the second strategy paper (GoM 2006) projects growth in domestic revenues of around 0.5 percentage points per year for the period 2005–9.

In light of the above, the motivation for persisting with optimistic forecasts needs to be uncovered. Taking the principal-agent framework proposed by Danninger (2005) (see also Danninger *et al.* 2005), one hypothesis is that (high) targets are used to influence collection effort when the true effort of the collection agency cannot be fully controlled by its principal. On the assumption that revenue shortfalls are somewhat costly to the agent, optimistic or overstated targets will be employed as long as the benefits of higher collection surpass the costs to the principal of overstated budgets. Recalling that revenue forecasts in Mozambique are the outcome of negotiations with the IMF, it can be assumed for simplicity that the agent is the government and the (final) principal is the IMF.[13] From this perspective, there are various costs to the government of failing to meet the revenue target, including jeopardizing the country's relationship with the IMF.

In order to examine these issues, the relationship between the actual and forecast tax effort measures, as well as other proximate variables which may affect collection performance, comes into focus. The null hypothesis, incompatible with a principal–agent dynamic, is that the actual level of collection effort is uncorrelated with both its forecast and other strategic variables. This rests on the previous findings of substantial stability in the actual tax effort (elasticity) and persistently optimistic forecast errors. To test this hypothesis the actual effort is regressed on its forecast, controlling for the previous period actual effort as well as current macroeconomic conditions; formally:

$$z_t^a = \alpha_t + z_t^f + z_{t-1}^a + p_t + g_t + t \tag{6}$$

where z^f and z^a are the forecast and actual levels of tax effort, p the (change) in prices for the period, g real growth, t time and α a constant. Note that inclusion of the macroeconomic variables, as well as the time trend, reflects earlier results concerning the influence of these factors on revenue forecast errors. The model is estimated for internal revenues only, allowing the slope coefficients on the forecast effort regressor to vary for each of the revenue groups identified in Section 4.2. The panel-based estimator discussed in Section 3.4 is applied once again (although the feasible GLS estimator is also used for comparison).

The results, summarized in Table 9.5, indicate that approximately 80 per cent of the variation in actual tax elasticity (effort) is explained by the model. Hansen tests for parameter stability confirm the validity of the results despite the partial pooling applied. Importantly, the positive and significant coefficients on the forecast effort suggests there is a positive association between forecast and actual tax effort across revenue lines and over time. Although a simple interpretation of this result would be that the forecasts are accurate, this can be rejected on the basis of previous analysis. Indeed, it is precisely the combination of these results alongside persistent forecast optimism that is highly suggestive of the employment of forecasts-as-targets. Integral to this interpretation, which runs against the null hypothesis, is the fact that the coefficients on the forecast effort regressors are positive but less than one (≈ 0.3), showing only a partial (imperfect) effect of the forecasts on collection effort.

Results for the other regressors in the model confirm that the agent retains a considerable degree of strategic flexibility in his or her choice of behaviour. First, the absence of a significant relationship between the current tax effort and its lagged value indicates the absence of longer-term (unexplained) determinants of actual tax effort. The coefficients for the macroeconomic variables demonstrate that when the macroeconomic environment is conducive to a higher nominal tax take, via high inflation or robust output growth, the tax effort falls. This reading is particularly apposite as the Mozambican tax authorities employ nominal revenue targets (stated in the budget) to monitor their progress. Thus high levels of real growth and/or inflation enable these targets to be met passively, without extra effort. In summary, the results provide convincing support for the proposition that revenue targets are employed to influence taxation effort, but that the collection agency retains considerable flexibility in its choice of final effort. Of course, this is not the only possible explanation of the relationships in the

Table 9.5 Determinants of Tax Effort (internal revenue lines only)

	PCSE	*FGLS*
Forecast effort, g1	0.33	0.31
	(0.07)***	(0.07)***
Forecast effort, g2	0.31	0.27
	(0.07)***	(0.07)***
Forecast effort, g3	0.31	0.29
	(0.07)***	(0.07)***
Lag actual tax effort	0.10	0.07
	(0.12)	(0.08)
Growth	−0.91	−1.00
	(0.33)***	(0.39)***
Inflation	−0.46	−0.46
	(0.09)***	(0.10)***
Trend	−0.01	−0.01
	(0.00)***	(0.00)***
Constant	2.07	2.23
	(0.42)***	(0.47)***
R^2	0.79	–
χ^2	42.72	46.65
N	80	80

* $p<.1$, ** $p<.05$, *** $p<.01$; standard errors in parentheses
Notes: actual tax effort is the regressand; pools of revenue lines are denoted by: g1 (VAT, income and luxury taxes), g2 (border taxes), and g3 (all other internal revenues); PCSE and FGLS indicate panel corrected standard errors and feasible generalized least squares estimators respectively, both of which adjust for the time-series cross-sectional nature of the data.
Source: Government of Mozambique (various, see text), author's estimates

data. However, this thesis represents a highly intuitive explanation of the characteristics of the forecast errors.

It remains pertinent to ask whether this is the best possible strategy to stimulate collection effort. From a theoretical position (Danninger 2005), there is no doubt that mechanisms of this kind are second best (at most) given that they do not fully internalize the principal–agent problem. This is proven in this instance by the remaining strategic behaviour of the agent. The very absence of sustained growth in the domestic revenue ratio and the negative coefficient on the time-trend regressor also supports this view. However, it has been shown that the use of *nominal* targets enables the agent to choose his or her effort depending on macroeconomic fluctuations. This suggests that simple modifications to revenue targets could at least reduce some elements of strategic behaviour. Even so, it may be the case that the use of forecasts-as-targets suffers from a rational expectations critique – knowing that the forecasts are deliberately optimistic, the agent has no incentive to fully meet the targets and they lose effectiveness. This also may be behind the negative coefficient on the time-trend regressor.

According to the above framework, optimistic targets will be applied as long as the benefits outweigh the costs from the principal's point of view. This says nothing of the aggregate social costs of optimistic targets, which may be significant. These include undermining the efficiency and quality of government services, as well as the credibility of the overall budget process. In addition, where normative factors dominate the forecasting process, technical contributions may be undervalued, which, in turn, weakens their influence on fiscal decisions. While these points cannot be developed here, the assumption that the principal is an external actor, as opposed to the general public, would be compatible with a failure to take these wider costs into account.

A final issue refers to *how* improved forecasting might be achieved without prejudicing taxation effort. On the one hand, mechanisms which separate technical forecasts from normative targets may be useful. These might include formal forecasting rules which limit the scope of normative inter-ferences. On the other hand, a valuable contribution may come from efforts to develop a consensus view among all key actors, including the private sector, as to realistic medium-term macroeconomic and fiscal projections. According to the analysis in Chapter 5, Mozambique's domestic taxation performance is neither an outlier nor is it far below its expected level in comparative terms. If this is broadly correct, then harmonization of medium-term taxation expectations around such a view could reduce short-term pressures on revenue forecasts.

6 Conclusion

This study has undertaken a careful review of the quality of government fiscal forecasts in Mozambique, focusing on revenue forecasts in parti-cular. A methodological toolkit has been presented and its considerable practical value demonstrated. Persistent forecast bias in an optimistic direc-tion has been found to affect all major variables, excluding external revenues. There is also robust evidence for an upward time trend in the forecast errors for core domestic revenue lines. Despite enhanced macroeconomic and fiscal stability, neither revenue nor macroeconomic forecasts have shown any marked improvement overall. In turn this suggests that forecast errors derive from a more systematic process than in the past. Differences in forecast performance across revenue lines and over time, however, suggest the need to develop a more sophisticated understanding of the dynamics of individual tax instruments. This is especially important for larger revenue lines, such as VAT and income taxes, which have experienced policy reforms during the period.

It has been argued that government forecasts are not pure unconditional expectations but can be influenced by normative considerations. As such, persistent optimistic forecast bias may be explained by political pressure to realize sustained growth in the tax ratio and/or the desire to sustain an image of effective macroeconomic and fiscal management. With respect to revenue behaviour, the analysis provides strong evidence of a principal–agent problem in which optimistic nominal targets are employed to induce a higher collection effort. However, this does not appear to be wholly effective in light of the continued flexibility of the collection agency to choose his final effort. Moreover, this approach may undervalue the social costs of inferior budget credibility and execution efficiency arising from overstated forecasts. In response, alternative mechanisms are required both to stimulate strong collection performance and to reinforce budget quality. Further consideration should be given to actions which separate technical and normative forecasts in government planning, possibly by adopting formal forecast rules.

Notes

1 The focus of this study must be distinguished from research into the impact of IMF and World Bank programmes in developing countries. While this research often has an interest in the plausibility of macroeconomic forecasts (expectations) associated with adjustment programmes, they are not motivated by an explicit interest in the practice of forecasting *per se*.

2 The internal revenue lines are: income taxes (personal and corporate combined), VAT (internal and external), import duties, excise duties, taxes on luxury goods, fuel tax, other taxes and non-tax revenues; the external financing items are split between grants and credits.

3 A remark should be made about budget revisions. In certain years stated budget targets can become misleading and even unhelpful due to unexpected changes and/or errors in the original budget. In extreme cases this necessitates a formal revision, which, for the period under analysis, occurred in Mozambique in 2001. Given the magnitude of the revisions to the revenue forecasts made at this time, the dataset uses the revised as opposed to original figures. For all other years original budget figures are used.

4 It is beyond the scope of this chapter to discuss evaluation methodologies. For an overview, see Schuh (2001) and the contributions in Hendry and Ericsson (2001).

5 For further discussion, see Barrionuevo (1992). Note that bias is tested after the effect of any trend; to ensure average bias is captured, the trend variable is zero for the mid-point in the series.

6 For a discussion of these, see Beck (2001).

7 All estimations are implemented in Stata via either the *sureg* or *xtpcse* commands.

8 See note 5.

9 According to Hansen (1992), one can reject at the 5 per cent level the null hypothesis of parameter stability for those individual coefficients for which the given (L) statistic exceeds 0.47. For the macro variables in the SUR general specification the largest L statistic is 0.133, relating to the second period real growth error; for the specification as a whole the joint L statistic is 1.618, which with 36 degrees of freedom cannot be taken as indicative of instability at any reasonable confidence level.

10 From the general specification, a Wald test for equality of the serial correlation slope coefficients across revenue lines gives a chi square statistic of 23.6, meaning one cannot reject the null hypothesis of equality at the 0.5 per cent significance level.

11 This result derives from a simple regression of the actual tax elasticity on a constant plus dummies for each revenue line (internal only).

12 In the previous analysis no distinction is made between the sales and VAT tax as the latter simply replaced the former. Thus data for the sales tax are incorporated within the VAT line.

13 Note that this is an alternative to the principal–agent model outlined in Danninger (2005), where the principal is defined as the central government and the agent a semi-autonomous revenue collection authority.

Part III

Taxation at the border

10 Transmission of prices from the border to domestic markets

Xavier Cirera and Virgulino Nhate

1 Introduction

Mozambique has carried out significant trade liberalization in the last twenty years and is currently engaged in a process of tariff phase-down with its main trade partners under the SADC agreement. The main objective of this liberalization process is to increase Mozambique's economic integration with its regional partners and with the global economy. But are the potential gains from this trade liberalization process accruing to the Mozambican economy? Is the Mozambican economy becoming more integrated regionally and globally?

Obviously the answer depends on a large number of factors, such as the elimination of non-tariff barriers, the business and investment climate or the elimination of the significant constraints on domestic supply capacity. In this chapter, however, we focus on another, perhaps more simple, but equally important, factor for economic integration: the degree of border price transmission.

The degree of economic integration between countries depends on how well markets function and how well price signals are transmitted from one country to the other. Thus two countries are well integrated if price signals are correctly transmitted. This implies that producers and consumers adjust production and consumption decisions in response to existing excess supply/ demand conditions in other locations of the integrated area. As a result, integration is potentially welfare improving, since it implies a more efficient allocation of resources and higher consumption possibilities.

Trade reform, multilateral or regional, aims to eliminate restrictions to trade flows. In the absence of good price transmission from the border, price signals after trade reform may be imperfectly transmitted to the economy, jeopardizing the potential benefits in terms of resource allocation and higher consumption possibilities described above. For example, in the case of no border price transmission due to a monopolistic distribution sector, the price of imports may not be significantly reduced and the economy may not experience any significant increase in competition following trade reform.

The aim of this chapter is to assess the degree of price transmission from border to consumer prices for a sample of homogeneous products in three main urban markets in Mozambique. We do so by exploiting a unique dataset from the Mozambican Customs Authority that registers all import processes by border post in the country. This allows us to estimate the short-run elasticity between these import unit values and consumer prices at the specific market level. Furthermore, it allows the decomposition of price transmission into three different components: changes in the exchange rate, changes in border taxes and changes in import unit values.

The chapter is organized as follows. Section 2 briefly describes the theory behind price transmission and price equalization. Section 3 describes the methodology employed in the chapter. Section 4 summarizes the main data used in the estimations. Section 5 describes the main results and Section 6 concludes. The main finding of the chapter suggests a large and robust degree of exchange rate pass-through (ERPT) to consumer prices, while the degree of transmission of border price and trade tax changes seems to be low.

2 Price transmission and the law of one price

The law of one price (LOP) establishes that in the absence of any barriers to trade, costless trade and perfectly functioning markets, prices of the same good in different countries should be equal when evaluated in the same currency.

Several empirical papers have tried to test different versions of the LOP, and most of the evidence indicates that the LOP tends to be rejected (see Goldberg and Knetter 1997 for an overview).[1] For some authors this rejection is due to the violation of two main assumptions: costless trade and arbitrage and good homogeneity, especially when using aggregate indices. For others, however, the LOP failure implies the rejection of global monetarism and the existence of important price rigidities and imperfect competition.

Related to the failure of the LOP, the empirical literature has tested whether changes in exchange rates and tariffs are fully transmitted to domestic prices: exchange rate pass-through (ERPT) and tariff pass-through (Feenstra 1989).[2] Full or complete ERPT happens if there are constant marginal costs or there is a constant mark-up of price over cost. Thus lack of full ERPT implies some degree of imperfect competition, where firms can adjust margins according to their business strategy.

The evidence suggests that ERPT and tariff pass-through to border prices are far from perfect, indicating evidence of imperfect competitive markets. Estimated ERPT to import prices is around 60 per cent in the US (Campa and Goldberg 2005), and smaller countries tend to experience larger pass-through (Frankel *et al.* 2005). On the other hand, ERPT to consumer prices tends to be even lower than to border prices, between 13 per cent and 30 per cent (Campa and Goldberg 2006).

Some authors have also tested whether the extent of ERPT is symmetric, that is, whether firms respond to appreciations and depreciations in the same way when pricing. Pollard and Coughlin (2004) suggest that ERPT tends to be asymmetric, and firm's pricing policies react differently to appreciations than to depreciations.

A critique of the existing empirical literature comes from papers that use threshold methodologies. These models have tried to test the existence of thresholds to arbitrage, where prices converge only if price differentials are above a certain threshold that makes arbitrage profitable (Obstfeld and Taylor 1997). Thus these studies tend to find higher pass-through once the thresholds or bands of inaction have been accounted for.

The source of incomplete ERPT can lie on the import or the export side. Krugman (1986) suggests as the source of incomplete pass-through the fact that exporting firms in an oligopolistic setting may use third-degree price discrimination when pricing in different markets, i.e. pricing to market (PTM).

The most recent literature has focused on the import side and the fact that border prices seem to be more sensitive than consumer or retail prices to exchange rate changes (Campa and Goldberg 2006; Frankel *et al.* 2005). There are three potential explanations of this result: (1) the existence of non-tradable goods in the Consumer Price Index (CPI); (2) the fact that the distribution sector reduces the foreign content value of imports; and (3) the fact that imperfect competition in the distribution sector implies double margin-alization, where distributors adjust profits and margins according to exchange rate fluctuations in order to expand their market share.

Campa and Goldberg (2006) find evidence of three channels that limit pass-through to consumer and retailer prices. First, they find that margins change with exchange rate changes. Second, the use of imported inputs in non-tradable goods is less than for tradable goods, which impacts pass-through. Finally, they find that non-tradables also use imported inputs, so the impact of the distribution sector is also important for non-tradable goods.

Goldberg and Hellerstein (2006) model pass-through in a Bertrand oligo-polistic setting with differentiated products, where retailers set prices according to the ones given by wholesalers. In this setting, firms adjust margins in response to exchange rate changes, reducing full pass-trough. Hellerstein (2004) analyses the market for beer and finds that the effect of exchange rate changes is dampened by strategic interactions between domestic and foreign firms in the traded and the non-traded sector.

Summing up, the evidence on border price transmission indicates that foreign and domestic prices do not tend to converge in the short run. This is mainly due to imperfect competition, both on the export side, where firms apply some degree of price discrimination, and on the import side, where distribution mark-ups impede perfect price transmission.

The following section describes the methodology used for estimating the degree of price transmission from border prices in Mozambique.

3 Methodology

As suggested above, the LOP stresses that the price of the same good sold in different markets should be the same when evaluated in the same currency. The assumption for the LOP to hold is that trade and arbitrage are costless, and markets efficient. Thus price differences should be explained by transport, distribution costs, price discrimination and variable margins/mark-ups. As an example, in the case of an imported good the consumer price should equal to the FOB price adjusted for insurance and freight, tariffs and other border taxes, transport costs and the commercialization margin.

Mozambique's capacity to affect the FOB export price is negligible, since it is a small country and more than 50 per cent of imports originate from neighbouring South Africa.[3] For this reason, this chapter focuses on the degree of price transmission from the border to consumer prices. This allows us to look at the sources of inefficiency in the domestic market, and has clear implications in terms of domestic competition policy and the potential impact of trade reform.

As shown in equation (1), we can express consumer price P^c_{it} of good i in period t as a function of the FOB price converted to domestic currency and adjusted to insurance and freight (a^{cif}_{it}), taxes paid at the border (τ_{it}) (mainly import duties t_{it} and VAT), internal transport costs (tr_{it}) and the commercialization mark-up (η_{it}).

$$P^{fob}_{it} e_t (1 + a^{cif}_{it})(1 + \tau_{it})(1 + tr_{it})(1 + \eta_{it}) = P^c_{it} \tag{1}$$

$$P^{cif}_{it} = P^{fob}_{it}(1 + a^{cif}_{it}) \tag{2}$$

$$T_{it} = (1 + \tau_{it}) = (1 + t_{it})(1 + vat_{it}) \tag{3}$$

$$TR_{it} = (1 + tr_{it}) \tag{4}$$

Using equations (2), (3) and (4) and applying logarithms, we obtain equation (5). This reduced form equation allows us to decompose and estimate the elasticity of pass-through from changes in the exporter price, the exchange rate, import taxes, transport costs and mark-ups.

$$\ln P^c_{it} = \beta \ln P^{cif}_{it} + \lambda \ln e_t + \sigma \ln T_{it} + \chi \ln TR_{it} + \gamma \ln M_{it} + \varepsilon_{it} \tag{5}$$

Equation (5) assumes a product-specific and time-variant mark-up. This constitutes a problem in the estimations since there is a lack of data on distribution margins and mark-ups. Some authors (see Feenstra 1989) use competitive pressure indicators for the mark-up. The problem with this approach is that in our case we are interested on distribution margins at the product-specific level and the distribution sector in Mozambique appears to be very concentrated in a few firms. This implies that the same distributors may allocate domestically produced and imported goods for retail with a certain degree of monopolistic power. For this reason, and due to the lack of any relevant information on these margins, we adopt a strategy that treats the mark-up as constant and product specific.

Finally, we would like to add the monthly CPI for each province as a control variable for supply and demand shocks affecting the economy.

However, the CPI is highly correlated with the exchange rate.[4] Furthermore, no major shocks were observed in the three provincial urban markets during the period of study. Our baseline model is summarized by equation (6).

$$\ln P_{it}^c = \sum_i \alpha_i M_i + \beta \ln P_{it}^{cif} + \lambda \ln e_t + \sigma \ln T_{it} + \chi \ln TR_{it} + \varepsilon_{it} \qquad (6)$$

4 Data

The main source of data is the Trade Information Management System (TIMS), the primary database used by the Customs Authority to register import processes. It contains information specific to each separate import process: declared CIF value, customs valuation, taxes paid, currency priced, source, date and border post of entry. This information is available from 2000 to 2005.

One of the main constraints that we face is lack of data, especially regarding CIF unit values as compared to complete consumer price series. For this reason, we employ a panel data strategy in order to maximize the number of observations. We use monthly observations across a list of 25 agricultural and light processed products (see Table 10.1 for a list of the products). The selection of the products is based on the basket of products available in the consumer price indexes of Maputo, Nampula and Beira. The main criteria for product selection are: (1) product homogeneity; and (2) availability of data in order to compute CIF unit values.

A simple examination of computed unit values suggests that this measure contains a lot of noise. A first source of variance is the use of different units. We express all the units in kilograms in order that they are comparable with CPI data. Furthermore, two other problems emerge when working with border unit values. First, there are a significant number of typing errors when inputting the import value, especially related to wrong decimals and other typing mistakes. Second, it is likely that some substantial differences may correspond to quality differences. In order to overcome these problems, we apply Hadi's (1992) methodology to eliminate outliers at 99 per cent confidence level, to the de-trended unit values series. This allows us to eliminate extreme values due to typing errors or due to large quality differences.

Our panel is unbalanced due to the fact that for most products we do not observe imports every month. In addition, when estimating the province panels we eliminate products that do not have more than three observations in time. As a result, when we pool all the observations for the three markets we have 25 products and 1,140 observations: 24 products and 696 observations for Maputo; 18 products and 324 observations for Beira; and 8 products and 104 observations for Nampula.

Consumer prices are obtained from the provincial consumer price indexes calculated at the National Institute of Statistics (INE). Consequently, we use the monthly average CPI for Maputo, Beira and Nampula.

Table 10.1 Selected Products

HS	Product	Observations
2045000	Goat meat	15
2071200	Chicken	62
4051000	Butter	81
4070090	Eggs	64
7019000	Potatoes	42
7020000	Tomatoes	62
7032000	Garlic	54
7051100	Lettuce	89
7061000	Carrots	121
7082000	Butter Beans	40
7089000	Green Beans	6
7122000	Onions	9
8030000	Banana	11
8043000	Pineapple	20
8045000	Mangoes	7
8051000	Oranges	47
8052000	Tangerines	17
8055000	Lemons	41
8072000	Papaya	9
8081000	Apples	66
9012100	Coffee	33
9023000	Tea	60
12022090	Groundnuts	50
25010000	Salt	71
48181000	Toilet Paper	63
	Total	1140

Source: TIMS, Customs Authority, Mozambique, authors' calculations

The choice of the relevant reference price at the border is crucial to the analysis. In the case of Maputo, it is clear that the relevant border price is the one observed at the border posts of Maputo Province. However, this is less clear in the case of Beira and Nampula, and some products may be transported from the Maputo Province border posts towards the North of the country. For this reason we have considered two different specifications.

The first specification considers as border reference prices the average CIF import unit value observed in the same province border posts for every product. This implies that for Maputo we use the monthly average of all CIF unit values of that product observed in border posts in Maputo Province. In the case of Beira, we use those CIF unit values observed at Beira Province's border with Zimbabwe; and for Nampula, those observed at Nampula Province's border with Malawi.[5]

The second specification considers that the relevant border price is the one in Maputo Province. In this case, we use Maputo's CIF unit value for Beira and Nampula, and we adjust the transport costs proxies to reflect the increase in the relevant distance. For both specifications, we compute CIF unit values expressed in Rands, which is the most used currency regarding imports of these products.[6]

Regarding transport costs, we build two proxies. The first proxy uses the information regarding the calculation of the CIF unit values and computes the average distance from the relevant border post to the market. Since import processes from different border posts may be observed, this proxy calculates the average distance for all these import processes. The second proxy uses information on transport costs for maize in selected routes available from the SIMA database.[7] Data on transport costs are available for some months from 2001 to 2005. We use this information and build a transport cost index for those routes from the border to the three markets. Since observations are missing for some periods, we fit the data available for every route, border to market, with a regression in logarithms with a time trend, and use the predicted values as our transport costs proxy.

Import taxes are calculated according to the information provided by the customs database. Rather than using nominal tax rates existing in the tariff book, we calculate taxes as the ratio between total taxes effectively paid and the CIF value. This allows us to account for exemptions, since we only include taxes effectively paid at the border.[8,9]

As the exchange rate we use the Rand/Metical monthly official exchange rate, since most imports are priced in Rands.[10] Finally, as suggested on p. 192, we model the mark-up as product-specific dummy.

5 Results

Equation (6) is estimated at the national level, pooling all the observations, and at the provincial level. We start by discussing the results for the pooled specification, and later in the section we describe the results for each one of the provinces selected.

We consider different specifications at each level. For the national pooled case, we have four specifications, two using different reference prices for Beira and Nampula,[11] and two using different transport costs proxies. At the provincial level, in the case of Beira and Nampula we compute three specifications. In this case, we are forced to drop the specification that uses the transport cost index using Maputo reference border prices due to the existing high collinearity between the transport cost index and the exchange rate; both with no variation across the products of the panel.[12] In the case of Maputo, we estimate two specifications for each of the transport costs proxies.

5.1 Pooled sample

Equation (6) is estimated using all the observations of our sample and controlling for specific province effects using province dummies. The results for the four different specifications are summarized in Table 10.2.

Table 10.2 Price Transmission Panel Estimates – Pooled Provinces

| | Transport Costs: Distance | | | | | | Transport Costs: Maize Transport Cost Index | | | | | |
| | Neighboring border price | | | Maputo province border price | | | Maputo province border price | | | Neighboring border price | | |
	OLS	LSDV	RE	OLS	LSDV	RE	OLS	LSDV	RE	OLS	LSDV	RE
p^{caf}	0.1362*** [0.0168]	0.0165*** [0.0056]	0.0171*** [0.0057]	0.2178*** [0.0138]	0.0172*** [0.0056]	0.0188*** [0.0057]	0.2470*** [0.0147]	0.0014 [0.0048]	0.0025 [0.0048]	0.1352*** [0.0169]	0.0156*** [0.0056]	0.0161*** [0.0057]
ERPT	0.5986*** [0.1551]	0.7616*** [0.0489]	0.7605*** [0.0491]	0.5068*** [0.1183]	0.6741*** [0.0449]	0.6702*** [0.0454]	0.7720*** [0.2104]	0.2959*** [0.0570]	0.2957*** [0.0576]	0.5947*** [0.1599]	0.7804*** [0.0494]	0.7799*** [0.0496]
Tax	1.5121*** [0.3924]	-0.1434 [0.1381]	-0.14 [0.1385]	1.6343*** [0.3328]	-0.1135 [0.1514]	-0.11 [0.1528]	1.5227*** [0.3434]	-0.1462 [0.1223]	-0.1447 [0.1235]	1.5211*** [0.3929]	-0.1705 [0.1382]	-0.1678 [0.1386]
T. Cost	-0.0177 [0.0176]	-0.0164*** [0.0054]	-0.0165*** [0.0054]	-0.1656*** [0.0387]	0.0079 [0.0135]	0.0063 [0.0136]	-1.7124 [1.1850]	3.774*** [0.3210]	3.7529*** [0.3246]	-0.0394 [0.0549]	-0.0642*** [0.0167]	-0.0647*** [0.0168]
Beira	-0.2772*** [0.0653]	-0.0529*** [0.0203]	-0.0538*** [0.0204]	0.4947*** [0.1811]	-0.1430** [0.0630]	-0.1366** [0.0637]	-0.2362*** [0.0494]	-0.1024*** [0.0133]	-0.1027*** [0.0135]	-0.2521*** [0.0639]	-0.0263 [0.0202]	-0.027 [0.0202]
Nampula	0.2664*** [0.0981]	-0.1783*** [0.0307]	-0.1769*** [0.0308]	0.5908*** [0.2028]	-0.2121*** [0.0706]	-0.2047*** [0.0714]	-0.0607 [0.0499]	0.007 [0.0135]	0.0069 [0.0136]	0.2772*** [0.1031]	-0.1479*** [0.0322]	-0.1463*** [0.0323]
Constant	4.5797*** [1.2579]	5.2802*** [0.4043]	3.9655*** [0.4293]	5.5423*** [0.9768]	5.5524*** [0.3803]	4.5963*** [0.3962]	11.4201*** [4.5471]	-9.8077*** [1.2572]	-10.84*** [1.2764]	4.5706*** [1.3020]	5.1017*** [0.4107]	3.7964*** [0.4351]
Obs.	1140	1140	1140	1835	1835	1835	1865	1865	1865	1140	1140	1140
R^2	0.11	0.93	0.03 (0.25)	0.18	0.91	0.04 (0.20)	0.18	0.94	0.03 (0.35)	0.11	0.93	0.03 (0.26)
Products	25	25	25	25	25	25	25	25	25	25	25	25

Standard errors in brackets, * significant at 10%; ** significant at 5%; *** significant at 1%. The R^2 in ( ) corresponds to the 'within' R^2 for the panel estimates

Source: TIMS, authors' estimates

The first column of each specification reports the result of the Ordinary Least Squares (OLS) estimation without controlling for product-specific heterogeneity. The main results show that the border price elasticity transmission is low, around 0.2 on average. That means that a 1 per cent change in the border price is translated into a 0.2 per cent increase in the consumer price. Second, the degree of exchange rate pass-through is high, between 50 per cent and 75 per cent depending on the specification. These results imply some kind of adjustment in distribution margins when exporters increase their price, or, perhaps, substitution to local sources; meanwhile, there is high transmission of exchange rate changes to retail pricing.

Another interesting result is the high transmission elasticity of border tax changes with the OLS estimation. Changes in trade taxes seem to be fully transmitted to consumer prices. However, some caution is required when interpreting this result. No major tariff changes have occurred during the period of study, therefore there is little time variance and most of the variation is related to exemptions at the border across products. Thus this coefficient may be capturing product-specific effects.

More puzzling is the negative sign associated with the transport costs proxy. One potential explanation is that transport costs from the border to the three markets studied are not very relevant when pricing, due to the fact that road corridors are in very good condition and the substantial transport costs from the origin to the border posts are already included in the CIF price. However, this is unlikely to be the case for Beira and Nampula when using Maputo's border prices, since the large distance to the border should impact the price.

We use province dummies to control for provincial effects. The coefficients indicate a lower intercept for Beira with respect to Maputo for most specifications, and for Nampula it changes sign according to the specification. If the intercept is mostly capturing a constant margin, this implies lower margins in Beira.

A problem that arises with the OLS specification is the fact that it does not control for margin heterogeneity. The assumption is that all margins are constant through time and products and are captured by the intercept. We apply an F-test to test whether we can eliminate heterogeneity. The result of the test, however, supports the rejection of the restricted OLS model (constant common intercept), indicating, as in equation (6), the presence of product-specific effects.

In order to introduce product-specific effects we estimate in columns 2 and 3 of Table 10.2 the specifications for Least Squares Dummy Variables (LSDV) and Random Effects (RE). The Hausman and the Breusch–Pagan Lagrangian multiplier (LM) test indicate the significance of product-specific effects, and the RE model seems to be preferred to OLS.

The first important result is that product-specific effects absorb most of the transmission elasticity of border prices and trade taxes, the last one becoming statistically not significant. This indicates weak elasticity estimates or the importance of product-specific effects. Especially relevant is the large drop in the tax elasticity, indicating, as suggested above, that the coefficient in the

OLS specification was capturing product-specific effects. Second, the coefficient associated with ERPT is still high, suggesting a robust, significant, large pass-through. The estimated ERPT coefficients drop on the third specification using the maize transport index, but this is likely to be the result of collinearity between this index and the exchange rate.[13]

Summing up, the results for the pooled specifications indicate that, once controlled for product heterogeneity, border price and trade taxes transmission elasticity estimates are very low and not statistically significant. On the other hand, ERPT is high and robust across specifications, while product-specific margins may also be significant in explaining price transmission. The results are robust using different transport costs proxies and different reference border prices for Beira and Nampula.

5.2 Maputo Province

Table 10.3 shows the results from estimating equation (6) for Maputo Province. We consider two specifications using the two different proxies for transport costs. The results are very similar to the ones obtained at the pooled country level (see Table 10.2). We perform an F-test for the significance of product-specific effects and we reject the null of common intercept. This is also confirmed by the Breusch–Pagan LM test supporting RE as opposed to OLS, and by the FE estimation that rejects the possibility of a common product effect.

The Hausman test cannot be performed due to the fact that the model fitted on these data fails to meet the asymptotic assumptions of the test. Nevertheless, coefficient estimates appear to be very similar between models and the estimated correlation between the error term and the regressors for the FE model is very low (0.02). This indicates that the RE model is more efficient than FE.

The results show that the ERPT elasticity remains very high and significant. On the other hand, border price elasticity is low, around 0.15, and once we account for product-specific effects, it becomes very low. Trade tax elasticity is very volatile and not robust across specifications.

The R^2 of the panel estimates is very low. Most of the variance explained corresponds to the 'within' R^2, around 0.5. Nevertheless, the model poorly explains 'between' variance. This is also reflected in the fact that 99 per cent of the variance is due to product effects. The most likely explanation is the lack of significant data variation cross-section. The panel has large gaps for every cross-section, especially until 2003, when the average number of observations per period is around six.

An important issue that arises when working with price equations is the fact that prices tend to have some inertia and persistence in price formation. This is confirmed by the modified Durbin–Watson test (Bhargava *et al.* 1982), which indicates the presence of autocorrelation in the error term in our data (Baltagi 2003). Therefore, we need to deal with time dependence and potential autocorrelation problems, which may bias our estimates if data are not properly corrected.

Table 10.3 Price Transmission Panel Estimates – Maputo Province

	Transport Costs: Distance				Transport Costs: Maize Transport Cost Index			
	OLS	RE	GLS (AR1) FE	PCSE	OLS	RE	GLS (AR1) FE	PCSE
pcif	0.1482*** [0.0217]	0.0247*** [0.0050]	0.0181** [0.0078]	0.0260*** [0.0052]	0.1498*** [0.0224]	0.0252*** [0.0051]	0.0187** [0.0079]	0.0240*** [0.0049]
ERPT	1.0206*** [0.2247]	0.9147*** [0.0488]	1.2824*** [0.0103]	1.3825*** [0.0095]	0.9019*** [0.2295]	0.8791*** [0.0483]	1.2763*** [0.0099]	1.3765*** [0.0091]
Tax	2.3994*** [0.6196]	-0.2152 [0.1620]	0.156 [0.1404]	0.2410* [0.1431]	2.2463*** [0.6244]	-0.2538 [0.1623]	0.1607 [0.1407]	0.2296 [0.1425]
T. Cost	-0.2147*** [0.0451]	-0.0269*** [0.0095]	-0.0210** [0.0101]	-0.0303*** [0.0072]	-0.2715*** [0.0823]	-0.0215 [0.0181]	-0.0112 [0.0218]	-0.0386** [0.0185]
Constant	1.3513 [1.8422]	2.7848*** [0.4418]	-0.2583*** [0.0099]		1.8506 [1.9130]	3.0188*** [0.4436]	-0.2699*** [0.0100]	
Obs.	696	696	672	696	696	696	672	696
R^2	0.15	0.04 (0.47)	0.04 (0.98)	0.99	0.14	0.04 (0.46)	0.03 (0.98)	0.999
Products	24	24	24	24	24	24	24	24

Standard errors in brackets, * significant at 10%; ** significant at 5%; *** significant at 1%.
The R^2 in ( ) corresponds to the 'within' R^2 for the panel estimates
Source: TIMS, authors' estimates

The third column of each specification (GLS AR1 FE, Table 10.3) corrects for panel-specific autocorrelation and heteroscedasticity[14] using fixed effects. Once autocorrelation is corrected, some coefficient estimates change significantly, supporting the idea of correlation between the explanatory variables and the error term, and indicating FE as preferred. In addition, the within R^2 for the FE model doubles the RE R^2. The results are very similar to the previous estimates, suggesting very high ERPT and low border price transmission.

Finally, the last specification (PCSE) performs the Prais–Winsten transformation for autocorrelation using OLS estimation (Greene 2003), also correcting for heteroscedastic panels. We control for product-specific effects using product dummies. The results, as expected, are similar to the fixed effects estimation with autocorrelation, where the ERPT elasticity is very high and border price elasticity very low. Across all specifications, border price transmission appears very low and statistically significant.

5.3 Beira Province

The results for Beira province are illustrated in Table 10.4. They are very similar to those found for Maputo. We cannot reject the presence of product-specific effects. Once we control for product effects, most elasticity estimates become not significantly different from zero. The only robust result is the ERPT elasticity and the product dummies. The ERPT elasticity is around 0.5, depending on the specification, but the coefficient is more volatile than for the previous panels. The different specifications explain most of the 'within' variance; however, due to lack of data and enough cross-section variation, very little 'between' variance is explained by the model.

5.4 Nampula Province

For this province we have fewer observations and therefore we find that the results are less robust (see Table 10.5). Despite the lack of robustness, the estimates are similar to those for the two previous provinces. Nevertheless, most elasticity estimates are not significantly different from zero, and the model performs badly at explaining retail price variance; we obtain a very low R^2 for both, 'within' and 'between' variances. The ERPT elasticity estimate is lower than in the previous cases, and only statistically significant and positive for a few specifications.

5.5 Main results

Several issues arise from analysing the previous estimates. First, as equation (6) suggests, estimates should be performed controlling for specific product effects. This may reflect specific product margins, but also other product-specific characteristics.

Table 10.4 Price Transmission Panel Estimates – Beira Province

	Transport Costs: Distance						Transport Costs: Maize Transport Cost Index		
	Neighboring border price			Maputo province border price			Neighboring border price		
	OLS	RE	GLS (AR1) FE	OLS	RE	GLS (AR1) FE	OLS	RE	GLS (AR1) FE
p_{cif}	0.1476*** [0.0387]	-0.0042 [0.0109]	0.002 [0.0087]	0.2524*** [0.0294]	-0.0012 [0.0078]	0.0234** [0.0095]	0.1234*** [0.0385]	-0.0046 [0.0109]	0.002 [0.0087]
ERPT	0.5590* [0.2935]	0.5064*** [0.0913]	1.2076*** [0.0264]	0.4015 [0.2496]	0.7212*** [0.0618]	0.2651** [0.1311]	0.2445 [0.2968]	0.4978*** [0.0937]	1.2075*** [0.0264]
Tax	1.4095 [0.9339]	-3.0835*** [0.6619]	0.6326 [0.5148]	0.7615 [0.6052]	-0.1483 [0.1882]	-0.0065 [0.1592]	1.332 [0.9245]	-3.0984*** [0.6617]	0.634 [0.5159]
T. Cost	0.0135 [0.0249]	0.0013 [0.0059]	-0.004 [0.0054]	-3.0597 [2.4287]	-0.8173 [0.6098]	1.1077*** [0.1463]	0.2398** [0.1018]	0.0092 [0.0246]	-0.0149 [0.0226]
Constant	4.5928* [2.4588]	7.0065*** [0.9394]	-0.0064 [0.0162]	27.7598* [16.3322]	9.9885** [4.1259]	-0.0647*** [0.0128]	7.1186*** [2.4793]	7.0805*** [0.9551]	-0.0092 [0.0161]
Obs.	324	324	306	529	529	509	324	324	306
R^2	0.09	0.0001 (0.34)	0.02 (0.98)	0.17	0.01 (0.29)	0.05 (0.99)	0.1	0.0002 (0.34)	0.02 (0.98)
Products	18	18	18	20	20	19	18	18	18

Standard errors in brackets, * significant at 10%; ** significant at 5%; *** significant at 1%. The R^2 in ( ) corresponds to the 'within' R^2 for the panel estimates

Source: TIMS, authors' estimates

Table 10.5 Price Transmission Panel Estimates – Nampula Province

	Transport Costs: Distance						Transport Costs: Maize Transport Cost Index		
	Neighboring border price			Maputo province border price			Neighboring border price		
	OLS	RE	GLS (AR1) FE	OLS	RE	GLS (AR1) FE	OLS	RE	GLS (AR1) FE
P^{cif}	0.0569 [0.0636]	-0.0326* [0.0176]	-0.0024 [0.0044]	0.2050*** [0.0379]	-0.0051 [0.0149]	0.0070* [0.0040]	0.0578 [0.0638]	-0.0339* [0.0177]	-0.0015 [0.0048]
ERPT	0.9616* [0.5790]	0.3317* [0.1837]	0.2573** [0.1012]	1.1307*** [0.4007]	0.9335*** [0.1502]	-0.1599* [0.0845]	0.9684* [0.5801]	0.3505* [0.1862]	0.4033*** [0.1034]
Tax	0.3941 [0.8742]	-0.6707** [0.2958]	0.0017 [0.0679]	2.2416*** [0.8421]	0.2264 [0.3516]	-0.0787 [0.0600]	0.5787 [0.8615]	-0.6962** [0.2967]	-0.0087 [0.0736]
T. Cost	-0.0286 [0.0452]	0.0067 [0.0147]	0.001 [0.0019]	-15.1826** [6.8713]	-15.3971*** [2.5851]	1.4290*** [0.0878]	0.0115 [0.1527]	0.0387 [0.0559]	-0.0062 [0.0085]
Constant	2.402 [4.5544]	7.5338*** [1.5020]	32.6903*** [0.0053]	116.3668** [51.2768]	120.6233*** [19.4039]	2.5308*** [0.0044]	2.1796 [4.5571]	7.3829*** [1.5237]	25.6366*** [0.0060]
Obs.	104	104	96	249	249	240	104	104	96
R^2	0.07	0.01(0.11)	0.05 (0.09)	0.23	0.09 (0.20)	0.01 (0.93)	0.07	0.01 (0.11)	0.05 (0.16)
Products	8	8	8	9	9	9	8	8	8

Standard errors in brackets, * significant at 10%; ** significant at 5%; *** significant at 1%. The R^2 in ( ) corresponds to the 'within' R^2 for the panel estimates
Source: TIMS, authors' estimates

Second, ERPT elasticity tends to be quite high and this result is robust across specifications. This indicates that exchange rate changes tend to be fully transmitted to retail prices. On the other hand, the elasticity of transmission from border CIF import unit values tends to be very small and statistically significant for the pooled and Maputo regressions. This suggests that retail prices seem to be very responsive to exchange rate changes, but not very responsive to border prices. We may expect this to happen only if retailers adjust retail margins and therefore they have some degree of market power.

Third, trade tax transmission elasticity tends to be small and not statistically different from zero. This may be explained by the fact that there is very little variation of trade taxes, both 'within' and 'between' panels. Furthermore, the coefficient associated with the transport costs proxy tends to be negative, which is somewhat puzzling. This may be related to the fact that these proxies may not accurately reflect transport costs for some products. In addition, another potential explanation is that the relevant transport costs for the retailer, transport costs from the exporter to the customs post, are already incorporated in the CIF import unit value.

These results are consistent across the three provinces studied. They are also consistent with specifications that control for autocorrelation due to time dependence in price formation, and for panel heteroscedasticity, likely to arise due to potential different measurement units across panels.

5.6 *Equality of coefficients across provinces*

We test for the equality of the coefficients between the pooled sample and the province-specific regressions. The same specification, based on a normal regression with product-specific dummies, is estimated for the pooled sample and each of the provinces and then we apply an F-test.[15] The F statistic rejects the restricted model and the null hypotheses that the coefficients are the same for all the provinces.

5.7 *ERPT symmetry*

We also look at whether the high ERPT elasticity is symmetric, that is, whether appreciations and depreciations are transmitted equally to retail prices. In order to do this, we employ an approach based on Pollard and Coughlin (2004), and replace the exchange rate term in equation (6) with two interactive terms. The first term is the product of a dummy variable A_{it}, with value 1 if the Rand/Mt appreciated that month, by the logarithm of the exchange rate. The second term is the product of a dummy variable D_{it}, with value 1 if the Rand/Mt depreciated that month, by the logarithm of the exchange rate. Thus we estimate the following equation:

$$\ln P_{it}^c = \sum_i \alpha_i M_i + \beta \ln P_{it}^{cif} + \lambda_1 (A_{it} \ln e_t) + \lambda_2 (D_{it} \ln e_t) + \sigma \ln T_{it}$$

$$+ \chi \ln TR_{it} + \gamma CPI_t + \varepsilon_{it} \tag{7}$$

Table 10.6 shows the results for the preferred specifications at the national and provincial levels using distance as transport cost proxy and neighbouring border prices.[16] We observe a monthly appreciation of the Metical with respect to the Rand in around 33 per cent of the months of our period of analysis. The results clearly indicate that ERPT tends to be symmetric. For all the cases, pooled and provincial, coefficient estimates are very close. We perform a Wald test for the equality of the coefficients and we accept the null hypothesis of equal coefficients only for the case of the pooled sample. Nevertheless, we accept the null that the appreciation elasticity is 1.05 times the elasticity of depreciation, which indicates only marginal differences and, more importantly, a symmetric ERPT.

6 Conclusions and policy implications

This chapter has attempted to address empirically the issue of price transmission from border to retail prices. We use a unique customs dataset that allows us to link average import unit values with retail prices for the same

Table 10.6 ERPT Symmetry Specifications

	Pooled LSDV	Maputo PCSE	Beira GLS (AR1) FE	Nampula GLS (AR1) FE
P^{cif}	0.0166***	0.0213***	0.0017	−0.0039
	[0.0056]	[0.0050]	[0.0087]	[0.0043]
e_apr (λ_1)	0.7668***	1.3935***	1.2058***	0.2934***
	[0.0494]	[0.0092]	[0.0262]	[0.1029]
e_dep (λ_2)	0.7651***	1.3862***	1.2016***	0.2912***
	[0.0491]	[0.0091]	[0.0264]	[0.1026]
Tax	−0.1417	0.1958	0.718	0.0028
	[0.1381]	[0.1403]	[0.5129]	[0.0653]
T. Cost	−0.0162***	−0.0255***	−0.005	0.0011
	[0.0054]	[0.0072]	[0.0053]	[0.0019]
Beira	−0.0531***			
	[0.0203]			
Nampula	−0.1783***			
	[0.0307]			
Constant	5.2460***		0.0091	31.1061***
	[0.4066]		[0.0161]	[0.0052]
Test H$_0$: $\lambda_1=\lambda_2$	Accept	Reject	Reject	Reject
Observations	1140	696	306	96
R^2	0.93			
Products		24	18	8

Standard errors in brackets, * significant at 10%; ** significant at 5%; *** significant at 1%
Source: TIMS, authors' estimates

product and the same provincial market. Thus this study provides evidence at the micro or product-specific level of the determinants of consumer price changes.

The main result of the estimations is that the ERPT elasticity tends to be very high and symmetric. Other transmission elasticity estimates, such as the ones associated with changes in CIF unit values or trade taxes, tend to be small and not significantly different from zero. This suggests that margins are used to offset changes in import unit values and trade taxes, while changes in the exchange rate are fully transmitted to consumer prices.

There are two main policy implications of these results. The first policy implication, related to monetary policy, is the importance of exchange rate stability in order to avoid increases in consumer prices. Large exchange rate volatility, as observed in some recent periods, is translated into volatile consumer prices, and steady appreciation is associated with significant price changes.

The second policy implication is related to competition policy. Despite the fact that more work is required in order to model mark-ups, the fact that consumer prices seem to be insensitive to changes in border prices and taxes indicates the use of mark-ups for offsetting these changes and departing from the perfect competition framework. Therefore, more work is required to analyse the size of these mark-ups and the degree of competition in the retail sector.

Notes

1 Several empirical studies have analysed the LOP in the context of specific goods. For applications, see Haskel and Wolf (2001) and Ghosh and Wolf (1994).
2 The degree of ERPT is of high importance since, for example, the Marshall–Lerner condition, the sensitivity of the trade balance to the exchange rate, depends on the degree of ERPT.
3 We should expect that South African exporters have some degree of market power when fixing the prices of exports to Mozambique. This implies that a discrepancy between the factory price of that product in South Africa and the FOB price should be expected, introducing a first wedge between the retail price in South Africa and in Mozambique.
4 This may be interpreted as an indicator of potentially high ERPT.
5 Concretely the border posts with observed unit values for those products are Espungabera and Beira port for Beira; and Cuamba, Nampula and Nacala for Nampula.
6 We also compute unit values in US dollars and reproduce the estimations using the US dollar as the relevant currency. Nevertheless, as discussed in Section 5, the results are very similar.
7 Sistema Integrado de Monitoria Agrícola (SIMA), Ministry of Agriculture.
8 Exemptions have to be previously granted by the Ministry of Finance and/or customs under the different exemption schemes: inputs for transforming industry, investment law and other ad hoc exemptions. Thus there is no possibility of duty drawbacks after the import process has crossed the border.
9 Smuggling may be significant for some products and therefore small changes in taxes may not be very relevant in affecting consumer prices. We do not have,

however, any registered data on smuggling products that would allow us to control for this effect.

10 We also estimate some specifications using CIF prices in dollars and the Dollar/Metical exchange rate for comparison, obtaining similar results.

11 One where the reference border price is calculated from neighbouring border posts and the other specification using Maputo Province border prices.

12 In the case where the transport cost index is used for cases of neighbouring border reference price, we use the average of transport cost index for all the processes from all the border posts observed that month. That gives us enough variation across products to avoid collinearity.

13 Due to this problem of collinearity, we have abandoned the specification that uses the maize transport cost index and Maputo reference border price for the provincial panels.

14 Heteroscedasticity may arise from problems with unit measurements between unit values, price per kg and market prices, which may represent price per units different from kg, especially for non-agricultural products.

15 $F_{k+1,N_1+N_2+N_3-3k-3} = \frac{(RSS_R - RSS_1 - RSS_2 - RSS_3)(N_1 + N_2 + N_3 - 3K - 3)}{(RSS_1 + RSS_2 = RSS_3)^*(K+1)}$

16 Tests for symmetry using different specifications regarding transport costs and border prices yield similar results.

11 Empirics of evasion

Channing Arndt and João E. Van Dunem

1 Introduction

The present chapter focuses on the causal relationship between trade tax rates and evasion in Mozambique. In so doing, it also investigates distinct forms of tax evasion. Clearly, the empirical problem presented when studying tax evasion is that, by its very nature, evasion is not easy to measure. The methodology employed, originally pioneered by Fisman and Wei (2004), permits the measurement of evasion with some precision by aligning and comparing (at the product level) bilateral trade flow data between Mozambique and its largest trading partner, South Africa.

The chapter is organized as follows. Section 2 provides a brief review of the public finance literature related to tax evasion in developing countries. Section 3 outlines the regression framework adopted to understand the empirical link between evasion and tax rates. Section 4 describes general aspects of the data used in the regression models, highlighting idiosyncrasies of Mozambique trade flow data. Section 5 discusses results and Section 6 simulates economic implications of alternative tax rates for tax evasion and customs revenue using the estimated results. Section 7 concludes.

The chapter tackles three central questions:

1 To what extent is there a connection between tax evasion at the border and trade tax rates in a typical Sub-Saharan African country? The results suggest a positive impact of tax rates on tax evasion, albeit half of that found by Fisman and Wei for an Asian country like China. On average, an increase in trade taxes of one percentage point prompts an upward response in tax evasion of about 1.4 per cent.
2 Given that higher tax rates induce higher levels of tax evasion, how does that evasion manifest itself? The empirical results provide evidence in favour of two forms of evasion: under-reporting in prices and fraudulent misclassification of imports.
3 What practical lessons for evasion and customs revenue can be offered from our results? The chapter finds – based on the preceding results – that the average level of evasion in Mozambique is large (close to 36 per cent

of total recorded imports) and is concentrated in more highly taxed product categories. The evasion rate for consumer goods, which are typically subject to higher rates, slightly exceeds half of total consumer product imports. Substantial evasion also occurs when similar products are taxed at differential rates. Finally, the results suggest that revenue losses from reducing tax rates at the border, such as tariffs, will be cushioned, but not fully offset, by reductions in evasion.

2 Literature review

The prominent role of tax evasion as part of the fiscal difficulties of developing countries is widely documented.[1] Burgess and Stern (1993) bluntly characterize tax evasion in developing countries as 'rife'. They argue that evasion hinges on cultural factors as much as on economic incentives and deficient tax collection agencies. According to Burgess and Stern, 'differences in the tradition of compliance probably explain as much of the worldwide pattern of taxation as do under-resourced or poorly organized tax administrations' (Burgess and Stern 1993: 799). In a survey of the literature on tax evasion, McLaren (1996) makes the case for a distinction in the relevant theory between two divergent strands of research. At one level, tax evasion related to fiscal corruption,[2] and evasion simply as an undeclared transaction. In the process, McLaren reviews a number of studies which attempted to estimate evasion. He reports, overall, that the degree of revenue erosion due to evasion seems to be not very far from actual tax receipts.

The connection between tax rates and evasion, from a theoretical point of view, was first formally explored more than three decades ago by Allingham and Sandmo (1972). They assert the existence of a positive association linking these two variables, under the assumptions of risk aversion and punishment for evasion if caught. This result has not been generalized. Later theoretical literature almost uniformly fails to establish predictions of the impact of tax rates on evasion. Slemrod and Yitzhaki (2000), in a review of the modern literature, suggest that predictions follow from the assumptions imposed.

While the theoretical literature does not necessarily point to a positive association between tax rates and evasion, existing empirical work seems to point in this direction. For example, Pritchett and Sethi (1994) examine the relation between average tariff rates (collection for a specific product divided by the recorded trade flows for that product) and the official, statutory rates of the tariff code for a sample of three developing countries. They report that growth in collected rates is significantly less than one-for-one following an increase in the official rates, due to a growing ratio of officially exempted imports as the tariff rate increases. It bears emphasizing that their approach relies solely on official statistics, thus ignoring tariff revenue losses due to smuggling, under-invoicing and incorrect declaration of items. As a result, the gap that they find between actual tax receipts and potential tax collections (that is, if all imports were properly reported and paid the official tax rate) is understated.

As mentioned in Section 1, Fisman and Wei (2004) find a significant and strong relationship between the tax burden at the border and evasion using product level data on imports by China from Hong Kong. According to the estimates generated by Fisman and Wei, China would actually increase revenue through the application of lower rates. The case country in question here, Mozambique, exhibits many of the symptoms discussed in the literature. In a recent survey of the business community, tax evasion was perceived as a major factor in explaining 'the large sums of money which remain outside the tax system' (Bolnick 2004a: 27). A separate survey of perceptions of governance and corruption found that tax collection agencies are viewed by the overwhelming majority of Mozambicans as among the most corrupt institutions in the country.[3] Macamo (1998), employing a marvellously simple study design, recorded easily observable but still illicit trade crossing relevant border posts with neighbouring countries. The study found an amount of illegal trade in 1996 close to 10 per cent of the total value of imports. As Macamo monitored less than half of total import volume and explicitly admits to missing certain forms of evasion, this estimate is clearly a lower bound. More recently, Arndt and Tarp (2004) have developed a trade model (with Mozambique as case study) where special attention is given to evasion and tariff revenues paid. Despite these efforts, a great deal remains unknown in relation to the full extent of evasion, its motivations, its characteristics and its linkages with tax policy. We turn to the specific methodology employed for filling this knowledge gap.

3 Model specifications

3.1 Baseline model specification

A central challenge when studying tax evasion concerns the issue of measurement. Evasion, due to its very nature, does not generate any statistical data, which implicitly means that an appropriate methodology for estimation is required. Following the approach explored by Fisman and Wei (2004), our base measure of evasion is determined by the ratio of the value of South African declared exports to Mozambique – defined hereafter as X – to the value of Mozambique's recorded imports from South Africa – defined hereafter as M. In principle, to the extent that errors of measurement and evasion are entirely avoided, the numerator and denominator should be precisely equivalent.[4] Put differently, a ratio X/M of unity is supposed to characterize a state with no evasion.

As a first step towards examining the causality between customs tax rates and tax evasion, a baseline model must be specified. The model posits a linear relationship between the logarithm of our evasion measure (X/M) and the *Taxes* variable, which consists of the sum of all applicable taxes levied at the border for any particular product.

The model, thus, is defined by:

$$Log\left(\frac{X}{M}\right) = \alpha + \beta Taxes + \varepsilon \tag{1}$$

In equation (1), a positive B indicates that tax evasion is positively related to overall tax rates. Because of the specification itself, the coefficient B indicates the responsiveness of tax evasion to tax rates, so that a marginal increase in the tax rate would have an impact in evasion of B per cent. Alternatively, with a positive B we could simply make the case that higher levels of taxation are associated with higher levels of evasion. The baseline model can be used, furthermore, to suggest an expression for the growth rate of evasion:

$$\left(\frac{dX}{X}\right) - \left(\frac{dM}{M}\right) = \beta(dTaxes) \tag{2}$$

Empirically, direct imports M cannot always be directly observed. What is in reality observable is M^*, a measure that encompasses both direct imports from South Africa and transhipments misreported as imports from South Africa. For the time period under investigation, the Mozambican customs tax system provided very limited incentives for deliberate misclassification of products as South African. Following Fisman and Wei, misclassified imports are simply assumed to be proportionally related to the size of genuine imports from South Africa. Allowing for a slight adjustment in the assumption made by Fisman and Wei in the Chinese case study,[5] misclassified indirect imports in the Mozambican case can be expressed as follows:

$$M_i^* = (1 + \theta_i)M_i \tag{3}$$

where θ_i is an independent and identically distributed random variable, with $0 \leq \theta_i \leq 1$.

Equation (3) leaves us now in a more suitable position to specify a transformed baseline model, which can be expressed as follows:

$$Log\left(\frac{X}{M^*}\right) = \alpha^* + \beta Taxes + v \tag{4}$$

where

$$\alpha^* \equiv \alpha + E(\varepsilon_i - \log(1 + \theta_i))$$

and

$$v = \varepsilon_i - \log(1 + \theta_i) - E(\varepsilon_i - \log(1 + \theta_i)) \sim N(0, \sigma^2)$$

The transformed model in (4) includes a new constant term, α^*, and a new error term, v. The error term, v, is assumed to be identically and independently distributed. In the remainder of the analysis, equation (4) will be used to evaluate the sensitivity of evasion to tax rates.

3.2 *Augmented model specification*

Evasion, of course, can occur in a host of forms. One distinct form of evasion is misclassification of merchandise. Detecting whether or not higher taxed goods are being mislabelled as lower taxed goods requires an extension to our baseline model. In order to investigate for product misclassification, an augmented model with a new variable, *Av_Tax_Sim*, defined as the average tax of similar products, is specified. For each product, *Av_Tax_Sim* is defined as the average of the tax rate applied to products sharing the first four digits of the commodity classification code as the product in question.

Note that the error term maintains the properties specified earlier in equation (4). The augmented model hence yields:

$$Log\left(\frac{X}{M^*}\right) = \alpha * + \beta_1 Taxes + \beta_2 Av\_Tax\_Sim + v \tag{5}$$

Product mislabelling may be captured by a negative and statistically significant β_2. Holding the tax of a given product constant, lowering the tax of similar products enhances the incentives to misclassify our given product as a similar one.

In addition to this, the augmented model can be further extended. For example, equation (6) includes a squared *Taxes* variable as a regressor to ascertain whether the relationship between tax rates and evasion is non-linear:

$$Log\left(\frac{X}{M^*}\right) = \alpha^* + \beta_1 Taxes + \beta_2 Taxes^2 + \beta_3 Av\_Tax\_Sim + u \tag{6}$$

Similar specifications in terms of quantities, as opposed to values, can also be employed. Let us define *Qx* and *QM* as new variables that capture the quantities exported and imported, respectively, for each product. The basic and augmented models then take the following forms:

$$Log\left(\frac{Q_x}{Q_M}\right) = \alpha + \beta_1 Taxes + v \tag{7}$$

$$Log\left(\frac{Q_x}{Q_M}\right) = \alpha + \beta_1 Taxes + \beta_2 Av\_Tax\_Sim + v \tag{8}$$

4 Data and empirical application

Cross-border trade data between South Africa and Mozambique were obtained from the South African National Statistics Agency and the Mozambican Customs Service. Data from 2003 were structured at the tariff code item level (conforming to the Harmonized System). The recent adoption of a more detailed classification system for tradable goods (that is, eight digits) by both Mozambique and South Africa bolsters the analysis by permitting a more disaggregated approach, which improves the precision with which evasion can be measured.

Data on trade taxes, just like data on M^*, were taken from the customs central database. Essentially, a measure of taxation designed to capture the total tax burden at the border has been created by adding up, for every single listed product, the taxes that respectively apply. For the 2003 period, the (ad-valorem) tariff schedule in Mozambique ranges from 0 to 25 per cent. The tariff structure prescribes, grosso modo, the following rates: (1) 0 per cent tariff rates for medicines and SADC raw materials; (2) 2.5 per cent for non-SADC raw materials and for cereals; (3) 5 per cent for capital equipment and most oil products; (4) 7.5 per cent for rice, sugar and intermediate goods and (5) 25 per cent for consumer goods. Further, 17 per cent VAT tax is levied on the quasi-totality of imports, whereas excise and surcharge taxes are imposed on selected products.[6] Summary statistics on imports and taxes are displayed in Table 11.1.

The UN system of product classification leaves countries room for discretion in choosing the levels of disaggregation beyond the six-digit coding. This led to a number of product code mismatches between the Mozambican and South African datasets. In total, after reorganizing the dataset and focusing on clearly comparable product categories, the final sample contains 2,486 observations. Our dataset is further supplemented by flows in quantities and related units of measurement. For regressions in quantities (see equations (6) and (7)), every time it was not possible to match units of measurement from the respective data sources it was deemed necessary to discard the product in question from the regression.

5 Regression results

5.1 Baseline and augmented model results

In this sub-section, the focus is on results for the baseline and augmented models. Table 11.2 presents a first set of results for equation (4). According to Table 11.2, the estimate of B is positive and statistically significant. An estimate value of 1.38 suggests that if the tax rate increases by one

Table 11.1 Import and Taxes: Summary Statistics

	Mean	*Median*	*Min*	*Max*	*St. Dev.*	*No. of obs.*
Log (X)	18.91	19.097	7.98	27.74	2.728	4543
Log (M)	19.08	19.312	9.44	26.80	2.567	3481
Log (X/M)	0.29	0.282	−11.28	11.71	2.246	2486
Log (Qx)	7.11	7.139	0.00	20.58	3.393	4536
Log (QM)	7.27	7.203	-3.51	19.40	3.661	3434
Log (Qx/QM)	0.29	0.288	−12.28	14.26	3.109	2460
Taxes	0.30	0.245	0.00	1.07	0.141	3481
Av_Tax_Sim	0.30	0.245	0.00	1.07	0.134	3095

Source: Mozambique and Republic of South Africa customs data for 2003

Table 11.2 Results – Transformed Baseline Model

Variable	Coefficient	Total sample	Excl. first and last percentile	Excl. first and last 0.05 quantile
Constant	α^*	–0.12 (0.11)	–0.12 (0.09)	0.02 (0.08)
Taxes	β	1.38 (0.32)	1.43 (0.29)	0.99 (0.23)
R^2		0.0074	0.01	0.0082
Obs.		2486	2437	2237

Note: standard deviations in brackets
Source: Author's estimates

percentage point, the ratio quantifying evasion X/M will increase by nearly 1.4 per cent. Alternatively put, the result shows that a higher fiscal burden on trade in Mozambique leads to a larger amount of relative tax evasion. These results are robust to various exercises to test for undue influence of outliers.

It is important to draw attention to the poor fit of the regressions. In spite of the significance of the B coefficient, the tax rate cannot explain more than 1 per cent of the variation in evasion across the different results. The study of 'missing' imports in China conducted by Fisman and Wei encountered the same phenomenon of relatively poor explanatory power. In the Mozambican case, aggregation eliminates noise and enhances explanatory power. For example, collapsing the dataset by using the mean of X/M for each different tax rate enhances the R_2; statistic to close to 13 per cent, while the estimate of B rises to 1.9.

This first set of results reveals that higher tax levels are strongly associated with higher levels of under-reporting of import values. A different proposition is to attempt to detect the presence of misclassification of goods for tax advantage purposes. Table 11.3 displays results for the augmented model, which introduces the new variables Av_Tax_Sim and $Taxes_2$ into the baseline model. The coefficient on the Av_Tax_Sim variable is statistically significant and less than zero (one-tailed tests) except in the case where the lowest and highest 5 per cent of sample tax rates are excluded. Note that when the taxes applied to similar products are the same as the rate applied

Table 11.3 Results –Augmented Model

Variable	Coefficient	Omitting $Taxes^2$	Full regression	Excl. first and last 0.05 quantile
Constant	α^*	–0.07 (0.12)	–0.32 (0.17)	–0.08 (0.12)
Taxes	β_1	2.72 (0.75)	4.24 (1.05)	1.95 (0.77)
$Taxes^2$	β_2	–	–2.08 (1.00)	–0.63 (0.74)
Av_tax_Sim	β_3	–1.61 (0.80)	–1.53 (0.80)	–0.46 (0.59)
R^2		0.0094	0.0113	0.0109
Obs.		2219	2219	2003

Note: standard deviations in brackets
Source: Author's estimates

to the product in question and when the variable *Taxes^2* is omitted, the augmented specification collapses to equation (1). In this case, the coefficient on the variable *Taxes* effectively becomes 2.72–1.61 = 1.11, which is similar to the 1.38 found in the basic specification. However, when the average tax on similar products is less than the tax on the product in question (*Av_Tax_Sim* < *Taxes*), the propensity to evade increases markedly. Hence, results point to the presence of fraudulent classification of merchandise.

These findings are consistent with the existing empirical literature. A heterogeneous trade tariff menu seems to nourish corruption among customs officials as the standard deviation of trade tariffs across goods is robustly correlated with measured corruption across countries (see, for instance, Gatti 1999). Our results reinforce the case for harmonization of trade tariffs within classes of similar products. Gatti (1999) believes that setting trade tariff rates at a uniform level limits public officials' bribe taking behaviour, allowing countries to obtain efficiency gains as well as delivering higher revenue levels. Winters (2004) uses Chile as an illustration of simpler, more transparent and non-discretionary trade policies.

5.2 Regressions in quantities

The results thus far highlight the presence of under-invoicing and fraudulent product classification. Under-invoicing can potentially occur in two ways: under-pricing and under-reporting of quantities. To investigate these possibilities, we employ the same basic regression frameworks in 'quantity model' specifications as in equations (7) and (8). Results for the quantity models are presented in Table 11.4. Under-reporting of quantities requires the estimated coefficient for B_1 to be positive and significant. When the full sample is used, the estimated coefficients for both equations (7) and (8) suggest that there is no evidence of under-reporting of quantities. Caution is required due to the quality of data on quantities. Results are somewhat more robust when the lowest and highest 5 per cent of tax rates are excluded. Higher taxes result in significant evasion in quantities and point to the existence of merchandise misclassification.

Table 11.4 Results – Quantity Model

Variable	Coefficient	Omitting Av_Tax_sim (7)	Full regression (8)	Excl. first and last 0.05 quantile (8)
Constant	α*	0.19 (0.16)	0.22 (0.18)	0.34 (0.14)
Taxes	β_1	0.30 (0.50)	1.49 (1.10)	1.76 (0.85)
Av_tax_Sim	β_2	–	–1.48 (1.17)	–1.93 (0.91)
R^2		0.0002	0.0009	0.0026
Obs.		2201	1965	1784

Note: standard deviations in brackets. Regressions with the same units of measurement; when the units of measurement are not the same, the observations were dropped.
Source: Author's estimates

5.3 *Functional form*

So far, it has been implicitly assumed that the responsiveness of evasion to tax rates is constant, so that the elasticity of evasion is continuously equal to approximately 1.4 regardless of tax rate levels. However, the actual elasticity may vary as a function of the rate. The second specification in Table 11.3 permits nonlinearity in the relation between tax rates and tax evasion. Results using the full sample show a concave relationship with tax rates. The propensity to evade remains strongly positive over the domain of the data. Also, similar to the average tax for similar products, the significant concave relationship disappears with exclusion of the first and last 5 per cent quantiles.

For confirmation purposes, an alternative testing method was conducted using a specification with quartile dummy variables to measure differential coefficients. The specification employed is given by:

$$Log\left(\frac{X}{M^*}\right) = \alpha^* + \beta_1 Taxes + \beta_2(Q_2 Taxes) + \beta_3(Q_3 Taxes) + \beta_4$$

$$\times (Q_4 Taxes) + v \tag{9}$$

where Q_n refers to the variable *Taxes* quartile n and n = 1, ... , 4.

With this type of specification, β_2, β_3 and β_4 are differential coefficients by reference to β_1. The test, in this case, aims at evaluating potential shifts in the elasticity of evasion across the different quartiles, by looking both at the magnitude and the significance of those differentials. Table 11.5 shows the results. It indicates that the estimates of β_2, β_3 and β_4 are not statistically significant.

6 Implications of regression estimates for evasion and customs ~ tax revenue

In this section of the chapter, the implications of tariff rate changes for evasion and revenue are simulated using the regression coefficient estimates. Consider first the average value of *Taxes*, which is about 30 per cent. Let us assume for simplicity that the probability of error in merchandise country of

Table 11.5 Results – Nonlinearity Test with Quartile Dummies

	Coefficient	*Standard Error*
Constant	–0.05	0.21
Taxes	1.30	1.15
Q2 * Taxes	–0.61	0.60
Q3* Taxes	0.04	0.74
Q4* Taxes	–0.15	0.99
R^2	0.0084	
Obs.	2486	

Note: Dependent variable is Log (X/M*)
Source: Author's estimates

origin classification is insignificant, which translates to θ equal to zero. Employing mean values, the augmented model with full regression (see Table 11.3) gives a predicted X/M ratio of 1.357.[7] This implies that for every import transaction recorded the genuine import value is on average 1.357 times larger. Given the predominance of smuggling in highly taxed products, the consequences of evasion for revenue are stronger than the consequences for import volumes.[8]

Consider now the more specific case of a typical consumer good, subject to the top tariff rate. For this kind of product, the statutory trade tariff is 25 per cent and VAT applies at a rate of 17 per cent. Thus the aggregate tax, *Taxes*, equals 42 per cent. With a value for *Taxes* of 42 per cent, the augmented model predicts, in turn, an X/M ratio of 1.57. In sum, these results indicate that smuggling of consumer goods in 2003 amounted to more than half of reported imports of consumer goods.[9]

The implications of evasion for total revenue can also be considered. Figure 11.1 displays a 'Laffer Curve'. For an initial tax rate of 0 per cent, the corresponding value of imports is, hypothetically, 1,000 units. As tax rates increase, declared imports decline according to the estimated relationship for the total sample presented in Table 11.2. It is important to highlight that this analysis assumes that overall import demand is completely price inelastic (for example, a total of 1,000 units is imported either officially or unofficially regardless of the applied tariff rate). Under these assumptions, Figure 11.1 displays an indicator of tax revenue collections which reaches its maximum point when the tax rate is slightly less than 72 per cent. The actual peak of the Laffer Curve would be at a lower level of taxation if price responsiveness of total import demand were considered. Nevertheless, simulations with plausible elasticity values illustrate that nearly all Mozambican rates are to the left of the peak of the Laffer Curve, implying revenue losses with reduced tariff rates.[10]

7 Conclusion

Tax rates have a strong and positive effect on tax evasion in Mozambique. For every percentage point increase in the customs tax rates, evasion increases by about 1.4 per cent. In comparative terms, the degree of responsiveness obtained for this representative Sub-Saharan country corresponds to about half of the response found for China.

Customs tax evasion operates through two identifiable channels: under-invoicing and fraudulent misclassification of merchandise. Using the full sample, there is no evidence of under-declaration of quantities, suggesting that under-reporting in the value of imports acts through under-reporting in unit values. Noisy data on quantities, however, indicate that prudence is required in the interpretation of these results. Evidence for evasion in quantities begins to appear after exclusion of the first and last 5 per cent of tax rates in the database employed.

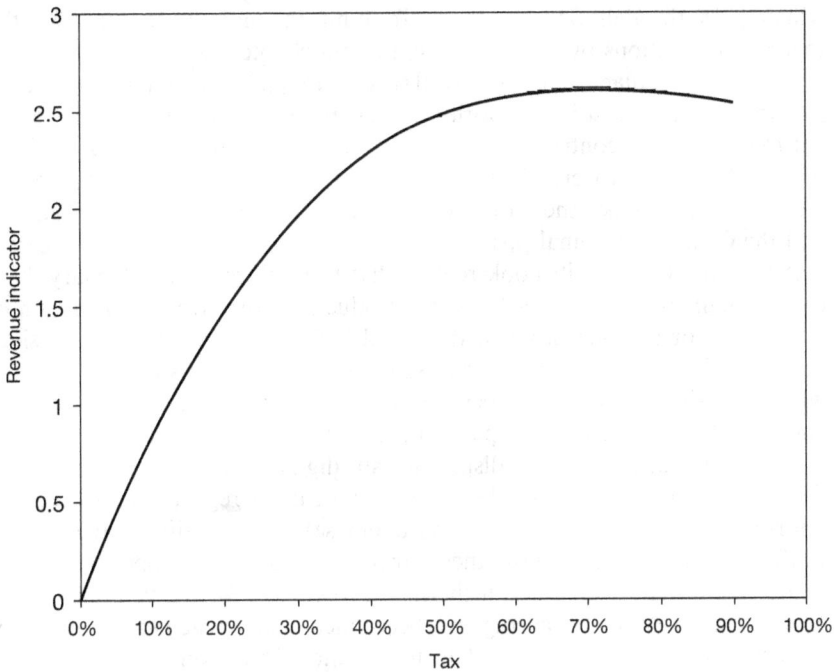

Figure 11.1 The Laffer Curve

We also build on regression results in order to infer levels of evasion. Using average tax rates, the general rate of evasion is estimated to be equal to 36 per cent of recorded imports. For consumer products, where the top tariff rate is applied, the evasion rate climbs to nearly 57 per cent of declared imports. This pattern of increasing concentration of unrecorded trade in products with higher protection rates is consistent with Macamo (1998) and Arndt and Tarp (2004).

The presence of substantial evasion combined with the sensitivity of evasion to tax rate levels implies that the negative revenue implications of trade liberalization may be softened or even reversed (as Fisman and Wei found for China). In this case, simulations imply that formalization of trade following trade liberalization softens but does not reverse the revenue impact. Hence, the difficult issue of replacing lost border tax revenue must be confronted as trade liberalization proceeds in Mozambique.

8 Annex: further data details

An effort was made to clean the original trade information and eliminate obvious inconsistencies detected in the data. Chapter 87 of the tariff book, covering motor vehicles and its spare parts, includes a substantial amount of indirect trade. An example is imported cars from Japan, the large majority of which pass through South Africa. To limit the noise introduced in the regression equations by indirect trade, the full chapter has been eliminated.

The lack of available data for Mozal (Mozambique's first aluminium smelter and the fourth largest in the world) and energy imports in the Mozambican Customs database contributed to further data exclusion.[11] Selected products imported by Mozal were identified and subsequently removed from the original database, as per the indications provided by the Mozal border agency and the Customs terminal post.

Additionally, the tariff book reform that took place in mid-January 2003 caused changes in duty rates for a few products. In the face of duplication of tariff rates for a single product, it seemed logical to systematically consider the prevailing rate after the reform, since it virtually covers the full year (so when choosing, for example, between a pre-reform tariff rate of 0 per cent and a post-reform rate of 2.5 per cent, the latter has been selected).

Moreover, tariff headings displaying six digits were not included in the database. As such cases invariably involve errors in the registration of the trade information in TIMS (the Customs database) and identifying the correct tariff heading is a delicate task, these tariff headings were scrapped along with related eight-digit positions. Furthermore, to correct for the volatility in the sugar surcharge, a simple average has been calculated for each variety of sugar.

Lastly, our dataset contains data for X and M* converted in CIF value terms. The existing 'simplified regime' of imports in Mozambique (small imports cleared at border points and of a value less than US$500) could be perceived as a likely source of discrepancy between Mozambican and South African trade data. This type of trade flow is not captured by the Mozambican trade statistics database, but due to its insignificance as a proportion of total imports this aspect is overlooked.

Notes

1 For instance, Gauthier and Gersovitz (1997), along with Gauthier and Reinikka (2001), provide surveys of widespread tax evasion among businesses in two African countries, Cameroon and Uganda, respectively.
2 Tirole (1986) constitutes one of the first attempts to formalize hierarchical collusion using a principal–agent framework.
3 *Savana Notícias* (local independent newspaper), 5 August.
4 Exact features of the Mozambican and South African data that might lead to a ratio different from one such as treatment of transport costs are examined in later sections and in the Annex to this chapter.
5 In Fisman and Wei, the magnitude of misclassified imports depends on a constant and the import value of the product (subject to some random error).
6 Sugar and one class of cement are two of very few products in Mozambique enjoying protection from import taxes above a typical consumer product in 2003.
7 It has been assumed in the simulations that the average tax of similar products equals the tax of the corresponding product.
8 Arndt and Tarp (2004) find a level of forgone revenue due to smuggling and legal tax avoidance equal to about 60 per cent of the total statutory tariff revenue.

9 If θ equals 0.1 (that is, 10 per cent of South African recorded imports were misclassified), the evasion rate increases by approximately 15 percentage points.

10 Reinhart (1995) estimates regional elasticities of import demand. Africa registers a price elasticity of 1.36. This is higher than the price elasticities estimated for Latin America (0.36) and Asia (0.40).

11 The export value for energy declared by the Repbublic of South Africa substantially underestimates the official import figure reported by Motraco (a private company operating under a concession contract that authorizes the import of energy into Mozambique).

12 Mozambique and regional integration

Andrea Alfieri and Xavier Cirera

1 Introduction

Mozambique has been implementing a gradual process of trade liberalization since the start of its Economic Rehabilitation Programme in 1987, when market-oriented economic reforms were first introduced. On the import side, duty rates have been lowered and harmonized into five ad-valorem tariff bands from 0 to 20 per cent. On the export side, the country is eligible for non-reciprocal duty-free access into most developed country markets for most products (for example through the European Union's Everything but Arms scheme or the United States' African Growth and Opportunity Act [AGOA] concessions).

During the same period, Mozambique has also demonstrated a commitment to regional integration in Southern Africa by participating in the SADC Trade Protocol, which led to the creation of a free trade area among a dozen countries in Southern Africa in 2008 (with certain product-specific exceptions until 2015). The country has separately been invited to join the five-member Southern Africa Customs Union (SACU).[1] Both SADC and SACU include South Africa, which is by far the largest and most advanced economy in sub-Saharan Africa, as well as Mozambique's largest, most diversified and most consistent trade and investment partner.

The government of Mozambique is now presented with strategic options for its trade policy. It can decide to continue implementing only the SADC Trade Protocol, leading to a free trade area in the region; it can advance towards a customs union through SACU; or it can accelerate the process of unilateral liberalization on a Most-Favoured Nation (MFN) basis for all trade partners worldwide.

The purpose of this chapter is to estimate and discuss the expected impact on Mozambique's trade and revenue flows, as well as on welfare, of reforming international trade under these different policy scenarios. A simple static partial equilibrium methodology is used, in order to disentangle the reform impact at the product-specific level. Product-specific estimates show where, and in what way, most of the gains and losses from granting trade preferences are likely to be concentrated, so they can help trade negotiators and policy makers to design trade and fiscal policies to maximize the benefits while minimizing the losses.

The chapter does not focus directly on the impact on exports, mainly due to the fact that Mozambique is already eligible for duty-free access for most products in most of its important partner country markets (including South Africa and the European Union, EU), so no additional tariff reductions are possible. Nevertheless, the chapter does discuss briefly the likelihood that regional integration would have a positive impact on exports through different channels: increased foreign investment, the elimination of non-tariff barriers or the elimination of rules of origin, especially in the case of a customs union.

The chapter is organized as follows. Section 2 describes the context of trade policy in Mozambique and the existing tariff and tax structure. Section 3 briefly illustrates the partial equilibrium methodology employed in the analysis. Section 4 summarizes the main results from the estimations. Section 5 discuses the revenue implications of the different trade reform scenarios considered. Section 6 analyses the main implications for trade and tax policy of the results of the chapter. Section 7 concludes with policy implications of the results and a list of issues for further research.[2]

2 Context of trade policy

2.1 Mozambique

Mozambique's total recorded imports in 2004 amounted to US$2.0 billion.[3] South Africa was by far the largest partner (55 per cent of total imports; see Figure 12.1), with all other SACU and SADC countries representing only 5 per cent of imports altogether (2 per cent for SACU members and 3 per cent for non-SACU SADC members). The EU was a major source of imports (16 per cent), while the USA, China and India each represented less than 5 per cent of Mozambique's total imports.

In the same year, Mozambique exported a total of US$1.5 billion (see Figure 12.2).[4] The EU was the major destination, with 68 per cent of total exports (due largely to Mozal aluminium). South Africa was the second-largest importing partner, receiving 14 per cent of Mozambique's exports, while exports to the rest of SACU and SADC were marginal (6 per cent).

Mozambique's exports are mostly limited to a small number of industrial 'mega-projects' such as the Mozal aluminium smelter, the Cahora Bassa hydro-electric dam and the Sasol natural gas pipeline, as well as certain agricultural/forestry/fishery commodities such as prawns, sugar, cotton and wood. Except for Mozal aluminium, there are very few value-added manufacturing exports. Imports are diversified and include fuel, electricity (for Mozal), vehicles, machinery, consumer goods, wheat, etc. (see Table 12.1).

As a result of the implantation of mega-projects, as well as the recovery and development of the agricultural sector since the end of the civil war, exports have grown rapidly over the last few years. Rapid import growth has

Imports by origin, 2004

Exports by destination, 2004

Rest of
World 24%

European
Union 16%

South
Africa 55%

Other Southern
Africa 5%

Rest of
World
12%

South
Africa 14%

Other Southern
Africa 6%

European
Union 68%

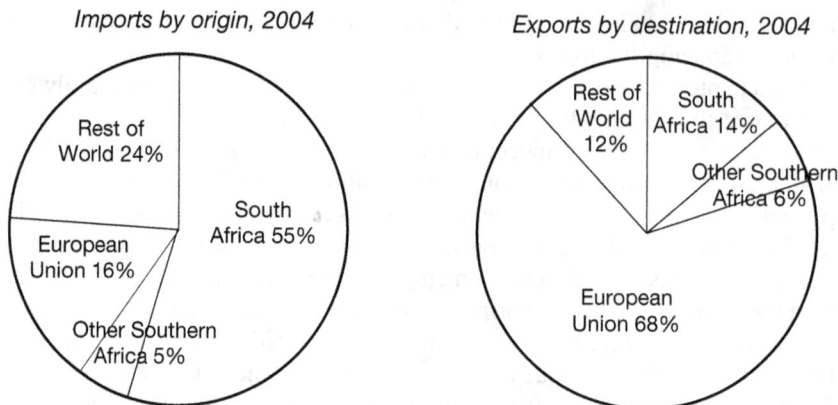

Figure 12.1 Import and export shares of Mozambique's trading partners
Source: INE, authors'calculations

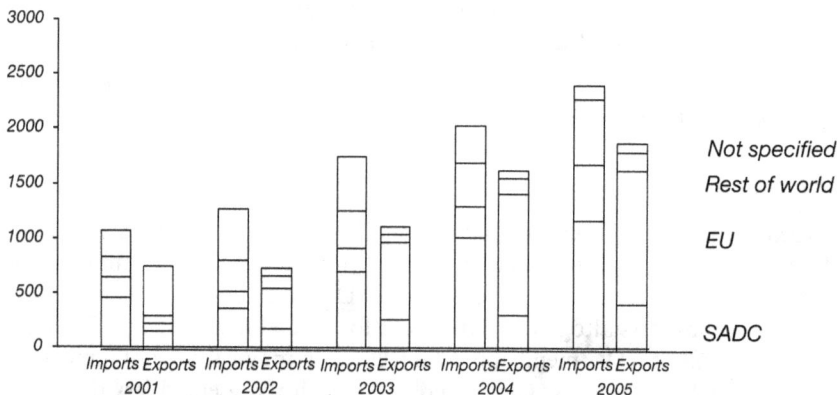

Not specified

Rest of world

EU

SADC

Imports Exports Imports Exports Imports Exports Imports Exports Imports Exports
      2001   2002   2003   2004   2005

Figure 12.2 Mozambique's evolution of trade (2001–05, US$ million)
Source: INE, authors'calculations.

been driven by the needs of the mega-projects and by the emergence of a
class of consumers with disposable income, especially in Maputo. The consistent trade deficit has been made possible by foreign exchange inflows due
to foreign aid, mega-project investments, remittances from migrant labour
abroad and certain service industries, especially tourism.

Mozambique reformed its applied MFN duty structure significantly
during the 1990s in agreement with the adjustment programmes proposed by
the World Bank and IMF. Overall rates have been reduced, all duties have
been converted into ad-valorem tariffs and the number of bands has been
harmonized to the existing five. In 2004 the simple average MFN applied
tariff was 12.1 per cent (see Table 12.2), while the weighted average tariff
amounted to 8.5 per cent. Tariff liberalization has continued since then, with

Table 12.1 Key Imported and Exported Product Groups, 2004

	Imports						Exports				
HS	USD Million	From SADC (%)	From EU (%)	From ROW* (%)	% of all imports	HS	USD Million	To SADC (%)	To EU (%)	To ROW* (%)	% of all exports
99	332	–	–	–	16.3	76	915	0	100	0	60.8
27	308	98.9	0.1	0.9	15.1	27	136	100	0	0	9.0
87	171	64.6	9.9	25.6	8.4	03	107	12.1	72.0	15.9	7.1
85	167	41.0	41.9	17.1	8.2	84	58	93.2	0.4	6.4	3.9
10	145	5.8	4.7	89.5	7.1	17	48	0	62.6	37.4	3.2
84	134	48.0	36.9	15.1	6.6	24	41	100	0	0	2.7
90	68	76.1	18.5	5.4	3.3	52	34	12.3	21.4	66.3	2.3
40	53	21.4	66.5	12.1	2.6	44	30	14.6	6.9	78.5	2.0
73	52	66.4	9.7	24.0	2.6	08	30	3.7	4.7	91.5	2.0
48	39	83.1	4.9	12.1	1.9	12	12	10.5	17.9	71.6	0.8

*: Rest of the world
Source:INE, authors' calculations

Table 12.2 MFN Tariff Structure, 2004

MFN duty (%)	Number of lines	% total lines	Imports ($1,000)	% total imports*	Average imports ($1,000)
0.0	116	2.16	83,871.6	12.19	723.03
2.5	1,151	21.46	94,101.6	13.68	81.76
5.0	662	12.34	134,269.1	19.52	202.82
7.5	1,564	29.16	253,812.3	36.89	162.28
25.0	1,871	34.88	121,912.6	17.72	64.95
All lines	5,364		687,967.2		
Average MFN tariff (%)				12.10	
Weighted average MFN tariff (%)				8.50	
Standard deviation				9.67	

*: Figures calculated using the total volume of trade net of good classified under Ch.99.
Source: Mozambique tariff book and INE, authors' calculations

the highest duties falling from 25 per cent to 20 per cent in 2006 and set to fall further in future years.

High duties are used mainly for the purpose of revenue collection rather than for the protection of import-competing industries. These higher rates fall mostly on consumer goods, while inputs – raw materials, capital goods and intermediate goods – are taxed at lower rates.

Special duty exemptions are granted in certain cases:

- about 50 manufacturing firms that are able to demonstrate yearly revenue of more than US$250,000 and value addition greater than 20 per cent on imported inputs benefit from a special exemption programme, the Regime Aduaneiro para a Industria Transformadora;
- registered investors may claim duty exemptions on 642 tariff lines (11 per cent of all lines) considered to be 'capital goods';
- 'mega-project' investments (those exceeding US$500 million) may benefit from special incentives and exemptions, granted on a case-by-case basis by the Council of Ministers;
- certain projects with a strong social component (such as those related to health or education) may be granted exemptions on a case-by-case basis;
- finally, VAT on inputs re-exported after processing or assembly should be reimbursed, although in practice firms are not reimbursed directly but are granted a credit for duties payable on future imports.

There are no specific duties currently being applied, nor are any anti-dumping, countervailing or safeguard measures being implemented. However, there are a small number of fixed and variable surcharges applied on top of normal duties to protect some 'sensitive' products (see Table 12.3). The most

Table 12.3 Applied Tariff Surcharges

Tariff line code	Product description	Surcharge
17011100	Raw cane sugar	Variable duty (average 2004: 77%)
17011200	Raw beetroot sugar	Variable duty (average 2004: 77%)
17019100	White sugar with flavourings or colourings	Variable duty (average 2004: 54%)
17019900	Other white sugar	Variable duty (average 2004: 54%)
25232900	Portland cement	10.5%
72104100	Corrugated iron or steel sheets	20%
73063000	Round tubes of iron or steel	10.5%
73066000	Other tubes of iron or steel	10.5%

Source: Mozambique tariff book and National Sugar Institute

important surcharge is in the case of sugar, where the surcharge was given as an incentive to foreign investors in the sector. It is being debated whether these surcharges should be maintained.[5]

In addition to duties and duty surcharges, goods imported to Mozambique may also be subject to excise taxes and VAT. These taxes are calculated cumulatively. That is, customs duties are calculated as a percentage of CIF import values, excise (where applicable) is a percentage of CIF plus duties, and VAT is a percentage of CIF plus duties plus excise.

Excise taxes on specific luxury products such as cars and alcoholic drinks range from 15 to 65 per cent. However, few products (2.7 per cent of tariff lines) are currently covered by such a tax. By contrast, VAT is charged on 97 per cent of tariff lines at a uniform rate of 17 per cent. Exempted products are mostly organic chemicals, pharmaceuticals, fertilizers, mechanical products, cereals and other basic agricultural products. VAT exemptions are also granted to specific industries (e.g. sugar, certain mega-projects) and government-supported projects (e.g. in education or health).

Taxes on imports are an important source of government revenue. In 2004 customs duties (including surcharges) represented 14 per cent, excise on imported goods 3 per cent and VAT on imports 21 per cent of total government revenue raised through taxes.[6]

Mozambique grants duty preferences to members of the SADC Trade Protocol. Through this agreement, duties are being progressively lowered and a free trade area is presently being established in Southern Africa, although certain 'sensitive' goods are exempted until 2012 or even 2015 in some cases. In 2004 SADC countries benefited from duty-free access into Mozambique on 30 per cent of tariff lines (see Table 12.4), equivalent to 53 per cent of total SADC imports. South Africa benefits from preferential access on roughly the same number of lines (28.1 per cent), with 21.7 per cent of imports originating in South Africa.

Table 12.4 SADC and South African Market Access into Mozambique, 2004

South Africa

MFN duty (%)	Number of lines	% Total lines	Imports ($1,000)	% Total imports*	Average imports ($1,000)
0.0	1,509	28.10	202,068.7	21.67	133.91
2.5	10	0.19	8,224.0	0.88	822.40
5.0	554	10.32	337,892.9	36.23	609.92
7.5	1,437	26.76	230,140.6	24.68	160.15
25.0	1,860	34.64	154,312.7	16.55	82.96
All lines	5,370		932,638.9		

Average tariff (%)   11.19
Weighted Average tariff (%)   7.80
Standard deviation   9.01

SADC

MFN duty (%)	Number of lines	% Total lines	Imports ($1,000)	% Total imports*	Average imports ($1,000)
0	1,613	30.04	43,651.8	53.22	27.06
2.5	6	0.11	0.1	0.00	0.02
5	548	10.20	5,455.4	6.65	9.96
7.5	1,405	26.16	18,472.3	22.52	13.15
25	1,798	33.48	14,440.5	17.61	8.03
All lines	5,370		82,020.1		

Average tariff (%)   10.85
Weighted Average tariff (%)   6.42
Standard deviation   10.44

*: Figures calculated using the total volume of trade net of good classified under Ch.99
Source: Mozambique tariff book and Comtrade, authors' calculations

On the export side, Mozambique is eligible for duty-free access into most of its major markets (the EU through the Cotonou Convention and Everything but Arms, the USA through AGOA, South Africa through the accelerated implementation of the SADC Trade Protocol). However, in practice preference utilization rates are low, due in part to the cost of complying with restrictive rules of origin but mostly because of the limited supply capacity of Mozambican producers.

2.2 SACU

SACU is the oldest customs union in the world, dating from 1910. The agreement was modified in 1969 and most recently in 2002. Botswana, Lesotho, Namibia, South Africa and Swaziland are equal members, although traditionally South Africa has dominated decision-making.[7]

SACU members have a common external tariff with 6,690 product-specific lines. Customs duties are charged on the basis of the FOB transaction price, in contrast to international standard practice which is based on the CIF value of goods. Duties are calculated in a variety of ways depending on the product, including ad-valorem, specific, mixed and compound tariffs and formula duties based on reference prices. Around 97 per cent of tariff lines have one of the 39 different ad-valorem rates (see Table 12.5). The simple average tariff is 8 per cent and the maximum applied tariff is 55 per cent. Over half the tariff lines are duty free; the highest ad-valorem rates are concentrated mostly among textile and clothing products. Specific and mixed duties are imposed almost exclusively on agricultural products.

In addition to customs duties, goods imported into the SACU area may be subject to excise taxes, levies and VAT (or sales tax). Customs duties, customs valuation, trade remedies and excise taxes have been harmonized between SACU members, but this is not true of all rebates and exemptions or of VAT.

Regarding excise taxes, SACU countries levy ad-valorem, specific and formula excise taxes on a total of 149 tariff lines. Excises are calculated on

Table 12.5 SACU MFN Tariff Structure, 2004

Type of duty	Number of lines	%
Ad valorem	6491	97.0
Specific	103	1.5
Compound	1	0.0
Mixed Total	90	1.4
Type 1 (25% or 70c/kg)	66	1.0
Type 2 (325c/kg with a maximum of 39%)	24	0.4
Formula	5	0.1
Total lines	6690	

Source: SACU tariff book, authors' calculations

the basis of the FOB reference price plus 15 per cent and any non-rebated customs duties. Ad-valorem excise rates range from 5 to 7 per cent and are levied mainly on manufactured products. Specific excise taxes are levied on prepared foodstuffs; beverages and spirits; tobacco; mineral products; and products of the chemical industries. The excise duty on certain categories of tractors, motor vehicles and chassis are calculated on the basis of a formula, with a maximum rate of 20 per cent. Specific levies are also charged on fuel.

Each SACU country applies a different VAT regime. Botswana charges a VAT rate of 10 per cent, Lesotho and South Africa 14 per cent, and Namibia 15 per cent, while Swaziland levies a sales tax at a rate of 14 per cent. All rates are lower than Mozambique's 17 per cent. The lack of harmonization of VAT is an obstacle to the free circulation of goods inside the union, since monitoring and control of trade flows within SACU are required in order to administer the diverging VAT regimes.

Import duties and excise taxes are collected in the common customs area through a common revenue pool distributed according to a sharing formula. The revenue sharing formula is made of two separate pools: the customs pool and the excise pool, this latter further split into an excise component and a development component. The customs pool is distributed among member states according to their share of intra-SACU imports (providing an additional incentive for member states to monitor closely trade flows within SACU), while the excise component (85 per cent of the excise pool) is distributed according to the country's share of SACU GDP and the development component (15 per cent) is assigned inversely to GDP per capita.

Prior to 2002, individual SACU members could enter into bilateral trade agreements with countries outside the customs union. Under the 2002 agreement this is expressly prohibited (Article 31) but existing arrangements can be maintained. This is problematic since in 2000 South Africa signed a Trade, Development and Cooperation Agreement (TDCA) with the EU establishing reciprocal duty-free access into each other's market for substantially all products by the end of a 12-year transitional period. Botswana, Lesotho, Namibia and Swaziland (the BLNS countries) found EU products entering their markets duty free via South Africa. Furthermore, Namibian ports were losing business to competing South African ports because of the differences in duties for European cargo shipments. Thus the BLNS have found themselves obliged to apply the TDCA preferences, and it is likely that they will formally adhere to a modified version of the TDCA as an outcome of the Economic Partnership Agreement (EPA) negotiations with the EU.

2.3 The SADC Trade Protocol

The SADC Trade Protocol is being implemented by 11 countries in Southern Africa, including Mozambique and all SACU countries.[8] Although a fully fledged free trade area was achieved in 2008 (and will be in 2015 in the case of all 'sensitive' products), many goods have already for some time enjoyed duty-free or preferential treatment. For example, Mozambique has duty-free access to the South African market for almost all goods and provides duty-free access to other SADC members on about one-third of its tariff lines.

Two sectors have special arrangements within SADC. Sugar will be liberalized only by 2013, subject to suitable economic conditions within the region. In the meantime preferential trade is limited by a quota system.[9] For textiles and clothing, access to SACU countries under favourable rules of origin (single transformation) is limited by a quota for the Least Developed Countries (LDCs) within SADC, all other members being required to demonstrate that products have undergone double transformation in order to benefit from preferential treatment.

The regional integration process should continue, and the mid-term review process of the protocol suggests the creation of a customs union by 2010 and a monetary union by 2012. Both targets are overly optimistic due to implementation delays[10] and double membership in other regional agreements.[11]

Until recently, Mozambique's regional integration strategy was premised on the existence of a common sense of purpose among all countries of Southern Africa. Since recent developments in regional trade negotiations are suggesting otherwise, there is a growing perception within the government of Mozambique that it is time to re-evaluate a number of other strategic trade policy options, including increased collaboration with SACU and unilateral liberalization. It is in this context that this chapter has been prepared.

3 Methodology

The methodology used in the chapter is based on that developed by Panagariya (2000) and extended by Milner *et al.* (2005). The methodology has all the caveats associated with static partial equilibrium analysis; however, it allows the estimation of revenue loss and welfare effects at the specific product level with a relatively low data requirement.

3.1 Main assumptions

A *static partial equilibrium* model is used. This implies that any dynamic gains or the path of adjustment from trade reform cannot be analysed and these dynamic gains are often substantially large and important. Furthermore, the partial equilibrium nature of the model implies that linkages between sectors and impacts on the labour market and main macroeconomic variables cannot be analysed.

Markets are *perfectly competitive* and *constant returns* are assumed, ruling out the possibility of economies of scale and market power, which may vary the potential impact of preferential integration by affecting prices and therefore the terms of trade between countries.

Imported products are *perfect substitutes* between different import sources and between foreign and domestic products. Since the analysis is carried out at the most disaggregated level possible (eight-digit national tariff lines, or six-digit Harmonized System tariff lines in the scenarios involving the SACU tariff book due to incompatibility with Mozambique's trade data at eight-digit national tariff lines), in the case of agricultural and primary products it is reasonable to assume that the elasticity of substitution between products sourced in different countries is very high. But this may not be the case for manufactured products.

There is *perfect transmission* of tariff reform. It may be the case that tariff reductions in some products will not be translated into price reductions. This is related to the possibility of market power by exporters in the source country or importers in the destination country and/or of products not being perfect substitutes. Furthermore, trade reform may be transmitted quite unevenly across space. Cirera and Arndt (2006) show lack of integration in maize markets in Mozambique between the different provinces of the country. This implies that the estimates of the impact of the different reform scenarios quite likely will indicate the impact in the Southern provinces neighbouring the South African border, but will over-estimate the impact further north.

Price elasticities are assumed. Lack of data availability implies that the import demand own price elasticity needs to be assumed based on other empirical work (see Milner *et al.* 2005). Regarding export price elasticity, it is assumed that for the rest of the world and the EU it is very high or infinity, while for South Africa, following the small country assumption, it is assumed that it is positive and equals one for simplicity.

There are *Trade data limitations*. It is assumed that 2004 trade data are accurate on the whole, although some adjustments are made (e.g. customs evasion is considered when computing revenue implications). Furthermore, it is assumed that 2004 is an appropriate base year for analysing reforms which would be completed many years in the future, when the economic situation might be very different.

Lack of production data at the product level implies that it is not possible to incorporate supply data in the analysis. Thus we will assume that demand refers to the net demand for imports. The demand and supply for home goods are unknown and the impact of the analysis on domestic products depends on the elasticity of substitution between home and foreign goods. Thus, when domestic and imported goods are perfect substitutes, the implication of the analysis on domestic production is that when prices do not change domestic producers keep their market share and only trade is diverted from the rest of the world towards preferential partners. On the other hand, when prices decrease (increase), consumption effects occur and imports are increased (reduced). In this case, we would expect a reduction (increase) in domestic producer share, the extent of which will depend on the degree of substitution between imported and domestically produced goods.

It is important to keep in mind the implications of the assumptions described above when interpreting the results. The estimations are rough estimates considering these assumptions; nevertheless, they give a clear orientation of the sign and magnitude of the changes expected in imports and revenue as a result of the different reform scenarios.

3.2 Scenarios

The purpose of the chapter is to analyse the impact of different trade reform scenarios. The fact that a static model is used implies that two periods in time are needed: the situation before the trade policy changes being investigated (i.e. the year with the most recent available data, 2004) and the situation after the trade policy changes, once the reform process is completed. While the initial period is easy to characterize (since the trade policy environment of 2004 is known already), the post-reform period in every scenario is subject to uncertainty.

As far as possible, known changes to trade policy after 2004 (e.g. the reduction in Mozambique's top duty rate from 25 per cent to 20 per cent) are incorporated into the post-reform period in the scenarios. However, there are many problems. For example, how the current SACU institutional arrangements might be modified if Mozambique were to negotiate its entry into the union is open to speculation. Indeed, Mozambique, with a population of about 20 million, could probably exert a great deal more influence over South Africa (with a population of 44 million) than the BLNS countries (none of which has a population exceeding 2 million). Rather than trying to guess what might happen, the SACU scenarios used in this chapter are based on the SACU common external tariff and related institutional arrangements *as they currently stand*. This makes the post-reform results 'unrealistic' but it allows trade negotiators and policy-makers to see what aspects of the current arrangements are most favourable and which are most unfavourable to Mozambique.

The scenarios and their implications are described in Table 12.6. The FTA scenario represents a successful implementation of the SADC protocol or, in case of problems during the implementation of the SADC protocol (and since South Africa is Mozambique's main trade partner), a free trade agreement between Mozambique and SACU. This scenario implies that Mozambique keeps its planned MFN tariff structure.[12]

There are two SACU scenarios. As highlighted in Section 2.2, the BLNS are *de facto* applying TDCA preferences due to the problems associated with tariff-jumping through South Africa. Mozambique might be able to avoid similar problems, but equally it might not. For this reason, SACU membershipwith and without EU preferences is considered as two separate scenarios.

For a significant proportion of product lines (28 per cent), South Africa already had duty-free access to the Mozambican market in 2004. This implies that these cases are already in the FTA scenario. Therefore the only changes that apply to these product lines are an MFN change to 20 per cent in the FTA scenario and the adoption of the SACU common external tariff in the two SACU scenarios.

Table 12.6 Trade Reform Scenarios

Scenario	Description
2004	This is not a scenario as such but the starting-point for the simulations in each of the scenarios. The base year is 2004. Thus: • The institutional and policy environment is as described in part 2.1 of this chapter.
FTA	This scenario is characterized by the formation of a free trade area (FTA) between Mozambique and SADC countries. The end result is equivalent to the SADC Trade Protocol once fully implemented (i.e. after 2015). The scenario is characterized by the following policies: • SADC countries have duty free access to the Mozambican market for all products. • MFN rates for those products taxed at 25%, final goods, are reduced to 20% as planned for 2006. • Consumption tax and VAT structure stays the same.
SACU 1	In this scenario, Mozambique joins SACU under existing SACU arrangements, thus liberalizing trade with SACU countries and adopting the SACU CET. This means that: • SACU countries have duty free access to the Mozambican market for all products. • Mozambique adopts the existing SACU MFN tariff structure. • Mozambique adopts the SACU excise structure, but keeps its own existing VAT structure. • Mozambique participates in the existing SACU revenue-sharing mechanism.
SACU 2	This scenario is the same as SACU 1 except that it includes the Trade, Development and Cooperation Agreement (TDCA) liberalization schedule with the EU. Therefore Mozambique also gives duty free access to all imports from the EU to the same extent as South Africa does by the end of the implementation period.
MFN	This scenario is characterized by the reduction of tariffs on all imported goods to 5%, keeping the existing consumption tax and VAT structure.

Finally, we assess the impact of a scenario ('MFN') envisaging a reduction of all duties on an MFN basis to a flat 5 per cent for all products.

The results of the different reform scenarios need to be compared with the present situation and with each other. When doing so, however, an important problem arises. The level of revenue effectively collected does not correspond to the level of imports. This is due to several factors:

• As mentioned in Section 2.1, some imports are exempted from paying duties or other taxes at the border. However, it is difficult to compile all information on project exemptions. For this reason, an adjustment factor is calculated. This is based on the difference between the 'theoretical' initial revenue level (calculated by applying the 2004 tariff and tax structure to the actual 2004 imports) and the actual level of revenue collected in the same year.

- Due to smuggling and evasion, some imports are not registered. The likelihood of fraud at the border decreases when duties are lower because the margin from smuggling the good is narrower. Van Dunem and Arndt (2005) provide an estimate of 1.4 for 'fraud elasticity' in Mozambique. This is applied to the results of the different scenarios.

3.3 The model

The model used here is extensively described by Alfieri *et al.* (2006). It has three regions: Mozambique, SADC (including South Africa) and the rest of the world (ROW).[13] For each product line, the total demand for imports, M, is equal to the sum of exports, X, from all sources. For a given level of income, the total demand for imports depends negatively on the price of the good in the market, while the export supply from each source depends positively on the existing price in the market. The equilibrium price in the market equals the international price at the border, p^*, plus an *ad-valorem* tariff τ_n (and other applicable taxes). The tariff may be equal for all n sources of imports or different, depending on whether the tariff structure gives preference to this good under the SADC protocol. The model is represented by the following two equations:

$$M(P, \bar{y}) = \sum X_n(P, \bar{y}) \tag{1}$$

$$P = (1 + \pi_n)P^* \tag{2}$$

This corresponds to the diagram shown in Figure 12.3.

In order to estimate the effects of the trade reform scenarios we benchmark the initial export supply and import demand functions for each product line, using information on the initial total value of imports from each source and ad-valorem tariffs for the product. The initial observed prices can be normalized to one (i.e. import quantities are taken to be equivalent to import values in the base year), dispensing with the need to obtain data on imported unit quantities.[14]

Finally, in order to complete the benchmarking exercise the different import demand and export supply price elasticities need to be identified. Import demand elasticities are not available for Mozambique, and therefore are taken from those sector-specific import demand elasticities calculated by Stern *et al.* (1976).[15] Export supply elasticity is initially assumed to be 1 for SADC and very high or infinity for the ROW.

Once the equations are benchmarked, different reform scenarios can be simulated by changing the import tariffs. This gives the new vector of import quantities for every source and the new price in the market. The new import quantities and prices can then be used to estimate the levels and changes of revenue associated with duties, excise and VAT, and also measures of consumer surplus and welfare, for every scenario.

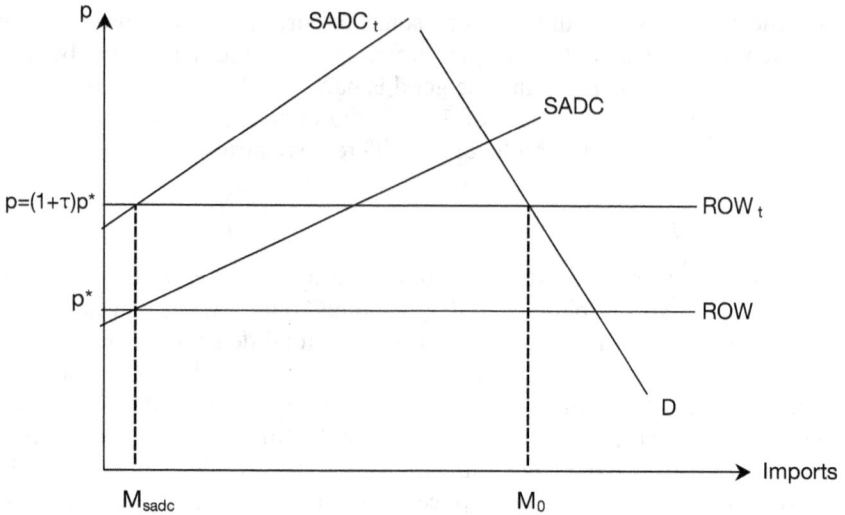

Figure 12.3 Impact of tariff on import quantities and prices

4 Results

This section describes the results from the estimations. Nevertheless, the results related to revenue are only indicative of potential levels of revenue due to the fact that they need to be adjusted to take account of tax exemptions, as well as misclassified and unregistered (smuggled) imports. These adjustments are carried out in Section 5.

4.1 Scenario comparison

The main results of the estimations can be summarized as follows:

- The greatest overall increase in imports takes place under the scenario in which Mozambique enters SACU and implements the TDCA, followed by the MFN liberalization scenario and then by a free trade area in Southern Africa (i.e. the SADC Trade Protocol). By contrast, SACU membership without the TDCA implies the lowest increase in the value of imports (Table 12.7).
- The weighted average price reduction is close to 18 per cent for the SACU TDCA scenario, 15.4 per cent for the MFN scenario, 14.9 per cent for SACU without the TDCA and 13.3 per cent for the SADC FTA. This implies that in all scenarios the increase in the *value* of imports is smaller than the increase in the *volume* of imports.
- The scenarios that imply more liberalization are clearly associated with larger revenue loss. However, these results need to be adjusted for existing exemptions and, in the SACU scenarios, for the transfer of revenue from the revenue pool (see Section 5).

- An interesting result is the fact that despite the increase in imports for most of the scenarios, VAT revenue only increases slightly. This is due to the fact that VAT is applied in cascade to the other taxes and the tax base is reduced because of reductions in prices and duties.
- Greater liberalization is associated with higher consumer surplus (see Table 12.8). However, we have to bear in mind that, in practice, this also depends on the degree of price transmission from the border to consumers.[16]
- The revenue losses are larger than the consumer gains in almost all scenarios, implying overall national welfare losses as compared to 2004. However, in the SACU with TDCA scenario the welfare change is positive due to the large reduction in prices. We need to recall, though, that for both SACU scenarios these results change when adjusted for revenue transfer from the common pool.

Table 12.7 Estimated Aggregate Impact on Value of Imports

	% change in value of imports from			
Scenario	*Southern Africa*	*European Union*	*Rest of the world*	*Total*
FTA	14.07	Included in 'Rest of the world', see decimal	–3.86	6.82
MFN	8.79	Included in 'Rest of the world', see decimal	9.10	8.91
SACU no TDCA	10.66	Included in 'Rest of the world', see decimal	0.40	6.19
SACU with TDCA	4.64	84.46	–27.39	9.73

Source: Authors' calculations based on simulations

Table 12.8 Estimated Aggregate Impact on Revenue and Welfare (before adjustment)

	Change in USD millions (% change)					
Scenario	*Duty revenue*	*Excise revenue*	*VAT revenue*	*Total revenue*	*Consumer surplus*	*Net welfare*
FTA	–100.3 (–66.6%)	0.6 (2%)	2.92 (1.2%)	–96.8 (–23.3%)	38.3	–58.42
MFN	–113.1 (–75%)	1.76 (6.9%)	8.04 (3.3%)	–103.3 (–24.4%)	99.86	–3.47
SACU no TDCA	–113.5 (–75%)	7.43 (29%)	3.98 (1.16%)	–102 (–24.4%)	57.28	–44.81
SACU with TDCA	–139.95 (–92.7%)	9.12 (35%)	11.35 (4.7%)	–119.4 (–28%)	130.65	11.18

Source: Authors' calculations based on simulations

The results from the estimation are, of course, partial equilibrium results. These ignore general equilibrium effects such as terms of trade changes, cheaper inputs, reallocation of resources and the impact on domestic production or income changes, which the partial equilibrium setting used here does not capture. Therefore these results should be interpreted as a first-order approximation of the impact of different reform scenarios on imports and revenue at the product level. The following sub-sections describe in greater detail the results of the different reform scenarios.

4.2 FTA scenario

This scenario involves the complete implementation of the SADC Trade Protocol, with all other policy arrangements taken as they stand for Mozambique in 2006.[17] It is important to point out that in the base (pre-reform) year, 2004, Mozambique was already partially implementing the free trade agreement, with 1,509 product lines duty free for South Africa, corresponding to 21 per cent of imports by value.

The estimations imply an increase in the value of imports of 6.79 per cent and a weighted average decrease in prices of 13.3 per cent. However, the increase in consumer surplus due to cheaper imports does not compensate for revenue losses.

The product groups where there is a larger loss of revenue and larger increase in consumer surplus are those with a greater value of imports (such as chapter 87, vehicles, or chapter 27, fuel), or higher taxes (such as chapter 17, sugar).

4.3 MFN scenario

This scenario corresponds to the case of unilateral liberalization and the reduction of tariffs and duty surcharges to 5 per cent, while keeping existing VAT and excise taxes. In this case the level of imports increases by 8.91 per cent. Also, consumer surplus significantly improves by US$99 million due to a reduction in prices amounting to 15.4 per cent (weighted average).

Those chapters with greater imports and with higher taxes such as vehicles (87), fuel (27) and sugar (17) experience the largest loss of revenue, even though the former two also experience large increases in consumer surplus. The net impact on welfare, even though slightly negative overall, shows a mixed pattern across chapters. For fuel (27) and medical appliances (90) it is overall negative, while for other chapters, like machinery (87) and clothing (63), it shows a positive sign.

4.4 SACU without TDCA scenario

Regarding the SACU scenario when the TDCA agreement with the EU is not considered, it is interesting to notice that the resulting weighted average tariff (4 per cent) is nearly half of that currently being implemented. Consumer surpluses increase on aggregate by 7.7 per cent, and particularly for sugar (17), medical appliances (90) and machineries (84 and 85). Conversely, the new SACU Common External Tariff implies a decrease in consumer surplus for chapters such as vehicles (87), rubber products (40 – including tyres) and textiles (63). Revenue change and net welfare effects depend on the application of the SACU revenue sharing mechanism, which is examined in Section 5.

4.5 SACU with TDCA scenario

This scenario is similar in terms of liberalization to the unilateral MFN liberalization due to the fact that there is liberalization for the two main sources of imports, Southern Africa (i.e. South Africa) and the EU. This scenario is the one which achieves the highest increase in imports (9.7 per cent) and decrease in prices (–18.3 per cent weighted average). The resulting weighted average tariff is down to a mere 1.15 per cent. Regarding consumer surplus, the sectors with the largest increases in consumer surplus are sugar (17) and electrical (85) and mechanical machinery (84). The final impact on revenue and welfare depends on the transfer from the SACU revenue pool. Interestingly, for vehicles the TDCA implies a positive shift in consumer welfare compared to the previous scenario.

5 Implications of revenue adjustments

Before drawing any conclusions from the results in the estimations in Section 4, it is fundamental to adjust expected revenue flows to take account of tax exemptions, as well as misclassified and unregistered (smuggled) imports. Indeed, the model used in this chapter heavily over-estimates expected revenue for the 2004 base year, as compared to actual collected revenue in 2004. This implies that the potential for revenue losses arising from the trade reforms modelled in the scenarios is in reality much lower than estimated in Section 4. Additionally, in the case of the SACU scenarios, it has to be taken into account that customs revenue is pooled and redistributed according to a formula. When expected revenue is adjusted for these factors, the MFN and SACU scenarios *become welfare improving* (see Tables 12.10 and 12.15).

An additional consideration to bear in mind, with respect to the FTA and MFN scenarios, is that one could design a revenue-neutral reform by reducing the average rate of taxation on imports at the same time as removing exemptions and improving the actual collection of taxes due (thus keeping the *effective* average rate of taxation at the same level). This in turn would have the double advantage of leading to greater transparency in the trade policy environment (with positive implications for good governance) and requiring fewer resources to implement and monitor exemptions schemes.

5.1 Exemptions

The estimations in Section 4 omit 16 per cent of imports that are mis-classified in chapter 99 as 'other products from other countries'. For these imports, there is no information about the country of origin or the applicable taxes. In addition, the large number of exemptions granted (as described in Section 2.1) implies that revenue collected is always lower than the theoretical revenue that would be obtained from taxing imports as specified in the customs tariff book.[18] The revenue totals obtained in Section 4 need to be adjusted to reflect these discrepancies.

Table 12.9 summarizes the adjustments required. The first column reflects actual revenues collected in the national currency, as reported in the state accounts. These are converted to US$ in the second column. It should be noted that, when divided by actual imports, these values translate into very low effective taxation rates: a 4.84 per cent average tariff rate, a 1.05 per cent excise rate (across all products) and a 7.27 per cent VAT rate. The fourth column indicates the theoretical level of revenue expected for the 2004 base year, applying tax rates as they appear in the tariff book, without any exemptions, to actual 2004 imports (disaggregated by tariff line and by country of origin). These yield expected average taxation rates of 8.9 per cent, 1.5 per cent and 14.0 per cent, respectively, for duties, excise and VAT, all of which are significantly higher than the actual effective rates.

In the second-last column, the amount of expected revenue is adjusted upwards to take into account the fact that some 16 per cent of imports are mis-classified as chapter 99. The expected taxes for these goods are calculated by applying a linear approximation that assumes the same average effective tax rates as for other goods. Finally, the last column shows the ratio of collected

Table 12.9 Actual and Expected Trade-related Revenue in 2004

Trade-related revenue	2004 actual revenue (MZM billion)	2004 actual revenue (USD million)	Effective average rate of taxation (%)	Theoretical revenue expected for 2004 (USD million)	Expected average rate of taxation (%)	Theoretical revenue expected for 2004 incl. Ch.99 (USD million)	Actual revenue as % of expected revenue in 2004
Duties & surcharges	2,223	98.4	4.8	150.9	8.9	180.25	54.60
Excise on imports	485	21.5	1.1	25.4	1.5	30.37	70.65
VAT on imports	3,340	147.9	7.3	238.4	14.0	284.84	51.92
Cumulative total	6,047	267.8	13.2	414.7	24.4	495.46	

Source: General State accounts and INE, authors' calculations

to expected revenue for every type of tax. The ratios are low, implying that around half of imports are effectively exempted from paying duties and VAT.

Taking the required revenue adjustments for the 2004 base year as a starting point, and assuming a constant relationship between actual and expected revenue among all scenarios, adjustments can be made to the revenue estimations in all scenarios, as shown in Table 12.10. The theoretical revenue for the 16 per cent misclassified imports (chapter 99) is added to the estimated total revenue reported in Section 4, and then the effective collection ratio as listed in the last column of Table 12.11 is applied to this intermediate result, to take exemptions into account.

The values in bold in Table 12.10 are the total expected revenue, after adjustment: US$204.5 million in the FTA scenario, US$200.3 million in the MFN scenario, US$203.7 million in the SACU (no TDCA) scenario and US$192.5 million in the SACU (with TDCA) scenario. These values correspond to effective taxation rates (total effective revenue over total imports), very close to 9 per cent for all four scenarios.

The revenue adjustments required to account for exemptions and misclassified imports are highly significant. Once adjusted, expected revenue collection both in the 2004 base year and in the post-reform scenarios is reduced significantly, reducing the expected revenue loss – and thus the negative impact on welfare – from reform. Table 12.11 recalculates the impact of the FTA and the MFN scenarios with the adjusted level of expected revenue flows. In the FTA scenario, the negative net welfare effect is considerably lower than originally estimated, at US$37.8 million, and in the MFN case the net welfare effect actually becomes positive.

As with the results in Section 4, however, consumer surplus is probably still over-estimated because of the assumption of perfect transmission of price changes to consumers. This probably leads to a positive bias in the net welfare effect of reform.

5.2 Fraud

The reduction in tariff rates reduces the incentives to smuggle goods by decreasing the price spreads between legally and illegally imported goods. Van Dunem and Arndt (2005), based on Fisman and Wei (2004), calculate the relationship between trade taxes and the level of unregistered imports. They regress estimated unregistered imports (obtained by observing the ratio between the CIF export value to Mozambique registered by South Africa and the CIF value of imports from South Africa registered in Mozambique for each product line), with respect to the level of import taxes for each product line. They find a 'fraud elasticity' of 1.4, suggesting that for every 1 per cent increase in taxes there is an increase of 1.4 per cent in imports not registered.

This elasticity coefficient can be applied to the results obtained in Section 5.1 to account for a potential reduction in non-registered imports arising

Table 12.10 Adjusted Aggregate Revenue Estimations

Trade-related revenue (USD Million)	FTA			MFN		
	Estimated theoretical revenue	Estimated theoretical revenue incl Ch.99	Anticipated effective revenue	Estimated theoretical revenue	Estimated theoretical revenue incl Ch.99	Anticipated effective revenue
Duties & surcharges	241.30	288.30	149.71	246.4166	294.41	152.88
Excise on imports	26.03	31.10	21.97	27.18416	32.48	22.95
VAT on imports	50.32	60.12	32.87	37.52993	44.84	24.52
Cumulative total	317.65	379.51	**204.55**	311.13	371.72	**200.35**

	SACU no TDCA			SACU with TDCA		
Duties & surcharges	244.37	291.96	151.61	251.71	300.73	156.17
Excise on imports	32.86	39.26	27.74	34.55	41.28	29.16
VAT on imports	37.41	44.70	24.44	10.98	13.11	7.17
Cumulative total	314.64	375.92	**203.79**	297.23	355.12	**192.50**

Source: Authors' calculations based on simulations

Table 12.11 Estimated Aggr. Impact on Revenue and Welfare (after adjusting for exemptions, mill. USD)

Scenario	Change in USD millions (% change)					
	Duty revenue	*Excise revenue*	*VAT revenue*	*Total revenue*	*Consumer surplus*	*Net welfare*
FTA	−65.55	0.51	1.82	−63.22	25.40	−37.82
	(−66.60%)	(2.39%)	(1.23%)	(−23.61%)		
MFN (5%)	−73.91	1.49	4.99	−67.43	99.86	32.43
	(−75.09%)	(−314.25%)	(3.37%)	(−25.18%)		

Source: Authors' calculations based on simulations

from tariff reduction. Concretely, the following equation is applied to every product line in every scenario:[19]

$$Log(X/M) = \beta Taxes + \varepsilon$$

where the estimated parameter $\beta = 1.38$. Given that M, the expected level of imports registered by Mozambique, is known for each scenario in 2004, we can apply the equation above and solve for X, which can be interpreted as the potential level of imports without smuggling in 2004. Then the different scenarios are re-estimated to obtain the new X^*. Finally, to the new potential registered imports X^* we apply the formula again to obtain the final expected imports M, which account for both the liberalization exercise and the potential increase in registered imports from reducing taxes at the border.

Table 12.12 shows the results in terms of imports change. Clearly there is a significant increase in the level of imports resulting now from the combined trade and fraud reduction effects when reducing trade taxes. Registered imports increase from 35.9 per cent in the FTA case to 53.1 per cent in the SACU with TDCA scenario.

Two important issues should be stressed in this section. As suggested above, it is unlikely that price transmission is complete in the presence of high transport costs and a not very competitive retail sector, which imply the over-estimation of the consumer surplus. Nevertheless, the existing level of smuggling may put downward pressure on domestic prices, below the price plus the wedge introduced by taxes, compensating for part of the over-estimation of the consumer surplus.

The second issue is related to the fact that the level of exemptions and effective taxation do not necessarily have to remain constant. It is possible to combine an effective reduction of trade duties with a reduction in exemptions. This could bring about two positive outcomes. First, it would add more clarity and transparency to the exemptions system, since there would be a very short list of exemptions, which could be more easily implemented and monitored. Second, it partially offsets the effective reduction in tax

Table 12.12 Estimated Aggregate Impact on Value of Imports (after adjusting for fraud)

| Scenario | % change in value of imports from | | | |
	Southern Africa	European Union	Rest of the world	Total
FTA	48.13	Included in 'Rest of the world'	17.92	35.92
MFN	52.74	Included in 'Rest of the worl'	51.15	52.10
SACU with TDCA	69.14	Included in 'Rest of the world'	29.46	53.11
SACU no TDCA	53.70	190.65	-8.03	38.44

Source: Authors' calculations based on simulations

revenue arising from liberalization, and these resources could be used to finance adjustment costs from liberalization.

5.3 Revenue sharing in SACU

In the scenarios involving SACU membership, revenue flows depend on the results of applying the revenue sharing formula, as introduced in Section 2.2. Therefore once tax revenue collection is calculated, final retained revenue has to be extrapolated from an estimation of revenues collected in all SACU member states. The formula for the revenue pool is described in the Annex to this chapter.

In the absence of a regional CGE model, it is impossible to calculate the impacts in terms of exports and imports for other SACU countries. For this reason simplified calculations are made, adding the estimated revenue flows obtained in the two SACU scenarios to the pool contributions in 2004. Despite being a simplification, this helps to approximate the revenue impact of SACU membership in static terms.

The calculations have been carried out according to information about the revenue pool in 2004.[20] For duties, the revenue allocation depends on each country's share of imports from other SACU members. We add the resulting SACU imports from the simulations and the observed exports from Mozambique to SACU in 2004 (see Table 12.13). Adjusting the other countries' shares to include Mozambique's imports from SACU and exports to SACU in total intra-SACU imports yields a share of imports of approximately 10 per cent in both scenarios.

Clearly, all SACU countries would experience a reduction in the share of the pool as a result of Mozambique's membership. However, and due to the significance of Mozambique's exports of electricity to South Africa, the customs pool share for South Africa would remain constant, while being significantly reduced for the BLNS.[21] This may be a significant element of conflict between SACU countries when considering Mozambique's membership. In addition, a controversial element when implementing the formula is the incentive to

Table 12.13 SACU Revenue Shares with Mozambique's Membership

Customs Pool shares	Botswana	Lesotho	Namibia	Swaziland	South Africa	Mozambique		Total
						Imports from SACU	% Pool share	Intra-SACU imports
SACU 2004	2,404.69	1,153.93	2,414.37	1,592.06	1,906.76			9,471.81
(%)	25.39	12.18	25.49	16.81	20.13			
SACU 2004 incl Moz exports	2,405.49	1,154.07	2,414.57	1,595.01	2,139.46			9,708.60
SACU no TDCA (%)	22.21	10.65	22.29	14.73	19.75	1,122.85	10.37	10,831.45
SACU TDCA (%)	22.33	10.72	22.42	14.81	19.86	1,061.76	9.86	10,770.36
SACU no TDCA (fraud adj) (%)	22.08	10.59	22.17	14.64	19.64	1,184.90	10.88	10,893.50
SACU TDCA (fraud adj) (%)	22.26	10.68	22.35	14.76	19.80	1,096.10	10.14	10,804.70
Excise pool shares (%)	3.67	0.58	2.31	1.02	90.07		2.35	
Development pool shares (%)	16.49	16.77	16.64	16.70	16.55		16.81	

Source: Authors' calculations based on simulations

over-declare higher intra-SACU imports in order to obtain more revenue from the duties pool.

The excise component of the formula (worth 85 per cent of total excise revenue) is based on the relative GDP size of each member. Using GDP at current US\$ from the World Development Indicators (World Bank 2006c), Mozambique's share in SACU GDP in 2004 was 2.4 per cent. Finally, the development component (worth 15 per cent of excise revenues) is more or less equally shared among members, although the SACU formula introduces a very minor bias in favour of those members with lower GDP per capita. Based on 2004 World Bank (2006c) GNI per capita, Mozambique obtains 16.81 per cent of this component, marginally higher than the average for all members (16.66 per cent).

An important element to consider is the fact that excise taxes on domestic products also have to be transferred to the revenue pool. It is not possible to estimate the total size of excise taxes collected in Mozambique with the model used in this chapter, since domestic production is not modelled. An assumption is made that excise revenue on domestic production in Mozambique would be the same under the SACU scenarios (applying the SACU excise structure) as was actually the case in 2004, namely about US\$34.86 million.[22]

Table 12.14 shows the results of applying the formula to both scenarios – SACU no TDCA and SACU TDCA – and taking into account the adjustment due to exemptions. Under both scenarios, SACU membership implies generated revenue of more than US\$300 million. Clearly, SACU membership would imply a positive redistribution of revenue to Mozambique with respect to its contribution – net revenue transfer of US\$126.18 million for the SACU no TDCA scenario and US\$118.12 million for the SACU TDCA scenario. These figures represent around US\$58–62 million more than the revenue collected in 2004. The fact that SACU membership allows a country to raise and keep its own VAT implies that revenue is maximized under SACU membership. The figures in terms of total revenue transferred from the SACU revenue pool are very similar under both scenarios due to the fact that Mozambique contributes a very small share to the pool.

These results are somewhat different from those of Kirk and Stern (2005), who indicate a general loss of revenue from implementing SACU. The authors suggest a 3 per cent decrease in government revenue, as opposed to an increase in our scenarios ranging from 19 to 20 per cent compared with the revenue actually collected in 2004 (US\$302.6 million). Kirk and Stern (2005) also suggest a positive net transfer from the revenue pool of 12 per cent, while our estimates indicate a ratio between SACU transfer and contribution in the order of 2.45 and 2.88.[23]

Once the impact of the SACU transfer on revenue is accounted for, the picture of the final impact of the reform scenarios changes significantly. As shown in Table 12.15, the SACU scenarios become welfare improving, with a higher level of welfare than the MFN and FTA scenarios. This is due to the fact that the net revenue transfer from SACU more than compensates for the higher MFN consumer surplus.

Table 12.14 SACU Revenue Pool Calculations (adjusted for exemptions, mill. USD)

Revenue Component	Revenue Pool 2004		Mozambique	SACU no TDCA		SACU with TDCA	
	Rand Million	USD Million	Share (%)	Revenue pool incl. Moz	Revenue transfer	Revenue pool incl. Moz	Revenue transfer
Duties	8,479.00	1,234.21	10.37 / 9.86	1258.65	130.52	1241.38	122.40
Excise	10,523.85	1,531.86	2.35	1555.43	36.55	1556.64	36.58
Development	1,857.15	270.33	16.81	274.49	46.14	274.70	46.18
Total	20,860.00	3,036.39		3088.57	**213.22**	3072.72	**205.16**
VAT					151.61		156.17
Total Revenue after SACU transfer					**364.83**		**361.32**
Net transfer (SACU transfer – overall contribution)[a]					126.18		118.12
Change with respect to actual revenue collected in 2004 (base year)[b]					62.17		58.67

a: Overall contribution includes duties and excises collected on domestic and imported products
b: Including domestic excises
Source: Kirk and Stern (2005) and WDI (2005), authors' calculations

Table 12.15 Estimated Aggregate Impact on Revenue and Welfare (after adjustment and SACU transfer mill. USD)

	Change in Total revenue	Consumer surplus	Net welfare
SACU no TDCA	62.17	57.28	119.45
SACU with TDCA	58.67	130.65	189.32

Source: Authors' calculations based on simulations

An important implication of these results is that if regional integration is an important goal of Mozambique's external trade policy, SACU membership seems a better option than the current SADC process.[24] This is mainly due to the extent of revenue transfer in the SACU scenarios as they have been set up.

Despite the importance of this result, it is important to point out that with the process of MFN liberalization being carried out in South Africa it is expected that the customs component, which is the main source of redistributed revenue, will decrease significantly in coming years. The size of the pool, of course, will also depend on the trend in consumption and import growth in SACU countries.[25] In addition, lack of data on the impact of applying SACU excises domestically implies that the revenue transfer figure is likely to be over-estimated because of higher average excise tax under SACU. Therefore, the figures reported should be taken as upper limits of the transfer.

6 Conclusions

This chapter has estimated the likely impact of four trade policy reform scenarios, SADC integration, SACU membership with and without the TDCA, and MFN unilateral liberalization,[26] on imports and revenue at the product-specific level. We should keep in mind, however, the important limitations of the analysis. First, we do not account for general equilibrium impacts of trade reform, especially regarding import competing and export sectors. Second, the model is static and therefore fails to capture dynamic gains, which may be substantial. Despite these problems, the results are indicative of the size and directions of the impacts expected under the four scenarios and are informative at the product level.

The main results indicate that the SACU TDCA scenario and MFN liberalization yield the larger increase in imports. Price effects are significant in all scenarios and ranging from 9 per cent to close to 50 per cent for almost all chapters, excluding fertilizers and pharmaceutical products. This suggests a substantial increase of competition from regional and international suppliers for the local industry across the board.

In all four scenarios the increase in consumption surplus does not fully compensate for the loss of revenue when no revenue adjustments are made to the model. VAT and excise increase slightly due to the increase in imports and despite the fact that the tax base is being reduced through tariff and price reductions.

The revenue (and hence also welfare) effects, however, need to be adjusted considerably. First, due to the large number of tax exemptions granted, actual trade revenue collected is around 50 per cent of its potential level for duties and VAT, and around 70 per cent for excise. Effective tax rates are thus lower than the nominal rates, at 4.8 per cent for duties, 1.1 per cent for excise and 7.3 per cent for VAT. When the calculations are adjusted to account for exemptions, the revenue loss decreases significantly and the MFN scenario becomes welfare improving, while the FTA scenario still shows negative welfare change. SACU scenarios need a further adjustment to take into account the SACU redistribution mechanism.

A second type of adjustment is required due to the fact that lower trade taxes reduce the incentive for smuggling and therefore increase the level of registered and taxed imports. Using Van Dunem and Arndt's (2005) estimates, the data is adjusted to account for the reduction of fraud and re-estimate the scenarios. In this manner, the anticipated trade effect is compounded by an additional fraud reduction effect. The results indicate a much larger increase in registered imports, ranging from 53 per cent in the SACU TDCA case to 35 per cent in the FTA case. This implies a lower revenue loss and more favourable welfare impact for all reform scenarios.

A final adjustment required concerns the SACU scenarios. The revenue related to these scenarios is transferred to the SACU revenue pool, after which it is redistributed to the member countries according to a formula. When the formula is applied, the results indicate that the levels of redistribution in favour of Mozambique, the difference between contribution and transfer, is high, and ranges from US$118 million to US$126 million according to the SACU scenario – although this figure is likely to be reduced by larger revenue collected by higher SACU excise taxes on domestic production and the future reduction of the pool as a result of ongoing MFN and preferential liberalization by South Africa. This, in addition to VAT revenue (the main source of trade-related tax revenue), which is not shared, leads to the largest welfare gain for the SACU with TDCA scenario, when compared with all other scenarios.

These results suggest that, given Mozambique's intention to pursue a path of regional integration, SACU membership may be an attractive option – or at least that its costs are unlikely to be unreasonably high, and are likely to be accompanied by significant benefits, especially if accompanied by additional liberalization. SACU, however, is not free from problems and has substantial issues that need to be addressed, such as having a complex tax structure, the predominance of South African trade policy interests, problems in the implementation of the revenue sharing formula, the TDCA or VAT tax coordination.

It is important to point out, however, that SACU membership alone would not be sufficient to attract investment, and would only be useful for this purpose as one supporting element among others in a coherent and credible strategy for the improvement of the business environment. Most importantly, without policies to foster exports and to enhance competitiveness, investment gains might not materialize and the trade balance would become difficult to sustain.

From a tax policy perspective, the estimations illustrate that, with the exception of SACU scenarios, any liberalization will bring about a significant reduction in tax revenue. This implies the need to diversify the tax structure and reduce the dependency on trade related taxes. In order to maximize the benefits of trade reform, tax reform must complement trade liberalization.

7 Annex: the SACU revenue sharing formula

According to SACU Trade Policy Review 2003 (WTO 2003), the revenue sharing formula of the 2002 SACU Agreement, for a given financial year, is:

$$R_i = C \cdot \frac{A_i}{A} + 0.85E \cdot \frac{GDP_i}{GDP} + 0.15\frac{1}{n} \cdot E \cdot \left(1 - \left(\frac{Y_i}{Y} - 1\right)\right)$$

where:

R_i: revenue share of SACU country i;
I: Botswana, Lesotho, Namibia, South Africa or Swaziland;
C: all customs duties actually collected on goods imported into SACU, less the cost of financing the Secretariat, the Tariff Board and the Tribunal, less the customs duties rebated or refunded;
A_i: CIF value (at the border) of imports of SACU country i from all other SACU members, less re-exports;
A: total CIF value (at the border) of intra-SACU imports, less re-exports;
E: all excise duties actually collected on goods produced in the SACU area, less the cost of financing the Secretariat, the Tariff Board, and the Tribunal, less the excise duties rebated or refunded;
GDP_i: gross domestic product of SACU country i;
GDP: total gross domestic product of SACU members;
n: number of countries in SACU;
Y_i: gross domestic product per capita of SACU country i;
Y: average gross domestic product per capita of all SACU members.

The customs component: C (A_i/A)

The pooled customs revenue will be distributed according to intra-SACU imports, excluding re-exports and net of rebates. Even though country shares are expected to remain stable over time, the size of the customs pool (C) will depend upon the value of imports and changes to the SACU tariff regime.

The excise component: 0.85 E (GDP_i/GDP)

The size of the excise component has been set initially at 85 per cent of the excise pool, and will be distributed on the basis of the GDP of each of the SACU countries.

The development component: $(0.15) (1/n) E (1-((Y_i/Y)-1))$

The size of the development component has been set initially at 15 per cent of the excise pool, and will be distributed inversely to each country's GDP per capita: the smaller the GDP per capita, the greater the share of the development pool.

The data for the calculation of the income shares accruing to each country are obviously a source of conflict among member states. Discrepancies in tracking intra-SACU imports between SARS (South Africa) data and National Statistics from BLNS countries are quite significant, leading to prolonged discussions.

Notes

1 Mozambique is also committed in principle to forming a customs union with other SADC Members by 2010. However, this deadline is unlikely to be met, for the reasons outlined in Section 2.3. In practice, the SADC customs union, if it happens at all, is likely to come about through the expansion and metamorphosis of SACU, since all SACU members are also members of SADC.

2 A more exhaustive treatment of the methodology and results is included in the working paper version of this chapter (Alfieri *et al.* 2006).

3 National Institute of Statistics (INE) data, CIF values. Subtracting goods of unknown classification (Harmonized System chapter 99), the result is US$1.7 billion. Comtrade mirror data report imports worth US$1.8 billion (FOB values), or US$1.5 billion excluding chapter 99.

4 INE data, FOB values. The value of goods of unknown classification is not significant. Comtrade mirror data yield essentially the same results.

5 The sugar surcharge depends on a fixed reference price. Currently, existing high prices in the international market imply that the CIF import price is above the reference price and therefore the surcharge is currently set to 0 per cent.

6 Calculations based on the General State Accounts for 2004.

7 With the new SACU agreement, decisions about the Common External Tariff need to be agreed among all members. This is expected to water down South Africa's dominance of decision-making.

8 The Members of the SADC Trade Protocol are: Botswana, Lesotho, Malawi, Mauritius, Mozambique, Namibia, South Africa, Swaziland, Tanzania, Zambia and Zimbabwe. Angola and Madagascar are in the process of acceding to the protocol.

9 Non-SACU sugar-producing countries with a surplus (defined as domestic production minus preferential deliveries to the EU and USA minus domestic consumption) obtain a duty-free quota into the SACU market. This quota is based on an initial level of 138,000 tonnes adjusted upwards yearly according to market growth in SACU.

10 Malawi, Zambia and Zimbabwe have in recent years experienced significant delays in implementing their tariff cuts as agreed under the Trade Protocol, and Malawi remains behind schedule; meanwhile non-tariff issues such as restrictive rules of origin and escalating non-tariff barriers remain unresolved.

11 Angola, Democratic Republic of Congo, Madagascar, Malawi, Mauritius, Swaziland, Zimbabwe and Zambia are all members of COMESA as well as of SADC, and COMESA too has been in the process of creating a free trade area and designing a customs union; meanwhile, Tanzania is a member of the EAC customs union with Uganda and Kenya.

12 This implies, however, a reduction from 25 per cent to 20 per cent of the rate for final goods as planned for 2006.

13 For the SACU scenario where the TDCA is included, there are three regions: SADC, the EU and ROW. Because non-SACU SADC trade with Mozambique is marginal, the SADC and SACU regions are considered to be equivalent for data purposes.

14 This means, in effect, that a hypothetical unit of quantity is created for this exercise. If prices are affected as a result of the trade reform scenarios, then values and quantities are no longer equivalent post-reform and new import values need to be calculated using the new prices and the new hypothetical quantities.

15 The assumption on import demand elasticties, as well as export price elasticities, impacts significantly the quantity and price estimates. However, to our knowledge Stern *et al.* (1976) is the best source of price elasticities, better than any guess estimate.

16 Traders may have market power and may be able to absorb some or all of the change in prices, reducing the benefits of liberalization for consumers. Moreover, the evidence on incomplete spatial market integration in maize markets suggests that consumers in central and northern parts of Mozambique will not benefit as much as implied by the estimations (Cirera and Arndt 2006).

17 This implies a reduction in the tariff for final products from 25 per cent to 20 per cent. In addition, the variable duty surcharges on sugar have been taken at their average rates in 2004.

18 It must be made clear that the term 'exemptions' in this chapter does not include the concept of preferential trade: thus, an import from South Africa claiming duty-free status under the SADC Trade Protocol is *not* considered to have been exempted.

19 The intercept originally in the equation is used to adjust imports from re-exports. Since the original model in Van Dunem (2005a) is only applied to South Africa's imports, and in our case we estimate imports from all the sources, we have only used the slope coefficient as a rough estimate of the elasticity without adjusting for re-exports from one source.

20 The official figures of SACU generated revenue in 2004 are 8,479 million rand for custom duties and 12,381 rand for excise duties. SACU revenues increased significantly in 2005, mainly due to a consumption boom. Thus we may expect that if the revenue shares remain more or less constant, SACU payments from 2005 may increase significantly. On the other hand, we may also expect in the future a reduction in the customs pool due to the implementation of the TDCA and other MFN liberalization.

21 Due to the significant increase in Mozambique's exports of gas to South Africa starting in 2005, we should expect that South Africa may even slightly increase its share of the duties pool.

22 Note that this figure is likely to underestimate the real excise revenue collection applying the SACU excise structure, since SACU excises are higher than current excises in Mozambique.

23 Kirk and Stern (2005) use 2002 as the base year, while the base year in this chapter is 2004, and the simulation methodologies for the impact of the liberalization scenario under SACU are different.

24 This result is highly dependent on whether SADC will effectively be a customs union, the type of revenue redistribution that will be established and the timing and costs of adjustment for both scenarios.

25 The size of the revenue pool increased significantly in 2005.

26 Setting the MFN tariff uniformly at 5 per cent.

13 Trade policy reform and missing revenue

Channing Arndt and Finn Tarp

1 Introduction

In many African countries, actual government revenues differ substantially from the amounts implied by multiplication of tax rates with the presumptive tax base. Estimates of this 'missing revenue' are almost invariably large enough to be of macroeconomic interest. Following a review of attempts to measure tax evasion, McLaren (1996) characterizes the extent of tax evasion in general in many LDCs as 'staggering'. The studies reviewed by McLaren suggest that the value of taxes avoided is often close to the value of actual collections for major taxes. With respect to trade policy, avoidance of taxes at the border is often combined with a complex patchwork of legal exemptions. Tsikata (1999) and Pritchett and Sethi (1994) find actual tariff revenues at levels between 44 per cent and 87 per cent of the amounts implied by published tariff rates and estimated import volumes for selected developing economies in Africa and elsewhere. In addition, Pritchett and Sethi find a significant positive relationship between the importance of exemptions and posted tariff rates. Their simulations reveal that reductions in peak tariff rates would likely have minimal revenue effects. These two studies relied on official imports data, so focus is on legal exemptions.

Fisman and Wei (2004) examine bilateral trade data between Hong Kong and China in an attempt to identify both legal exemptions and smuggling. They report an elasticity of evasion with respect to the tariff rate of approximately three. According to their findings, tariff rate declines, particularly for highly taxed items, would result in substantial *increases* in revenues. They conclude that there are widespread practices of under-reporting and mislabelling from highly to lightly taxed product categories.

Given the magnitude of the issue, the study of exemptions and tax evasion has received considerable attention in the public finance literature. Sandmo (2004) provides a general review of the theory of evasion. Burgess and Stern (1993) review the public finance literature with a specific focus on developing countries. They delve into, among other items, the perennial problem of the application of high rates to relatively small bases with attendant strong incentives for evasion. In more recent work, McLaren (1998) develops a model where evasion incentives drive the optimal tax pattern. McLaren's model is consistent with the well-documented tendency for poorer countries, with weak tax administrations, to focus revenue raising efforts on a few relatively easy to administer choke points within the economy, while more advanced economies tend to employ more broad-based revenue raising approaches (see, for example, Tanzi and Zee 2000). Bliss (1992) develops a model that explicitly recognizes the limited availability of tax handles in poor economies and the concomitant important role that taxes levied at the border often play in these economies.

While public finance economists highlight the importance of border taxes in financing activities of the state for poor countries, trade economists frequently tout the benefits of openness for growth prospects.[1] The work of Fisman and Wei (2004) and Pritchett and Sethi (1994) indicate that these views are not necessarily in conflict in light of the fiscal realities present in many developing countries. Given the ubiquity of tariff exemptions and evasion, it is possible that revenue neutrality can be maintained despite reductions in tariffs through accompanying reductions in the volume of official exemptions and the empirically observed tendency for rate reductions to reduce incentives to evade.

Nevertheless, the degree of disconnect, particularly in analyses of poor countries, between the role of revenue in the analysis of border policy and the role of the border in revenue analysis is striking. For example, even though trade taxes provide significant revenue to poor countries, analyses of the implications of global trade liberalization for developing countries under the auspices of the World Trade Organization (WTO) rarely contain more than a cursory discussion of revenue issues.[2] Furthermore, even though evasion and exemptions are known to be widespread, they are rarely accounted for explicitly in empirical trade policy analyses for developing countries. So, while computable general equilibrium (CGE) models are widely recognized to have been influential in the formulation of trade policies for developing countries over the past two decades, relatively few trade policy applications of a CGE model specifically account for evasion or exemptions.

In the context of official exemptions and revenue considerations, it is important to emphasize that some official exemptions are applied for specific and potentially justifiable reasons. In particular, rationale exists for policies, such as exemptions or rebates, which allow exporters to operate at world market prices for intermediates and investment goods. This is especially true when critical factors of production are internationally mobile, such as in the case of textiles and wearing apparel. Some work in the trade literature has focused on these cases. For example, Bach *et al.* (1996) model exemption of imported textiles later exported as wearing apparel. Ianchovichina (2005) considers whether these exemptions/duty drawbacks are really worth the administrative effort. She concludes, using China as a case study, that the wisdom of these schemes depends upon initial conditions and objectives. They may or may not be good policy.

So, some share of the 'missing revenue' can potentially be justified by appealing to export competitiveness, particularly for footloose industries where imported intermediates constitute a high cost share in the exported product. The remaining share of the 'missing revenue' is difficult to justify. High levels of evasion are hardly to be celebrated, especially from a governance perspective. Even considering exports, the case for official exemptions weakens considerably when one considers export of natural resource based products. In these cases, the critical factor of production, the natural resource, is immobile. The natural resource rent should be distributed reasonably equitably across the population. Taxation is one way, and oftentimes the only way, to achieve this objective. Official exemptions for consumption goods and for intermediate purchases for non-exporting industries are also difficult to justify.[3]

In the context of African economies, especially poor African economies, the value of exemptions targeted for the specific and justifiable purposes considered by Ianchovichina (2005) is often very small. For example, information on five African countries (Malawi, Mozambique, Zambia, Tanzania and Uganda) from version 6 of the GTAP database (see Dimaranan and McDougall 2005) indicates that exports from these countries are overwhelmingly natural resource based. Sectors, especially manufactures, where access to imported intermediates at world prices is crucial to competitiveness, represent less than 10 per cent of total exports in these five country cases.

In short, in the context of poor African economies, the share of 'missing revenue' attributable to the sorts of exemptions featured in the trade literature is likely to be small. Yet the value of taxes avoided, though difficult to measure, is clearly very large. The authors are unaware of any CGE application that captures the patchwork of exemptions and evasions that bring tariff collection rates down to the levels observed by Tsikata (1999) Pritchett and Sethi (1994) and Fisman and Wei (2004).

This chapter seeks to take a first step towards integrating the perspectives of public finance and trade economists in the analysis of developing country border policy. To do so, a simple stylized model of tariff avoidance through exemptions and/or smuggling is developed. The insights from this model are subsequently incorporated into a detailed CGE model to consider the implications of trade policy reform in a representative sub-Saharan country (Mozambique). The CGE model explicitly considers exemptions and evasion, and since the right to import duty free while others must pay tariffs (for example via an exemption) has a value, the distributional implications of trade policy reform are also considered.

The chapter is structured as follows. Section 2 presents a simplified model of international trade in order to investigate theoretical issues associated with duty free imports. Section 3 examines the extent and nature of duty free importation for the case of Mozambique specifically. Section 4 presents the CGE model employed for the analysis. Section 5 presents model simulations and results, while Section 6 summarizes and concludes.

2 A simple model of trade and tariffs with missing revenue

We seek to examine the issues of exemptions and evasion in the simplest possible way. Our model contains three goods: an importable that is not produced domestically (M), an exportable that is produced, but not consumed, domestically (E), and a non-tradable that is produced and consumed domestically (D). There are h households with identical Cobb–Douglas preferences. Each household has a labour endowment z_h. Production technology is linear in labour units, and standard neoclassical behavioural assumptions apply.[4]

The mathematical form of the model is as follows:

Consumer demand for M	$M_h P_m = (1 - \alpha) Y_h$	(1)
Consumer demand for D	$D_h P_d = \alpha Y_h$	(2)
Consumer budget constraint	$Y_h = z_h W + T_h$	(3)
E production technology	$E = a L_E$	(4)
D production technology	$\Sigma_h D_h = b L_D$	(5)
E first order condition	$W = a p_{we} R$	(6)
D first order condition	$W = b P_d$	(7)
Trade balance	$p_{we} E = p_{wm} \Sigma_h D_h$	(8)
Price transmission	$P_m = p_{wm}(1 + t) R$	(9)
Government balance	$\Sigma_h T_h = t \Sigma_h M_h p_{wm} R$	(10)
Numeraire definition	$R \equiv 1$	(11)
Factor market balance	$L_E + L_D = \Sigma_h z_h + WAL$	(12)

Ignoring subscripts, L represents labour allocations, W the wage, P prices (p_w indicates fixed world price), R the exchange rate, t the tariff rate applied to imports, α the share of the household budget devoted to good D, and T transfers. Variables are in upper case while parameters are in lower case. The variable WAL effectively drops the factor market balance equation (12) in accordance with Walras' law. Note that tariff revenue is distributed back to households in the form of direct transfers (equation (10)). Also, note that the model, as given above, is incomplete as the distribution of transfers, T_h, across households is left unspecified. Finally, note that by solving for P_m and P_d and substituting into equation sets (1) and (2), the model boils down to a system of linear equalities (assuming the allocation mechanism for transfers is linear). Accordingly, the model can be solved as long as the matrix of parameters is invertible.

For our purposes, the closed form solution is not strictly necessary. Rather, it suffices to note that all prices, including the wage, can be determined as a function of the tariff rate t, the production parameters a and b, world prices p_{we} and p_{wm} and the exchange rate R, which serves as numeraire. As a result, from an individual household perspective, income is exogenously determined by the household specific labour endowment and the level of government transfer. Production side issues are essentially abstracted from and changes in welfare are determined uniquely by changes in prices (through, for example, changes in the tariff rate) and changes in transfer income.

The model is used to consider three separate situations:

1 a tariff where particular groups obtain access to imported goods duty free, either via smuggling/corruption or via legal exemption, when these groups face no supply constraints;
2 a tariff with a legal exemption scheme under which particular groups are allowed access to goods duty free but are constrained from satisfying full domestic market demand;
3 a tariff with smuggling/corruption where those who are engaged are constrained from satisfying full domestic market demand.

Situation 1 implies no supply constraints on exempted imports or smuggling, so market demand will be completely filled at world market price. Hence, the *de jure* tariff is completely ineffective, and the operational tariff rate is zero. There is no revenue to distribute. The model arrives at the free trade solution. Analytically, situation 1 is not a particularly interesting case. It is, however, worth noting that the same solution can be obtained via an offsetting consumer subsidy on the importable good. The addition of a consumer subsidy on the purchase of imports can be achieved by modifying two equations of the model as follows:

Consumer demand for M $$M_h P_m (1 - s) = (1 - \alpha) Y_h \qquad (1a)$$

Government balance $$\Sigma_h T_h = t \Sigma_h M_h p_{wm} R - s \Sigma_h M_h P_m \qquad (10a)$$

It is straightforward to show that, if $(1 - s)(1 + t) = 1$, the free trade equilibrium is re-established.

Situation 2 recognizes the existence of official tariff exemptions. For example, expatriates and locals, who travel frequently, are often able to legally avoid paying import tariffs up to some specified value of imports. Government regularly exempts itself from import tariffs, and large investment projects negotiate special import treatment (see Gauthier and Reinikka 2006 for discussion of these phenomena in the case of Uganda). Situation 2 differs from situation 1 in that the ability to import duty free is extended only to certain actors and only on a specified volume of imports. The situation is analogous to a tariff rate quota where the in-quota import volume arrives duty free and the out-of-quota import volume pays posted tariff rates.

We model this situation by dividing the market for imports. Some groups import and consume with tariff laden prices, while others import and consume at world prices. We focus on division of markets across households in our simplified model. This situation requires further modification to the model. The market division can be achieved in at least two ways. First, a subscript h could be added to the tariff rate, t. In this case only certain groups pay the tariff. This modification also requires an h subscript on the domestic price of imports, P_{hm}. Alternatively, an offsetting consumption subsidy to specific households, s_h, can achieve the same outcome when a single tariff rate is applied in a manner analogous to the ineffective tariff situation considered above. These modifications are shown below.

Consumer demand for M $\qquad\qquad M_h P_{hm}(1 - s_h) = (1 - \alpha)Y_h$ (1b)

Price transmission $\qquad\qquad\qquad P_{hm} = p_{wm}(1 + t_h)R$ (9b)

Government balance $\qquad\quad \Sigma_h T_h = t_h \Sigma_h M_h p_{wm} R - s_h \Sigma_h M_h P_{hm}$ (10b)

Any given household j faces free trade prices if $(1 - s_j)(1 + t_j) = 1$. Further, in this simple model, if household j also receives zero transfers, it faces the free trade equilibrium. Note that situation 2 is captured through manipulation of indirect tax rates.

Situation 3 captures the basic elements of smuggling and/or corruption. Suppose that household j possesses the means to illicitly import duty free. It both imports commodities duty free for direct consumption and imports and resells commodities at the tariff laden price. As in situation 2, duty free importation for direct consumption can be modelled by setting $(1 - s_j)(1 + t_j) = 1$ (for household j only). Resale of imported products at the tariff laden price by household j is captured by imposing the posted tariff rate t on imports of these goods that are resold but directing the value of this tariff revenue to household j in the form of a transfer, T_j. Effectively, household j consumes at world prices and benefits from additional income by importing at world prices and selling at tariff laden domestic prices.

In order for situation 3 to exist in equilibrium, something must prevent the volume of imports from re-establishing the free trade equilibrium as in situation 1. As pointed out in Allingham and Sandmo (1972), risk-averse individuals may engage in evasion given positive returns despite a positive probability of detection and a penalty associated with detection. If one assumes that both the probability of detection and the penalty associated with detection increase with the scale of evasion, then individual willingness to evade will be circumscribed. Under these conditions, the free trade equilibrium is not possible as some returns are required to compensate for penalties, such as fines, loss of import licence or time in jail, associated with detection. A second avenue involves complicity in evasion by government officials. In this case, the smuggler effectively obtains an unofficial exemption with the power of the state directed to enforcing compliance on other importers. In this instance, some degree of discretion in the volume of goods imported on the part of the smuggler and the enabling government official(s) is required in order to avoid detection and to prevent collapse of the free trade equilibrium.

For the Mozambican case that we are to consider shortly, two empirical observations support the existence of some barriers preventing collapse of the free trade equilibrium. First, prices for commodities, particularly consumer goods that are highly taxed, traded between South Africa and Mozambique are almost invariably substantially higher in Mozambique.[5] Second, collapse of the free trade equilibrium when border taxes are significant would almost surely imply that honest importers would be forced out of business. This does not appear to be the case, as the relative success of large South African retailers, such as Game and Shop Rite, who are highly unlikely to engage in broad-scale smuggling, indicates.

Situations 2 and 3 are similar to the rent-seeking models developed by Krueger (1974) in that rents exist. They differ in that real resource absorption (rent-seeking) in the allocation of these rents is assumed to be small relative to the size of the actual rents. Krueger considers the opposite extreme where the presence of rents generates real resource allocations in rent-seeking equivalent to the value of the rents. In other words, the supply curve for smuggled goods is upward sloping and fairly steep. However, Krueger also explicitly points out that other outcomes are possible and goes on to indicate that the degree of real resource consumption allocated to rent-seeking depends upon the manner and environment in which the rent is generated. As is argued in Section 3 below, the evidence for Mozambique does not point to substantial real resources allocated to smuggling, especially relative to the size of the rents. As the Krueger result for the case of relatively steep upward sloping supply curves for smuggled goods (a large scale misallocation of real resources) is well established, and as this case appears to be of limited relevance for the case of Mozambique, we confine our analysis to situations 2 and 3.[6]

Reality is, of course, much more complicated than the simple model presented. However, the role of our model is to capture the essential features of the phenomena of interest. In the next sections we seek to examine empirically the interactions between revenue and trade considerations in the context of significant exemptions and evasions. Rather than constructing an archetype economy, we choose to focus on a representative poor African country (Mozambique) where about 50 per cent of government revenue comes from taxes (tariffs, value added and assorted consumption taxes) levied at the border. This has the advantage of directly confronting the challenge of estimating exemptions and evasion in a particular case and incorporating these estimates into a CGE model, a class of models frequently used for trade policy analysis.

3 Mozambique as case: import values, tariff revenues, and rents

A direct attempt at valuing unrecorded trade flows for the case of Mozambique was undertaken by Macamo (1998). He systematically attempted to observe unrecorded cross border trade at major border checkpoints with neighbouring countries. He estimated US$98 million in illegal trade for the year 1996.[7] This amounts to about 10 per cent of the value of total imports in 1996. While already large, this estimate likely substantially understates inflows that avoid border taxes. Macamo focused on cross border trade with Mozambique's neighbours, while significant imports also arrive from overseas. In addition, Macamo focused on small, relatively unsophisticated operators, with larger, presumably more sophisticated operators 'not necessarily' included (Macamo 1998: 12). Also, Macamo did not observe legal exemptions, which constitute a significant share of duty free imports.[8] Finally, if, as is likely, smuggling is concentrated in highly taxed products, then the implications for revenue would be much stronger than the implications for import volumes.

Mozambican National Accounts effectively estimated the combined value of evasion and official exemptions for 1997 by estimating import volumes based on a combination of import data for Mozambique, export data from important trade partners, and capital account data from the Central Bank. The results are shown in Table 13.1. In all, actual revenue collections amount to less than 40 per cent of the value implied by multiplying import volumes with the published tariff rates. Further, product categories with high tariff rates tend to exhibit higher volumes of missing revenue.

More recent analysis of South Africa–Mozambique trade data confirms the general picture. In total, the value of declared exports to Mozambique from South Africa exceeded the value of imports registered in Mozambique from South Africa by about 24 per cent in 2004 (Van Dunem and Arndt 2005).[9] Revenue implications would be stronger since the detailed data indicate higher discrepancies between declared South African exports and declared Mozambican imports for items in more highly taxed product categories. South Africa is, by far, Mozambique's largest trading partner.

Table 13.1 Import Values, Tariff Rates, and Tariff Revenues for 1997

Sector	Import Value	Published Tariff Rate (%)	Implied Tariff Revenue	Actual Tariff Revenue	Share Missing (%)
Primary Ag. Crops	662	10.0	66	60	9.6
Primary Ag. Livestock	85	10.0	8	6	29.5
Forestry and Firewood	5	46.1	2	2	0.0
Extraction	77	12.5	10	9	3.2
Food Processing	1,803	35.0	631	117	81.4
Beverages and Tobacco	298	35.0	104	17	83.4
Primary Product Processing	1,046	35.0	366	62	83.1
Chemicals	2,022	15.0	303	165	45.7
Other Manufactures	4,172	15.0	626	381	39.0
Other Services	168	0.0	0	0	0.0
Construction	0	0.0	0	0	0.0
Commerce	0	0.0	0	0	0.0
Transport and Communication	140	0.0	0	0	0.0
Insurance and Finance	1,308	0.0	0	0	0.0
Public Administration and Def.	0	0.0	0	0	0.0
Education	0	0.0	0	0	0.0
Health	0	0.0	0	0	0.0
Labor Intensive Services	0	0.0	0	0	0.0
Big Projects	0	0.0	0	0	0.0
Big ProjectImports	45	0.0	0	0	0.0
Total or Weighted Average	11,831	17.9	2,117	820	61.3

Note: All value figures are in billions of meticais. In 1997, the exchange rate was approximately 11,406 meticais to the US dollar.
Source: National accounts (1997) and MPF (2002)

So, while the degree of precision in all of these figures leaves much to be desired, the available information paints a qualitatively similar picture of large volumes of goods entering duty free. Nevertheless, as indicated earlier, retail prices for imported goods, particularly consumer goods, are almost invariably substantially higher than any reasonable calculation of CIF costs, indicating the presence of rents for those with access to imports duty free. The presence of rents corresponds with situations 2 and 3 identified within the framework of the stylized model presented in Section 2.

As discussed earlier, basic correspondence with situations 2 and 3 also requires small consumption of real resources relative to the size of the rents. Hence the degree of competition for these rents merits further discussion. Macamo (1998) does find evidence of real resource use in smuggling. For example, border traders wishing to evade tariffs often divide goods into small lots and hire numerous transporters to bring the goods across the border before re-amassing the contraband for transport to consumption centres. This is clearly much more expensive than simply trucking the goods across the border.

Nevertheless, the evidence collected by Macamo confirms that the large majority of unrecorded cross border transactions (with neighbouring countries) pass either through or very close to official entry points.[10] Some simply pass straight through in trucks, with very minor to no increment in transport costs relative to official imports. Even when disassembled into smaller lots, the incremental transport cost appears to be small compared to the value of the tariffs avoided. Macamo considers beer transported by the head, which draws an incremental transport cost of only about 10–15 per cent of the value of the tariffs avoided. Regarding international seaports, one would expect incremental transport costs to be relatively small since the options in terms of physical transport are much more limited. Incremental transport costs are almost surely about zero for officially exempted goods.

Payments made to corrupt customs officials in order to facilitate smuggling or to public officials in order to gain access to exemptions are properly accounted for as transfers, not real resource allocations. Overall, the evidence points to the existence of rents and a relatively small quantity of real resource allocated in pursuit of these rents. Situations 2 and 3 described in the simple model in Section 2 therefore guide the construction of a more formal empirical model of Mozambique.

Since substantial volumes of goods enter Mozambique duty free, as is the case in other developing countries, the overall average tariff rate (total tariff revenue divided by the total CIF value of imports) in 1997 was relatively low at 6.9 per cent. Nevertheless, substantial volumes of imports do arrive through official channels and pay duty at the published or marginal rate, which is typically well above the average rate. The marginal import appears to be tariff inclusive; so the price of traded goods within the country reflects the world price and the associated marginal tariff rate. When tariff rates are high, significant benefits therefore accrue to those individuals with the ability to import duty free either through legal exemptions or through smuggling/corruption at official border points.

Table 13.1 shows import values and actual tariff revenue according to the commodity classification employed in the social accounting matrix (SAM) underlying the computable general equilibrium (CGE) model employed for analysis in this chapter.[11] About 44 per cent of the value of imports entered the country duty free in 1997 despite positive posted tariff rates. However, as indicated in Table 13.1, duty free imports tend to be concentrated in sectors with higher posted tariff rates.[12] Therefore, as indicated above, tariff revenue forgone due to unrecorded trade and legal exemptions amounts to about 60 per cent of the total tariff revenue implied by the multiplication of posted tariff rates with actual import volumes.

Protection rates are highest for Food Processing, Beverages and Tobacco, and Primary Product Processing (which includes textiles, clothing and leather products). The rates for exemptions and unrecorded trade in these categories are estimated to be particularly high as well, with more than 80 per cent of the value of these products entering the country duty free (value shares and shares of tariff revenue forgone are the same in this instance since a flat rate of 35 per cent was applied to all goods in these three categories). The commodity composition observed by Macamo also reflects this concentration of unrecorded trade in these three commodity categories.

Finally, it is worth noting that Processed Food, Beverages and Tobacco, and Primary Product Processing represent an important part of consumer budgets. The 1997 SAM indicates that these products accounted for about 29 per cent and 37 per cent of total expenditure for rural and urban households, respectively. Consequently, price changes for these commodities have the potential to impact household welfare fairly strongly.

4 Modelling approach

4.1 The Mozambique CGE model and SAM

The empirical CGE model used in this chapter addresses the issue of exemptions/evasion in the spirit of the theoretical model in Section 2. Specifically, access to imported goods at world prices (either via smuggling or official exemption) is assumed to generate rents that are large relative to resources allocated to rent-seeking. In addition, some agents are assumed to import duty free goods and consume them directly; hence consumption decisions for these agents are made on the basis of world market prices. Other agents import duty free and resell on the domestic market at tariff laden prices. Profits from these resales are modelled as transfers of virtual tariff revenue. A final set of agents do not have access to goods at world market prices. The latter two groups of agents base consumption decisions on tariff laden prices. More standard elements of the model took as their point of departure an existing model of Mozambique described in Tarp *et al.* (2002). Relatively straightforward elements are briefly summarized first.

The model assumes profit maximization by producers under translog technology and utility maximization with Cobb–Douglas preferences by consumers. Investment and government consumption are allocated in a Leontief fashion (a fixed basket of goods). The Armington (1969) assumption is employed, with constant elasticity of transformation functions on the export side and constant elasticity of substitution functions on the import side. The external sector of the model is closed by fixing foreign currency inflows (primarily aid) and allowing the exchange rate to adjust. Investment is driven by available savings. Finally, the government deficit is fixed (more details on government closure are provided in the Section 5.1). The model numeraire is the consumer price index. Finally, detailed accounting for marketing margins is accomplished as described in Arndt *et al.* (2000).

Following the stylized model from Section 2, the Mozambique model as applied here involves the simultaneous capturing of average and marginal tariff rates when these diverge. As shown in Table 13.1, such differences are substantial in Mozambique. When confronted with this situation the CGE modeller has traditionally faced a choice. One can apply the average tariff rate, which gets revenue correct. This is clearly desirable in public finance applications. However, this approach understates the true import tariff wedge at the margin, which is in focus in trade policy analysis. Alternatively, one can apply the published rate, which overstates tariff revenue but captures the distortions inherent in trade policy.

In practice, modelling goals (and expedience) have guided analytical choices. For example, the Global Trade Analysis Project (GTAP) data usually reflect published (marginal) tariff rates since most users are trade policy focused and the model is relatively poorly suited to public finance applications (Dimaranan and McDougall 2005). On the other hand, a series of studies of southern African economies conducted by the International Food Policy Research Institute (IFPRI) typically employed average tariff rates since the public finance dimensions of these studies maintained a higher profile (see, for example, Tarp *et al.* 2002).

While the choice has typically been one or the other, both the average and the marginal rates can in fact be captured in a CGE model using the analytical model derived in Section 2. Conceptually, situations 2 and 3 described in Section 2 can be modelled in a manner similar to a tariff rate quota where a certain volume of imports enters the country duty free and the remainder enters the country at a strictly positive tariff rate (i.e. the published tariff rate). As in the case of a tariff rate quota, the ability to import duty free (or at the within quota rate) has a value. For those with access to goods duty free, the tariff revenue forgone by the government effectively represents income in the form of either a rent or an implicit subsidy. With relatively few modifications, the basic machinery for modelling tariff rate quotas can be applied to the issue of low rates of tariff revenue collection.[13]

In this particular case, the implicit value of tariffs avoided is calculated for each commodity. The actual tariff inclusive import value of all commodities is then augmented by the respective amounts of tariff payments avoided through (legal or illegal) duty free importation in order to obtain the CIF value of imports plus the full amount of tariff revenue implied by published rates. From the theory discussion presented in Section 1, the destination of the virtual tariff revenue (the tariff revenue not actually collected by government) depends upon the use of the imported commodity. If it is imported and then consumed directly, the importing/consuming agent could be viewed as paying the import tariff and receiving an exactly offsetting consumer subsidy. If the good is imported and then resold at tariff laden prices, then the importing agent could be viewed as receiving a transfer from the government equivalent to the value of the tariff revenue avoided.

There is very little information to indicate the share of duty free imports that is consumed directly and the corresponding share that is resold at tariff laden prices. Legal exemptions would tend to fall into the former category, while smuggled goods would tend to fall into the latter. The available evidence indicates that both of these categories are important. However, for Beverages and Tobacco, Food Processing and Primary Product Processing, where tariff rates and tariff avoidance are the highest, the share that is resold at tariff laden prices likely predominates. In this light, we assume that 33 per cent of duty free imports are consumed directly and the remaining 67 per cent are imported and resold. Further, we assume that government, investment and urban household accounts have some ability to import duty free and consume directly. Rents (modelled as transfers) from importing duty free and reselling at tariff laden prices are assumed to accrue to urban households.[14] Rural households, on the other hand, are assumed not to have access to duty free goods.

In the model, price linkage equations remain exactly as before. So, for example, import prices are equal to the world price converted to domestic currency times the sum of one plus the marginal tariff rate (plus any marketing margins). The tariff revenue side differs. Similar to the perspective of duty free imports as a tariff rate quota, we assume on a commodity by commodity basis that a certain fraction of imports enters the country duty free while the remaining fraction pays marginal tariffs. Actual tariff revenue in the government revenue equation becomes this fraction multiplied by the value of tariffs implied by the full marginal tariff rate. The remaining amount, the value of tariffs avoided, is divided between consumption subsidies (relating to goods that are consumed directly) and direct transfers to urban households (relating to goods that are imported and then resold).

5 Simulations and results

5.1 Simulations

Table 13.2 illustrates the simulations undertaken with the model. In the first, labelled 'All Products Pay', the share of products imported duty free is set to

Table 13.2 Simulations

Label	Description
Base	Base data in billions of meticais.
All products pay	The share of products imported duty free drops to zero while tariff rates are adjusted proportionately to maintain revenue neutrality.
Flat tariff rates	All positive tariff rates are reset to a single level that maintains revenue neutrality. The share of products imported duty free remains constant.
Both	The share of products imported duty free drops to zero and all positive tariff rates are reset to a single rate. This rate is adjusted to maintain revenue neutrality.

zero, while all tariff rates are adjusted proportionately to maintain revenue neutrality with respect to all indirect taxes (not just tariff revenue). Consumption subsidies reflecting direct consumption of products imported duty free are also set to zero. This corresponds to a fictional scenario where all legal exemptions are eliminated and all smuggling is stopped. In the second, labelled 'Flat Tariff Rates', all non-zero tariff rates are reset to a single level that maintains revenue neutrality with respect to all indirect taxes.[15] The share of products imported duty free remains constant. Consumption subsidies adjust to offset the level of virtual tariff revenue associated with direct consumption of duty free imports. In the third, labelled 'Both', the share of products imported duty free drops to zero and all positive tariff rates are reset to a single rate. This rate is adjusted to maintain revenue neutrality with respect to all indirect taxes.

The simulations are designed to investigate the implications of a lower tax rate applied to a wider base, a common public finance application. As in most public finance applications, careful attention is given to the maintenance of revenue neutrality. Maintenance of total indirect tax revenue was also targeted since these are the taxes that interact with the price system. The value of indirect taxes (less output subsidies) represented 75 per cent of government revenue in 1997. Changes in revenue from indirect taxes have implications for welfare analysis. As shown by Robinson and Thierfelder (1999), changes in indirect tax rates that change indirect tax revenue invalidate wages as an acceptable welfare indicator. With the revenue closure adopted, wages remain an acceptable welfare indicator (at least for the large majority of the population that lacks rights to import duty free).

The third scenario combines the first two scenarios to create a scenario of policy interest. This scenario asks the question: 'What flat tariff rate applied to all imported commodities (excluding commodities with a tariff rate of zero in the base) would be required to maintain revenue assuming all imported goods paid tariffs at the published rate, and what are the welfare implications of this policy?'

5.2 Results

Macroeconomic results are illustrated in Table 13.3. Trade expands in all scenarios. Growth in trade is led by increased imports of Processed Food, Beverages and Tobacco, and Processed Primary Products, which are associated with the highest initial rates of protection. Reductions in tariff rates applied to these products are large in all scenarios. In scenario 1, the existing rate structure is reduced by nearly two-thirds (see the Tariff Rate Expansion Factor at the bottom of the table). Consequently, rates on these three commodities decline from 35 per cent to about 12 per cent. In scenario 2, duty free shares remain constant but tariffs are reset to a single flat rate of about 17 per cent (the flat tariff rate is equal to the Tariff Rate Expansion Factor). For most commodities, this involves a tariff rate increase, which tends to reduce trade volumes. However, for the three highly taxed commodities mentioned above, tariffs decline by 18 percentage points. The net effect is a very small increase in trade volumes in this scenario.

Scenario 3 involves the elimination of exemptions and the application of a flat tariff rate. Under these conditions, revenue neutrality can be maintained with a 7 per cent tariff rate. This involves a substantial tariff rate cut for each of the commodity aggregates. However, trade expands less than in scenario 1 (All Products Pay) since importing duty free and consuming directly is no longer an option. All products are assessed duties.[16] The expansion of imports induces a devaluation of the currency in order to stimulate import competing and exporting sectors. Due to the large level of external financing

Table 13.3 Macroeconomic Results

	Base	All products pay (%)	Flat tariff rates (%)	Both (%)
Exchange Rate	1.00	5.0	1.4	5.0
Real GDP	40,609	0.1	0.1	0.1
Total Absorption	48,357	0.0	0.4	0.3
Imports	11,831	1.7	0.0	1.4
Exports	4,083	4.9	0.1	4.2
Investment	8,173	3.9	−0.3	3.0
Tariff Rate Expansion Factor*	1.00	0.35	0.17	0.07

Note: All base value metical figures are in billions. Also, the levels of some macroeconomic aggregates differ slightly from published values due to more explicit accounting for the rents associated with duty-free importation.
*: The tariff rate expansion factor is not in percentage terms and the interpretation of this factor differs by scenario. In scenarios 'Base' and 'All products pay', the factor multiplies existing marginal tariff rates. In scenarios 'Flat tariff rates' and 'Both', the factor still multiplies all tariff rates; however, these are all set to one. So, the expansion factor is the unique tariff rate applied to all goods with strictly positive tariff rates in these two scenarios.
Source: CGE Model Simulations

received by Mozambique, the value of imports exceeds the value of exports. As a result, exports must grow by proportionately much more for a given proportional change in imports in order to maintain external balance. Real gross domestic product (GDP) changes little in all scenarios, but total absorption – a measure of economy-wide welfare – increases mildly in the 'Flat' and 'Both' scenarios.

Table 13.4 provides information on the contribution of each sector to real GDP at factor cost in the base, the level of value added generated by each sector and the percentage change in real value added generated by each producing sector for each scenario. Focusing on the third scenario ('Both'), one observes some changes in the composition of value added, but they are not dramatic. Small sectors that enjoy substantial protection, such as Beverages and Tobacco, shrink when protection is removed. Increases in production are observed in Insurance and Finance. Import penetration in this sector is fairly large at about 30 per cent of the value of domestic consumption, and initial levels of protection were zero. The devaluation enables this sector to compete more effectively against imports and hence increase value added. The devaluation also increases the local currency value of foreign capital inflows. Since most of these inflows fund investment expenditure, investment spending increases spurring activity in, for example, the

Table 13.4 Real Value Added by Sector

	Base Share (%)	Base Level	All products pay (%)	Flat tariff rates (%)	Both (%)
Primary Ag. Crops	27.4	9,963	–0.4	0.8	0.0
Primary Ag. Livestock	2.2	795	–2.1	0.3	–1.6
Forestry and Firewood	3.2	1,156	0.2	0.2	0.3
Extraction	4.3	1,570	2.4	0.5	2.3
Food Processing	3.3	1,198	–1.6	–1.2	–1.9
Beverages and Tobacco	0.9	313	–5.3	–3.1	–5.9
Primary Product Processing	2.2	802	–3.0	–3.2	–4.0
Chemicals	0.6	231	–1.7	0.4	–1.3
Other Manufactures	1.1	410	0.3	0.6	0.4
Other Services	8.3	3,018	–0.9	–0.4	–1.0
Construction	6.5	2,375	3.3	–0.2	2.6
Commerce	20.1	7,337	–0.2	–0.3	–0.3
Transport and Communication	8.9	3,236	0.0	–0.2	–0.1
Insurance and Finance	4.6	1,682	3.1	0.1	2.6
Public Administration and Def.	2.8	1,007	0.0	0.0	0.0
Education	1.6	601	–0.7	–0.2	–0.7
Health	0.5	179	–0.5	–0.1	–0.5
Labor Intensive Services	1.5	550	0.4	0.1	0.4

Note: All base value metical figures are in billions.
Source: CGE Model Simulations

construction sector. An intuitive explanation of the decline in value added produced by the livestock sector will be deferred for later.

Table 13.5 provides information on factor prices. In all scenarios, all wages and rental rates increase relative to the base. The increases range from about 1.5 per cent to 1.8 per cent for all factors. This implies that all households lacking access to duty free imports benefit from the policy change. These are compelling results that are relatively simple to explain. Two broad effects dominate these increases in real wages.

First, the figures reported in Table 13.5 are real factor prices, with deflation being performed by the consumer price index (the numeraire). As indicated above, the three commodities with the highest rates of protection (Processed Food, Beverages and Tobacco, and Processed Primary Products) represent a significant share of the consumer consumption bundle. When protection is removed, prices for these commodities decline. The level of the consumer price index (CPI) cannot decline by definition. Only relative prices matter in a CGE model. As a result, other prices, including factor prices, tend to rise relative to the CPI in order to achieve a relative decline in the prices of the basket of goods comprising the CPI.

Second, as indicated earlier, the rents that accrue from importing duty free and reselling on the domestic market at tariff laden prices function in a manner analogous to imposing a tariff and having the government reimburse these 'tariff payments' back to those relatively few individuals with the right to import duty free. In a macroeconomic sense, the rents from duty free importation and subsequent resale function like a tariff (an indirect tax) that is later reimbursed (a direct transfer) to selected individuals.[17] Reductions in these 'transfers', through tariff rate reductions (which lower the implicit value of the rents) or reductions in the share of goods imported duty free, function like reductions in standard tariffs with concomitant reductions in transfers.

The macroeconomic impact on wages can best be perceived by considering the fundamental national accounting identity:

Table 13.5 Real (CPI deflated) Wages

	Base	All products pay (%)	Flat tariff rates (%)	Both (%)
Unskilled Ag Labor	1.63	0.6	2.1	1.6
Skilled Ag Labor	2.66	0.5	2.2	1.6
Unskilled Non-Ag Labor	6.99	1.4	0.5	1.5
Skilled Non-Ag Labor	23.96	1.9	0.2	1.8
Highly Skilled Non-Ag Labor	57.03	1.9	0.2	1.8
Capital	0.15	1.5	0.9	1.8

Note: All base values for wages are in millions of meticais per year.
Source: CGE Model Simulations

$$C + I + G + (X - M) = GDP = GDPfc + IT$$

where C is consumption, I investment, G government expenditure, X exports, M imports, GDP gross domestic product, GDP*fc* GDP at factor cost, and IT total indirect taxes. The right hand side of the above expression can be rewritten as:

$$\sum E_i w_i + TR^o + TR^r + IT^o$$

where E_i represents the quantity of each factor employed, w_i the wage for each factor, TR^o official tariff revenue, TR^r rents from resale of goods imported duty free, and IT^o other sources of indirect tax revenue. The sum of employment of endowments (in this case various categories of labour and capital) multiplied by their respective wages yields GDP at factor cost. The sum of the three tax components gives total indirect taxes.

In the simulations considered here, endowment supplies are fixed and fully employed. Hence the only way to increase nominal GDP at factor cost is to increase wages. By assumption in each scenario, the sum of $TR^o + IT^o$ is held constant. The remaining term represents the rents from resale of goods imported duty free, TR^r. In scenarios 1 and 3, this value is reduced from about 2.4 per cent of GDP at factor cost to zero. If nominal GDP remained constant and TR^r were the only source of indirect tax revenue, average wages would have to increase by about 2.4 per cent. In the event, nominal (CPI-deflated) GDP declines by about 0.6 per cent and other indirect tax revenue sources remain in place (at a constant value). Simple calculations indicate that average factor prices must rise by slightly more than 1.7 per cent, which is approximately equal to the change in the weighted average factor price one obtains from Table 13.5.

This effect on nominal wages often leads to the erroneous conclusion that trade liberalization increases household and economy-wide welfare due to the wage effect. As pointed out by Robinson and Thierfelder (1999), this is not necessarily the case. For example, if the tariff revenue is replaced by direct taxes such as income taxes, households might find that the increase in income taxes more than offsets the 'wage increase' which follows from reductions in indirect tax revenue. In this instance, the household is not better off. More generally, using factor prices as a welfare indicator in trade liberalization scenarios will tend to overstate the benefits of trade liberalization if the implications of reductions in government tariff revenue are not accounted for.

In order to conduct an acceptable welfare analysis using wages, we must account, not for the reduction in tariff revenue actually collected (which remains essentially constant), but for the reduction in rents accruing to those with the ability to import duty free. Even though we know relatively little about these people, it is safe to assume that they are not particularly numerous and that they are not poor. For these relatively few individuals (such as corrupt border guards) the reductions in the rents received will almost surely exceed the average increment to wages predicted by the model. Hence, their welfare declines. However, for the large majority of working people who lack access to duty free imports, wages are an acceptable welfare indicator. The results indicate that wages for these people will rise (with no offsetting reduction in rents).

A composite view of welfare effects on households can be obtained by examining household equivalent variation. This is done in Table 13.6. As shown, urban household welfare declines very substantially, while rural household welfare increases significantly.[18] The decline in urban household welfare is attributable entirely to the disappearance of rents from resale of products imported duty free, which formerly accounted for about 5.6 per cent of total income. If the information existed to divide urban households into those receiving rents and those not receiving rents, simple calculations indicate that urban households not receiving rents would experience welfare gains of about 2 per cent.[19]

6 Conclusions

Tax exemptions and smuggling are basic characteristics of many African countries. *De facto* tax collections are consequently far below revenue implied by published (marginal) or *de jure* tax rates. Efforts to address this problem have therefore been a key component of economic reform programmes geared at macroeconomic stabilization and promoting a better balance in public finances. Yet there is a curious lack of consistency between the way in which, respectively, public finance and trade policy analysts have treated average and marginal tax rates. Public finance studies typically rely on average tariffs, which get revenue right. Yet this approach underestimates the distortions inherent in trade policy, which are a prime concern of trade analysts. These have therefore traditionally resorted to using published rates, even if this leads to overstating revenue.

The above disconnect is unsatisfactory, in both theory and practice. In Section 1 we therefore developed a simple theoretical model to clarify the conceptual issues involved in capturing average and marginal tariff rates simultaneously in a common analytical framework. Motivated by this model, we proceeded in Section 3 to demonstrate that the key methodological challenge faced in this chapter can in large measure be viewed as a tariff rate quota (TRQ) within a model of international trade where a certain volume of imports enters a country duty free whereas the remainder enters at

Table 13.6 Household Welfare (measured by equivalent variation)

	Base	All products pay (%)	Flat tariff rates (%)	Both (%)
Urban	15890.9	−4	−1.1	−3.8
Rural	20,102	1.6	1.1	1.9

Note: All base value metical figures are in billions.
Source: CGE Model Simulations

a strictly positive tariff rate. We also noted that the ability to import duty free has a value as in the case with a TRQ. For those with access to duty free goods, the tariff revenue forgone by the government effectively represents income, in the form of a rent or as an implicit subsidy.

In sum, we demonstrated that the basic machinery known from modelling TRQs can be applied to the combined public revenue and trade issue at hand. On this basis, we revised a standard CGE model of international trade, so it could be applied to conduct a trade policy analysis with specific attention to capturing the importance of divergence between average and marginal tariff rates. We took as our point of departure the fact that CGE models represent an attractive framework for the analysis of public finance issues for low income African countries, and proceeded to detailed accounting of revenue from the border, which is a natural extension from models focused on trade policy. Similarly, improved representation in the model of the actual implementation of trade policies is clearly important for the items of classic interest to trade economists such as the structure of production, welfare and income distribution.

The model was implemented with Mozambique as case study. We argue that the analytical approach developed here is easily replicable and could be brought to bear on a series of other countries across the African continent. Moreover, our results in Section 4 indicate that there are considerable possibilities for increasing both efficiency and equity. Losers from trade reforms include those households (urban households by assumption), who benefited from their ability to import duty free one way or the other. It is highly unlikely that these rent-creaming households are particularly poor. In contrast, the welfare of poor rural families increases following trade reform. In the scenario 'Both', where a flat tariff rate is applied and all duty free importation ceases, rural household welfare as measured by equivalent variation increases by about 1.9 per cent. The implications for wages are strongly positive and remarkably uniform, indicating that the large majority of the urban population that does not enjoy access to duty free goods becomes better off following reforms. All in all, we appear to be as close to a win–win policy recommendation as one can in practice hope for.

Notes

1 See Winters (2004) for a balanced view.
2 Winters and Hertel (2005) is a recent exception.
3 If the tariff rate schedule is flat or broadly upward sloping from capital goods/ imported intermediates to final domestic consumption goods (as is typically the case), exemption on imports of intermediates by non-exporters results in increases in effective protection rates. Exemption is easier to justify in the case of negative effective protection but these cases are rare.
4 The model is motivated by the 1-2-3 model of Devarajan *et al.* (1990). This model is simplified by assuming perfect transformation between domestics (D) and exports (E).
5 This is true even for the capital, Maputo, which is located less than 100 km from the South African border by very good road.
6 Pitt (1981) presents a model where legal imports must exist in order to disguise illicit importation. In the Pitt model, market prices for imports settle within an

intermediate range between the CIF price and the tariff laden price such that the gains from smuggling and selling at above the CIF price are exactly offset by the losses from importing officially but selling at less than the tariff laden price. If real resource costs of smuggling are zero, smuggling acts like a reduction in tariffs and is welfare enhancing. Note that in a competitive version of the Pitt model all honest importers would be forced out of business.

7 More precisely, Macamo estimated unrecorded trade for the period December 1995 to November 1996.

8 Van Dunem (2005a) calculated the value of official exemptions at about 15 per cent of the value of the theoretical tariff taken for the period 2002–4.

9 Differences between FOB and CIF values are accounted for in the analysis.

10 Given the underdeveloped state and characteristics of the existing transport infrastructure, this is not surprising.

11 The SAM and modelling code can be obtained from the authors on request.

12 In many cases, the same posted tariff rate does not apply across all the goods comprising the aggregate commodities shown in Table 13.1. As a result, aggregation of posted tariff rates is necessary in order to determine the actual tariff rate that should be applied. A number of complex conceptual issues are associated with appropriate aggregation of tariff rates. These issues are explored in Bach and Martin (2001), among other sources. In Table 13.1, the posted tariff rates reflect weighted averages of import volumes with a small corrective factor to account for the fact that higher tariffs tend to drive down import volumes.

13 See Elbehri and Pearson (2000) or Rutherford (1995) for general equilibrium analysis of tariff rate quotas.

14 To simplify the modelling, the real resource costs associated with importing duty free are assumed to be zero. If real resource outlays to avoid tariffs are indeed a relatively small share of the value of tariffs avoided, as the available evidence suggests, then this simplification is harmless. The other case, involving significant real resource outlays, has, as already discussed above, been examined in the seminal paper by Krueger (1974), among others.

15 As Table 13.1 indicates, the tariff rate applied to some imports, particularly services, is zero in the base. These rates remain at zero in all simulations.

16 As indicated earlier, deriving an appropriate aggregate tariff rate for an aggregate commodity is complex. In 1997, some components of some aggregates were taxed at a rate lower than 7 per cent, so the 7 per cent flat rate does represent a tariff rate increase for some commodities when a more detailed level of disaggregation is considered.

17 Direct consumption of duty free imports, on the other hand, functions as if the government had imposed a tariff at the border and then given back the revenue in the form of a commodity specific consumption subsidy. These two indirect taxes exactly offset one another.

18 These are large numbers for trade policy simulations, where welfare changes are often of the order of 1 per cent.

19 This aggregation of urban households into a single average helps to explain the somewhat counterintuitive decline in livestock production shown in Table 13.4. Urban households are, on average, considerably wealthier than rural households; and they direct a much larger fraction of their income to meat consumption. When average urban household income declines, direct demand for livestock products declines as well. In addition, marketed meat products (butchered animals) are considered processed foods. With declines in domestic processed food production following reductions in tariffs, intermediate demand for livestock products falls as well. A more detailed analysis with more disaggregate data would provide a more precise insight into production effects for the livestock sector.

Part IV
Domestic taxation

14 Taxation and the cost of capital

Shakill Hassan

1 Introduction

1.1 Relationship to firm financing

A firm's cost of capital is the rate of return which investors (or lenders) require in order to invest in it. Firms are not exclusively owned by shareholders. A firm's value depends on its ability to transform some collection of resources into output, which when sold generates income. The inputs are acquired using the funds provided by equity and debt holders. Lenders are entitled to a predetermined fraction of the firm's income. Once debt obligations are met, the government collects its (direct) share of firms' profits. Shareholders own the residual claim to a portion of this stream of income.

The crucial distinction between the claims of equity holders and debt holders is not that interest payments are fixed and known in advance, while dividends are not. The payments on variable rate loans are neither fixed nor known in advance. The norm in the Mozambican credit market is for interest rates to be indexed to a money market rate. And dividends will be fixed if managers and shareholders decide that they should be so – if the firm has the cash to pay.

The distinction is in the set of circumstances in which the providers of capital can exercise control. For as long as an indebted firm can meet its obligations towards its lenders, equity holders control the firm. This assumes owner-managed firms, which is of course the dominant form of governance in Mozambique and most other developing countries. Once the firm fails to meet such obligations, however, control passes to lenders.

When a firm approaches a financial intermediary to raise external finance, debt and equity are alternative instruments through which the intermediary will gain access to some portion of the firms' revenues. The regulations that govern Mozambique's financial system recognize this by permitting banks to hold equity, as well as debt, in the corporate sector. But the tax system does not. It treats income from owning a priority claim to firms' earnings (i.e. from lending) and income from residual claims (i.e. from owning equity) differently, by effectively taxing the latter more heavily (see GoM 2002a). This note seeks to explain clearly and precisely how, to what extent and with what implications for the cost of capital.

1.2 Double taxation of equity income and financial sector development

In Mozambique (not uniquely), individuals and corporations are taxed separately. The tax liability of shareholders is assessed independently of the tax liability of the corporations they own. In particular, and in contrast to interest payments, dividends do not count as expenses in the computation of the paying firm's tax liability. Yet, like interest income, dividend income is fully taxable in the hands of the receiving shareholder. A corporate tax rate of 32 per cent and personal income tax of 32 per cent (in the highest bracket) imply a tax rate on income from risky equity investment of 54 per cent.

Internationally, the effect of the double tax on equity income is at least partly mitigated by a lower capital gains tax.[1] The return from equity investment is not only, nor even primarily, due to dividend income. There is a liquid capital appreciation component, due to the tradability of equity shares. Gains from increases in the value of shares, which exceed dividends as the source of returns, are taxed at the capital gains rate. The latter is normally lower than ordinary income tax, under which interest (and dividend) income falls. The effect is the following. Although interest income is paid from earnings before tax and dividends are paid from after-tax earnings, the personal tax rate on equity can be close to, and is usually lower than, the rate on interest income. (See Poterba and Summers 1985 for a classic and extensive treatment of the effect of dividend taxation on capital allocation).

In addition, numerous countries have introduced measures that reduce the double tax even when equity returns flow mainly through dividends, which is the case for unlisted firms. Greece and Norway allow dividends to be deducted from corporate taxes; Australia, Canada, France, Germany, Italy and the UK have an imputation system, where dividends received create a tax credit for part or all of the taxes paid by the corporation.[2] Similar measures are currently absent from the Mozambican tax code. They are as important in Mozambique as elsewhere.

Since Mozambique's stock market consists of little more than a handful of illiquid shares listed, the benefits from owning equity capital accrue almost exclusively through dividends. Thus the tax penalty on equity can be particularly high. The consequence is an incentive for potential investors to benefit from business activity by lending, rather than acquiring equity (a firmer, longer-term commitment), or not investing at all. With respect to financial sector development, the relative unattractiveness of equity investment contributes to the slow expansion of the stock market, and the virtual non-existence of private equity investment – which is arguably the form of alternative financing that the Mozambican private sector could benefit the most from.

Given frequently expressed concerns of the private sector about the restricted availability and high cost of external financing (see IMF 2004c; DNEAP and KU 2006) and the central importance of private sector investment for sustained economic growth (see Jones 2006 for Mozambican evidence), the effect of corporate taxation on the attractiveness of equity investment is not consistent with the central role of private sector growth in the government of Mozambique's economic growth plan.

2 Relative attractiveness of alternative forms of ownership

Consider a standard one-period risk-neutral setting. (King 1974; Grinblatt and Titman 1998; Amaro de Matos 2001; Auerbach 2002). Suppose a firm is financed by a combination of owners' equity capital and debt. Let E represent the initial equity investment, and D the amount initially borrowed, at the rate of interest r_D. So the amount to be repaid to lenders is $(1 + r_D)D$ (most bank loans in Mozambique have short maturities). Let X denote end of period payoff, before interest and tax. After repaying debt and corporate taxes, at rate τ_C, and assuming no cash is retained for future investment or working capital, profits available for distribution are equal to $[X - (1 + r_D)D](1 - \tau_C)$. If this entire sum is paid out to the providers of equity capital, the investor is liable for personal income tax on the dividends received, at rate τ_E. The (maximum) amount received by investors is thus

$$[X - (1 + r_D)D](1 - \tau_C)(1 - \tau_E)$$

So the rate of return on equity, after corporate and personal taxes, is

$$r_E(1 - \tau_C)(1 - \tau_E)$$

where $r_E = (X - (1 + r_D)D)/E$ is the pre-tax return on equity. Lenders pay income tax on interest received, so the after-tax return on debt is $r_D(1 - \tau_D)$.

The condition for indifference between investing in equity and lending as alternative ways of owning a firm's cash flows is that the after-tax return from each be equalized:

$$r_E(1 - \tau_C)(1 - \tau_E) = r_D(1 - \tau_D) \tag{1}$$

Consider only investors whose total personal income puts them at the highest threshold for personal taxation. In Mozambique, $\tau_C = \tau_E = \tau_D = 0.32$. The above condition for indifference simplifies to $r_E(1 - \tau_C) = r_D$, or $r_E = r_D/(1 - \tau_C)$, implying that for any positive corporate tax rate investors will only be indifferent between debt and equity if the pre-tax return on the latter strictly exceeds the former, $r_E > r_D$.

A reasonable estimate of the weighted average rate of interest on one-year bank loans in Mozambique for 2005 is circa 25 per cent.[3] Take this rate as the pre-tax return on debt. Then, given the corporate tax rate of 32 per cent, after-tax return equivalence requires that $r_E = 0.25/0.68$, i.e. 36 per cent return on equity, or 47 per cent larger than the return on debt.

Hence the result is: in the absence of non-debt tax shields, investors with the possibility of acquiring private sector debt obligations (i.e. lending) in Mozambique will find equity in the same firms a more attractive investment only if the expected pre-tax return on equity is strictly larger than 1.47 times the interest rate on the loan.

A few remarks and further results follow.

2.1 One reason why banks do not invest more in equity

Banks in Mozambique are the dominant participants in the financial sector. In addition to extending loans, commercial banks are allowed to hold equity in the corporate sector. But very few, if any, ever do. The result above partly explains why.

2.2 Why Treasury bills seem so attractive

Banks can lend to the government by investing in Treasury bills and government bonds.[4] The average rate of interest on one-year government bonds issued in July 2006 was over 18 per cent.[5] Moreover, the income earned from holding Treasury bills is tax free.[6] That is, in case of government debt we have $\tau_D = 0$. When comparing equity investment with buying government debt, the condition for investor indifference is thus

$$r_E(1 - \tau_C)(1 - \tau_E) = r_{GD}$$

Using the fact that for investors in the highest income tax bracket $\tau_C = \tau_E = 0.32$, a tax-exempt rate of return of 18 per cent on government bonds implies that the above condition is only satisfied when the pre-tax return on equity reaches 39 per cent.

The cost to the government of its securities is determined in the primary market for government debt, where participation is restricted. Before drawing conclusions on the scope for raising more funds for each unit of future interest payments (i.e. obtaining a higher price for debt obligations issued), consider the relative attractiveness of government and private sector debt. With a weighted average rate of interest on loans of 25 per cent, the after-tax return from private lending is 17 per cent. Private loans require significant overheads and involve default risk. Treasury bills do not yet offer comparable after-tax returns.

Thus the general result is: in the absence of non-debt tax shields, investors with the possibility of acquiring government debt obligations in Mozambique will find private sector equity investment more attractive only if the expected pre-tax return on equity is at least 2.1 times greater than the return on government debt; and private sector lending (more attractive than government debt) only if the rate of interest, net of default, is at least 1.47 times larger than the return on government debt.

2.3 Implications for public debt management

First, government borrowing crowds out private sector investment through two channels: banks facing high default rates from corporate borrowers and/ or high overheads associated with lending will prefer default free government securities; and any other investor with no tax exemptions prefers government bonds to equity. Second, the government seems to be selling bonds too cheaply, paying a higher rate of interest than necessary.

Hence there is scope for both reducing the cost of government borrowing in the domestic market as well as promoting private sector investment by raising the price of government debt securities (i.e. reducing the rate of interest on government debt obligations). This may be achievable by promoting increased competition in the primary market for government securities, where participation is currently restricted; re-examining the design of government securities auctions; and carefully managing government borrowing requirements (which determine the supply of securities).

Should the government start taxing interest earned on Treasury bills and/or bonds? Not necessarily. If it imposes taxes, it will receive additional revenue from these taxes, but it will have to pay a higher pre-tax rate of interest. The interest currently paid represents the required after-tax return from holding government securities – given the existing auction rules. If the income from holding these is taxed, bidding institutions will (all else constant) simply bid lower prices for buying the bonds, so that the higher pre-tax interest permits a sufficient attractive after-tax return. What is a sufficiently attractive after-tax return given the current financial sector conditions? Precisely the rate received under the tax exemption.

A preferable solution is to increase competition in the primary market for government securities. All else constant, the increased demand will raise bond prices, reducing the interest rate on bills. The private sector will benefit through a lower benchmark interest rate; and the government will benefit through a lower cost of domestic financing (receiving more metical in each auction for each metical it will be liable to pay in the future) – even without removing the tax exemption on interest from holding government securities. It might also be of interest to subject the auction rules to careful examination given the well-documented sensitivity of optimal bidding behaviour to auction design. Evidently, sporadic large increases in Treasury bill issues will always push bond prices down and interest rates up. The preceding recommendations presume the minimization and careful timing of issues.

2.4 Allowing for non-debt tax shields

So far the analysis has ignored the existence of non-debt tax shields. Mozambican entrepreneurs, as well as foreign firms operating in Mozambique, receive non-trivial allowances which can substantially reduce firms' tax liabilities. (This is especially so in the case of large foreign investments, which command significant bargaining power when negotiating for concessions before committing (for more on this, see Chapter 15). Such tax shields and exemptions significantly reduce the effective corporate tax rate.

Take the extreme case where tax exemptions or non-debt tax shields reduce the effective corporate tax rate to zero. Now reconsider the comparison above between buying government bonds and investing in equity. The condition for indifference becomes:

$$r_E(1 - \tau_E) = r_{GD}$$

With the rate of tax on received dividends at 32 per cent, and a tax free return of 18 per cent on government bonds, this condition translates to approximately $r_E = 0.26$.

In brief, when non-debt tax shields reduce the effective corporate tax rate to zero, equity investment becomes more attractive than buying government debt obligations if the pre-tax return on equity is at least 1.47 times the yield on government debt.

Similarly, comparing the after-tax returns from equity investment with corporate lending when the effective corporate tax rate is zero but the income from dividends and interest is taxed equally, equity investment will be as attractive as corporate lending if simply $r_E = r_D$. This sounds trivial. But bear in mind it only applies *when the effective corporate tax rate is zero.*[7] For any positive effective corporate tax rate, the required return on equity is strictly larger than the required return on debt. The fewer the exemptions, the larger this difference must be. The closer the effective corporate tax rate is to the standard rate, the larger will the excess return on equity have to be. Ignoring risk and agency issues, the required return on equity equals the required rate of interest on debt only when non-debt tax shields reduce the effective corporate tax rate to zero.

Note that this is true before any adjustments for the higher risk associated with equity investment. We are considering only the tax effects. Reliable measures of the equity premium in Mozambique do not exist. But it is safe to conjecture that it is larger than in neighbouring South Africa, where the long-term equity premium is estimated at between approximately 6 and 8 per cent.[8]

2.5 Depreciation and other special allowances

Mozambique has a complex and partly ad-hoc system of special tax exemptions. Simultaneously, the rates of tax on interest and dividend income are equal. But interest payments are tax-deductible, while dividends are paid from after-tax profits. Because of very low financial development (the existence of only a trivial and illiquid stock exchange in particular), lower capital gains tax cannot be relied on to keep the effective tax on equity income lower than that on interest income, thus compensating for the tax disadvantages of dividends. The consequence is that equity investments offering expected returns which elsewhere may be regarded as highly profitable are only attractive in Mozambique if there are special tax allowances.

There are good reasons to either eliminate or change substantially the system of fiscal exemptions (see Chapters 2, 5 and 6). But the preceding analysis suggests that any such changes will impact on the after-tax cost of capital and therefore require changes in the combination of taxes on corporate profits, interest income and dividend income, to mitigate the effect of the reductions in exemptions on the after-tax cost of capital.

3 Effect of taxes on mix of debt and equity in firms' balance sheets

In the absence of non-debt tax shields, a firm with taxable profits will be indifferent between debt and equity financing if the after-tax cost of debt equals the after-tax cost of equity.[9] Under the Mozambican IRPC, interest payments reduce taxable profits and thus the firm's tax liability, while dividend payments do not. Dividends are paid from after-tax profits. Hence, from the viewpoint of the firm, and ignoring risk (which is firm or project specific), the condition for indifference (in terms of minimizing the cost of capital) between the two forms of external financing is that

$$r_D(1 - \tau_C) = r_E \tag{2}$$

It follows that, as long as the corporate tax rate is non-negative, debt and equity will be equally costly only if $r_E \leq r_D$ (specifically, in the Mozambican case, this means that at a minimum, $r_D = r_E/0.68$. Usually, in countries with non-integrated tax systems, the average tax rate on equity income can be equal to or lower than the tax on interest income. This is due to low capital gains tax reducing the effective tax rate on equity income, as explained previously. That is, $\tau_D > \tau_E$, so that $(1 - \tau_D) < (1 - \tau_E)$ and conditions (1) and (2) can be simultaneously satisfied under various combinations of τ_C, τ_D, and τ_E larger than zero.

From the viewpoint of investors in Mozambique, however, the preceding analysis shows clearly that there will be no incentive for equity investment unless $r_E \geq r_D$. If the firm faces an effective corporate tax rate of zero, it was seen that we can have $r_E = r_D$. In this extreme case, we can have both conditions (1) and (2) satisfied provided $(1 - \tau_E) = (1 - \tau_D)$, which is ensured by the fact that $\tau_E = \tau_D$. But if the firm pays any corporate taxes, it was seen that $r_E > r_D$ if equity is to be attractive, in which case condition (2) cannot be met – the after-tax cost of debt is lower than the cost of equity for any level of return on equity that investors will be happy with.

4 Recommendation and remarks

4.1 Summary and recommendation

The primary market interest rate on government securities sets a lower bound on the cost of private sector borrowing. From the viewpoint of banks: interest paid by private sector borrowers is not tax-exempt; private sector lending involves larger operational costs than simply buying Treasury securities; and it carries larger default risk. In turn, the interest rate on private sector debt, through the Mozambican tax treatment, sets a premium on the lower bound on the required return on equity – over and above the usual risk factor. Because equity investment is only attractive if the pre-tax return on equity exceeds the rate on loans, the average cost of capital is kept strictly above the rate of interest on loans. Hence the double taxation of equity income contributes to under-investment, leading to slow renewal of capital stock and slower economic growth.

Obviously, tax policy is not the sole impediment to sustainable growth, and it is not through tax reform alone that this central objective will be achieved. It is equally obvious that the judicious use of state revenues can have a significantly positive effect on growth. But changes to alleviate its adverse effects on the cost of financing would help. Such changes would have to involve either (1) exempting dividends from personal income tax or (2) permitting dividends to be paid from pre-tax earnings.

This leads to the following recommendation: removing the fiscal bias against equity investment requires either that dividends received be exempted from personal income tax or that dividend payments be made from earnings before tax, thus reducing the firm's tax liability – or an alternative measure to the same effect.

The second measure is likely to have a stronger impact on private sector investment, and the least harmful short-term effect on government tax revenues. Due to significant credit constraints, it is estimated that circa 80 per cent of private sector investment in Mozambique is funded by retained earnings.[10] A firm's profit before tax has to match the sum of its tax liability, dividends paid and retained earnings. Permitting dividends to reduce the corporate tax liability leaves more retained earnings for any given combination of dividends paid and profits before tax, relaxing the firm's financing constraints. Detailed empirical research suggests that reductions in the effective taxation of retained earnings can have significant sustained effects on private sector investment and economic growth in economies with under-developed financial sectors.[11]

As discussed in other chapters in this volume,[12] corporate tax revenues as a share of GDP declined substantially from 1999 to 2005. Personal tax receipts are now twice the volume of corporate taxes. Moreover, the effective corporate tax rate is already lower, for at least some firms, than 32 per cent. If dividend income becomes tax-exempt, equity investment in such firms may become essentially tax free. That is, the state does not receive much from taxing the firms' profits, or from the dividends received by its owners. Thus the second measure (treating dividend payments as expenses for the purposes of computing firms' tax liabilities, rather than exempting dividend income from personal taxation) is likely to have the smaller negative impact on aggregate tax receipts. All firms will benefit from a reduction in the corporate tax burden, and the double taxation of equity income will be mitigated; but the government collects taxes on dividend income.[13] It would, however, further reduce the effective corporate tax rate.

4.2 Informal remark on the level of the corporate tax rate and growth

Investment occurs when the expected return on investment exceeds the return investors require (i.e. can obtain elsewhere), given the prospect's risk. The investors' required rate of return is the firm's cost of capital. Then the higher the average cost of capital, the smaller the set of investments which will be attractive.

The results of systematic empirical studies on the effect of taxes on growth are ambiguous.[14] There are a number of reasons for this, including measurement difficulties and the difficulty with isolating the effects of taxes. Low taxes stimulate corporate activity and private sector investment. High taxes permit higher public investment. Lowering taxes increases the former at the cost of the latter. The net effect on economic growth depends on the marginal productivity of private versus public investment. There is no reason to expect that all countries will experience a higher rate of productivity from one form of investment over the other across time. There may be variations over time for a given country.

For a cross-section of African countries, Skinner (1987) found that for the 1965–73 period the benefits from public investment outweighed the negative effects of the taxes raised to finance them; but for the 1974–82 period the productivity of public investment fell to the point that tax-financed public investment reduced output growth. In the Mozambican case, Jones (2006) finds that over the post-war period the contribution to output growth from private investment largely exceeds that of public investment, but no definite conclusions are made regarding investment productivity.

The anecdotal evidence can also shed some light. Data from a recent survey by KPMG, an international auditing firm, imply that the corporate tax rate in Mozambique (see Table 14.1) is not high in comparison to most low growth developing countries in Africa.[15] It is, however, higher than the rates in two of the most well-governed countries in Africa: Botswana, one of the world's fastest growing economies over the past decades, and Mauritius – both with corporate tax rates at or below 25 per cent. Moreover, the Mozambican corporate tax rate exceeds the average rate in the Asia-Pacific region, Latin America and the European Union, where a number of countries have been steadily reducing rates in the past decade.[16]

Table 14.1 Corporate Tax Rates (selected countries)

Country or Regional Average	Corporate Tax Rate, 2006
Mozambique	32
Botswana	25
Mauritius	25–15
Asia Pacific	30
Latin America	28
European Union	25

Source: KPMG (2006b)

The same study suggests that worldwide the average rate of corporate tax reduced from 38 to 27 per cent between 1993 and 2006. In some cases, reductions in corporate taxes are followed by periods of increased economic growth. A remarkable example is Ireland, the so-called 'Celtic Tiger'. The initial impulse for the very high growth rates it experienced through the 1990s is largely attributable to very low corporate tax rates: 12.5 per cent by 2004, reduced from 40 per cent prior to 1993. EU countries are dropping corporate tax rates to lure (or prevent flight of) investment and stimulate economic growth. In 2005 the average corporate tax rate in the European Union had dropped to 25 per cent – well below the Mozambican rate. Increasingly, only very large economies with enormous domestic markets and numerous other sources of competitive advantage manage to retain comparatively high corporate tax rates and robust economic growth, particularly the USA, at 40 per cent. Mozambique seems to have largely ignored worldwide reductions in corporate tax rates.

4.3 Informal remark on timing

Of course there are two issues to bear in mind. There is an urgent need for increased investment and sustained growth in Mozambique. But simultaneously, there is a pressing need for increased domestic revenues to fund the government budget. However, first, private sector-led economic growth will generate more profits, so that reduced tax rates need not cause reductions in income tax revenue. Second, in the long term it is unlikely that Mozambique will be able to apply higher corporate tax rates than developed countries with far higher capital and labour productivity, and expect to attract much investment.

In this regard, there is an important question of timing. Development funding to Africa has received considerable attention recently. The number of African countries which simultaneously have a pressing need for aid and satisfy the emerging requirements for funding, in terms of macroeconomic management, democratic governance and other criteria regarded as desirable in the donor community, has diminished considerably. Mozambique occupies what is arguably a particularly good position as an aid recipient. Assuming the country remains on its developmental path, there are no indications of large reversals of foreign aid in the near future. Indeed, improved governance may lead to increased funding. This may present an opportunity to bear the possibility of a short- to medium-term reduction in tax revenues due to a reduction in corporate taxes without much strain on the budget. Once the effects of lower taxes feed through to higher domestic growth, this temporary loss can be compensated for.

5 Conclusion

Mozambique is characterized by a combination of (1) comparatively high corporate tax rate and (2) non-integration of corporate and personal income tax systems. The associated double tax of equity income creates an incentive for lending rather than equity investment, and raises the required rate of return on the latter. Given the high levels of real interest rates on domestic currency loans, this translates to a high cost of capital and consequently under-investment by domestic entrepreneurs. Removing this fiscal bias requires either that dividend payments be made from pre-tax profits, thus conferring on dividends the same treatment as interest, or that dividend income be exempted from taxable income.

Notes

1 Note also that in countries under a classical tax system (no integration) it is usual for small firms to be largely or completely exempt from corporate taxes. In Mozambique, very few firms can be meaningfully categorized as anything other than small to medium-sized firms.

2 See, for example, McKenzie and Thompson (1996) and Grinblatt and Titman (1998).

3 Data from Banco de Moçambique, the central bank, indicate a simple arithmetic average nominal interest rate on one-year loans of 23.5 per cent for July 2006.

4 Other institutions and individuals can only buy Treasury bills in the secondary market.

5 According to Banco de Moçambique data, the rate of interest paid on one-year Treasury bonds issued in July 2006 was 18.25 per cent. It dropped to 16 per cent by September 2006, and was unaltered, at 16.5 per cent, from December 2006 to mid-January 2007. See various issues of 'Sintese de Situação Financeira', available at the Banco de Moçambique website: www.bancomoc.mz.

6 See Decreto 22–2004, Artigo 13, República de Moçambique.

7 Of course, equity is normally a riskier form of corporate investment. This last result implies that on a risk-adjusted basis the pre-tax required return from equity has to exceed the return from lending – even if the effective corporate tax rate is zero.

8 See Biljon and Hassan (2007).

9 Depreciation is the most common example of a non-debt tax shield. We are evidently ignoring agency and information-theoretic aspects of financing. This chapter is focused exclusively on tax effects.

10 See Chapter 4 and DNEAP and KU (2006).

11 See Hsieh and Parker (2006).

12 See Chapters 2, 5 and 6.

13 There may be also an advantage in the facility of tax collections. Firms would have an incentive to declare dividend payments, which can then be used to track taxable dividend receipts.

14 See, for example, Easterly and Rebelo (1993) and Easterly (2002).

15 It is common to see comparisons of Mozambique with countries at a comparable level of development. Intuitively, this seems natural. The obvious problem is that countries at such a low level of development tend to be poorly governed. Their economic policies are not usually an example to follow.

16 Behind the EU average are some notable reductions, motivated by the need to revive competitiveness as an investment destination. Two examples are: the reduction in Austria from 34 to 25 per cent in 2004; and Germany's decision in 2005 to reduce the average rate from 38.7 to 29, by 2008.

15 Fiscal treatment of mega-projects

Alice Kuegler

1 Introduction

Since 2002 tax incentives in Mozambique have been governed by the Code of Fiscal Benefits. The creation of this legislation was a major step towards formalizing fiscal regimes, and only allows for discretion with respect to tax incentives for projects of large dimension, so-called mega-projects. Even for investment projects of normal dimension, however, previous decrees and a myriad of incentives and deductions provide for a complex incentive system. Due to complexities and a lack of emphasis on recording, figures of forgone revenue for Mozambique have not been available in the past. This lack of data has inhibited cost control and detailed impact analyses of various tax incentives.

As a percentage of GDP, fiscal revenues for the Mozambican government added up to 14.4 per cent of GDP in 2006. This ratio is one of the lowest in Africa, in line only with the revenue-to-GDP ratios of Uganda and of Tanzania (FIAS 2006). While fiscal revenues are relatively low, a variety of fiscal incentives have been granted, which are specifically marked for mega-projects. In 2006, revenues of Mozambique's largest company and first post-war mega-project, Mozal, were equivalent to 6 per cent of GDP. Whereas corporate income tax is set at 32 per cent for normal firms, Mozal paid an equivalent income tax of approximately 3 per cent in 2006.[1] Incentive schemes have been similarly extensive for more recent mega-projects.

This chapter provides an overview of the various fiscal incentives available for investors in Mozambique and presents an initial analysis. Section 2 shows more generally that empirical evidence on the effectiveness of tax incentives is inconclusive and several shortcomings urge caution regarding their application as policy instruments. Section 3 discusses the beneficiaries and the different types of tax incentives applied in Mozambique. Where data are available, the impact of these incentives on state revenues is demonstrated. Estimates show that the Mozambican government in 2006 lost over US$120 million in revenues from income tax incentives granted to Mozal alone, which is equivalent to 12 per cent of the state's total revenue and 124 per cent of total income taxes collected. Section 4 outlines different policy implications and highlights the necessity for further analysis of the fiscal incentive regimes in Mozambique. Section 5 concludes.

2 The need to rationalize the current tax incentive schemes

Tax incentives are thought to attract capital that would not be invested in the absence of these fiscal benefits. If fiscal incentives are only granted partially or for a limited period of time, these additional investments would eventually lead to increased government revenues. Even with nearly full tax exemptions or unlimited benefit periods, additional investments can have positive effects for economic development via spillover effects to the domestic economy.

Politically, tax incentives may have an advantage over other investment promotion initiatives, because such incentives do not require additional budget allocations up front but occur as *post hoc* expenditures. Due to the lacking counterfactual, however, it is often cumbersome to demonstrate analytically the intuitive benefit of tax incentives. According to the literature, the empirical evidence on the cost effectiveness of tax incentives in stimulating investment is highly inconclusive (Shah and Toye 1978; Zee *et al.* 2002). In Mozambique, measuring the costs and benefits of tax incentives has proven difficult as precise data on the magnitude of incentives have been lacking at the individual firms level, by the size of firms and by sectors.

While evidence on the benefits of tax incentives is inconclusive, Bolnick (2004a) shows that the revenue costs incurred by governments can be significant, especially if the investments would have been viable without tax incentives. He argues that due to the shortcomings of the business environment, investments undertaken in Sub-Saharan Africa are generally projects that are profitable by a larger margin than the one provided through tax incentives. An additional shortcoming of fiscal incentives is posed by the fact that some incentives for foreign investors will be offset by the taxation policies of the source countries. In such a case, a company may pay fewer taxes in Mozambique, but will pay the difference in its country of origin. As a consequence, potential advantages from fiscal benefits granted in Mozambique would be futile.

Due to weak fundamentals in the Southern African region the majority of investments in these countries are likely to be location specific (Ogley 2006), which is particularly true for resource-seeking or factor-driven foreign direct investments. In Mozambique, some of the mega-projects are the firms that benefit most from tax incentives, in absolute as well as in percentage terms. These projects are active in exploration and export of minerals (for instance Kenmare Moma and Limpopo Corridor Sands), hydroelectric power production (Hidroeléctrica de Cahora Bassa), production of natural gas (different Sasol subsidiaries) and the production of aluminium (Mozal). For these projects, the availability of natural resources and cheap electricity are key reasons for locating in Mozambique. For the South African conglomerate Sasol, for instance, the impetus to invest in Mozambican gas fields was provided by the size of the country's natural gas deposits, combined with the need of the South African industry to find a more environmentally friendly and relatively cheap source of energy (Grobbelaar 2004). According to a survey by Macamo (2002), three-quarters of businesses surveyed said they would have invested in Mozambique regardless of the tax incentives that they benefited from.

In Mozambique, tax incentives are available for specific sectors, for underdeveloped regions and for projects of large dimension. Tax incentives, however, that do not result in a uniformly lower tax code will bias certain types of investments. As a result, tax preferences can introduce serious economic distortions, which reduce economic efficiency and productivity. Otherwise less productive activities are encouraged, and tax-favoured investments may sidetrack business from fully taxable producers. As a further cost of incentives, Bolnick (2004a) highlights that tax incentives will divert administrative resources from revenue collection tasks. An additional shortcoming arises if the accountability and transparency of the fiscal benefits granted are inadequate.

In Mozambique, the head of the Central Revenue Authority (Autoridade Tributária de Moçambique), Rosário Fernandes, underlined the difficulty of enforcing a complex and varied incentive scheme.[2] As further discussed in Chapter 6, the Mozambican tax administration largely relies on the self-compliance of companies for collecting firms' due fiscal obligations. Fernandes highlighted, for instance, that due to the administration's capacity constraints many firms continue to pay preferential tax rates after their incentive periods have expired.

While tax incentives might be more readily used than policies that require additional expenditure, significant trade-offs are involved in granting fiscal incentives. In an intertemporal framework, tax incentives give rise to considerable fiscal expenditures, which reduce the state's budget for spending on alternative initiatives. In addition, fiscal incentives may not be effective policies for attracting investment. For instance, it would be desirable to analyse the degree to which a new agricultural investor in rural Mozambique benefits from an income tax exemption. Potentially, government policies that enhance the local infrastructure, education and health of workers, the provision of cheap credits or of advisory services can trigger more additional investment than tax benefits.

Moreover, if the favourable treatment of some taxpayers creates inequities, this can undermine the compliance of less favoured investors, in particular in a country such as Mozambique which relies heavily on fiscal self-compliance. Bolnick (2004a) highlights that a tax system should be effective, efficient, predictable and equitable in its impact on different groups in society. If tax incentive regimes favour certain taxpayers over others in similar economic conditions, there must be a clear expectation that the tax incentives will 'truly and substantially foster equitable growth and job creation' as compensation for these inequities (Bolnick 2004a: ch. 1, 4).

One way to assess alternative expenditures is the marginal effective tax rate (METR) analysis, which, for example, allows the comparison of effective tax rates across sectors (see Section 3.1). The METR is defined as the cost of tax payments to the investor, expressed as a percentage of the incremental investment. METR analysis can be a useful indication of the impact of the tax system on the tax burden faced by an investor on additional investment.[3] While lower METRs indicate better investment conditions, the METR analysis does not incorporate revenue considerations by the government (FIAS 2006).

As discussed above, tax incentives for certain sectors, regions or projects are potentially not the most cost effective way to promote economic development in Mozambique, and impose additional constraints on the efficiency of the tax administration. A way of addressing these concerns is to ensure that careful analysis of the tax incentives system can be carried out.

3 Standard fiscal benefit regimes and mega-projects

This section provides an overview of the different types of tax incentives available in Mozambique, outlines the tax expenditure that arises for the Mozambican government and describes who benefits from these incentives. The current tax incentive scheme gives rise to distortions with respect to firm size, geographical regions and sectors.

In 2002 the Mozambican government summarized a previously dispersed and fragmented legal framework of tax incentives in the Code of Fiscal Benefits. The Code of Fiscal Benefits specifies the objectives of tax incentives and defines fiscal benefits as

> tax measures that reduce the amount of taxes payable in order to benefit activities having a recognized public, social or cultural interest as well as promoting the Nation's economic development. Fiscal benefits include tax and customs incentives, namely: deductions from taxable income, deductions from the amount of tax assessed, accelerated depreciation, tax credits, exemption from tax and the reduction of the rate of taxes and other fiscal payments, the deferment of the payment of taxes and other special fiscal measures.
>
> (Code of Fiscal Benefits, GoM 2002b: Article 2)

The Code of Fiscal Benefits contains little detail specifying the objectives of investment in Mozambique. Investment objectives are more specifically referred to in the Law on Investment and include, amongst other objectives, the creation of jobs and the raising of professional skill levels, the increase and diversification of exports, improvements in the balance of payments and government revenue, and technological as well as infrastructure development (GoM 1993a).

Tax incentives are categorized in the Code of Fiscal Benefits according to (1) a general incentive scheme, (2) specific sectoral incentives for agriculture, tourism and mining, rapid development zones and investments under the Petroleum Law, as well as (3) an incentive scheme for large-scale investment projects and industrial processing zones.

3.1 The standard incentive scheme

Any investments in Mozambique that are approved by the Investment Promotion Centre (Centro de Promoção de Investimentos, IPC) benefit from tax incentives as defined in the Code of Fiscal Benefits. Most foreign investors process their investments through the IPC, as they are not allowed to repatriate their profits out of Mozambique without the IPC certificate. The threshold investment value to apply for IPC benefits for foreign investors is US$50,000; for domestic investments this amount is set at a minimum of US $5,000. An additional requirement is that firms must have audited accounts, which excludes many small investors from applying for the IPC certificate. Table 15.1 outlines the standard incentives available for a firm holding an IPC certificate.

Further to these generic incentives, investments in agriculture and the tourism sector, in rapid development zones, along with investments under the Mining and the Petroleum Law, benefit from additional fiscal incentives. In agriculture, undertakings benefit from an 80 per cent reduction in the tax rate applicable to profits until 2012. For the tourism sector, tax credits apply as in the standard incentive scheme, but are augmented by an additional 3 percentage points, and therefore range from 8 to 18 per cent. Until 2010, investments carried out under the Mining Law and whose initial investment values exceed US$500,000, benefit from a 25 per cent reduction in the rate of the income tax, for the first five years from the commencement of production (Code of Fiscal Benefits, GoM 2002b: Article 42). This clause results in an effective income tax rate for mining operations of 24 per cent. For investments under the Petroleum Law, Article 44 specifies that enterprises carrying out petroleum operations are exempt from import and export duties, as well as from value added tax. According to Article 45, these investments benefit from a 25 per cent reduction in the rate of income tax during the first eight years from the start of production (until 2010). Due to controversy about their generosity, however, the Mozambican Parliament was considering dropping Articles 42 and 45 from the Code of Fiscal Benefits.

Further to these sectoral specifications in the Code of Fiscal Benefits, the Zambezi Valley, Niassa Province, Nacala District, Moçambique Island and Ibo Island are defined as rapid development zones. Investments in these zones benefit from an investment tax credit of 20 per cent of total realized investment, deductible from corporate income tax for the first five years, and firms are further exempt from property transfer tax. The rapid development zone scheme will be in force until the end of 2015.

Provisions in the Code of Fiscal Benefits such as investment tax credits, initial investment allowances and accelerated depreciations link available benefits to capital investments, and are therefore most useful for capital-intensive investments (Bolnick 2004b). By contrast, other countries of the Southern African Development Community (SADC) provide incentives that more specifically target training and employment. In Mozambique there is only

Table 15.1 Generic Incentive Provisions as Defined in the Code of Fiscal Benefits

Exemptions

Exemption from import duties for all capital goods
Exemption from stamp tax for the first five years

Investment tax credits

Investment tax credit for five years, equal to 5 per cent of the total investment realised
In the case of investments realised in Gaza, Sofala, Tete and Zambézia Provinces, this investment tax credit shall be 10 per cent
For investment projects in Cabo Delgado, Inhambane and Niassa Provinces, the percentage of income tax credit is 15 per cent

Depreciation allowance

Accelerated depreciation allowance, at twice the normal rate set by law

Deductible expenditures

Expenses on technology, up to 15 per cent of taxable income for the first five years
Expenses on the training of Mozambican staff, up to 5 per cent of taxable income for the first five years
Expenses on training up to 10 per cent deduction of taxable income for the first five years if the training is for the use of technologically advanced equipment
Tax deduction of 120 per cent for expenditures related to infrastructure in the city of Maputo
150 per cent of such expenditures for the rest of the provinces
50 per cent of the expenditures on art and Mozambican culture

Reductions

50 per cent reduction of the property transfer tax for agricultural, industrial, and hotel activities

one provision which concerns training costs, and normal firms can deduct up to 5 percent of taxable income for such costs (GoM 2002b: Article 18).

As tax incentives were only consolidated into the Code of Fiscal Benefits in 2002, many firms' tax obligations are still governed by previous laws and regulations. While generic income tax reductions now last for five years, firms authorized before July 2002 have benefited for periods from five to 25 years. Table 15.2 outlines the amount of fiscal expenditure arising for the government due to corporate income tax incentives granted to normal firms. In 2005, for instance, income tax benefits for these firms cost the Mozambican government US$21.9 million. This figure does not include tax incentives granted to mega-projects.

Table 15.2 Standard Income Tax Incentives Granted 2001–2005 (excluding mega projects)

	2002	2003	2004	2005
Foregone revenues (in thousands of Meticais)	622,724	344,955	341,900	477,032[a]
Foregone revenues (in million US Dollars)	26.3	14.5	15.1	21.9
Foregone revenue as percentage (%) of total corporate income tax collected	N.A.[b]	52	33	32

a: This figure has been updated by the author.
b: As corporate income was taxed differently in 2002, total corporate income tax figures are not comparable with subsequent years. Foregone revenues are high due to elevated investment values realised in 2002.
Source: National accounts (2003, 2004, 2005)

Until 2005, firms self-declared their deductible expenditures and attributed these costs to the most appropriate of seven categories of tax-deductible expenditures.[4] This procedure has resulted in a lack of information on the types of deducted costs. In 2004, for instance, 98.6 per cent of deductions were listed in the category 'other deductions'; the remaining 1.4 per cent were not attributed at all. This lack of information on tax-deducted expenditures has been addressed in the design of new tax benefit declaration forms, and firms have been required to provide more detail on the nature of their deductions from 2005 onward.

In addition, prior to figures for 2005, the records of the National Tax Directorate did not contain information regarding the sectors or the size of firms that benefit from the standard incentive regime. As further discussed in Chapter 4, alternative data from firm surveys in Mozambique indicate that large enterprises benefit disproportionately from tax exemptions compared to micro-, small and medium-sized firms, even if mega-projects are not accounted for in the analyses.

A 2006 report by the Foreign Investment Advisory Service (FIAS)[5] attempts to analyse the effect of the taxation system on investment decisions in Mozambique by means of calculating marginal effective tax rates. Under the normal tax regime, METRs in Mozambique range from 16 per cent for the agriculture sector to 57 per cent for the finance sector (see Table 15.3). For investments that have been approved by the IPC and to which the Code of Fiscal Benefits applies, the METRs fall to their lowest level of 5 per cent for the mining sector and are at a high of 46 per cent for the finance sector (FIAS 2006). The METR analysis shows that distortions arise between sectors. The finance sector, for instance, appears to be the most heavily taxed sector in Mozambique.

The METR analysis carried out by FIAS allows for a comparison between Mozambique and South Africa, Lesotho, Rwanda and Tanzania, for the agriculture sector, for manufacturing, for the tourism sector and for

Table 15.3 Mozambique's METRs vis-à-vis Regional Peer Economies

METR in %	Mozambique	Mozambique (with CPI)	Rwanda	South Africa	Tanzania	Lesotho
Agriculture	16	6	7	6	23	18
Manufacturing	40	11	7	21	15	11
Tourism	40	16	13	14	15	43
Financial Services	57	46	28	30	30	51
Mining	51	5	N.A.	N.A	N.A.	N.A.

Source: FIAS (2006)

financial services. This comparison shows that under the normal tax regime investors face a relatively high tax burden in Mozambique. When investors, however, have been approved by the IPC and therefore qualify for the application of the Code of Fiscal Benefits, Mozambique's tax rates are in line with those faced by investors in the other four countries.

The FIAS report underlines the critical role of the IPC for the access of investors to attractive tax rates. As a consequence, the current tax regime discriminates against small businesses, which do not hold an IPC certificate. FIAS calculates that for firms whose initial investment value falls below the required threshold for IPC benefits the METR ranges from 71 to 78 per cent. Even firms above the IPC thresholds report that the bureaucracy to access the tax incentives contained in the Code of Fiscal Benefits can be so cumbersome and costly that the benefits are not worth the effort. Consequently, FIAS suggests making the incentives of the Code of Fiscal Benefits automatically available to all investors. In order to protect against the resulting revenue loss for the government, FIAS advises making the Code less generous. Such a change to the fiscal legislation would be a critical step toward the necessary further simplification of the tax codes in Mozambique.

3.2 Industrial processing zones and mega-projects

The Code of Fiscal Benefits provides certain fiscal discretion for large-scale projects, whose initial investment value exceeds US$500 million or which are investments in infrastructure for the public domain (GoM 2002b: Articles 29–32). The Code determines that such mega-projects may benefit from exceptional incentives with regard to import duties, income tax, property transfer tax and stamp duty. These exceptional incentives are subject to proposal by the Minister of Finance and are granted under a contractual regime by the Council of Ministers, for a period up to 10 years. To qualify for the exceptional incentives, the undertakings shall (1) materially promote and accelerate national economic development, (2) materially reduce the regional imbalances and (3) create at least 500 jobs or induce the creation of at least 1,000 jobs within the maximum period of three years.

Mega-projects such as Mozal, Sasol, Beluluane Industrial Park, Limpopo Corridor Sands and Kenmare Moma were negotiated before the Code of Fiscal Benefits came into force in 2002. As a result, previous legislation applies to these projects, which are benefiting from more generous fiscal incentives and longer exemption periods than are provided for in the Code. Mozal has been able to negotiate its special fiscal regime for 50 years, renewable for a further 50 years, and the contracts of Limpopo Corridor Sands and Kenmare Moma are valid for 20 years each, renewable for a further 20 years.

Mozal, Beluluane Industrial Park, Limpopo Corridor Sands and Kenmare Moma are mega-projects that were also granted industrial processing zone status. In Mozambique, export processing zones are called industrial processing zones (Zonas Francas Industriais, ZFIs).[6] According to Article 1 of the Industrial Processing zone Regulation, a ZFI is an area

> where the goods that are imported into such a zone are not considered to have entered the country's customs territory for the purposes of the duties and other imposts that are payable.
>
> (GoM 1999: Article 1)

Operators in industrial processing zones benefit from exemptions of import duties, value added tax, property transfer tax and specific consumption tax. Investors holding a ZFI certificate benefit from a 60 per cent reduction in the rate of income tax for a limited period of 10 years, which results in an effective ZFI income tax of 12.8 per cent. An industrial processing zone is approved by the Council of Ministers and therefore the Mozambican government. The Council of Ministers in turn establishes the Council of Industrial Processing zones, which is given a particular mandate to deal with the issues arising for the ZFIs.

Initially, the industrial processing zones legislation was aimed to attract labour-intensive manufacturing projects. Instead of labour-intensive projects, however, ZFIs have been created around capital-intensive mega-projects. Within the Beluluane Industrial Park, for instance, 13 companies enjoy industrial processing zone status. According to their terms of authorization, each of these firms is on average required to employ 43 employees.

Considering mega-projects, Mozal, for example, employed a total of 1,102 workers in 2005 and Sasol Petroleum Temane had 120 employees (KPMG 2006a). For Limpopo Corridor Sands, the IPC predicted the creation of 2,000 jobs during the construction phase, shrinking to 600 employees needed for normal operations. Kenmare Moma expected to employ 1,362 workers in the construction phase and to have 450 employees running its standard operations. The employment provisions of the Industrial Processing zones Regulation hold that the authorization for the establishment of a ZFI is subject to the existence, in the industrial processing zone overall, of at least 500 permanent positions for employees of Mozambican nationality, provided that each of the enterprises operating in the ZFI employs a minimum of 20 employees. By contrast, labour-intensive textiles and apparel firms in export processing zones are the largest employer in Lesotho, with 50,000 employees in 2004 (FIAS 2006).

In addition to increased employment, an often cited positive impact of attracting mega-projects is the projection of a positive investment climate internationally. Further advantages of large-scale projects are in general their effect on the balance of payments, on GDP and on the trade balance. From 1997 to 2004, mega-projects contributed significantly to Mozambique's buoyant performance in exports, which grew at an average rate of about 29 per cent (FIAS 2006).

Mega-projects in Mozambique, however, have been criticized for creating relatively little new employment and for repatriating a large share of their profits. Furthermore, the positive contribution of large-scale projects to fiscal revenue has been diminished by generous tax incentive schemes (see the Annex to this chapter for a summary of fiscal incentives granted to mega-projects with industrial processing zone status in Mozambique). Along with exemptions on value added tax, property transfer tax, import and export duties, several mega-projects do not pay income taxes. In these cases, a substitute 1 per cent tax on sales figures applies, which is called taxa liberatória. Even compared with sectoral and regional incentives available through the Code of Fiscal Benefits, income tax incentives for mega-projects are generous (see Table 15.4).

The fiscal incentives of mega-projects are enshrined in their terms of authorization, which are approved by the Council of Ministers and signed by the Prime Minister. Penalties in the event of breach of contract by the government

Table 15.4 Income Tax Rate Reductions for Specific Sectors, Zones and Mega Projects

	Income tax	Taxa liberatória	Period of validity
Standard fiscal regime	32.0	–	–
Agriculture	6.4	–	until 2012
Petroleum Law	24.0	–	until 2010, for the first eight years
Mining Law (exceeding US$ 500,000)	24.0	–	until 2010, for the first five years
Rapid development zones	25.6	–	until 2015, for the first five years
Industrial free zones	12.8	–	for the first ten years
Large scale projects (exceeding US$500 million)	negotiable	negotiable	for the first ten years
Mozal	–	1	until 2047 renewable, applicable after the first two years
Parque Industrial de Beluluane	–	1	until 2049 renewable, applicable after the first seven years
Kenmare Moma	–	1	until 2022 renewable, applicable after the first seven years
Limpopo Corridor Sands	–	1	until 2022 renewable, applicable after the first seven years

Source: Author's review of existing legislation and agreements

are clearly defined and potential changes in the fiscal legislation will have no effect on the tax payment obligations of mega-projects. For instance, in Limpopo Corridor Sands' terms of authorization, Clause 14.17 specifies that 'no additional taxes will have to be paid' in case of changes to any taxes, tariffs, deductions or other imposts.

While these contracts have been negotiated between the mega-projects and the government, several of the large-scale projects in Mozambique have attracted international support through financing by international donors and the IFC, and were guaranteed by the World Bank's Multilateral Investment Guarantee Agency (MIGA). Kenmare Moma and Sasol Petroleum Temane, for instance, hold MIGA guarantees which insure them against political unrest and instability as well as against breach of contract.

The issues at stake in granting casuistic tax incentives to mega-projects are exemplified by Mozambique's first post-war investment of large dimension, Mozal. Mozal is an aluminium smelter located near Maputo, and was authorized in 1997 with an initial investment value of US$1,300 million. Mozal is owned by the South African multinational BH Billiton, which is the world's largest mining company, the Industrial Development Corporation (South African) and Mitsubishi (Japanese). It produces approximately 560 million tons of aluminium annually, most of which is exported, and it has one of the best production rates per day per oven in the world (KPMG 2006a). Since 2003 – its first year of production – Mozal has been Mozambique's largest company. Consequently, it has significantly contributed to Mozambique's GDP, reduced the country's trade deficit by up to one-third and has had an important positive impact on the balance of payments (Castel-Branco and Goldin 2003). Mozal received the title 'World's Best Project for 2001', and due to Mozal's involvement in a program to combat malaria, BH Billiton, Mozal's principal shareholder, was awarded the World Social Responsibility Prize in London in June 2005 (KPMG 2005).

Initial expectations were that the establishment of Mozal would give an impetus to Mozambique's economy, by means of technology spillovers, linkages with local firms and employment of workers. At a presentation by Mozal's South African sister firm Alusaf to a Mozambican delegation in Richards Bay,South Africa, Alusaf's General Director explained that the creation of Mozal will lead to 'a process of knowledge transmission through linkages between local and international firms, resulting in a massive local participation'.[7]

Several critical advantages exist for Mozal in Mozambique. Primarily, the company benefits from access to cheap electricity, as discussed further in Chapter 16. Due to the Everything but Arms Initiative and the Cotonou Convention, exports by Mozambican firms to the European Union are duty and quota free. For aluminium products these preferential agreements grant duty-free market entry against a Most Favoured Nation tariff of 6 per cent. In addition, Mozal benefits from highly favourable tax incentives. Mozal negotiated its fiscal regime with the government of Mozambique and was exempt from paying income tax. In place of income tax at 32 per cent, Mozal is liable to pay a 1 per cent taxa liberatória on the volume of quarterly sales.[8]

As official figures about forgone state revenue arising from Mozal's income tax incentives do not exist, the author used publicly available data in order to estimate the expenditure that arises for Mozambique (KPMG 2006a, 2004; Mozal 2006). To calculate the state revenue forgone by raising a 1 per cent taxa liberatória instead of 32 per cent income tax from Mozal, the taxa liberatória payable was estimated by multiplying revenue figures by 1 per cent. This approach results in a taxa liberatória payable of US$12.4 million in 2006 (see Table 15.5). This value does not take into account additional deductions that Mozal is entitled to. As a share of net profits, the taxa liberatória in 2006 is therefore equivalent to a corporate income tax of 2.9 per cent. If Mozal were to pay income tax at 32 per cent, this would amount to approximately US$133 million (resulting from the multiplication of net profits by 32 per cent). Deducting the taxa liberatória from this amount, we arrive at a figure for forgone state revenue of roughly US$120 million in 2006. This value is equal to 124 percent of all income tax paid in Mozambique and accounted for 11.9 per cent of total government revenue in 2006.

Additional fiscal incentives, such as deductions from expenditure on infrastructure and training of employees, value added tax, personal income tax of expatriate staff, excise exemptions and others have not been taken into account in these estimates.

Even if a revision of Mozal's fiscal regime may be desirable, revising its contract with the government will not be straightforward. The Clause of Stability (Article 22) in Mozal's terms of authorization holds that benefits and incentives specified in its contract with the government cannot be revoked or reduced, unless

Table 15.5 Mozal – Operating Indicators and Tax Approximations

In million US Dollars	2003	2004	2005	2006
Revenues	379.52	1,014.30	1,090.02	1,203.75
Net profits	21.01	272.27	306.94	414.41
Number of workers	1,083	1,080	1,102	1,126
Net profits/GDP	0.4	4.6	4.6	6.0
Taxa liberatória at 1 * (without deductions)	3.8	10.14	10.9	12.04
Income tax payable at 32 *	6.72	87.13	98.22	132.61
Foregone state revenue due to replacing income tax by *taxa liberatória* for Mozal *	2.93	76.98	87.32	120.57
Foregone revenue from income of Mozal/Total income tax collected	10	170	146	124
Foregone revenue (Mozal)/Total government revenue	0.5	10.9	10.4	11.9

* Values estimated by the author
Source: KPMG (2006), Mozal Annual Reports (2006, 2004), Ministry of Finance

the beneficiaries do not comply with their obligations. The government has committed not to alter the terms of authorization and guaranteed that any new legislation, regulations or resolutions of the government, including new taxes, will not be applicable to Mozal if such changes do not result in a favourable treatment for the project and the entities that are involved in it.

Since Mozal was authorized in 1997, mega-projects in subsequent years have received slightly less favourable tax incentive schemes. For instance, Kenmare Moma and Limpopo Corridor Sands were authorized in 2002, and their exemption periods have fallen to 20 years renewable, a marked decrease from the 50 years available for Mozal. For Sasol Petroleum Temane, the negotiated incentive scheme is less generous than the regimes for previous mega-projects. Income tax has been reduced to 17.5 per cent for the first six years, losses can be carried forward as tax deductions for eight years, and foreign staff are exempt from personal income tax.

It is notable that tax concessions for a number of the mega-projects have been granted to large multinational mining firms. Limpopo Corridor Sands, for instance, is 90 per cent owned by the Australian mining company Western Mining Corporation, which now is a subsidiary of BH Billiton. The remaining 10 per cent is held by the Industrial Development Corporation of South Africa, and Limpopo Corridor Sands therefore belongs to similar owners to Mozal. In this context, the International Monetary Fund (IMF) speaks of generous tax exemptions, which Mozambique has granted particularly to mega-projects related to natural resource extraction (IMF 2005a). As these projects are not typically labour intensive, the IMF advises that the authorities reconsider such exemptions in the future. Moreover, increased attention should be paid to other types of incentives, notably to improving the business operating environment.

At the moment of publication, the Brazilian company Companhia Vale do Rio Doce, the world's biggest iron ore producer, was negotiating the terms for its investments in Moatize with the Mozambican government. While the project seeks to exploit one of the largest unexploited coal deposits in the southern hemisphere and is therefore location specific, the company referred to fiscal incentives granted to previous mega-investments to negotiate a favourable tax incentive regime. In such considerations, historic cost–benefit analysis is critical in informing current and future fiscal policy and the specific design of incentives. The availability of systematic data for the fiscal expenditure arising from different tax incentives for all mega-projects is a prerequisite for such analysis.

4   Policy implications

Currently, fiscal bias in Mozambique favours the agriculture, tourism and mining sectors. Little analysis, however, has been carried out by the government on the effects of this sectoral distortion. With respect to tax incentives for the agricultural sector, for instance, FIAS outlines that taxation is not an impediment to the development of the sector, and efforts would be better focused on issues such as land tenure security, rural infrastructure and enhanced extension services (FIAS 2006). According to a World Bank Investment Climate Assessment for Mozambique, tax rates and the tax administration are only the seventh and tenth most cited business constraints, respectively (World Bank 2003). Further analysis would be useful to assess the incentive structures for investments in certain regions, rapid development zones and industrial processing zones.

A representative survey of South African firms which have invested in Mozambique shows that large investors consistently rate the Mozambican business environment more positively than smaller investors (Grobbelaar 2004). This outcome is attributed to the relative insulation of larger firms from bureaucratic bottlenecks that smaller companies face, which exacerbates the effects of disproportionate tax burdens for firms of different sizes in Mozambique. Further constraints listed by South African firms operating in Mozambique were, amongst others, corruption, the small size of the domestic market, a weak legal system, lack of access to finance and infrastructure, the inefficiency of the bureaucracy, smuggling and theft. In 2007, for instance, it took a business 361 days to deal with all licences required for its operation in Mozambique, compared to 139 days in Namibia or 100 days in Kenya (World Bank 2007). By contrast, as a percentage of profits the World Bank's 'total tax rate' was only 39 per cent in Mozambique, while the regional average for Sub-Saharan Africa was 71.2 per cent in 2006 (World Bank 2006a).[9]

In a prosperous business environment, companies are able to earn adequate returns on their investments. If tax rates are too high, lowering overall tax rates seems to be the appropriate policy response. While for the efficiency of an investment, the optimal tax level will be zero, this is only true as long as public expenditures are held constant. In Mozambique, the trade-off between granting tax incentives and forgone government revenue and expenditure should be carefully assessed. It will be important to link forgone revenue figures with alternative expenditures in a framework that accounts for dynamic trade-offs.

As shown in Section 2, it is an urgent priority to produce data and cost–benefit analyses of the tax incentives in place, in order to define well-targeted and clearly formulated policy objectives. If mega-projects create little new employment, and spillover effects to the local economy are negligible, tax incentives will be too generous. Ogley (2006) speaks of 'ring-fencing' if tax incentives are granted for activities which are isolated from the domestic economy and have little or no impact on the national tax base. Tax incentives are especially problematic when granted to projects that are depleting non-renewable resources, such as mining activities. By contrast, large potential revenue gains for the Mozambican government could come from emulating Botswana, where state revenues from the exploitation of natural resources have financed a large expansion of public services and even enabled the government to lower other taxes (Bolnick 2004b).

This chapter presents indicative figures and estimates of the cost of tax incentives incurred by the Mozambican government. It will be necessary to further develop these calculations to arrive at a more complete figure of tax expenditures. These calculations need to take account of all types of exemptions, such as exemptions from value added tax, property transfer tax, taxes on salaries paid to foreign workers, offsetting of losses carried forward against profits, investment tax credits, deductions, customs duty and excise reductions, as well as accelerated depreciations. Such an effort is especially necessary for mega-projects with casuistic fiscal regimes and complex tax obligations. Analysis of this type will be an important step in ensuring that the budgetary cost involved in securing investment is proportionate to the policy objectives.

Furthermore, the lengths of exemption periods granted have so far received little attention. It has been shown that governments tend to over-estimate the potential benefits and underestimate the costs of tax incentive regimes (Bolnick 2004a). Given the uncertainties regarding these benefits, the exemption periods made available in Mozambique seem excessively long, especially for investment projects authorized before the Code of Fiscal Benefits came into force in 2002. Ogley (2006), for instance, argues that it is inadvisable to grant tax holidays beyond a five-year period.

The development of common policies in the Southern African Development Community, of which Mozambique is a member, could provide a push factor for member states to adopt a coherent approach to tax incentives, eliminating discretion and ensuring at the same time that the tax incentives are effective. Article 4 of the SADC Memorandum of Understanding specifies that

> [SADC] member states will endeavour to achieve a common approach to the treatment and application of tax incentives and will, amongst other things, ensure that tax incentives are provided for only in tax legislation.
>
> (SADC 2002: 5)

Member states will 'endeavour to avoid harmful tax competition' as may be evidenced by, amongst other thing, zero or low effective rates of tax, lack of transparency and restricting tax incentives to particular taxpayers. In addition, SADC member states have committed to developing a fiscal framework for tax incentives that will focus on the effectiveness of proposed tax incentives in achieving their stated policy goals, states' revenue costs as a result of proposed tax incentives, or the effects of tax incentives on the overall distribution of the tax burden within a member state.

Bolnick (2004a) further points out the need for SADC member states to refer to the IMF Code of Good Practices on Fiscal Transparency (IMF 2001b), and more specifically to commit to transparent tax incentives, procedures and criteria, public disclosure of discretionary tax incentives granted, transparent cost control and effective monitoring mechanisms.

5 Conclusion

At initial assessment, the tax incentive schemes in place in Mozambique seem to produce sectoral distortions, to favour large companies over small and medium-sized ones and to be biased toward capital-intensive mega-projects. By granting tax incentives to location-specific investments, the Mozambican government is incurring substantial revenue losses. While the consolidation of myriad tax incentives in the Code of Fiscal Benefits in 2002 has been a step toward more efficient incentive schemes, the post-war eagerness to attract investment even at high fiscal costs is still manifest in the design of the Code.

As a consequence, the need to examine the tax incentives in place remains a critical task. It will be useful to define investment objectives more narrowly, along with scrutinizing sectoral and regional biases as well as the magnitude of incentives and exemption periods, and assessing the desirability of easing fiscal obligations of location-specific multinational mega-projects. Increased emphasis will have to be paid to data collection, to allow for cost–benefit analyses of incentives granted as well as for more effective monitoring and auditing of the beneficiaries.

One of the goals for a more efficient incentive scheme should be simplification. All incentives need to be included in the fiscal legislation, with no leeway for discretion regarding large-scale investment projects. Simplification could, for instance, entail an automatic application of tax incentives to all firms in Mozambique, thereby lowering the overall corporate tax burden and increasing the effectiveness of tax collection.

In the past, mega-projects have received funding from international donors and investments were guaranteed by MIGA. Internationally and domestically, the intuitive assumption that attracting mega-projects promotes economic development in Mozambique needs to be qualified and discussed in relation to the large government revenues forgone due to tax incentives, in particular for the earlier mega-projects. Regional integration in the Southern African Development Community and reference to international best practices offer an opportunity to rationalize the incentive scheme in place in Mozambique. For the drafting of fiscal regimes for new mega-projects, public discourse and cost–benefit analyses will be of critical importance.

6 Annex: mega-projects with industrial processing zones status in Mozambique

Mozal	Mozal was created by Decree 45/1997 for 50 years, with a possible further 50-year extension, under the condition of employing at least 800 Mozambican nationals. Mozal is an aluminium smelter which produces for exporting. The main tax benefits enjoyed by Mozal are exemptions from corporate income tax, value added tax, excises, customs duties on imported capital goods, stamp tax, property transfer tax, and the municipal tax on rental income. A 1 per cent substitute corporate income tax has been levied on Mozal, which was first payable two years after its creation. Allowable deductions include expenses related to staff training and the improvement of the infrastructure of the industrial free zone. Below certain limits, foreign employees and suppliers of services and information and technology to Mozal also benefit from exemptions in personal and corporate income taxes respectively.
Beluluane Industrial Park	Beluluane Industrial Park was created by Decree 61/1999 for 50 years, renewable for another 50 years. The Park was aimed to stimulate investment projects of large dimension. From its seventh year of authorization, it is liable to pay 1 per cent of quarterly gross receipts as taxa liberatória. It is exempt from customs duties, value added tax, specific consumption tax, income tax and property transfer tax. Further deductible from the royalty paid are expenditures on infrastructure for public use, on the training of Mozambican nationals, and on Mozambican culture and art. Shareholder funds are tax exempt.
Kenmare Moma	Kenmare Moma was created by Decree 45/2002 for 20 years, with a possible further 20-year extension. Activities carried out in the zone are construction and operation of a heavy sand-processing unit for the production of minerals for export. Moma's main tax benefits are exemptions from corporate income tax, value added tax, excises, customs duties on imported capital goods, the real property transfer tax, and the municipal tax on rental income. A 1 per cent substitute corporate income tax has been levied on enterprises operating in free zones, payable after seven years of their creation. Foreign workers cannot represent more than 15 per cent of the total workforce.
Limpopo Corridor Sands	Limpopo Corridor Sands was created by Decree 7/2002 for the exploitation of heavy mineral sands in Chibuto. Its main tax benefits are exemptions from value added tax, excises, customs duties on imported capital goods, the stamp tax, property transfer tax, and the municipal tax on rental income. A 1 per cent substitute corporate income tax applies to its industrial free zones operations after seven years after its creation. Allowable deductions include expenses related to staff training and improvement of the infrastructure of the free zone. Below certain limits, foreign employees and suppliers of services, information and technology to ZFI Limpopo Corridor Sands also benefit from exemptions in the personal and corporate income taxes, respectively. In-kind remunerations of Mozambican workers are not subject to the personal income tax.

Source: Respective Terms of Authorization, IMF (2005b)

Notes

1 This percentage is an estimate using the fact that Mozal paid 1 per cent substitute income tax on its revenue figures in 2006 (see the estimate in Section 3.2). This figure, however, does not account for additional expenditure deductions from the 1 per cent substitute income tax that Mozal is entitled to.

2 Rosário Fernandes, 'Welcome Speech' on the occasion of taking over the presidency of the Central Revenue Authority, Matola, 22 December 2006.

3 For instance, if the marginal rate of return to an investment before tax is 50 per cent, and the marginal rate of return after tax payments is 30 per cent, then the METR is calculated as 20/50 = 40 per cent (Ogley 2006).

4 Until 2005, the National Tax Directorate recorded seven categories of tax-deductible costs: Expenditures on equipment, installations, agricultural infrastructure, public construction works, training of employees, art and 'other deductions'.

5 FIAS is a joint service of the International Finance Corporation (IFC) and the World Bank.

6 The Industrial Free Zone Regulation was approved by Decree 62/1999, with changes incorporated by Decree 35/2000 and Decree 16/2002.

7 Speech of Alusaf's General Director on 6 November 1997. National Tax Directorate 1997: Minutes of the delegation's visit at Alusaf in Richards Bay, South Africa.

8 The amount of the taxa liberatória collected is linked to the price of aluminium, as total sales results from multiplying the price of aluminium (calculated as the three-month lowest medium on the London Metal Exchange) by the number of ton dispatched per month (Mozal – Terms of Authorization, Chapter III, Article 15).

9 The World Bank defines the 'total tax rate' as the tax a medium-sized company must pay or withhold in a given year, as well as measures of the administrative burden in paying taxes.

16 Prospects for an electricity tax

Aurélio J. Bucuane and Peter Mulder

1 Introduction

The energy sector plays an increasingly important role in the economic development of Mozambique. The main reason for this is that Mozambique has abundant and yet largely unexplored natural resources, which are attracting substantial foreign direct investment in large energy-intensive industries as well as in the mining, exploration and transformation sectors. These are projects of large dimension, often referred to as 'mega-projects'. So far, some mega-projects have been realized, such as the Mozal aluminium smelter near the capital Maputo, while several new projects are planned or already under construction (for an overview of mega-projects and their applicable fiscal incentives, see Chapter 15). It is to be expected that the recent transfer of ownership of the Cahora Bassa hydro dam from Portugal to Mozambique will accelerate the realization of various new mega-projects, such as the construction of the Mphanda Nkuwa hydro dam.

In this chapter we will argue that these mega-projects offer a good opportunity to extend the tax base in Mozambique for two reasons. First, with a typically small tax base in Mozambique, mega-projects offer a unique source to increase government revenue, thereby lowering the dependence on foreign aid. Second, electricity production, energy-intensive production processes and mining are known for their substantial negative impact on the environment. An energy tax is an important instrument to internalize these negative externalities.

With the exception of natural gas exploration as such, electricity is a key issue for all existing and future mega-projects in Mozambique. The industrial and mining projects all depend critically on the availability of cheap electricity in large quantities, while the other mega-projects are engaged in the production of electricity. Therefore we focus in this chapter on an electricity tax on mega-projects as a new policy instrument in Mozambique. This implies that we do not consider the taxation of non-renewable resource extraction, such as the exploration of natural gas or coal. Resource extraction is already subject to taxation, and it is outside the scope of this chapter to review this tax regime.

The chapter is organized as follows. In Section 2 we provide a brief description of the energy sector in Mozambique, focusing on electricity and the role of mega-projects. Section 3 elaborates upon the arguments in favour of an electricity tax on mega-projects. In Section 4 we explore the appropriate level and base of the tax. In Section 5 we present the potential revenues from implementing a tax on electricity *consumption* by mega-projects and a tax on electricity *production*, respectively. Section 6 discusses the possibilities and limitations of the various tax proposals. Section 7 concludes.

2 The energy sector and mega-projects

In this section we provide a brief overview of the energy sector in Mozambique for the period 2000–20, with a focus on electricity and mega-projects. Before 2000 the energy sector was characterized by decline, disruption and initial post-war reconstruction, while the year 2000 marks the beginning of a new era with the introduction of the Mozal aluminium smelter as the first mega-project in Mozambique.[1] Moreover, it is expected that the energy sector in Mozambique will undergo rapid expansion until 2020, mainly because of the realization of a number of new mega-projects. Our overview is based on original data for the period 2000–5, in combination with projections for the period 2006–20. With this aim, we used the software tool LEAP (Long-range Energy Alternatives Planning system), a scenario-based energy-environment modelling tool.[2] The LEAP scenarios presented in this chapter are based on comprehensive accounting of how energy is consumed, converted and produced in Mozambique under a range of assumptions on population, economic development, technology and so on. The figures below are all based on the reference scenario, representing the most likely development path.[3]

2.1 Production

Traditionally, primary energy production in Mozambique consists mainly of biomass, including predominantly fuel wood, but also charcoal. With the realization of the Cahora Bassa hydro dam (HCB) in 1974, Mozambique became a potential large producer of hydroelectricity (for export to South Africa), but destruction of the transmission lines during the post-independence civil war prevented this from happening for a long time. Post-war reconstruction allowed production to pick up in 1997, and since then the amount of electricity produced has been gradually increasing, and will continue to grow because of new generation projects. Large-scale natural gas production started in 2004 with the exploration of the Pande/Temane gas fields in the Inhambane Province by the South African company Sasol, and is expected to grow steadily over the coming years. Coal production used to be small scale and became marginal during the civil war. This situation is, however, going to change since the Brazilian Companhia Vale do Rio Doce

(CVRD) won a bid in 2004 to develop the Moatize coalfield in Tete Province, with expected coal production of 14 to 15 million tonnes per year, starting in 2009 (Yager 2005).

Notwithstanding the importance of natural gas and coal, electricity is the key issue when talking about the development of existing and new mega-projects. Figure 16.1 gives an overview of current and future electricity production in Mozambique, indicating spectacular growth in production from about 10,000 GWh in 2000 to about 42,000 GWh from 2014.

Virtually all electricity produced is hydroelectricity generated by HCB. Since 1997, the production by HCB has gradually increased and is currently close to reaching its maximum capacity (2,075 MW). HCB is and will be the main producer of electricity in Mozambique, exporting about 80 per cent of its production (mainly to South Africa), while the remaining 20 per cent is acquired by the national electricity company Electricidade de Moçambique (EdM). The latest information we have from the Ministry of Energy indicates that we may expect a second large hydro dam, Mphanda Nkuwa, to become operational in 2014, with a capacity of 1,300 MW, thereby increasing base-load hydroelectricity production capacity in Mozambique by more than 50 per cent. We expect that, of the total capacity of 1,300 MW, 650 MW will go to the extension of Mozal (hereafter referred to as Mozal III), while the other 650 MW will be exported.[4] Another new mega-project in the electricity sector is a 700 MW natural-gas-fired electricity plant fuelled by gas from the Pande/Temane fields and expected to become operational in 2010. The most likely scenario is that initially all its electricity will be exported to South Africa, while from 2014 about 100 MW might be acquired by EdM and from 2017 an additional 200 MW might go to the Chibuto Heavy Sands

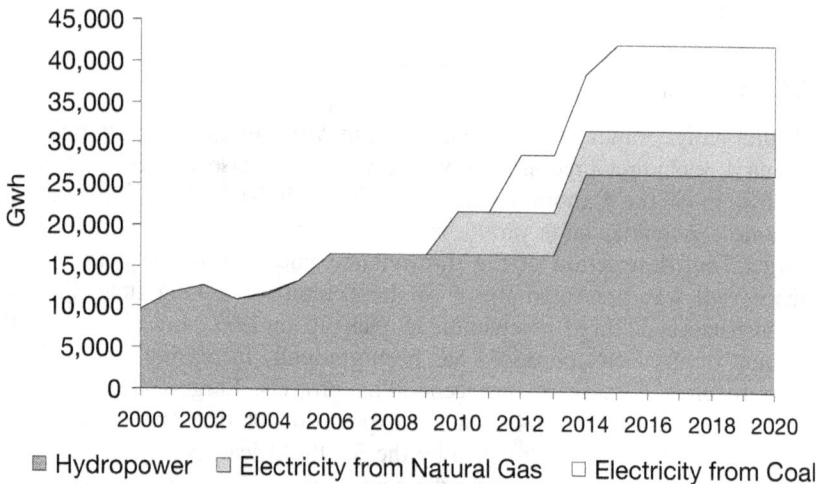

Figure 16.1 Electricity production
Source: Ministry of Energy (2007a).

project. Finally, the large-scale exploration of the Moatize coalmine in the near future has given rise to the possibility of constructing a coal-fired power station with a capacity of 1,500 MW. It is to be expected that 1,000 MW will become operational in 2012, while the remaining 500 MW will probably be available from 2015. We assume in this chapter that about 10 per cent of its electricity production will be consumed at the site of the Moatize coalmine itself and in the northern region of Mozambique, while 90 per cent will be exported. In sum, the current and new electricity generation plants together account for a total base-load electricity production equivalent to 5,575 MW and a total investment value of US$5.7 billion (for more details, see Table 16.A2 in the Annex to this chapter).

2.2 Export and import

Most energy produced in Mozambique is exported. With respect to the coal from the Moatize mine, we expect 15 per cent to be marketed in Mozambique, including consumption by the electricity plant, while the remainder will be exported for consumption by steel plants in Brazil (Yager 2005). The vast majority of natural gas is and will be exported to South Africa, although domestic consumption is increasing due to the completion in 2005 of a new pipeline to the Beleluane industrial park near Maputo and because of the natural-gas-fired electricity plant to be constructed.

Also in terms of electricity, almost all production is exported. About 75 per cent of Mozambique's major electricity generation at site HCB is exported, mainly to South Africa but also to Zimbabwe and Botswana, and in the future also to Malawi. It is to be noted that this fact is due to traditionally low domestic electricity demand as well as lack of transmission infrastructure from HCB (located in the northern Tete Province) to the southern region of Mozambique – the economically most vibrant part of the country. Thus, electricity consumption in the southern part of Mozambique, including the large electricity consumption by Mozal, has to be wheeled through South Africa, and/or imported from South Africa. As a result, we arrive at the somewhat peculiar situation in which Mozambique is currently an (almost equally big) exporter as well as importer of electricity.

As said before, the Moatize coal-fired electricity plant will mainly produce electricity for export (in this chapter we assume 90 per cent), implying a considerable increase in electricity exports as of 2012 (see Figure 16.2). As mentioned in Section 2.1, the new natural-gas-fired electricity plant is expected to produce primarily for export, while in the long run it will presumably also deliver electricity to EdM and the Chibuto Heavy Sands mine.

Concerning energy imports, those consist in Mozambique primarily of oil products and electricity. Given the absence of refineries, all domestic consumption of fuels is imported.[5] Electricity imports have been rapidly increasing since 2000, mainly due to the start-up of Mozal, which imports its electricity from South Africa.[6] From Figure 16.2 it can be seen that electricity imports will

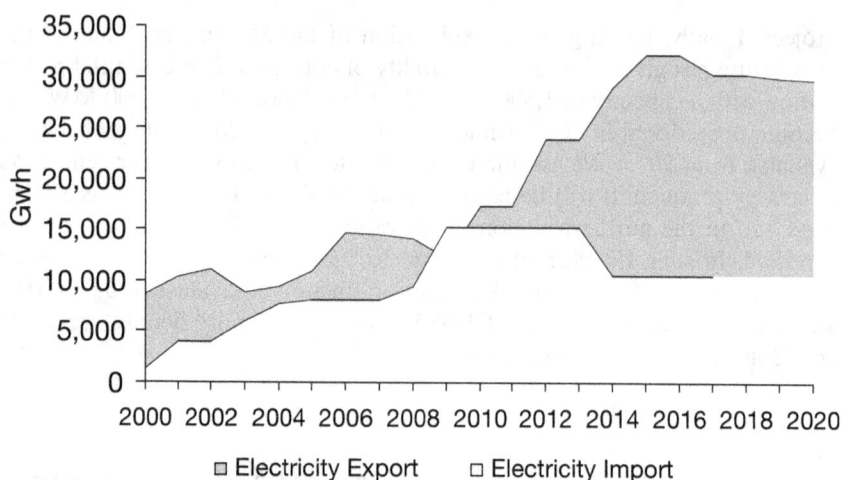

Figure 16.2 Electricity export and import
Source: Ministry of Energy (2007a).

increase substantially between 2009 and 2014. This is mainly due to the completion of Mozal III, due in 2009, which depends on electricity imports from South Africa until the Mphanda Nkuwa dam can take over electricity delivery as of 2014. The second most likely scenario here is that Mozal III will fail to import its electricity from South Africa due to the severe capacity problems of ESKOM, in which case we can expect the natural-gas-fired electricity plant to supply Mozal III until 2014 instead of exporting its electricity. Finally, although negotiations are not yet finalized, we assume that the Chibuto Heavy Sands mine in Gaza Province, which is expected to start in 2009, will also import its electricity initially from South Africa.

2.3 Consumption

Access to modern energy services is still very low in Mozambique, with about 80 per cent of the population relying entirely on traditional biomass to meet their energy needs. Electricity consumption is in principle very low: only about 8 per cent of the population have access to electricity, and electricity consumption in the service and industry sectors is still very limited due to the small scale of economic activity. The various mega-projects, however, (will) consume large amounts of electricity, about six to nine times as much as the rest of the country put together. This dual nature of the Mozambican electricity market is illustrated in Figure 16.3.

'Normal' demand for electricity will grow as a result of ongoing rural electrification and continuous economic growth. At the same time electricity consumption by mega-projects will sharply increase in the (near) future. By and large, Mozal is and will be the main electricity consumer in Mozambique.

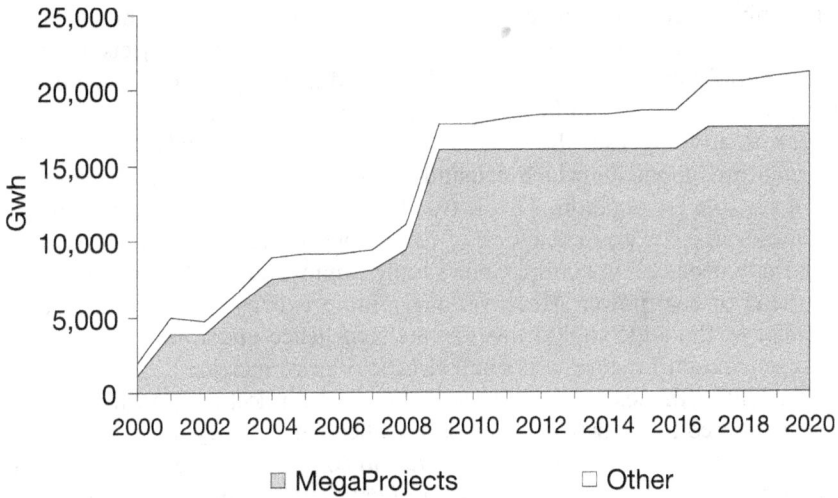

Figure 16.3 Electricity consumption
Source: Ministry of Energy (2007a).

As mentioned before, Mozal has been operating since 2000 (constructed in two phases, hereafter referred to as Mozal I+II) and we assume that Mozal III will begin operation in 2009. Furthermore, we assume the Moma Heavy Sands mine began in 2007, receiving its electricity from HCB through a newly constructed transmission line from Nampula. We suppose that the Chibuto Heavy Sands mine will start in 2009, with a second phase starting in 2017.[7] Finally, we assume the Moatize coalmine will start operating in 2009. Initially they will be supplied by HCB, while the new coal-fired plant is expected to take over electricity supply as of 2012. Together these mega-projects account for a total electricity consumption equivalent to 1,882 MW and a total investment value of US$5.5 billion (for more details, see Table 16.A1 in the Annex to this chapter).[8]

3 Principles of an electricity tax

We would like to highlight two reasons why mega-projects offer a good opportunity to extend the tax base in Mozambique: revenue-raising and negative externalities. In this section we will discuss these arguments, both from a theoretical point of view and in the particular context of Mozambique.

3.1 Revenue-raising

As a developing country, Mozambique is characterized by a typically small tax base due to, amongst other things, the relatively large scale of the informal economy and a traditionally weak fiscal institutional infrastructure. As a result,

Mozambique continues to depend on foreign aid, which account for about half of the government budget. The existence of mega-projects offers a unique opportunity to extend the tax base in Mozambique, thereby increasing government revenue and lowering the dependence on foreign aid.

Tax theory suggests that where the aim is to raise revenue for public expenditure, goods for which demand is least sensitive to price increases are most suitable for taxation. This is true for base-load electricity consumption by mega-projects, given the lack of technological alternatives to serve their electricity needs.[9] For example, one simply cannot run an aluminium smelter on diesel or heat power. Moreover, mega-projects constitute high sunk costs because of the large capital investments, and hence investors will not easily change location because of a small electricity price increase.

In addition, the costs of raising revenues through an electricity tax are relatively low compared to other tax instruments. Collecting ordinary taxes on imports, income and profit is relatively expensive and complicated compared to taxing mega-projects due to the large number of entities involved, as against a small number of mega-projects. Moreover, an electricity tax on mega-projects suffers neither from the problems raised by the large scale of informal economic activities nor from evasion problems (see, for example, Chapter 11).

While there are thus good reasons to tax mega-projects, so far these projects have been enjoying highly preferential tax treatment. For example, Mozal is entitled to pay a 1 per cent revenue tax only (against a standard tariff of 32 per cent) while enjoying a range of specific tax exemptions, resulting in an estimated annual tax benefit of about US$100 million. For more details we refer to Chapter 15, by Krueger. The issue here is that these large tax incentives are not necessary, because it is highly likely that mega-projects such as Mozal, Sasol and the Moma and Chibuto Heavy Sands projects would also have gone forward under a less favourable tax regime, given their dependence on the availability of cheap natural resources in Mozambique in combination with (port) infrastructure to facilitate exports. In this respect, Mozambique exhibits a large competitive advantage (also in comparison with most of its neighbouring landlocked countries) and will therefore remain an attractive location for mega-projects. Of course, economic feasibility requirements set a limit on electricity price increases, but currently low electricity prices in Mozambique suggest that we have not yet reached this limit, by a long way. Section 4.1 (Figure 16.4) shows that Mozambican industrial electricity prices are among the lowest in the world, and this is particularly true for mega-projects.

At the same time, the positive structural impact of capital-intensive mega-projects on the Mozambican economy is very limited: amongst other things, they provide only limited employment opportunities and do not create many links with other sectors (see, for example, Anderson 2001; Castel-Branco and Goldin 2003). Since all these projects enjoy substantial benefits from consuming or generating cheap electricity, an electricity tax provides a good opportunity to increase the social benefits of these mega-projects through their contribution to government funds.

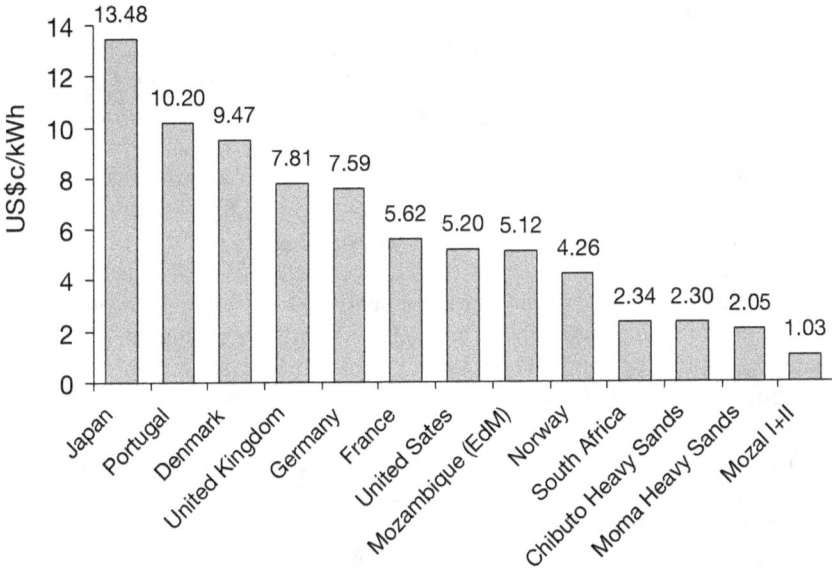

Figure 16.4 Industrial electricity prices (2005 prices)
Note: Mozambican prices include prices of Chibuto Heavy Sands, Moma Heavy Sands and Mozal I+II.
Source: IEA (2006), Ministry of Energy (2007a) and NER (2004).

3.2 Internalizing negative externalities

Electricity production, energy-intensive production processes and mining are known for their substantial negative impact on the environment. As described in Section 2.1, hydropower is and will be the most important source of electricity production in Mozambique. Contrary to electricity generation based on fossil fuel, hydroelectricity does not lead to air pollution, and is thus a clean technology from an air quality and climate change point of view. However, the construction of large dams does have substantial social and environmental impacts. Social impacts include the replacement and resettlement of inhabitants of the flooded area, while environmental impacts include reduction in wetland habitat, restricted fish migration and reduced biodiversity downstream of the dam, because of lower levels and changed patterns of water flow. For example, environmental impact studies have found that the Cahora Bassa dam has caused, amongst other things, a 40 per cent loss of mangroves, coastal erosion, a 60 per cent decline in prawn catch rates between 1978 and 1995, and a virtually non-existent bird and mammal life as compared to the 1970s (Davies *et al.* 2000).

As mentioned before, in addition to the proposed extension of hydropower capacity, concrete plans exist to build two thermal plants for electricity generation in Mozambique: one on the basis of natural gas (2010) and one on the basis of coal (2012–15). This will lead to local effects such as air pollution (nitrogen oxides, sulphur oxides, particulates), medium-distance effects such as acid rain, and long-range, long-term phenomena such as global warming from the emission of carbon dioxide and other greenhouse gases. Our scenario analyses indicate that the new coal-fired electricity plant will become by far the largest air polluter in the country, followed by air pollution from natural-gas-fired electricity generation.

An energy tax has proven to be an effective instrument to attempt to internalize these negative externalities from energy production and consumption. Externalities or external effects refer to effects that are not accounted for in the transactions between buyer and seller, and hence are not reflected in the price of the good or service. The aforementioned environmental effects are thus typical examples of negative externalities. According to economic theory, a socially optimal level of energy consumption, as well as an optimal distribution among different producers of energy, can be obtained if the full marginal costs of energy production and consumption (thus including externalities) are reflected in the price. If the energy prices are to reflect the total costs of energy production, all (social and environmental) externalities from production must be identified, valued and internalized in the price. As mentioned before, this internalization can be made with taxes.

The classic Pigovian view on efficient environmental taxes is that they should be direct and uniform, i.e. a uniform rate on emissions itself (Baumol and Oates 1988). In the end, it is pollution and not energy production or consumption per se that is the problem. An electricity tax on mega-projects violates this principle in two respects: it is an indirect environmental tax (one taxes electricity instead of emissions) and it is not uniform since it discriminates among various types of consumers (mega-projects only). However, recent theoretical developments in the literature indicate that indirect and non-uniform taxes can very well be efficient instruments in a second-best world (Bovenberg and Goulder 2001; Cremer *et al.* 1998; Cremer and Gahvari 2001). Without going into detail, the main reasons for this result are the existence of a revenue-raising government, heterogeneous administrative costs across different type of consumers, and the fact that it is difficult to adequately observe emissions and their marginal social damage (i.e. there is a constraint on policy instruments). As was noted in Section 3.1, the administrative costs of various taxes differ, with an electricity tax on mega-projects being a relatively cheap policy instrument. In addition, if there is a close link between energy and emissions and if pollution abatement costs are high, taxing energy instead of emissions might be the preferable option, particularly if administrative costs are low for taxing energy and high for taxing emissions (Smulders and Vollebergh 2001). It is clear that these conditions are met in the case of electricity generation on the basis of fossil fuels.[10]

4 Tax level

In this section we provide some building blocks for determining the appropriate level and tax base of an electricity tax. We follow the structure of the previous section by first discussing the electricity tax from a revenue-raising point of view, and then from the point of view of internalizing negative (environmental) externalities.

4.1 Revenue-raising motive

Setting a tax levy for mega-projects in order to raise government revenues inevitably includes some arbitrariness, given the absence in real life of theoretical constructs such as a well-defined objective function of a social planner (government), agents (firms and consumers) in a competitive equilibrium, an exogenously given level of expenditures, etc. It is, however, beyond doubt that using an electricity tax as an instrument to compensate for forgone revenues resulting from tax exemptions allowed to mega-projects would imply an excessively high electricity tax. For example, to compensate for the circa US$100 million annual tax benefit awarded to Mozal would require a tax levy of about 1.3 US$c/kWh over its electricity consumption, which is equivalent to a tax rate of about 125 per cent. While this is of course far from realistic (if desirable at all), it does indicate that any reasonably moderate electricity tax levy will by no means jeopardize the highly preferential tax treatment of existing mega-projects.

If we take a look at the international perspective, the average electricity tax on industries is in the range of 6–10 per cent, with some countries such as France (11.4 per cent) and Norway (18.8 per cent) imposing even higher electricity tax rates (IEA 2006). It is to be noted that those countries with relatively high electricity tax rates also have relatively low electricity price levels, implying that their overall electricity prices remain moderate so as to preserve the competitive position of their industries. This is also true for Mozambique, and even stronger: the electricity prices that the mega-projects currently pay are among the lowest in the world (see Figure 16.4).

Figure 16.4 shows that whereas the average EdM tariff of 5.12 US$c/kWh to small and medium-sized enterprises in Mozambique is already low from an international perspective, Mozal pays only 1.03 US$c/kWh and the Chibuto and Moma Heavy Sands projects are paying 2.3 and 2.05 US$c/kWh, respectively.[11] A moderate electricity tax of up to 10 per cent will not change this picture. When we look at energy taxes from a domestic perspective it is to be noted that EdM's industrial and commercial customers pay a fixed monthly tax, which translates into an average tax rate of about 3 per cent.[12] For residential EdM customers the fixed monthly tax implies an effective tax rate of 5–10 per cent, depending on the level of electricity consumption.[13] Moreover, all EdM customers are due to pay an additional 17 per cent VAT. In contrast, the mega-projects currently pay no electricity tax while also enjoying (general or specific) VAT exemptions.

Finally, implementing an electricity tax requires a definition of the tax base. The tax can be defined either as a percentage of the current electricity price, or as an amount per unit of electricity consumption/production (kWh). The main advantage of a (uniform) percentage price tax is to avoid disturbance of the current relative electricity prices across the various mega-projects. This is, for example, relevant with respect to appreciating the relatively low costs of hydropower compared with coal-based electricity from an environmental point of view. Unlike a percentage tax, a fixed tax per kWh would distort this price difference by making clean hydroelectricity relatively more expensive, and thus effectively rewarding dirty coal-based electricity generation. However, a percentage price tax does have a couple of practical disadvantages, mainly resulting from difficulties in defining the current electricity price that should serve as the basis for taxation. One source of indeterminacy is that power generation plants commonly apply price discrimination among their clients, often in the form of (long-lasting and frequently suboptimal) specific power purchase agreements. For example, South Africa (ESKOM), Zimbabwe (ZESA) and EdM all pay different tariffs for electricity acquired from the HCB. What, then, should be taken as the price of electricity generation?

Another important source of difficulty in defining the electricity price is the fact that some mega-projects invest in transmission lines themselves (e.g. the Moma Heavy Sands project), while others do not (e.g. the Chibuto Heavy Sands project). Although this in principle should not have any (significant) impact on the effective price per kWh, it does of course make a difference to the nominal tariff the mega-projects pay (in the case of electricity consumption) or ask (in the case of electricity generation). Should the basis for a percentage electricity tax, then, be the nominal tariff or the effective price per kWh? Taking the effective electricity price including transmission infrastructure costs requires information and consensus about the investment costs calculations, which might prove difficult in practice.[14] Applying a percentage tax to the nominal tariff, on the other hand, will imply an incentive for mega-projects to construct the transmission lines themselves since this lowers their tax base. That might actually be a good idea, since these (long-distance) transmission lines might well serve as important backbones for extending and strengthening the national grid, thereby facilitating rural electrification programmes. However, discrepancies between private and social benefits might give rise to disputes about the optimal route of transmission lines. Moreover, mega-projects differ in terms of new transmission line requirements and thus a nominal tariff-based tax might promote considerable discrimination across the various mega-projects. In any case, defining the current electricity tariff of mega-projects that will serve as a base for the percentage tax is likely to be less simple than it might look at first sight.

A fixed electricity tax per kWh produced or consumed will solve the aforementioned complications. However, as mentioned before, from an environmental point of view it does create a perverse incentive against relatively cheap hydroelectricity. On the other hand, the relatively low production cost of hydroelectricity in comparison with fossil-fuel-based electricity constitutes a free good, since the end-product (electricity) is the same. A relatively high increase in hydroelectricity prices as a result of taxation per kWh will then partly absorb the producer surplus that arises from this free good characteristic, which in principal is a good idea from a welfare point of view. In sum, we tend to argue in favour of an electricity tax per kWh consumed or produced. In Section 5 we will, however, explore both a percentage and a fixed tax levy.

4.2 Environmental externalities motive

Quantifying negative externalities is far from easy, because often it is difficult to define and observe all effects and also because the effects are typically characterized by a lack of markets and thus prices. For example, to determine the value of loss of biodiversity or negative health impacts one needs to place a price on species lost and on human life, respectively. Nevertheless, a range of methodologies exists to establish such prices, using all kind of indirect approaches such as shadow prices, willingness to pay and estimates of statistical life.

As noted before, the negative social and environmental impacts of electricity generation are diverse: amongst others things, they include resettlement of people and biodiversity loss as a result of hydro dams, and different kinds of air pollution (mainly NO_x, SO_2, CO_2) from fossil-fuel-based electricity generation. It is beyond the scope of this chapter to quantify all these effects for the different electricity generation sites in Mozambique. Instead, we make use of a methodology developed in the European Union (EU) to quantify the externalities of different power generation technologies applied in various EU countries (Bickel and Friedrich 2005). The methodology consists of an integrated assessment of the chain of processes linked to the generation of electricity from a given fuel. The impact assessment and valuation of this 'fuel cycle' include the effects of electricity generation on human health, crops, forests, freshwater fisheries and biodiversity. Methods range from the use of simple statistical relationships, in the case of occupational health effects, to the use of a series of complex models and databases, in the cases of acid rain and global warming effects. The underlying principle for economic valuation is the willingness to pay to avoid a negative impact. Table 16.1 summarizes some key results.

Table 16.1 Environmental Damage Costs

USDc/ kWh	Environmental Damage Costs EU	Environmental Damage Costs Best Average	Price electricity generation Mozambique	Environmental Damage Costs (Best Average) as % of price electricity generation
Coal	2.0–26.3	4.93	3.5	140.8
Gas	0.6–9.7	2.13	3.2	66.7
Hydro	0.04–0.64	0.45	2.7	16.7

Source: Bickel and Friedrich (eds) (2005)

The table shows that the estimated environmental damage costs of coal-based electricity generation range from 2–26.3 US$c/kWh, depending on the technology used and other site-specific characteristics. Environmental damage costs from electricity generation based on natural gas are substantially lower, varying from 0.6–9.7 US$c/kWh. On average, human health damages due to aerosols account for 5–25 per cent of the total environmental damage from these fossil fuel cycles, while global warming impacts account for 40–80 per cent and ozone damage due to NO_x emissions is roughly 5–20 per cent of the total damage. It is to be noted that global warming damage from the natural gas cycle is substantially lower than for the coal cycle. As compared to fossil fuel cycles, the environmental damage costs of the hydro cycle are small: they are estimated at 0.04–0.64 US$c/kWh. The most important components of the quantified externalities from hydroelectricity generation concern the impacts on natural ecosystems and especially on the different fauna species which live in the vicinity of the project.

Combining this information and the underlying characteristics of the plants in the EU with the characteristics of the Mozambican electricity generation sites allows us to come up with a rough best average estimate of environmental damage costs for the Moatize coal-fired electricity plant, the Pande/Temane gas-fired electricity plant and the Cahora Bassa and Mphanda Nkuwa hydro dams. As shown in Table 16.1, we estimate these costs at about 4.9 US$c/kWh for the coal plant, 2.1 US$c/kWh for the gas plant and 0.45 US$c/kWh for the hydro dams. In Table 16.1 we compare these rough estimates with the costs of electricity generation in Mozambique. This leads to the conclusion that internalizing all negative externalities would imply an electricity tax of 141 per cent for coal-based electricity, 67 per cent for gas-based electricity and 17 per cent for hydroelectricity. In sum, although the presented estimates of environmental damage costs are far from perfect, we can draw the conclusion that the negative externalities caused by electricity generation are considerable and that any reasonable electricity tax will only account for a small part of these, particularly in the case of coal-based electricity generation.

5 Tax revenues

In this section we present the estimated potential revenues from implementing an electricity tax on mega-projects. We distinguish between a tax on electricity consumption by mega-projects and a tax on electricity generation. Obviously, in order to avoid double taxation the government has to choose between implementing a tax on electricity production *or* on electricity consumption. Both tax systems are to be motivated by revenue-raising and internalizing environmental externalities, as discussed in the previous sections. Based on our calculations in Section 4, we evaluate a fixed electricity tax in the order of 0.1–0.2 US$c/kWh as well as a percentage tax of 5–10 per cent.

5.1 Taxing electricity consumption by mega-projects

To calculate the potential revenues from a tax on electricity consumption we consider the following mega-projects: the existing aluminium smelter Mozal (Mozal I+II) (2000–2), the Moma Heavy Sands mine (2007), the Chibuto Heavy Sands mine (2009, 2017), the Moatize coalmine (2009) and the extension of the Mozal aluminium smelter (Mozal III) (2009), with a total electricity consumption equivalent to 1,882 MW (circa 17,500 GWh). We refer the reader to Section 2.3 for more details on these projects. The value of electricity consumption by these mega-projects is calculated using constant electricity prices. More specifically, we use the actual price paid by Mozal I+II in 2005 (1.03 US$c/kWh) and the prices foreseen for the new mega-projects in their initial years, based on the respective feasibility studies and internal communication with EdM (i.e. Moma, 0.90 US$c/kWh; Chibuto, 2.30 US$c/kWh; Moatize, 2.50 US$c/kWh). Furthermore, recall that we use the nominal electricity tariffs, and thus exclud eventual own investment costs in transmission infrastructure (see Section 4.1). Finally, in line with the most likely reference scenario as discussed in Section 2 we assume that Mozal III will pay 1.5 US$c/kWh for imported electricity until 2014, and 2.7 US$c/kWh for electricity from Mpanda Nkuwa from 2014 onwards.

The resulting value of electricity demand by mega-projects ranges from about US$80 million in 2007 to US$328 million in 2020. In Figure 16.5, we present the annual potential revenues from a tax on electricity consumption by mega-projects over the period 2007–20 under different tax rates. The figure shows that a 5 per cent tax on electricity consumption will generate annual

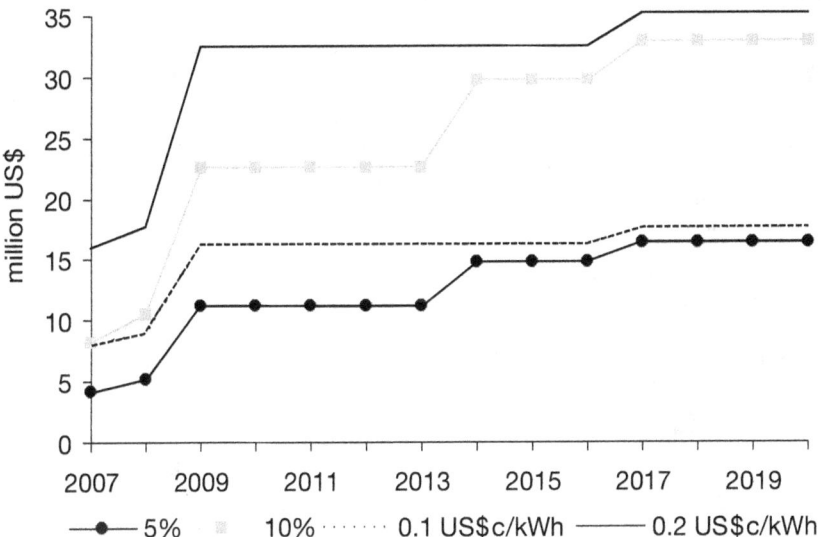

Figure 16.5 Potential revenues from tax on electricity consumption by mega-projects
Source: Authors'calculations.

revenues in the range of US$4–16 million during the period 2007–10. A 10 per cent tax doubles these revenues to about US$8–32 million annually. A tax of 0.1 US$c/kWh yields annual revenues of US$8–17 million, while a 0.2 US$c/kWh tax rate doubles these figures to US$16–35 million. In terms of total projected tax revenues in Mozambique, a 0.1–0.2 US$c/kWh tax on electricity consumption accounts for 1–3.5 per cent of this over the period 2007–20.[15]

In Table 16.2 we present a breakdown of these revenues for each megaproject for a tax regime of 10 per cent and 0.2 US$c/kWh. The table shows that at constant 2005 electricity prices the total accumulated revenues over the period 2007–20 will be about US$351 million at a 10 per cent tax rate, and US$433 million at a tax rate of 0.2 US$c/kWh. In the case of a percentage tax, 32 per cent of these revenues originate from Mozal I+II, while Mozal III will contribute another 45 per cent. The other mega-projects together roughly account for the remaining 24 per cent. A fixed tax rate per kWh, however, places the main burden on Mozal, in total 83 per cent, with the other mega-projects being responsible for the remaining 17 per cent.

This considerable difference in the tax burden between the two tax regimes is of course due to the combination of Mozal's high electricity consumption and a relatively low price, which is particularly true of Mozal I+II. To a lesser extent this is also true for the Moma Heavy Sands projects, due to its low nominal electricity tariff.[16] On the contrary, thanks to the relatively low electricity consumption and the high price of the other mega-projects

Table 16.2 Breakdown of Electricity Consumption Tax Revenues

MegaProject	Mozal I+II	Mozal III	Moma	Chibuto I	Chibuto II	Moatize	Total
Price (USDc/kWh)	1.03	1.50/2.70	0.90	2.30	2.30	2.50	
10% Tax							
After Tax Price (USDc/kWh)	1.08	1.58/2.84	0.95	2.42	2.42	2.63	
Average Annual Tax (million USD)	8.0	11.2	0.2	2.9	3.2	2.2	25.1
Cummulative Tax 2007–20 (million USD)	112.5	157.1	2.4	37.8	12.6	28.7	351.2
% contribution	32.0	44.7	0.7	10.8	3.6	8.2	
0.2 USDc/kWh Tax							
After Tax Price (USDc/kWh)		1.13 1.60/2.80	1.00	2.40	2.40	2.60	
Average Annual Tax (million USD)	15.6	10.2	0.4	2.5	2.7	1.8	30.9
Cummulative Tax 2007–20 (million USD)	217.8	142.8	5.4	32.9	11.0	23.0	432.9
% contribution	50.3	33.0	1.2	7.6	2.5	5.3	

Source: Authors' calculations

(compared with Mozal), their tax burden will be somewhat smaller under a fixed tax per kWh than under a percentage tax.

5.2 Taxing electricity production by mega-projects

To calculate the potential revenues from a tax on electricity production we take into account the following mega-projects: the Cahora Bassa hydro dam (HCB) (1974), the natural-gas-fired electricity plant (2010), the Moatize coal-fired electricity plant (2012, 2015), and the Mphanda Nkuwa hydro dam (2014), with a total electricity production equivalent to 5,575 MW (circa 42,000 GWh). We refer the reader to Section 2.1 for more details on these projects. The value of electricity consumption by these mega-projects is again calculated using constant electricity prices. More specifically, we use the weighted average of the actual selling price of HCB to its various clients (1.43 US$c/kWh),[17] while for the other projects we take the base-load price, which covers the cost price of generation as indicated in the most recent feasibility studies of these projects (gas plant, 3.2 US$c/kWh; coal plant, 3.5 US$c/kWh; Mpanda Nkuwa, 2.7 US$c/kWh). In doing so we again exclude eventual own investment costs in transmission infrastructure by the new projects (see Section 4.1).

The resulting value of electricity production by mega-projects ranges from about US$247 million in 2005 to circa US$1,032 million in 2020. In Figure 16.6 we present the annual potential revenues from a tax on electricity consumption by mega-projects over the period 2007–20 under different tax rates.

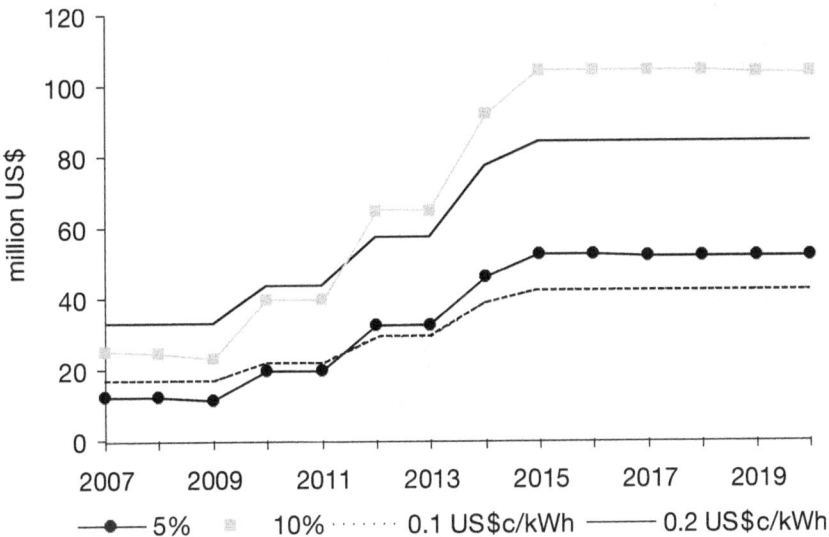

Figure 16.6 Potential revenues from tax on electricity production
Source: Authors'calculations.

The figure shows that a 5 per cent tax on electricity production will generate annual revenues of US$12–52 million during the period 2007–10. A 10 per cent tax doubles these revenues to about US$25–103 million annually. A tax of 0.1 US$c/kWh yields annual revenues of US$16–42 million, while a 0.2 US$c/kWh tax rate doubles these figures to US$33–84 million. In terms of total projected tax revenues in Mozambique, a 0.1–0.2 US$c/kWh tax on electricity production accounts for 1.6–5.1 per cent of this over the period 2007–20

In Table 16.3 we present a breakdown of these revenues for each mega-project. The table shows that at constant 2005 electricity prices the total accumulated revenues over the period 2007–20 will be roughly US$993 million at a 10 per cent tax rate, and US$881 million at a tax rate of 0.2 US$c/kWh.[18] In the case of a percentage tax, 33 per cent of these revenues originate from HCB, 29.6 per cent from the Moatize coal-fired plant, while the natural-gas-fired electricity plant and the Mphanda Nkuwa hydro dam each account for about 18 per cent of total revenues. A fixed tax rate per kWh,

Table 16.3 Breakdown of Electricity Production Tax Revenues

MegaProject	Natural Gas	Coal	Hydro	Hydro	Total
	Inhambane	Moatize	HCB	Mphanda Nkuwa	
Price (USDc/kWh)	3.2	3.5	1.4	2.70	
10% Tax					
After Tax Price (USDc/kWh)	3.52	3.9	1.6	3.0	
Average Annual Tax (million USD)	16.7	29.4	23.4	26.8	70.9
Cummulative Tax 2007–2020 (million USD)	183.5	294.3	328.2	187.3	993.2
% contribution	18.5	29.6	33.0	18.9	
0.2 USDc/kWh Tax					
After Tax Price (USDc/kWh)	3.4	3.7	1.6	2.9	
Average Annual Tax (million USD)	10.4	16.8	32.8	19.8	62.9
Cummulative Tax 2007–2020 (million USD)	114.7	168.2	459.5	138.7	881.1
% contribution	13.0	19.1	52.2	15.7	

Source: Authors' calculations

however, places the main burden on HCB, in total 52 per cent, with the other projects sharing the remaining 48 per cent almost equally.

This considerable difference in the tax burden between the two tax regimes is due to HCB's combination of high electricity production and a relatively low selling price. On the contrary, the Moatize coal-fired plant will face a considerably lower tax burden under a fixed tax per kWh than under a percentage tax (US$16.8 million instead of US$29.4 million, annually) due to the relatively high (cost) price of coal-fired electricity.

6 Taxing electricity consumption or production?

So far we have explored a tax on both electricity consumption and production by mega-projects. Obviously, to avoid double taxation the government of Mozambique (GoM) has to opt for either a tax on consumption or a tax on production. What is the best option? Standard tax theory argues that distortions should be confined to final consumption, leaving production undistorted (Diamond and Mirrlees 1971). However, this conclusion assumes the absence of any market failures. From the point of view of internalizing negative externalities, however, it makes more sense to tax electricity generation than consumption. As we argued in Section 3, it is the production rather than the consumption of electricity that causes negative environmental (and social) impacts. Moreover, in the context of international agreements (such as the Kyoto Protocol) the global pollution caused by electricity generation is assigned to the country where the electricity plant is located. In the case of Mozambique this implies, for example, that the pollution from the electricity consumed by Mozal is assigned to South Africa, from where Mozal imports its electricity. Implementing a tax on electricity consumption by Mozal on environmental grounds is therefore difficult, and might require coordination with South Africa.

In addition, a tax on electricity consumption might prove to be difficult, if not impossible, given the contracts between the GoM and the existing mega-projects. For example, Mozal's 50-year contract with the GoM includes a clause that guarantees indemnification if changes in the law were to impact its profitability (see also Chapter 15, by Kuegler). As shown in Table 16.4, a large part of the projected revenues from a tax on electricity consumption was to come from Mozal. Excluding Mozal from a tax on electricity consumption will not only considerably reduce the projected revenues but will also further discriminate fiscal treatment across the various mega-projects (with Mozal already enjoying the largest benefits).

A tax on electricity production might then be a way to circumvent the (too) generous tax regime for existing mega-projects since it is likely to serve as an indirect tax on electricity consumption by mega-projects, presuming that electricity producers will pass the tax burden on to their clients, as far as possible. This raises the question as to who will effectively pay the tax bill. In Table 16.4 we provide a breakdown of annual tax payment according to the (most likely) destinations of the electricity produced. From the table it can be

Table 16.4 Transfer of Electricity Production Tax

MegaProject	Natural Gas		Coal		Hydro		Hydro	
	Inhambane		Moatize		HCB		Mphanda Nkuwa	
		% share		% share		% share		% share
10% Tax								
Average Annual Tax (million USD)	16.7		29.4		23.4		26.8	
Of which:								
Export	13.4	80.5	26.5	90.0	20.6	87.8	13.4	50.0
EdM	1.5	9.1	1.0	3.3	2.7	11.4		
Chibuto Heavy Sands	1.7	10.4						
Moatize Coal mine			2.0	6.7				
Moma Heavy Sands					0.2	0.7		
Mozal III							13.4	50.0
0.2 USDc/kWh Tax								
Average Annual Tax (million USD)	10.4		16.8		32.8		19.8	
Of which:								
Export	8.4	80.5	15.1	90.0	25.7	78.4	9.9	50.0
EdM	0.9	9.1	0.6	3.3	6.7	20.4		
Chibuto Heavy Sands	1.1	10.4						
Moatize Coal mine			1.1	6.7				
Moma Heavy Sands					0.4	1.2		
Mozal III							9.9	50.0

Source: Authors' calculations

seen that while all new mega-projects that consume domestic electricity will probably face increasing electricity prices, by far the largest burden will fall on neighbouring countries through higher export prices.

In principle there is no need to tax exports of electricity. After all, Mozambique has a typical comparative advantage in producing cheap electricity, and classical trade theory suggests that increasing trade in this good will then enhance welfare. More specifically, increasing exports helps to improve the balance of payments, which currently shows a considerable deficit. However, there will be no complete trade-off between export benefits and tax benefits because of the low electricity prices in Mozambique (see Figure 16.4). To illustrate this point, Figure 16.7 compares the electricity generation costs in Mozambique, including a tax of 0.2 US$c/kWh, with those in South Africa, by far the most important buyer of Mozambican electricity (NER 2004). The figure shows that the relatively low costs of electricity generation in Mozambique, thanks to abundant natural resources, provide ample space to sustain its comparative advantage in electricity production, even after including a tax levy of 0.2 US$c/kWh. This is particularly true for hydroelectricity, while the room for price increases is smallest for coal-based electricity.

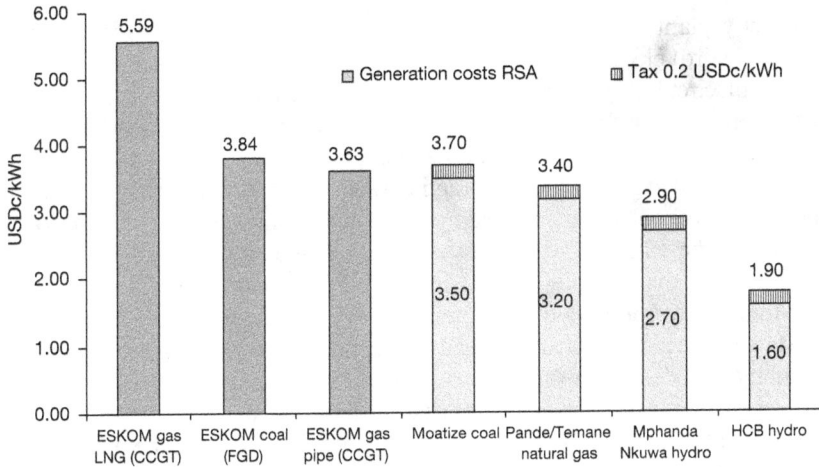

Figure 16.7   Electricity generation prices (Mozambique and South Africa)
Source: NER (2004) for South African ESKOM data, Ministry of Energy
Mozambique for other data.

Of course, Mozambique has to be careful about increasing its prices of electricity exports to South Africa, for the very reason that Mozambique depends on South Africa to sell its electricity, due to the combination of excess production capacity in Mozambique and the dominance of South Africa in the regional electricity market. This evidently places South Africa in a comfortable position to negotiate low prices for its electricity imports, a situation that has characterized the past and in particular the last decade, during which time South Africa had considerable excess capacity of its own. This situation, however, is rapidly changing, with South Africa entering a situation of excess demand (NER 2004; SAPP 2005). In spite of an increase in production capacity in South Africa up to 2010, as it returns several mothballed units to service, South Africa continues to face excess demand that can only be satisfied by a further increase in generation capacity. As shown in Figure 16.7, electricity generation costs in Mozambique are highly competitive even after taxation, implying that Mozambique is rapidly gaining market power in the regional electricity market, and will continue to do so even after 2010.[19]

So far we have assumed private ownership of the electricity generation capacity. However, in November 2006 an agreement was signed to transfer the majority ownership of HCB from Portugal to the GoM. In addition, it is not an unlikely scenario that the GoM will also become the major shareholder in the Mpanda Nkuwa hydro dam which is to be constructed. The latest developments concerning this project indicate that the Chinese Exim Bank is willing to finance the project in return for collateral in the form of natural resources like minerals. Since minerals are state property this in effect means that the GoM will become the owner of the dam. The fossil-fuel-based electricity plants will most likely develop as private enterprises. Imposing a tax on (hydro) electricity produced by state-owned enterprises is, of course, a means of circulating money. In this case, our plea to impose a tax on electricity production changes into a plea to set appropriate market-based electricity prices, with the 'tax revenues' to be interpreted as additional profit.

Finally, if it turns out to be practically or politically impossible to implement a tax on electricity consumption, one might consider the option of extending the existing EdM cross-subsidy scheme to include mega-projects. To facilitate the availability and affordability of electricity in rural areas, EdM currently applies a cross-subsidy scheme consisting of two components. First, the electricity tariff applied to domestic consumers is progressive, meaning that large consumers pay a higher price per unit than small consumers. Second, there is a uniform tariff structure across the country, while the costs of supplying electricity vary considerably – costs per unit are much higher in remote rural areas than in densely populated urban centres. This in effect implies a cross-subsidy from the southern and the central regions to the northern region of Mozambique. The current rural electrification programme means that the current cross-subsidy scheme will come under great pressure over the coming years because of the relatively sharp increase in the number of small (poor) customers in remote areas. One way to solve this problem is to extend the cross-subsidy scheme so that it also includes mega-projects. There are good reasons to do so. First of all, rural electrification generates substantial positive externalities, originating from increased productivity in the private sector, the freeing up of time and labour for education and/or income generating activities, and improved health and environmental conditions. Furthermore, due to the high costs of rural electrification, without subsidies there will be underinvestment in expanding the national grid from a social point of view, given the aforementioned positive externalities. Finally, mega-projects enjoy substantial private benefits from consuming large quantities of cheap electricity, while their positive impact on the Mozambican economy is currently very limited, as argued before. The calculations in Section 5 showed that a minor price increase for electricity consumption by mega-projects may generate considerable funds that could be used to subsidize the costs of electricity supply to small consumers (in rural areas), thereby contributing to economic growth and increased welfare while largely preserving the private benefits of mega-projects.[20]

7 Conclusions

Mega-projects offer a good opportunity to extend the tax base in Mozambique for two reasons. First, with a typically small tax base due to, amongst other things, the relatively large scale of the informal economy and a traditionally weak fiscal institutional infrastructure, they offer a unique source to increase government revenue, thereby lowering the dependence on foreign aid. Second, electricity production, energy-intensive production processes and mining are known for their substantial negative impact on the environment. An energy tax is an important instrument to internalize these negative externalities. In this chapter we have detailed these arguments, the appropriate level and tax base, as well as potential revenues from a tax on electricity *consumption* by mega-projects and a tax on electricity *production*, respectively. We conclude that, in particular, a tax on electricity production seems to be a promising instrument. Existing contracts between mega-projects and the GoM are likely to prohibit the implementation of a new tax regime on the consumption side. Furthermore, compensating for negative environmental externalities argues for taxing electricity production rather than consumption. We estimate annual tax revenues of 0.1–0.2 US$c/kWh on electricity production in the order of US$16–84 million during the period 2007–20. By and large, the burden of a tax on electricity production in Mozambique will fall on neighbouring countries due to the large share of electricity generation earmarked for export. We have shown that the regional electricity market provides ample space to increase electricity prices without compromising Mozambique's comparative advantage in electricity production. Finally, we have argued that any reasonably moderate electricity tax levy will by no means jeopardize the highly preferential tax treatment of existing mega-projects, while such a tax may contribute to realizing the social benefits of the presence of mega-projects. As such, an electricity tax on mega-projects is a valuable instrument to help transform Mozambique's natural resource abundance into increased welfare for the society as a whole.

8 Annex: electricity consumption and production by mega-projects

Table 16.A1 Electricity Consumption by Mega Projects

	Project	Year	MW	Location	Activity	Investor	Investment (million USD)
1	Mozal I + II	2000/2	850	Maputo	Production and Export of Aluminium	Biliton (UK), IDC (RSA), Mitsubishi (JP)	2,250
2	Heavy Sands Moma	2007	22	Nampula	Exploration and Export of Minerals	Kenmare Resources PLC (Ireland)	200
3	Heavy Sands Chibuto I	2008	155	Gaza	Exploration and Export of Minerals	SMC (RSA), IDC (RSA), WMC (Australia)	500
4	Moatize Coal Mine	2009	100	Tete	Exploration and Export of Coal	Companhia Vale do Rio Doce (Brazil)	1,000
5	Mozal III	2009	650	Maputo	Production and Export of Aluminium	Biliton (UK), IDC (RSA), Mitsubishi (JP)	860
6	Heavy Sands Chibuto II	2017	105	Gaza	Exploration and Export of Minerals	SMC (RSA), IDC (RSA), WMC (Australia)	700
	Total		**1,882**				**5,510**

Source: Ministry of Energy

Table 16.A2 Electricity Production by Mega Projects

	Project	Year	MW	Location	Activity	Investor/Owner	Investment (million USD)
1	Cahora Bassa hydropower plant (HCB)	1974	2,075	Tete	Production of electricity forexport (85%) and domestic consumption (15%)	Portugal (15%), Mozambique (85%)	1,300
2	Mphanda Nkuwa hydropower plant	2014	1,300	Tete	Production of electricity for export (25%) and domestic consumption (75%)	Unknown	2,300
4	Gas fired electricity plant	2010	700	Inhambane	Production of electricity for export (30–90%) and domestic consumption (70–30%)	Siemens, Sasol (RSA)	827
5	Coal fired electricity plant	2011	1,500	Tete	Production of electricity for export (90%) and domestic	Companhia do Vale do Rio Doce (Brazil)	1,300
	Total		**5,575**				**5,727**

Source: Ministry of Energy

Notes

1 Except, of course, for the Cahora Bassa hydro dam, completed in 1974.
2 For more information, see: http://www.energycommunity.org.
3 For the period 2007–20 we assume 2.4 per cent annual population growth, a household size of five persons and an annual GDP growth rate of 6 per cent. The information required concerning the new mega-projects in the reference scenario stems from personal communication with the Ministry of Energy as well as recent feasibility studies for the various projects.
4 A third large hydro project in Mozambique with a capacity of 600 MW is HCB North, to be built on the north bank of HCB's site. To be completed some time in the period 2010–15, HCB North is meant to meet peak-load demand in the SADC region. Since peak-load is a very different market from base-load, and not suitable to serve the base-load demand of mega-projects, in this chapter we do not take HCB North further into consideration (see also Section 5.2).
5 A plan exists to build refinery capacity, for example to produce LPG from natural gas, but so far it is very uncertain whether and when this will be realized.
6 It can be argued that the South African national power company ESKOM is able to provide Mozal with a large quantity of cheap electricity because it obtains cheap electricity from HCB. Hence, this implies that in effect ESKOM principally facilitates the transport of electricity from HCB to Mozal, which is similar to its role in transporting the electricity that EdM acquired from HCB for distribution in the south of Mozambique.
7 Recently, the investor BHP Billiton announced the probability of further delays in the project due to increased mining costs (*O País*, 2 March 2007). At the time of finishing this chapter, senior government officials within the Ministry of Energy, however, could not confirm the delay in the project and we cannot exclude the possibility of interpreting the news in terms of strategic behaviour in the context of ongoing negotiations over electricity supply, among other things.
8 Recently the Norwegian energy company NorskHydro relaunched a plan for a second aluminum smelter in Mozambique, most likely to be located at the port of Nacala in the northern province of Nampula. Electricity is supposed to be supplied by the Moatize coal-fired plant that is proposed to become operational in 2012. The plan is, however, too premature to be included in our analysis.
9 It is to be noted that this argument does not hold for peak-load electricity consumption, which is much more sensitive to marginal price increases. Recall that for this very reason we do not take the HCB North hydro dam into consideration (see Section 2).
10 Instead of taxing fossil-fuel-based electricity one could also opt to directly tax fossil fuels. On the one hand, taxing fuels provides an incentive to improve the efficiency of the electricity generation production process. On the other hand, taxing electricity has the advantage of discouraging electricity consumption as a relatively inefficient use of fossil fuel energy (conversion losses in the electricity sector are, on average, much higher than in the direct use of these fuels).
11 EdM 2006, personal communication. It is to be noted that the Moma Heavy Sands project pays a nominal electricity tariff of 0.9 US$c/kWh to EdM. However, Moma constructed the required 200km transmission line originating in Nampula itself at a cost of about US$13 milion. Given a 30-year economic lifetime of the line, a discount rate of 10 per cent and 193 GWh annual electricity consumption, this yields 1.15 US$c/kWh. Hence the effective electricity tariff to Moma is about 2.05 US$c/kWh (0.90 + 1.15 US$c/kWh).
12 Own calculations, based on Ministry of Energy (2007a, 2007b).
13 Own calculations, based on Ministry of Energy (2007a, 2007b). Note that residential customers eligible for the social tariff are exempted from the monthly tax.

14 For example, which discount rate is appropriate for an investment made in a developing country with high interest rates by a multinational with easy access to cheap foreign capital?

15 Total tax revenue projections up to 2010 come from the Quadro Macro model of DNEAP, while we assume a nominal annual growth of 10 per cent from 2010 to 2020.

16 Recall that this low nominal tariff is due to the fact that Moma invested itself in transmission infrastructure. See also Section 4.1.

17 We assume the following tariffs per client: ESKOM, 1.6 US$c/kWh as of 2007 (70 per cent of production); EdM, 0.8 US$c/kWh; Moma, 0.9 US$c/kWh.

18 By way of illustration one may also want to compare the total accumulated tax revenues of US$881 million over the period 2007–20 with the total investment of about US$850 million required to increase access to electricity to about 20 per cent by 2020 (EdM 2004), or the required payment of US$750 million to Portugal in order to secure transfer of HCB's ownership from Portugal to Mozambique.

19 The latter conclusion also holds after taking into account potential new capacity in other SADC countries, which mainly consists of relatively expensive thermal capacity, except for the giant potential of the Inga hydro dam (10,000 MW) in the Democratic Republic of Congo and the total of four medium-sized hydro dams in Zambia (1,290 MW). The Inga dam is, however, not likely to jeopardize Mozambique's competitive advantage in electricity generation because the unstable political situation in Congo prevents completion of the dam in the short and medium run, while its distance from South Africa implies relatively high transmission costs.

20 One may want to consider the option that if mega-projects invest in transmission lines they are allowed to subtract these costs from the amount of supposed cross-subsidy payment, since transmission lines also constitute a valuable contribution to rural electrification programmes, as argued before.

17 VAT and economy-wide modelling

*Channing Arndt, Bruce Byiers,
Sherman Robinson and Finn Tarp*

1 Introduction

The application of value added taxes (VAT) has expanded during the past couple of decades in developed and developing countries alike, including in Africa, where the number of countries with VAT increased from 2 to 30 in the 1990s (Ebrill *et al.* 2001). VAT is a tax on final consumption, collected by applying a tax on sales made at each stage of production, where enterprises are generally permitted to offset tax paid on inputs against that collected on sales of output. The corresponding net value represents the amount transferred to government as VAT revenue. Major advantages of VAT are that it avoids the cascade effect of turnover taxes and is viewed widely as a fair and efficient way to raise revenue.

While this rise in popularity may also be related to the role of VAT as a key element in IMF-sponsored fiscal reforms, it has also been advocated in the theoretical literature as an effective tool for 'reaping the efficiency gains of tariff reform' while strengthening public finances (Keen and Ligthart 2001: 491). Keen and Ligthart (2001) model a one-for-one increase in domestic consumption tax rates to offset tariff reductions and leave consumer prices unchanged, with a *ceteris paribus* resultant increase in welfare and public revenue for a small open economy. However, as they recognize, this result does not extend to include non-tradables, intermediate goods or the case of imperfect competition. Their approach also ignores the potential distributional effects caused by the impact of tariff reform on factor incomes.

Keen and Ligthart's (2001) theoretical analysis also disregards some potentially important developing country constraints on effective tax policy. Burgess and Stern (1993) highlight some of these, which include a large primary sector, segmented and fragmented markets, poor education levels, weak administrative capabilities, pervasive corruption, widespread tax evasion and a vast number of small-scale enterprises, many of which operate outside the tax system. As a consequence, 'even when broad-based taxes are used, the evidence suggests that in practice revenue is collected from only a fraction of the activity that by statute should be covered' (Gordon and Li

2005: 2). In particular, the presence of a large informal sector may hinder the potential for offsetting border taxes with domestic taxes.

Emran and Stiglitz (2005) develop a model to incorporate this additional feature which allows for an informal sector, with imperfect substitution of formal and informal goods.[1] In their analysis, a generalized uniform reduction in import tariffs reduces the distortion between tradable and non-tradable goods.However, the accompanying revenue-neutral increase in VAT creates distortions between the formal sector, which is subject to VAT, and the informal sector, which is not, with negative welfare effects. They further consider a selective tariff reduction and selective VAT reform and show that under 'plausible' conditions welfare is reduced. Although they recognize that VAT collected on imports may moderate this decline, they find this incompatible with the view that VAT is a more efficient tax, advocating the elimination of VAT collected at the border. Again, being a theoretical model, some aspects are ignored, such as the existence of non-tradables, intermediate goods, smuggling and the difference in administrative costs between applying border taxes and domestic taxes, although they claim that these are likely to add weight to their results.

Empirically, the behaviour and impact of VAT will depend on a variety of country-specific factors. How a VAT system is applied may vary in terms of the extent of use of exemptions, of zero-rating and the size threshold above which enterprises are required to register for and comply with VAT.[2] The importance of the informal sector in economic activity and administrative capacity will clearly also impact on how effective VAT is at fairly and efficiently raising revenue, and how its incidence compares with other taxes. The above considerations highlight the importance of country studies.[3]

The Mozambican VAT was introduced in April 1999 as part of a wave of fiscal reforms. The reform effort is ongoing, with the introduction of a new income tax code in 2003 and the establishment of a Central Revenue Authority (CRA) in 2006. Little or no in-depth economic analysis preceded the introduction of these innovations; so there is limited knowledge of how the VAT system actually behaves in Mozambique, in theory and practice. In particular, questions arise regarding (1) VAT incidence, (2) its ability to offset lost revenues from trade liberalization, (3) how VAT interacts with other taxes and (4) the potential impacts of changes in the application of VAT.

We address these questions in the present chapter, which is organized in five main sections. Section 2 provides a summary of key characteristics of the Mozambican economy. The CGE framework adopted here is described in detail in Section 3. It is well suited to the analytical requirements listed abovegiven its automatic inclusion of intermediate goods and non-tradables and its ability to trace the differential effects of VAT implementation under a variety of different scenarios.[4] Subsequently, we present and discuss the results of a variety of VAT scenarios in Section 4. Final remarks follow in Section 5.

2 Country background

The Mozambican VAT was introduced to replace the 'circulation tax', a conventional turnover tax. In its first full year of operation in 2000, VAT revenues accounted for 38.8 per cent of total revenues (5.0 per cent of GDP), compared with 29.2 per cent of revenues (3.3 per cent of GDP) from the turnover tax in 1998, its final full year of operation. By 2005, total revenues from all sources as a share of GDP had marginally declined, from 11.7 per cent in 2000 to 11.4 per cent. Total VAT in 2005 represented 4.3 per cent of GDP and 38.0 per cent of total revenues. In both 2000 and 2005, 58 per cent of total VAT was collected on imports and the remaining 42 per cent on domestic transactions. In sum, VAT revenues are important and are likely to have significant economic impacts that merit analysis.

The next major contributors to Mozambican revenues are taxes on trade, which represented 33.4 per cent of total revenues in 2000 and 29.0 per cent in 2005.[5] Trade tax revenues declined marginally more in percentage terms than VAT revenues over the same period but continue to represent a substantial part of government revenues. Mozambique, like many poor countries, is characterized by a continuing high level of dependence on trade taxes, in particular when one includes revenues from VAT on imports, and a low level of total revenues.

In terms of financing government expenditure, foreign aid typically finances about half of the national budget, putting aid on a par with total domestic revenues. In this environment, the interactions between tax revenues and aid are potentially important.

The structure of an economy determines the first-order impact of a shock, such as a change in tax rates. Hence a review of the basic structure of the Mozambican economy as presented in the 2003 social accounting matrix (SAM), which is the data system underpinning the CGE analysis, is worthwhile. Table 17.1 provides basic indicators for production and trade. Consider the second to bottom row, which provides information on the agricultural sector overall. From this row, one sees that the agricultural sector generates approximately one-quarter of GDP and slightly less than one-fifth of total exports. About 14 per cent of the total value of agricultural production is exported. Agricultural imports of relatively minor importance. Imports of agricultural products represent only 2.9 per cent of total imports, while imported agricultural products comprise only slightly more than 5 per cent of total domestic demand for agricultural products.

Other features from Table 17.1 include the high share of metals (aluminium) in total exports and the nearly complete dedication of metal production to exports. Though representing nearly half of exports, metals production represents only about 5 per cent of GDP at factor cost. In addition, the weight of services in value added and exports is noteworthy for a poor African economy.

Table 17.2 illustrates the structure of household expenditure. For expositional purposes, only the expenditure patterns for the second and top quintiles in rural and urban zones are presented (trends in shares across quintiles are

Table 17.1 Economic Structure from 2003 SAM

	Value Added Share	Export Share	Export/ Output Share	Import Share	Import/ Demand Share
Grains	5.4	0.2	0.8	2.0	17.1
Other subsistence	12.6	2.0	3.4	0.3	1.6
Cash crops	1.3	2.4	27.6	0.3	7.8
Other agriculture	6.7	13.8	29.3	0.3	2.2
Mining	0.3	0.3	5.1	0.2	7.2
Processed food	5.6	2.3	2.9	15.0	29.6
Light manufactures	1.9	3.9	20.0	14.3	60.3
Heavy manufactures	1.2	1.8	11.5	28.7	76.0
Metals	5.3	45.9	98.0	2.3	87.3
Energy	0.0	0.0	0.0	9.4	100.0
Construction	7.1	0.0	0.0	0.0	0.0
Trade	18.8	0.0	0.0	0.0	0.0
Hotels and restaurants	1.1	0.0	0.0	0.0	0.0
Transport	7.3	6.4	8.1	0.0	0.0
Public services	4.5	0.0	0.0	0.0	0.0
Private services	4.5	0.0	0.0	0.0	0.0
Other services	16.4	21.2	20.3	27.2	41.4
Total	100.0	100.0	12.4	100.0	25.2
Total agriculture	26.0	18.3	14.1	2.9	5.3
Total non-agriculture	74.0	81.7	12.2	97.1	28.2

Source: Mozambique social accounting matrix 2001

roughly linear). Key features include high shares of home consumption (comprised almost entirely of agricultural products), high food shares, low savings rates and low effective rates of income taxation even for the top quintile in urban zones. Reliance on home consumption tends to be higher in rural zones and higher among the less well off. Consistent with Engel's law, expenditure on food (home consumed or purchased) tends to decline as total expenditure increases. Tax rates and savings rates tend to increase with income.

Table 17.3 illustrates the principal indirect tax rates – VAT and tariffs. VAT rates are differentiated between those applied at the border and those applied domestically. Note that domestic applied VAT rates are typically lower compared with the border due to greater ease of collections. Note that investment goods and exports are zero rated. As a result, applied VAT rates are zero for construction, which is considered a pure investment sector, and metals, which is (very nearly) a pure export sector.

3 VAT–CGE model for Mozambique

In the model applied in this paper, we start from a standard, trade-focused computable general equilibrium (CGE) model,[6] which contains four basic elements: (1) behavioural specification of all economic actors; (2) simulation

Table 17.2 Household Expenditure Structure

	Rural		Urban	
	2nd Quintile	Top Quintile	2nd Quintile	Top Quintile
Home Consumption	42.7	25.8	11.7	5.4
Grains	2.4	2.0	2.3	0.7
Other subsistence	4.5	6.6	23.5	7.9
Cash crops	1.3	0.9	0.4	0.7
Other agriculture	5.2	2.5	10.4	6.3
Mining	1.7	0.8	0.7	0.2
Processed food	22.9	24.9	30.2	28.5
Light manufactures	4.1	10.3	2.9	6.8
Heavy manufactures	1.9	3.5	1.9	4.0
Energy	0.4	1.0	0.7	0.7
Trade	0.0	0.1	0.0	0.2
Hotels and restaurants	0.3	0.6	0.4	0.8
Transport	6.5	11.7	6.8	18.2
Public services	0.0	0.0	0.0	0.0
Private services	0.4	0.4	0.8	1.1
Other services	5.1	5.3	5.7	13.8
Income tax	0.1	1.7	0.7	2.9
Savings	0.5	1.8	0.9	1.8
Total	100.0	100.0	100.0	100.0

Source: Mozambique social accounting matrix 2001

Table 17.3 Tariff and VAT Tax Structure

	Domestic VAT	Border VAT	Average VAT	Border Tariff
Grains	0.0	0.0	0.0	2.6
Other subsistence	0.0	12.6	0.2	10.0
Cash crops	0.0	14.7	1.0	1.2
Other agriculture	0.0	13.9	0.3	2.4
Mining	10.2	14.0	10.5	5.2
Processed food	5.0	5.8	5.3	7.1
Light manufactures	4.7	10.8	8.3	10.0
Heavy manufactures	0.1	9.7	7.2	9.2
Metals	0.0	0.0	0.0	0.0
Energy	0.0	15.6	13.4	5.9
Construction	0.0	0.0	0.0	0.0
Trade	0.0	9.0	9.0	5.5
Hotels and restaurants	0.1	0.0	0.1	0.0
Transport	4.5	0.0	4.5	0.0
Public services	15.7	0.0	15.7	0.0
Private services	1.6	10.0	4.9	0.0
Other services	2.6	9.3	4.4	5.9

Source: Mozambique social accounting matrix 2001

of the operation of markets; (3) macro closure; and (4) detailed specification of the operation of the tax system, especially VAT.

3.1 Behavioural specification

The model has 17 'activities' (or sectors of production), 17 'commodities' (domestically produced or imported), 12 factors of production (with 7 labour categories differentiated by skill and sector, 2 land types and 3 types of capital), and 10 household types (rural and urban, each divided into income quintiles). There are 4 agricultural activities, which provide some detail on the sources of rural income. The model assumes profit maximization by producers under a sectoral translog technology. This treatment allows specification of separate substitution elasticities between labour in production, independently of substitution elasticities with respect to land and capital.

Households are assumed to demand commodities according to fixed expenditure shares, which is consistent with maximizing a Cobb–Douglas utility function. Investment and government expenditures are allocated across commodities with fixed real coefficients rather than fixed expenditure shares.

The model incorporates the division of labour types by skill and zone (rural and urban), which constitute separate inputs into the sectoral translog cost functions. The translog allows specification of different substitution elasticities between any pairs of factors. Elasticities across labour classes are based on Arndt (2006). There is limited labour mobility between zones, given the segmentation of rural and urban labour markets.

Foreign trade is specified using the Armington assumption. Exports, imports and domestically produced goods of the same commodity classification are assumed to be imperfect substitutes. There are constant elasticity of transformation (CET) functions that underlie sectoral export supply functions and constant elasticity of substitution (CES) functions underlying sectoral import demand functions. The commodity/sector export transformation elasticities used in this chapter were estimated econometrically by Arndt *et al.* (2002). Import substitution elasticities are based on data from the Global Trade Analysis Project (GTAP 2005).

3.2 Operation of markets

A CGE model simulates the operation of product and factor markets, solving for market-clearing prices and wages. It is a closed general equilibrium system, incorporating all elements of the circular flow of income and expenditure, and the corresponding real flows. Characteristic features of this type of model include the following:

1 households must respect their budget constraint;

2   the domestic price of commodity imports equals the CIF price multiplied by the exchange rate and the prevailing tariff rate plus any marketing margins, value added tax or additional domestic sales taxes;
3   the value of imports cannot exceed the availability of foreign exchange;
4   supply of commodities must equal demand for commodities (with inventory accumulation counted as demand);
5   firms collectively cannot use more of any factor than the total availability in the economy;
6   investment must be financed via foreign or domestic (private plus government) savings;
7   government consumption must be financed through tax revenue, foreign grants (aid) or borrowing on domestic and/or foreign markets.

In our model, aggregate supply of all labour types is exogenous and wages adjust to clear labour markets, with full employment of all labour categories. The model also accounts for marketing margins as described by Arndt *et al.* (2000) and Jensen and Tarp (2002). Prices and wages are solved endogenously to equilibrate supplies of and demands for commodities and factors. The model determines relative prices, and the numeraire is given by the consumer price index.

3.3 Macro closure

All economy-wide models incorporate macro balances. How equilibrium is achieved between savings and investment, the government deficit and the trade deficit constitutes the 'macro closure' of the model. This VAT–CGE model is used to explore different mixes of tax instruments, so we specify a macro closure consistent with standard practice in public finance analysis. The aggregate price level, the consumer price index, is fixed, defining the model's numeraire. Aggregate investment and government demand for goods are both fixed in real terms. Aggregate nominal government revenue is also fixed, with the analysis focused on considering the impact of different mixes of tax instruments that yield the same aggregate revenue through revenue replacement. The government deficit (and hence government saving) is endogenous, as are enterprise savings rates, to achieve savings–investment balance.[7] Foreign savings and aid are fixed exogenously, and the real exchange rate adjusts to achieve external balance through changes in aggregate exports and imports, operating through changes in the relative prices of traded and non-traded commodities.

3.4 Modelling VAT

The model incorporates a European-style destination value added tax with rebates on VAT paid on intermediate input and investment purchases. With this treatment, there is no cascading effect on prices of indirect taxes on intermediate goods.

We assume VAT is administered using the 'invoice method'. All transactions are taxed at a fixed proportional rate regardless of whether they are final or intermediate demand. Firms can deduct VAT taxes paid on intermediate inputs, and that tax amount is reported on the invoices for intermediates. Import sales are subject to VAT, export sales are not.

In the model, we assume that domestically produced goods sold on the domestic market are imperfect substitutes for imports. For each commodity, purchasers demand a 'composite' good, which is a CES aggregate of imports and domestically produced goods. Ignoring the commodity subscript:

$$Q = F(D, M), \tag{1}$$

where:

Q: composite good;
D: domestic good sold on the domestic market;
M: imports.

The demand for imports is a function of the relative prices on domestic markets of imports and domestic goods:

$$PDT = PD \cdot (1 + tvad)$$

$$PM = pwm \cdot ER \cdot (1 + tm) \cdot (1 + tvam) \tag{2}$$

where:

PDT: price of domestic goods including the value added tax, $tvad$;
PD: supplier price of domestic goods;
PM: domestic price of imports, including tariffs and value added tax, $tvam$;
pwm: world price of imports in foreign currency units;
ER: exchange rate.

The value of the composite good equals the value of its component imports and domestic goods:[8]

$$PQT \cdot Q = PM \cdot M + PDT \cdot D, \tag{3}$$

which defines the composite price, PQT, which includes the value added taxes. Note that VAT is not imposed on exports, only on goods sold on domestic markets.

Assuming that the value added tax rate is the same for domestic and imported goods, $tvad = tvam$, we can simplify the model. Assume that PQ is defined without the separate VAT on M and D, and then define a uniform VAT for the composite good, $tvaq$. Then demanders of the composite good pay $PQT = PQ(1 + tvaq)$. In practice, the VAT rates applied to domestics and imports differ, forcing recourse to the former, more complicated, model specification.

To calibrate the model, we assume the observed VAT tax revenue in the SAM is the net payment by sector.[9] Producers must pay VAT on all domestic sales and can collect a rebate on VAT taxes paid on intermediate inputs. For each production activity, we compute the rebate on intermediate expenditure using data on input–output relationships. We assume a Leontief production structure with fixed input–output shares defining intermediate demand.

The rebate to each activity is based on total intermediate input use (where a is the activity index and c is the commodity index):

$$REBATE(a) = \sum_c tvaq(c) \cdot PQ(c) \cdot QINT(c, a), \tag{4}$$

where:

$tvaq(c)$:   value added tax by commodity;
$PQ(c)$:   price of commodity c without VAT;
$QINT(c, a)$: quantity of intermediate commodity, c, purchased by activity, a.

The price of the aggregate intermediate input now includes the rebate per unit of aggregate intermediate input:

$$PINTA(a) = \sum_c PQT(c) \cdot ica(c, a) - REBATE(a)/QINTA(a), \tag{5}$$

where:

$PINTA(a)$: price of the intermediate aggregate input;
$PQT(c)$:   price of the composite commodity including VAT;
$ica(c, a)$: the intermediate input c per unit of aggregate intermediate input;
$QINTA(a)$: quantity of aggregate intermediate input into activity A.

The price, $PINTA(a)$ is used in the producer's first-order condition for profit maximization.

If *tvam* does not equal *tvad*, we assume that the rebate is based on an average *tvaq* for the commodity, computed so that:

$$PQ \cdot (1 + tvaq) \cdot Q = PD \cdot (1 + tvad) \cdot D + pwm \cdot ER \cdot (1 + tm)$$
$$\cdot (1 + tvam) \cdot M, \tag{6}$$

The net value added tax revenue paid to the government ($VATREV$) is:

$$VATREV = \sum_c tvaq(c) \cdot PQ(c) \cdot Q(c) - \sum_a REBATE(a) \tag{7}$$

Rebates on expenditures on investment goods are handled similarly, with the rebate being given to 'enterprises' in the model.

The model can easily accommodate sectors that are 'zero rated' by simply specifying that *tvaq* (or *tvad* and *tvam*) equals zero for those activities. While their VAT rate is zero, zero-rated activities are eligible to be reimbursed for VAT paid on intermediate inputs and capital goods. The model can also accommodate 'exempt' activities which neither pay VAT on their output nor are reimbursed for VAT paid on intermediate inputs and capital goods. In this case, *tvaq* and *REBATE* both equal zero.

4 VAT analysis

4.1 Simulations

Analysis of VAT focuses on three sets of simulations. The first set is a classic public finance application where VAT rates are moved proportionally up or down and the resulting revenue gains or losses are offset by proportional changes in personal income tax rates. The second set of simulations considers reductions in tariff rates with offsetting proportional increases in VAT rates. The final set of simulations harmonizes applied VAT rates at the border and domestically. This final simulation is motivated by the administrative ease of collecting taxes at the border and the consequent tendency for applied rates to be higher at the border. In all scenarios, revenue neutrality is maintained.[10] Analysis focuses on the incidence of the various simulations across households. The implications of the tendency for higher collection rates at the border are also considered.

Prior to considering the results of the simulations, the primary structural drivers of the results are presented.

4.2 Results

Table 17.4 summarizes results for simulation set 1, which proportionately moves VAT tax rates and offsets changes in revenue via proportionate changes in personal income tax rates. Under this scenario, VAT is shown to be broadly progressive, with lower income households in both rural and urban areas doing relatively better than higher income households. This result is driven primarily by the highly progressive nature of personal income taxes (see Table 17.2). Relative factor prices (not shown) are, for the most part, minimally affected by the simulation. This result, combined with the insulation afforded by home consumption and the relatively light taxation of agriculture, implies that VAT overall is, as implemented, a reasonably progressive tax. On the other hand, household welfare, in general, decreases marginally with an increase in the VAT rate offset by reductions in income tax rates.

Table 17.4 also illustrates that VAT acts like a tariff in a macroeconomic sense. A reduction in VAT causes the real exchange rate to depreciate, thus encouraging movement of factors of production from non-traded to traded sectors of the economy. As already noted, and similarly to static analyses of tariff reform, reductions in the VAT result in overall efficiency gains (as measured by absorption); however, these efficiency gains tend to be very small.

Table 17.4 Household Welfare and Macroeconomic Indicators (simulation set 1)

	Proportional Changes to VAT Tax Rates						
	–30	*–20*	*–10*	*0*	*10*	*20*	*30*
Rural1	0.80	0.53	0.26	0.00	–0.26	–0.52	–0.77
Rural2	0.88	0.59	0.29	0.00	–0.29	–0.57	–0.85
Rural3	0.68	0.45	0.23	0.00	–0.22	–0.45	–0.67
Rural4	0.95	0.63	0.31	0.00	–0.31	–0.61	–0.91
Rural5	–0.01	–0.01	0.00	0.00	0.00	0.00	–0.01
Urban1	0.73	0.48	0.24	0.00	–0.24	–0.47	–0.71
Urban2	0.53	0.35	0.18	0.00	–0.17	–0.35	–0.52
Urban3	0.35	0.23	0.12	0.00	–0.12	–0.23	–0.35
Urban4	0.40	0.27	0.13	0.00	–0.13	–0.27	–0.40
Urban5	–0.50	–0.32	–0.16	0.00	0.15	0.30	0.44
Total	0.10	0.07	0.03	0.00	–0.04	–0.08	–0.12
Real x-rate	1.04	0.69	0.34	0.00	–0.34	–0.68	–1.01
Absorption	0.07	0.05	0.02	0.00	–0.02	–0.05	–0.07

Note: Simulation set 1 proportionately moves VAT rates and offsets revenue gains/ losses with proportional changes in income tax rates.
Source: CGE Model simulations

Table 17.5 illustrates simulation sets 2 and 3. The first two columns focus on the incidence effects of either halving tariff rates or eliminating tariffs entirely and replacing the revenue with increases in VAT. VAT is shown to be mildly more progressive than the existing tariff structure. Elimination of tariffs with offsetting increases in VAT rates results in a small welfare gain for all households other than the top 40 per cent or earners in urban areas. This provides further evidence that VAT incidence is concentrated on relatively wealthy urban households.

The first two columns of Table 17.5 also underscore the macroeconomic result highlighted in Table 17.4. Halving or eliminating tariffs does cause the currency to depreciate. However, the depreciation is exceedingly mild (less than 1 per cent even with full tariff elimination), underscoring the tendency of VAT to function in a manner economically similar to an import tariff. Table 17.5 also illustrates that changes in aggregate welfare as measured by absorption are negligible.

The final column of Table 17.5 shows the implications of harmonizing applied VAT rates between border and domestic collections as well as across commodities (unless the commodity was zero rated in the base). As might be expected given earlier results, the relative expansion of the domestic component of VAT is mildly regressive. In addition, this simulation further highlights the role of VAT as a source of protection for the domestic tradable sectors. Similar to tariff reduction, the harmonizing of VAT rates results in a depreciation of the real exchange rate by a fairly considerable 3.6 per cent. In a similar manner to a tariff reduction, harmonizing of VAT rates results in a small gain in aggregate welfare.

Table 17.5 Household Welfare and Macroeconomic Indicators (simulation set 2
and 3)

	Tariffs (–50%)	*Tariffs (–100%)*	*Unify VAT rates*
Rural1	0.1	0.3	–0.5
Rural2	0.1	0.2	–0.2
Rural3	0.2	0.3	–0.3
Rural4	0.1	0.1	0.0
Rural5	0.1	0.2	0.2
Urban1	0.1	0.2	–1.0
Urban2	0.1	0.2	–0.8
Urban3	0.1	0.2	–0.6
Urban4	–0.1	–0.2	0.0
Urban5	–0.2	–0.4	0.6
Total	0.0	–0.1	0.2
Real x-rate	0.4	0.8	3.6
Absorption	0.0	–0.1	0.1

Note: Simulation set 2 (first two columns) proportionately reduces tariff rates by 50
percent and 100 percent with revenue losses offset by proportional increases in
VAT rates. Simulation set 3 equilibrates domestic and border VAT rates across all
commodities unless the product was zero rated in the base.
Source: CGE Model simulations

5 Conclusion

The value added tax is becoming increasingly important across developed
and developing countries alike, including the poorer African countries such
as Mozambique. Yet the process of reforming the tax system in Mozambique
has, as elsewhere, taken place with little prior in-depth economic analysis of
VAT behaviour and impact. More specifically, the knowledge about VAT
incidence, revenue and interaction with other taxes has been limited. The
present chapter aims at helping fill this gap. We began with the observation
that economic structure is important in shaping the first-order impact of shocks,
such as changes in tax rates. We summarized the characteristics of the
Mozambican economy as reflected in the 2003 SAM, and proceeded to outline
the CGE analytical model underlying this study. We paid particular attention to the modelling of VAT, and ran three sets of simulations: (1) a classic
public finance application where VAT rates were moved proportionally up
and down, including offsetting proportional changes in personal income
taxes; (2) reductions in tariff rates with offsetting proportional increases in
VAT rates; and (3) harmonization of VAT rates applied at the border and
domestically. In all simulations, revenue neutrality was maintained. Analysis
focused on incidence across five rural and five urban household types.

The results raise interesting policy-relevant issues, in particular with
respect to VAT's commonly espoused role as a revenue replacement mechanism
to accompany trade and other tax reforms. In particular, in its current guise
the Mozambican VAT is progressive relative to tariffs but regressive relative

to personal income taxes. If trade taxes are cut and VAT rates are increased to offset revenue losses, lower income households tend to become better off. Increases in personal income taxes with offsetting reductions in VAT also tend to favour lower income households. Our simulations also reveal that, as VAT is collected more easily on imports than on domestic transactions, it operates much like a tariff, thus maintaining distortions in production, particularly between tradable and non-tradable goods. On the plus side, VAT is a unified 'tariff' and provides a form of 'duty drawback'. Finally, our simulations suggest that attempts to increase the revenue contribution of domestic VAT relative to import VAT are likely to reduce progressiveness.

Notes

1 VAT on imports is classed a 'trade tax'.
2 Note that 'exemption' from VAT for a sector or good means that enterprises theoretically do not collect VAT on their sales but neither do they receive reimbursement for that paid on inputs. 'Zero-rating' also implies that VAT is not collected on sales, but in this case that paid on inputs is reimbursed by government. Zero-rating is generally applied to exports, while exemption applies to enterprises operating below the VAT size threshold.
3 See Fourie and Owen (1993) and Go *et al.* (2005) for two relevant VAT studies of South Africa.
4 In the model applied here to the case of Mozambique, the formal and informal sectors are not explicitly treated, although VAT is implicitly captured from the informal sector through the use of net VAT data by sector, while welfare impacts are captured through household survey data.
5 Trade taxes are here defined to include import duties, excises on imports and the tax on fuel.
6 See Löfgren *et al.* (2002) and Tarp *et al.* (2002) for a couple of standard references.
7 The government deficit changes very little in the tax scenarios, varying only with changes in relative prices of goods demanded by the government.
8 The CES import aggregation function is homogeneous, and the import demand function satisfies the adding-up condition that total expenditure on the composite good equals the expenditure on imports and the domestic good.
9 We use the effective tax rates based on tax collection data. The rates differ by sector and differ from the reported statutory rate of 17 per cent due to sector aggregation, the treatment of the informal sector and/or measurement error.
10 This also implies that the rate of tax evasion remains the same, regardless of rate changes, although in practise this is unlikely to be the case.

Annex

Documentation of social accounting matrix (SAM) development

Christen McCool, James Thurlow and Channing Arndt

1 Constructing the unbalanced prior social accounting matrix

The initial task in building a SAM involves compiling data from various sources into the framework outlined below. This information is drawn from national accounts, household surveys, foreign trade statistics, government budgets, balance of payments and various other publications. This information often uses (1) different disaggregation of sectors, production factors and socio-economic household groups, (2) different years and/or base-year prices and (3) different data collection and compilation techniques. Consequently, the initial or *prior* SAM inevitably includes imbalances between row and column account totals.

The underlying prior macro SAM is based on the National Accounts put together by the National Institute of Statistics (Instituto Nacional de Estatística, or INE).[1] The disaggregated micro SAM is built so that the aggregate totals from the macro SAM are preserved (i.e. shares are used from other sources rather than actual numbers). This Annex explains how each macro SAM entry is derived and then disaggregated to arrive at the prior micro SAM. Table A.1 shows accounts in the 2001 micro SAM, while Table A.2 shows the 2001 macro SAM for Mozambique. Each of the entries in the Macro SAM is discussed in detail below. The notation for the SAM entries is row then column, and the values are in billions of 2001 Mozambique Meticais.

It is important to emphasize that this documentation refers to the most disaggregated version of the SAM. In particular, an attempt at regional disaggregation is made. For the purposes of the analyses conducted in this book, the regional dimension was aggregated away. It is also important to emphasize that the documentation provided here details a process towards arriving at a balanced and consistent social accounting matrix reflecting existing information. As more or updated information is expected to become available with time, considerable effort was expended to make updating processes and/or improvements relatively simple to implement. The code and resulting files are available on the World Wide Web.

Table A1: Annex Accounts in the Mozambique 2001 SAM – Sectors

Activities (108, 27 for each of four regions)

Agriculture (56)
Maize (North, Center, South, and Maputo city – regional breakdown of all sectors)
Rice
Wheat
Other grains
Cassava
Beans
Other basic food crops (Vegetables, fresh fruit, etc.)
Cashews
Cotton
Other export crops (Citrus fruits, sugarcane, etc.)
Other crops (Peanuts, tea, etc.)
Livestock
Forestry
Fisheries

Industry (20)
Mining
Food processing
Light manufacturing
Heavy manufacturing
Metal industries

Services (32)
Energy
Construction
Trade and repairs
Hotels and restaurants
Transport services
Public administration
Education and health services
Other services

Commodities (27): Same as activities, not regionalized

Factors (33)

Labour (23)
Skilled labour

Semi-skilled labour, rural (North, Center, South)
Semi-skilled labour, urban formal (North, Center, South, Maputo city)
Semi-skilled labour, urban informal (North, Center, South, Maputo city)

Unskilled labour, rural (North, Center, South)
Unskilled labour, urban formal (North, Center, South, Maputo city)
Unskilled labour, urban informal (North, Center, South, Maputo city)

Capital (3)
Rural capital
Urban capital
Megaproject capital

(table continued)

Table A1: (continued)

Activities (108, 27 for each of four regions)

Land (7)
Land, rural (North, Center, South)
Land, urban (North, Center, South, Maputo city)

Households (35)
Rural, 20th expenditure percentile (North, Center, South)
Rural, 40th expenditure percentile (North, Center, South)
Rural, 60th expenditure percentile (North, Center, South)
Rural, 80th expenditure percentile (North, Center, South)
Rural, 100th expenditure percentile (North, Center, South)

Urban, 20th expenditure percentile (North, Center, South, Maputo city)
Urban, 40th expenditure percentile (North, Center, South, Maputo city)
Urban, 60th expenditure percentile (North, Center, South, Maputo city)
Urban, 80th expenditure percentile (North, Center, South, Maputo city)
Urban, 100th expenditure percentile (North, Center, South, Maputo city)

Other institutions (5)

Enterprises (3)
Rural enterprises
Urban enterprises
Megaproject enterprises

Government

Rest of the world

1.1 (Factors, Activities) ... 66,727

This is the value of gross domestic product (GDP) at factor cost or, alternatively, total value-added generated by land, labour and capital. Labour and capital (inclusive of land) value-added for 41 activities are captured in the INE's production-side GDP table, and the aggregate SAM entry is the sum of these sectoral values. The INE accounts include a single agricultural crop activity, which we separated into 11 sub-sectors. A total of 51 sectors were therefore recognized in the initial disaggregated national SAM, but given the limited availability of sub-national regional data, the final micro SAM contains only 27 sectors (14 agriculture, 5 industry and 8 services).

GDP within these 27 sectors is further broken down by region. The four regions recognized are North (Niassa, Cabo Delgado and Nampula provinces), Center (Sofala, Zambezia, Manica and Tete), South (Gaza, Inhambane and the province of Maputo, exclusive of Maputo city) and the city of Maputo. This regional disaggregation is accomplished using production shares calculated from a variety of sources. Regional value shares of food

Table A2: Annex 2001 Macro SAM for Mozambique (Billions of Mozambique Meticais)

	Activities	Commodities	Factors	Enterprises	HouseHolds	Government	Taxes	Investment	Rest of World	Total
Activities		113,297			11,336					124,633
Commodities	57,969	41,991			47,778	10,467		18,796	14,830	191,832
Factors	66,727									66,727
Enterprises			17,695			60				17,755
Households			49,032	11,416		137			337	60,921
Government				113			8,440			8,553
Taxes	-63	6,928		542	1,033					8,440
Savings				2,005	775	-2,112			18,129	18,796
Rest of World		29,616		3,680						33,296
Total	124,633	191,832	66,727	17,755	60,921	8,553	8,440	18,796	33,296	

Source: Author's calculations

crop production are derived from 2002 Ministry of Agriculture and Rural Development agricultural survey estimates (Ministry of Agriculture and Rural Development 2002). Cashew and cotton shares are taken from McMillan *et al.* (2003: Table 3) and Benfica (2005), respectively, and other export crop shares are also taken from the Benfica paper. Sectoral GDP figures for 1999 are used to calculate shares for livestock, forestry and fishing; and production value shares for all 14 agricultural sectors are adjusted to account for home consumption using the INE's 2002/3 National Household Survey (IAF). Food processing production shares are estimated using 1999 regional GDP as well as IAF own and marketed consumption numbers, and value shares for all other industry and service sectors are calculated from 1999 regional GDP figures, taking into account survey estimates of regional labour income by activity.

Within each region-specific activity, region-specific labour value-added is disaggregated by skill level using the IAF, a nationally representative household consumption survey. 'Skilled', 'semi-skilled' and 'unskilled' are the three potential skill categories, where unskilled labour is workers with maximum educational attainment less than grade 6, semi-skilled labour those with education between grade 6 and grade 10; and those with any higher education level are considered skilled. Rural, urban formal and urban informal labour are also distinguished, again using the IAF. The most skilled labour is aggregated into a single category, combining all regions and sectors, and this skilled factor is employed by all activities. Rural capital is disaggregated from urban capital value-added using rural–urban labour income shares for each region-specific activity, and 'mega-project' capital is separated from urban capital in the mining, heavy industry and metal sectors using provincial GDP estimates.[2] An estimate of land value-added is also separated from agricultural capital, and this land factor is both region and sector specific (i.e. rural or urban).

1.2 (Commodities, Activities) … 57,969

This is the value of intermediate inputs used in the production process. The value of intermediate demand by each activity is taken from the national GDP table, and the 1997 Input–Output matrix is used to disaggregate this demand across commodities. This value is scaled such that the total value of intermediate demand for a given commodity (i.e. the sum across all activities) is equal to aggregate intermediate demand from the INE's 2001 Supply–Use table. The sum of intermediate demand for all commodities as given in the Supply–Use table therefore provides the macro SAM aggregate shown in Table A.2. Intermediate demand is regionalized using the regional production shares outlined above, where commodities remain homogeneous (i.e. are not region specific). This implies a national commodity market for marketed commodities, which is a distinguishing feature of the final micro SAM.

1.3 (Taxes, Activities) ... –63

While the macro SAM in Table A.2 shows only a single row and column for taxes, this accounts actually consists of a number of distinct tax accounts. These include specific accounts for activity, income, sales and import taxes. The activity tax entry is negative, indicating a subsidy. The national GDP table provides the value of activity subsidies for each sector, and the macro SAM value is the sum total of these sectoral subsidies. Regional production shares are used to map subsidies to regional activity.

1.4 (Activities, Households) ... 11,336

The payment from households to activities represents households' consumption of own production. This production is measured at producer (or farm-gate) prices. The value of own consumption for each sector is taken from the national Supply–Use table, and the macro SAM value is therefore the sum of auto-consumption across all commodities in the Supply–Use table. Household consumption of own production is mapped between regional activities and region-specific households using own consumption data from the 2002/3 IAF. Households are further disaggregated by sector (rural or urban) and national expenditure quintile using the IAF.

1.5 (Activities, Commodities) ... 113,297

Total marketed output is the difference between gross output (124,633) and the value of own household consumption (11,336). This value is taken from the Supply–Use table, calculated as total domestic production (both formal and informal) minus home consumption. The SAM distinguishes between activities and commodities, and thus facilitates interactions between single/multiple activities and single/multiple commodities, as do expanded National Accounts, which, after disaggregating agriculture, distinguish 51 productive sectors and 144 commodities (i.e. some activities produce more than one good). Although our chosen disaggregation of 27 commodities maps directly to 27 activities, we do take advantage of the possibility of a non-diagonal mapping in the supply matrix. Activities are regionalized while commodities are not, and so each commodity is produced by up to four regional activities, capturing different production technologies and structures.

1.6 (Commodities, Commodities) ... 41,991

The payment from commodities to commodities is a condensed version of the treatment of trade margins in the final micro SAM. In the micro SAM there are separate margin accounts for the trade costs incurred through the marketing of each commodity. This value of transaction costs is further disaggregated to distinguish between the costs incurred by imports, exports and domestically produced and sold goods. Like many other entries in the SAM, this entry was first calculated on a disaggregated level and then aggregated to arrive at a final macro SAM value. Total trade margins for a given commodity were taken from the national Supply–Use table. These were distributed across imports, exports and domestic markets according to the value of each item in total demand or supply. The trade and repairs sector is assumed to provide all trade and marketing services.

1.7 (Taxes, Commodities) ... 6,928

The commodity tax entry can be disaggregated to include indirect sales taxes (1,598), value-added taxes collected on domestic sales (1,642), value-added taxes collected on imports (1,962) and import tariffs (1,726). Indirect or sales taxes include excise duties on petroleum products, beverages and tobacco, and vehicles, and are given in the Supply–Use table for all commodities. The Supply–Use table provides import tariff data as well, but while the Supply–Use total supplies the macro SAM value in the case of sales taxes, national accounts are used for the tariff aggregate value. An aggregate value for value-added taxes is also taken from the tax authorities, and the Medium Term Fiscal Framework model is used to split this value between tax receipts domestically collected and those effectively collected at the border. A single value-added tax rate is calculated for domestic goods from the share of the domestic value-added aggregate in domestically produced household marketed consumption. Similarly, a single value-added tax rate is calculated for imports from the share of the border value-added aggregate in non-investment import demand. This rate is applied to all non-exempted commodities, where exemption data are obtained from the National Directorate of Taxes and Auditing.

1.8 (Rest of World, Commodities) ... 29,616

The value of total imports of goods and services is taken from national accounts. The total value of imports is then scaled upwards by 20 per cent to reflect unrecorded imports and errors and omissions in national accounts. Import data is provided for individual goods in the Supply–Use table, and this information is used to disaggregate the macro SAM value into import values for each commodity.

1.9 (Commodities, Households) ... 47,778

Total household marketed consumption of each commodity is provided in the national Supply–Use table. Disaggregation according to household characteristics (region, rural or urban, and expenditure quintile) is accomplished by using consumption shares calculated from the IAF. The scaled-up imported values are assumed to be primarily consumed by households consistent with the results in Chapter 11.

1.10 (Commodities, Government) ... 10,467

Sectoral values of government consumption spending are taken from the national Supply–Use table. All of government spending is for the purchase of administrative services, education, health and social security services. In this way the government is treated as a sector producing government services as well as a demander of these services.

1.11 (Commodities, Investment) ... 18,314

The aggregate value and commodity-specific values of investment demand are taken from the Supply–Use table.

1.12 (Commodities, Rest of World) ... 14,830

The value of export demand for each commodity is taken from the national Supply–Use table, and macro aggregate is the sum of these sectoral values.

1.13 (Enterprises, Factors) ... 17,695

The residual of capital value-added (or gross operating surplus less land rents) is paid to enterprises. There are three enterprises, corresponding to the three categories of capital: rural, urban and 'mega-project'. All rural capital earnings, for example, are transferred to rural enterprises. These earnings are subject to direct/corporate taxes.

1.14 (Households, Factors) ... 49,032

This value is the sum of all land and labour value-added generated during production. The distribution of labour income across households is determined using household labour income shares as reported in the 2002/3 IAF, mapping labour disaggregated by region, skill level and sector (rural, urban formal or urban informal) to households disaggregated by region, sector (rural or urban) and expenditure quintile. Land income from a given region and urban/rural sector is transferred to households from that region and sector, distributing among households of different expenditure quintiles using IAF auto-consumption shares.

1.15 (Enterprises, Government) ... 60

This is the value of interest payments paid by the government to domestic financial enterprises. It is taken from national accounts. We assume that enterprise income from government occurs in urban sectors.

1.16 (Government, Enterprises) ... 113

Total transfers paid by enterprises to the government are taken from national accounts. They comprise interest on property, distributed income of corporations, property rent payments and social contributions paid by enterprises. We assume these are paid by urban capital.

1.17 (Taxes, Enterprises) ... 542

These are corporate taxes paid by enterprises to the government, and the total value is derived from national accounts. We assume that 'mega-project' enterprises pay taxes totalling 0.6 per cent of government revenue, and disaggregate the remaining value between rural and urban enterprises according to rural and urban capital value-added shares in non-agricultural sectors.

1.18 (Savings, Enterprises) ... 2,005

Enterprise savings are taken from national accounts and include allowance for depreciation or consumption of fixed capital. The aggregate value is split between rural, urban and 'mega-project' enterprises according to capital value-added shares.

1.19 (Rest of World, Enterprises) ... 3,680

This is income from abroad on properties owned by domestic enterprises. This is taken from national accounts, and is largely paid by mega-project capital (calculated as a residual so that mega-project enterprises transfer no income to households), with the remainder disaggregated according to non-agricultural value-added shares of capital.

1.20 (Households, Enterprises) ... 11,416

This is the value of mixed income received by households and is calculated as a residual of total enterprise income minus enterprise transfers to government, tax payments, enterprise savings and enterprise transfers abroad. It is assumed that 'mega-project' enterprises do not transfer any income to households. Rural capital value-added is distributed to rural households according to profit shares as recorded in the IAF. Urban households receive transfers from urban enterprises according to savings shares in addition to profit shares. The disaggregation of indirect capital returns is therefore based on proxy variables from the household survey.

1.21 (Households, Government) ... 137

Transfers from the government to households are taken from national accounts and include social benefits and domestic miscellaneous current transfers. They are distributed across different household groups according to the pensions and social grants that households reported receiving in the IAF.

1.22 (Households, Rest of World) ... 337

Aggregate household income from the rest of the world is taken from national accounts and is equal to international miscellaneous current transfers. This is distributed across households according to the cash and in-kind remittances received from abroad by households in the IAF.

1.23 (Taxes, Households) ... 1,033

The value of direct taxes on households is taken from national accounts. This value is initially distributed across households according to tax rates calculated from tax expenditure and income data from the IAF. Household taxes are then scaled up to match the value of actual direct tax collections as reported in national accounts.

1.24 (Savings, Households) ... 775

Household savings are taken from national accounts. Savings rates are calculated on the basis of savings as reported in the IAF, and these rates are used to distribute total savings among households. Household savings are then scaled up to match the value of savings reported in national accounts.

1.25 (Government, Taxes) ... 8,440

The tax accounts in the micro SAM are separated into activity subsidies, import tariffs, sales taxes and direct taxes. Each account sums tax revenue from all sources and then transfers these funds to the government.

1.26 (Savings, Government) ... –2,112

This is the fiscal deficit and is taken from national accounts.

1.27 (Savings, Rest of World) ... 18,129

This is the current account deficit or the total value of foreign savings. It is derived from national accounts.

2 The balancing process and flexible aggregation

The 2001 micro SAM for Mozambique includes regionalized activities, labour and households. We recognize, however, that other types of research may demand a different choice of sectors, factors and institutions, and the

SAM is constructed with this possibility in mind. To allow for flexibility in disaggregation, the construction of the SAM is organized into multiple stages. First a national micro SAM is built from national accounts, incorporating the most detailed level of sectoral disaggregation possible given our data (51 activities and 144 commodities). From this initial micro SAM, the final SAM is created. Sectors are aggregated and disaggregated as desired, and data from the IAF (household survey) is brought in to disaggregate factors and institutions. This two-stage process is designed to facilitate the construction of new SAMs, both when new national accounts data become available and when the research requires different levels of sectoral or institutional detail. The GAMS, Stata and Excel files used to construct a new SAM in either instance are discussed in Section 2.1.

2.1 Building the prior national micro SAM: 1datafile.xls and 1construct.gms

The first stage of the SAM construction process is the creation of the national (i.e. non-regional) micro SAM. This is accomplished using three primary files: the Excel file 1datafile.xls and the GAMS files 1construct.gms and 2balance.gms. The end-product of this first step is a balanced SAM consisting of 51 activities, 144 commodities, and single labour, capital, household and enterprise categories. This SAM is outputted to the 'AFINAL' tab of 2workfile.xls, from which it will be read at the beginning of the second stage. This entire first step may be skipped unless either national accounts data are to be updated or new production, consumption, trade or tax information is to be incorporated at the sectoral level. If only a change in the disaggregation of regional activity, or in the breakdown of factors and institutions, is desired, one can proceed immediately to the second stage, using the SAM stored in 'AFINAL' directly (or, equivalently, running 1construct.gms and 2balance.gms, leaving all files unchanged, to produce the 'AFINAL' SAM in 2workfile.xls).

The Excel file 1datafile.xls contains the prior macro SAM as well as national production, value-added, trade and demand data for all commodities and activities, including trade margin and tax information. It also contains information for GAMS, including set definitions (the 'Sets' tab) and an index which tells GAMS the location of all the information being read in from Excel (the 'Index' tab). If the new SAM will continue to use 2001 national accounts, no change is needed to this file. If, however, new national accounts data is to be incorporated, 1datafile.xls is the starting point, and the first step is the construction of a prior balanced macro SAM to be included in the 'Macro' tab of 1datafile.xls. It is important that this macro SAM remains in the same area of the worksheet as the current 2001 SAM (i.e. starting in cell A15) and that the account names are identical (i.e. 'mact', 'mcom', etc.) National accounts supply these macro aggregates. Other tabs in the Excel file can also be updated, if new data is available, specifically, 'GDPTable' and 'SUTable', which detail activity-level production and commodity-level demand and supply, respectively. The source of both of these worksheets is national accounts. Keep in mind that if 'GDPTable' is to be updated, the agricultural crop sector found in national accounts must be disaggregated into 11 sub-sectors, because, as with the macro SAM, account names must remain unchanged (i.e. 'amaiz' and 'arice' for the activities in 'GDPTable' and 'cp001' etc. for commodities in 'SUTable'). If these initial set elements are to be altered, more extensive work must be done. The 'IOTable', 'ActHhd' and 'ComHhd' tabs will not change unless new input coefficients or household survey data are obtained.

The GAMS file 1construct.gms reads in the data from 1datafile.xls and uses it to construct the prior national micro SAM. Little or no change should be needed to the code contained in 1construct.gms. The code is written so that the sectoral data contained in 'GDPTable' and 'SUTable' is used to disaggregate macro aggregates through the use of shares rather than absolute values. For example, import supply is calculated as follows:

$$SAM('ROW', C) = \frac{SUTAB(C,'IMPORT')}{SUM(CP, SUTAB(CP,'IMPORT'))} MSAM('MROW','MCOM') \quad (1)$$

rather than as $SAM('ROW', C) = SUTAB(C,'IMPORT')$. This means that there is no problem if the macro SAM is updated to new national accounts numbers, but the activity- and commodity-level data are not, because 1construct.gms automatically applies the shares implied by the 2001 data to the new macro aggregates.

The micro SAM we created takes home and marketed consumption numbers from the Supply–Use table. Another choice would be to use household survey data to disaggregate consumption across commodities. The 2002/3 IAF data on household consumption of own and marketed output are already stored in 1datafile.xls under 'ActHhd' and 'ComHhd'. In order to calculate consumption shares from this survey data rather than from 'SUTable', the variable 'UPDATE' need only be changed from a value of '0' to a value of '1'. Another example of an instance in which the code in 1construct.gms might be changed is if the method for calculating tax or transaction cost rates were to be altered. Other than these few small changes, however, any update of 1datafile.xls will automatically be accommodated.

2.2 Balancing the prior national micro SAM: 2balance.gms and 2workfile.xls

The SAM created in 1construct.gms is unbalanced, and so column and row totals must be reconciled before moving on to stage two. This is done in 2balance.gms, and the resulting balanced SAM is then stored in the 'AFINAL' tab of 2workfile.xls (the prior unbalanced SAM created in 1construct.gms is stored in 'APRIOR'). The unbalanced SAM from 1construct.gms is transferred to the balancing file 2balance.gms using a method known as a 'save/restart'. When executing 1construct.gms, it is necessary to enter the following into the command line box:

$$s = \frac{save}{1construct}$$

In turn, when executing 2balance.gms, one must enter

$$r = \frac{save}{1construct}$$

This basically allows 2balance.gms to resume where 1construct.gms left off, with all definitions and calculations retained.

2.3 Building the final micro SAM: 2datafile.xls and 3aggregate.gms

The SAM outputted from the first stage of the construction process is extremely disaggregated in one sense (it contains the maximum number of sectors and commodities possible given current data) and extremely aggregated in another sense (it makes no regional, urban/rural or formal/informal distinctions, and recognizes only one aggregate household institution, one aggregate labour factor, etc.) The purpose of the second stage is to bring in data from sources other than national accounts in order to create the level of disaggregation desired for the final micro SAM. In our case, this means aggregating activities and commodities into a smaller number of sectoral categories, adding the regional detail missing in the national SAM, as well as incorporating survey data to flesh out the factor and institutional accounts. An outline of the work involved in choosing a different disaggregation along any of these dimensions is provided in Section 2.1, including discussion of the associated files.

As with the first stage, the Excel file (2datafile.xls in this case) is the primary place to make any changes to the SAM. Like 1datafile.xls, 2datafile.xls stores set definitions as well as an index for GAMS; 2datafile.xls also includes the data that will be used to disaggregate activities, factors and households. Additionally, this is the place to make a change in the aggregation of activities and commodities – i.e. to reduce or increase the number of non-regionalized categories from the current 27. This is done by updating set definitions, including mapping sets which link, for example, aggregate activities (e.g. 'atrans') to the associated disaggregated ones ('arail', 'aroad', 'apipe', 'amari', 'aaero' and 'aotrn'). The global set ACOLD includes the initial disaggregation, as outputted by the first stage, including all 51 activities and 144 commodities. To change the number of activity or commodity categories in the final micro SAM, update the set AAG (in the case of activities) or C (in the case of commodities), as well as AC in both cases. If, for example, only two sectors are desired, agriculture and non-agriculture, AAG and C should be altered to include only two elements each ('aagr' and 'anagr', and 'cagr' and 'cnagr'), replacing the old activity and commodity set elements with these new ones in AC as well. Further, the mapping sets 'MAPACACOLD' and 'MAPAAGC' need to updated to reflect the mapping between aggregate and disaggregated activity accounts and the mapping between the new activity and commodity accounts, respectively. The 'Notes' tab, which provides the documentation for this file, should reflect these changes.

Of course if the aggregate activity account AAG is updated, corresponding changes must be made to the region-specific account elements in set A. For example, 'aagr11' would need to replace 'amaiz11', 'arice11', 'awheat11', etc. The process for accomplishing this can be generalized into a discussion of disaggregating sectors, factors and institutions along regional, rural/urban, formal/informal, expenditure quintile or any other dimension. This process involves two steps: first, updating set definitions in the 'Sets' tab of 2datefile.xls as well as the GAMS include file 3sets.inc; and, second, updating the information used to make the disaggregation, in the 'ActReg', 'ActHhd', 'ComHhd', 'LabAct', 'HhdLab' and 'HhdMisc' tabs. Once again, any changes should also be documented in 'Notes'. Updating the appropriate sets should be somewhat uncomplicated. A change in the sectoral aggregation as described in the previous paragraph, for example, would necessitate updating AC to include the new regionalized elements, replacing the old set definitions in AAGR, ARUR and AURB with the new ones, updating the mappings in MAPAAGA and MAPRA in 'Sets', as well as updating the mapping sets MAPMACAC, MAPAAP and MAPRUA in 3sets.inc. Similarly, a change in household categories would result in changes in the set definitions of AC, H, HRUR, HURB, INS and MAPRH, as well as the mappings MAPMACAC and MAPRUH found in 3sets.inc. This should all be rather straightforward if careful attention is paid to the set definitions in 2datafile.xls and 3sets.inc, so that relevant sets are easily identified and updated. This involves not only the sector/factor/institution sets themselves but also supporting sets. If, for example, the number of regions recognized changes, the set R must be updated as well as the R element of the many mapping sets. Also, if a new dimension, such as gender, is added, new supporting sets may be useful (such as FLABFEM and FLABMALE). This can be done either in Excel (adding to or subtracting from the 'Index' tab) or directly in GAMS. Remember that even if the new set is defined in Excel, the set must still first be declared in GAMS. Similarly, if an old dimension is removed, some sets may cease to be relevant (e.g. FLABR and FLABU if the rural/urban distinction is removed for labour).

The first step of the disaggregation process, as described above, provides the new account elements for the SAM. The second step inputs the information required to assign values to the new elements of the SAM. This information is included in the 'ActReg', 'ActHhd', 'ComHhd', 'LabAct', 'HhdLab' and 'HhdMisc' tabs of 2datafile.xls. These tabs are organized in different ways; some provide shares directly (i.e. 'ActReg' and 'LabAct'), while others provide values from which shares are calculated in GAMS. This data can come from any source and can be adjusted as desired; the only requirement is that the account names match up with 'Sets' definitions. Our method of disaggregating production along regional lines is in 5 Regional GDP Disaggregation.xls, for example, but all of those background calculations are 'hidden' from

GAMS – all that GAMS requires is the final table of shares in 'ActReg'. The other data tabs summarize IAF survey findings. This work with the survey data is done in Stata using the do file 0master.do. Household and factor definitions can be altered in the supporting files 1hhdclass.do and 2facclass.do, and these alterations will carry through the rest of the master do file. Tables are outputted from Stata into comma separated values files that can be opened in Excel and pasted directly into the 'ActHhd', 'ComHhd', etc. tabs. An example of an alternative set definition is provided in 2facclass-gender. do. In addition to region and sector, this file disaggregates labour according to gender rather than skill level. The only change needed to incorporate this alternative definition is to remove the asterix (*) from in front of the

do 2facclass-gender.do

command in 0master.do and to place it in front of

* do 2facclass.do

When pasting the data into Excel, be sure not to move the tables (all must remain located on the appropriate worksheet, beginning in cell A7) unless the 'Index' tab is updated to reflect the move.

The GAMS file 3aggregate.gms reads in the definitions and parameter values from 2datafile.xls and creates a SAM which incorporates the desired set elements and data. Most of the aggregating and disaggregating is done automatically, but it is still important to scan the GAMS code as well. This is because while most of the GAMS file refers only to sets, and therefore requires no updating, it is sometimes necessary that a specific sector, factor or institution be treated individually. In this case, the individual set element is referred to by name, and if that name has changed, any attempt to run the file will result in an error. Additionally, there is some discretion possible in the way certain values are allocated, for example how land value-added is separated from agricultural capital or how enterprises transfer capital earnings to households.

2.4 Balancing the prior micro SAM: 4balance.gms and 4final.xls

When all desired changes have been made to 2datafile.xls and 3aggregate. gms, run 3aggregate.gms. This will output the unbalanced micro SAM to the DPRIOR1 and DPRIOR2 sheets in 2workfile.xls. The final step of the SAM construction process is to balance the SAM using cross-entropy econometrics. This is done in 4balance.gms, which reads in the prior SAM from 2workfile.xls and balances it. A final aggregation is also made, removing the rural/urban distinction in activities, using the set definitions and mappings in 3datafile.xls. The final balanced micro SAM is outputted to the 'Final1' sheet of 4final.xls.

References

Abramowitz, M. and Stegun, I.A. (eds) (1972) *Handbook of Mathematical Functions with Formulas, Graphs, and Mathematical Tables*, 9th edn, New York: Dover.

Acemoglu, D., Johnson, S. and Robinson, J.A. (2000) 'The colonial origins of comparative development: an empirical investigation', NBER Working Paper 7771, National Bureau of Economic Research, Inc.

Adam, C. and Bevan, D. (2001) 'Fiscal policy design in low-income countries', Discussion Paper 2001/67, World Institute for Development Economics Research (WIDER).

Addison, T. and Osei, R. (2001) 'Taxation and fiscal reform in Ghana', Discussion Paper 2001/97, World Institute for Development Economics Research (WIDER).

Alfieri, A., Cirera, X. and Rawlinson, A. (2006) 'Estimating the impact on Mozambique of different trade policy regimes: SADC, SACU or MFN?', DNEAP Discussion Paper 29E, National Directorate of Economic Studies and Policy Analysis, Ministry of Planning and Development, Mozambique.

Allingham, M.G. and Sandmo, A. (1972) 'Income tax evasion: a theoretical analysis', *Journal of Public Economics*, 1: 323–38.

Amaro de Matos, J. (2001) *Theoretical Foundations of Corporate Finance*, Princeton, NJ: Princeton University Press.

Anderson, P.A. (2001) 'The impact of the mega projects on the Mozambican economy', Discussion Paper 2001/18, Ministry of Planning and Finance, Maputo, Mozambique.

Andreoni, J., Erard, B. and Feinstein, J. (1998) 'Tax compliance', *Journal of Economic Literature*, 36: 818–60.

Armington, P.S. (1969) 'The geographic pattern of trade and the effects of price changes', *International Monetary Fund Staff Papers*, 16(2): 179–201.

Arndt, C. (2006) 'HIV/AIDS, human capital, and economic prospects for Mozambique', *Journal of Policy Modeling*, 28: 477–89.

Arndt, C. and Tarp, F. (2004) 'On trade policy reform and the missing revenue: an application to Mozambique', Discussion Paper 04–19, Institute of Economics, University of Copenhagen.

Arndt, C., Jones, S. and Tarp, F. (2007) 'Aid and development: the Mozambican case', in S. Lahiri (ed.) *Theory and Practice of Foreign Aid* (vol. I), Amsterdam: Elsevier B.V.

Arndt, C., Robinson, S. and Tarp, F. (2002) 'Parameter estimation for a computable general equilibrium model: a maximum entropy approach', *Economic Modeling*, 19: 375–98.

Arndt, C., Jensen, H.T., Robinson, S. and Tarp, F. (2000) 'Agricultural technology and marketing margins in Mozambique', *Journal of Development Studies*, 37(1): 121–37.

Artis, M. and Marcellino, M. (2001) 'Fiscal forecasting: the track record of the IMF, OECD and EC', *Econometrics Journal*, 4(1): S20–S36.

Auerbach, A. (1999) 'On the performance and use of government revenue forecasts. Berkeley Olin Program in Law and Economics', Working Paper Series 1000, Berkeley Olin Program in Law and Economics.

—— (2002) 'Taxation and corporate financial policy', in A. Auerbach and M. Feldstein (eds) *Handbook of Public Economics,* (vol. III), Amsterdam: Elsevier.

Bach, C.F. and Martin, W. (2001) 'Would the right tariff aggregator for policy analysis please stand up?', *Journal of Policy Modeling*, 23(6): 621–35.

Bach, C.F., Martin, W. and Stevens, J.A. (1996) 'China and the WTO: tariff offers, exemptions, and welfare implications', *Weltwirtschaftliches Archiv*, 132(3): 409–31.

Baer, K. (2002) 'Improving large tax payer compliance: a review of country experience', Occasional Paper, 215, International Monetary Fund.

Baltagi, B. (2003) *Econometric Analysis of Panel Data*, 2nd edn, West Sussex: John Wiley and Sons.

Barrionuevo, J.M. (1992) 'How accurate are the World Economic Outlook projections?', in *Staff Studies for the World Economic Outlook*, Chapter II, International Monetary Fund.

Baumol, W.J. and Oates, W.E. (1988) *The Theory of Environmental Policy*, Cambridge: Cambridge University Press.

Beck, N. (2001) 'Time-series cross-section data: what have we learned in the past few years?', *Annual Review of Political Science,* 4: 271–93.

Benfica, R. (2005) 'The economics of smallholder households in tobacco and cotton growing areas of the Zambezi Valley of Mozambique', PhD dissertation, Department of Agricultural Economics, Michigan State University.

Bhargava, A., Franzini, L. and Narendranathan, W. (1982) 'Serial correlation and fixed effects model', *Review of Economic Studies,* 49: 533–49.

Bickel, P. and Friedrich, R. (eds) (2005) *ExternE – Externalities of Energy Methodology 2005 Update*, Luxemburg: European Communities.

Biljon, A.V. and Hassan, S. (2007) 'The equity premium in South Africa', mimeo, University of Cape Town.

Bird, R. (2004) 'Administrative dimensions of tax reform', *Asia-Pacific Tax Bulletin*, 134–50.

Bird, R.M. and Zolt, E.M. (2005) 'Redistribution via taxation: the limited role of the personal income tax in developing countries', Working Paper 0508, International Tax Program, Institute for International Business, Joseph L. Rotman School of Management, University of Toronto.

Bird, R.M., Martinez-Vazquez, J. and Torgler, B. (2004) 'Societal institutions and tax effort in developing countries', Working Paper 0411, International Tax Program, Institute for International Business, University of Toronto.

Blackwell, J.L. (2005) 'Estimation and testing of fixed-effect panel-data systems', *The Stata Journal*, 5(2): 202–7.

Bliss, C. (1992) 'The design of fiscal reforms in revenue-constrained developing countries', *Economic Journal*, 102(413): 940–51.

Bolnick, B. (1999) 'The role of financial programming in macroeconomic policy management', HIID Development Discussion Paper 720, Harvard Institute for International Development.

— (2004a) 'Tax reform and the business environment in Mozambique: a review of private-sector concerns', unpublished report, Nathan Associates, USAID/Mozambique. Online. Available at http://www.fiscalreform.net/library/pdfs/mozambique_tax_reform_and_business_environment.pdf (accessed 29 May 2008).

—— (2004b) *The Effectiveness and Economic Impact of Tax Incentives in the SADC Region*, USAID/RCSA and SADC Tax Subcommittee, Nathan Associates.

Bovenberg, A.L. and Goulder, L.H. (2001) 'Neutralizing the adverse industry impacts of CO_2 abatement policies: what does it cost?', in C. Carraro and G. Metcalf (eds) *Distributional and Behavioral Effects of Environmental Policy*, Chicago, IL: Chicago University Press.

Burgess, R. and Stern, N. (1993) 'Taxation and development', *Journal of Economic Literature*, 31(2): 762–830.

Campa, J. and Goldberg, L. (2005) 'Exchange rate pass through into import prices', *Review of Economics and Statistics*, 87(4): 679–90.

—— (2006) 'Distribution margins, imported inputs, and the sensitivity of the CPI to exchange rates', NBER Working Paper 12121, National Bureau of Economic Research, Inc.

Castel-Branco, C.N. and Goldin, N. (2003) *Impacts of the Mozal Aluminium Smelter on the Mozambican Economy*, Final Report presented to Mozal, Maputo, Mozambique.

Centro de Promoção de Investimento (2004) Investment Data, Centro de Promoção de Investimento.

Chabal, P. (2001) *A History of Post-Colonial Lusophone Africa*, London: C. Hurst and Co.

Chen, D., Matovu, J.M. and Reinikka, R. (2001) 'A quest for revenue and tax incidence in Uganda', IMF Working Paper 01/24, International Monetary Fund.

Cirera, X. and Arndt, C. (2006) 'Measuring the impact of road rehabilitation and the liberalization trend on spatial market efficiency in maize markets in Mozambique', mimeo, Maputo, Mozambique.

Comtrade (2008) United Nations Commodity Trade Statistics Database. Online. Available at http://comtrade.un.org/ (accessed 17 June 2008).

Cremer, H. and Gahvari, F. (2001) 'Second-best taxation of emissions and polluting goods', *Journal of Public Economics*, 80: 169–97.

Cremer, H., Gahvari, F. and Ladoux, N. (1998) 'Externalities and optimal taxation', *Journal of Public Economics*, 70: 343–64.

Crown Agents (2006) 'Customs Reform Programme 1997–2006: the modernisation of Alfândegas de Moçambique', Maputo: Crown Agents. Online. Available at www.crownagents.com/uploads/public/documents/downloads/Our%20Work/Public%20Financial%20Management/Mozambique%20Customs.pdf (accessed 14 May 2008).

Dabla-Norris, E., Gradstein, M. and Inchauste, G. (2005) 'What causes firms to hide output? The determinants of informality', IMF working paper 05/160, International Monetary Fund.

Dalgaard, C.-J., Hansen, H. and Tarp, F. (2004) 'On the empirics of foreign aid and growth', *Economic Journal*, 114(496): F191–F216.

Daneshkhu, S. (2006) 'Low corporate tax boosts countries' competitiveness', *Financial Times*, 1 November 2006.

Danninger, S. (2005) 'Revenue forecasts as performance targets', IMF Working Paper 05/14, International Monetary Fund.

Danninger, S., Cangiano, M. and Kyobe, A. (2005) 'The political economy of revenue-forecasting experience from low-income countries', IMF Working Paper 05/2, International Monetary Fund.

Davidson, R. and Duclos, J.-Y. (1997) 'Statistical inference for the measurement of the incidence of taxes and transfers', *Econometrica*, 65(6): 1453–66.

Davies, B.R., Beilfuss, R.D. and Thoms, M.C. (2000) 'Cahora Bassa retrospective, 1974–97: effects of flow regulation on the Lower Zambezi River', *Verhandlungen Internationale Vereinigung für Theoretische und Angewandte Limnologie*, 27: 1–9.

De Soto, H. (1989) *The Other Path: The Invisible Revolution in the Third World*, New York, Harper and Row.

Deaton, A. (1989) 'Rice prices and income distribution in Thailand: a non-parametric analysis', *Economic Journal*, 99(395), Supplement: Conference Papers: 1–37.

—— (1997) *The Analysis of Household Surveys: A Microeconometric Approach to Development Policy*, World Bank, Baltimore, MD and London: The Johns Hopkins University Press.

Devarajan, S., Lewis, J.D. and Robinson, S. (1990) 'Policy lessons from trade-focused, two-sector models', *Journal of Policy Modeling*, 12: 625–57.

Diamond, P.A. and Mirrlees, J.A. (1971) 'Optimal taxes and public production I: production efficiency', *American Economic Review*, 61: 8–27.

Diebold, F.X. and Mariano, R.S. (1995) 'Comparing predictive accuracy', *Journal of Business and Economic Statistics*, 13(3): 253–63.

Dimaranan, B.V. and McDougall, R. (2005) 'Global Trade, Assistance, and Production: The GTAP 6 Data Base', Center for Global Trade Analysis, Department of Agricultural Economics, Purdue University.

DNEAP and KU (2006) 'Enterprise development in Mozambique: results based on manufacturing surveys conducted in 2002 and 2006', DNEAP Discussion Paper 33E, National Directorate of Economic Studies and Policy Analysis, Ministry of Planning and Development, Mozambique, and Department of Economics, Copenhagen University. Online. Available at http://www.mpd.gov.mz/gest/publicat.htm (accessed 12 May 2008).

Don, F.J.H. (2004) 'How econometric models help policy makers: theory and practice', *De Economist*, 152(2): 177–95.

Dreher, A. and Schneider, F. (2006) 'Corruption and the shadow economy: an empirical analysis', Working Paper 2006–01, Center for Research in Economics, Management and Arts, Basel.

Dunne, T., Roberts, M.J. and Samuelson, L. (1988) 'Patterns of firm entry and exit in US manufacturing industries', *RAND Journal of Economics*, 19(4): 495–515.

Easterly, W. (2002) *The Elusive Quest for Growth: Economists Adventures and Misadventures in the Tropics*, Cambridge, Mass.: MIT Press.

Easterly, W. and Rebelo, S. (1993) 'Fiscal policy and economic growth', *Journal of Monetary Economics,* 32 (December): 417–58.

—— (1994) 'Fiscal policy and economic growth: an empirical investigation', NBER Working Paper 4499, National Bureau of Economic Research, Inc.

Ebrill, L., Keen, M., Bodin, J. and Summers, V. (eds) (2001) *The Modern VAT*, Washington, DC: International Monetary Fund.

Economic Commission for Africa (2005) 'The ESPD–ECA macroeconomic forecasting framework', Technical Report, Economic and Social Policy Division, Economic Commission for Africa.

EdM (2004) *Mozambique Electricity Master Plan Study*, Maputo: Electricidade de Moçambique (Norconsult/SwedPower).

Elbehri, A. and Pearson, K. (2000) 'Implementing bilateral tariff rate quotas in GTAP using GEMPACK', Global Trade Analysis Project, Technical Paper 18, Center for Global Trade Analysis, Department of Agricultural Economics, Purdue University.

Emran, M.S. and Stiglitz, J.E. (2005) 'On selective indirect tax reform in developing countries,' *Journal of Public Economics*, 89: 599–623.

Engle, R.F., Hendry, D.F. and Richard, J.-F. (1983) 'Exogeneity', *Econometrica*, 51 (2): 277–304.

Enterplan (2004) 'Mozambique: evaluation of multi-donor tax reforms', November 2004, Department for International Development.

Ernst and Young (2004) 'A reforma da tributação das pequenas actividades empresariais em Moçambique', Technical Report, Ernst and Young, Mozambique.

Evans, D.S. (1987) 'The relationship between firm growth, size, and age: estimates for 100 manufacturing industries', *Journal of Industrial Economics*, 35(4): 567–81.

Feenstra, R.C. (1989) 'Symmetric pass-through of tariffs and exchange rates under imperfect competition: an empirical test,' *Journal of International Economics*, 27(1/2): 25–45.

FIAS (2006) 'Study on the impact of taxes, customs, licenses and other fees on the investment climate: Mozambique', Foreign Investment Advisory Service, International Finance Corporation and World Bank. Online. Available at http://www.tipmoz. com/page.php?lang = ENG&cat1 = 107&cat2 = 207&cat3 = 499 (accessed 12 May 2008).

Fisman, R. and Wei, S.J. (2004) 'Tax rates and tax evasion: evidence from "missing imports" in China', *Journal of Political Economy*, 112(2): 471–96.

Fjeldstad, O. and Rakner, L. (2003) 'Taxation and tax reforms in developing countries: illustrations from sub-Saharan Africa', *Chr. Michelsen Institute Report R 2003:6*, Chr. Mikkelsen Institute, Bergen, Norway. Online. Available at http://www. cmi.no/publications/publication/?1551=taxation-and-tax-reforms-in-developing-cou ntries (accessed 12 May 2008).

Fourie, F. and Owen, A. (1993) 'Value-added tax and regressivity in South Africa', *South African Journal of Economics*, 61(4): 282–319.

Frankel, J.A. (2002) 'Promoting better national institutions: the role of the IMF', Panel Discussion Remarks, Third Annual Research Conference, November 7–8, International Monetary Fund.

Frankel, J.A., Parsley, D. and Wei, S. (2005) 'Slow pass-through around the world: a new import for developing countries?', NBER Working Paper 11199, National Bureau of Economic Research, Inc.

Gatti, R. (1999) 'Corruption and trade tariffs, or a case for uniform tariffs', Policy Research Working Paper 2216, World Bank.

Gauthier, B. and Gersowitz, M. (1997) 'Revenue erosion through exemption and evasion in Cameroon, 1993', *Journal of Public Economics*, 64: 407–24.

Gauthier, B. and Reinikka, R. (2001) 'Shifting tax burdens through exemptions and evasion: an empirical investigation of Uganda', Policy Research Working Paper 2735, World Bank.

—— (2006) 'Shifting tax burdens through exemptions and evasion: an empirical investigation of Uganda', *Journal of African Economies*, 15: 373–98.

Gemmell, N. (2004) 'Fiscal policy in a growth framework', in T. Addison and A. Roe (eds) *Fiscal Policy for Development: Poverty, Reconstruction and Growth*, New York: Palgrave Macmillan.

Gemmell, N. and Morrissey, O. (2003) 'Tax structure and the incidence on the poor in developing countries', CREDIT Research Paper 03/18, Centre for Research in Economic Development and International Trade (CREDIT), School of Economics, University of Nottingham.

Gerson, P.R. (1998) 'The impact of fiscal policy variables on output growth', IMF Working Paper 98/1, International Monetary Fund.

Geweke, J., Horowitz, J. and Pesaran, M.H. (2006) 'Econometrics: a bird's eye view', CESiof Working Paper 1870, Center for Economic Studies and Ifo Institute for Economic Research, Munich, Germany. Online. Available at http://econpapers. repec.org/scripts/redir.pl?u = http%3A%2F%2Fwww.cesifo.de%2F%2FDocCIDL% 2Fcesifo1_wp1870.pdf;h = repec:ces:ceswps:_1870 (accessed 14 May 2008).

Ghosh, A.R. and Wolf, H.C. (1994) 'Pricing in international markets: lessons from the economist', NBER Working Paper 4806, National Bureau of Economic Research, Inc.

Ghura, D. (1998) 'Tax revenue in sub-Saharan Africa: effects of economic policies and corruption', IMF Working Paper 98/135, International Monetary Fund.

Go, D., Kearney, M., Robinson, S. and Thierfelder, K. (2005) 'An analysis of South Africa's value added tax', Policy Research Working Paper 3671, World Bank.

Goldberg, P. and Hellerstein, R. (2006) 'A framework for identifying the sources of local-currency price stability with an empirical application', 2006 Meeting Paper 625, Society for Economic Dynamics.

Goldberg, P. and Knetter, M. (1997) 'Goods prices and exchange rates: what have we learned?', *Journal of Economic Literature*, 35: 1243–92.

Golosov, M. and King, J. (2002) 'Tax revenue forecasts in IMF supported programmes', Working Paper 02/236, Fiscal Affairs Department, International Monetary Fund.

GoM (1978a) Lei 2/78 (Código do Imposto de Reconstrução Nacional), *Boletim da República*, No. 20 Série I, 16 February.

—— (1978b) Decreto No. 4/78 (Código dos Impostos sobre o Rendimento), *Boletim da República*, No. 27, Série I, 4 March.

—— (1978c) Lei 3/78 (Código do Imposto de Circulação), *Boletim da República*, No. 27, Série I, 4 March.

—— (1982) Lei 6/82 (Reformulação do Código do Imposto sobre a Reconstrucção Nacional), *Boletim da República*, 23 June.

—— (1987a) Lei 3/87 (Reformulação da Política Fiscal), *Boletim da República*, No. 16, Série I, 20 January.

—— (1987b) Decreto 1/87 (Código do Imposto de Circulação), *Boletim da República*, No. 4, Série I, 30 January.

—— (1993) Decreto 14/93 (Regulamento da Lei de Investimento), *Boletim da República*, 21 July, altered by Decreto 36/95, 8 August 1993, in *Legislação Fiscal*, Moçambique, 1st edn, 2005.

—— (1995) Decreto 36/95 (Revisão do Regulamento da Lei de Investimento), *Boletim da República*, 8 August.

—— (1998a) Lei 3/98 (Introdução do Imposto sobre o Valor Acrescentado e o Imposto sobre Consumos Específicos no Sistema Tributário Nacional), *Boletim da República*, No. 1, Série I, 8 January.

—— (1998b) Decreto 51/98 (Código do Imposto sobre o Valor Acrescentado), *Boletim da República*, No. 38, Série I, 29 September.

—— (1999) Decreto 62/99 (Regulamento das Zonas Francas), *Boletim da República*, 21 Setembro de 1999. Online. Available at http://www.cpi.co.mz/e107_files/downloads/regulifz.pdf (accessed 25 June 2008).

—— (2000) Decreto no 27/2000, *Boletim da República*, No. 40, Série I: 176, 10 October.

—— (2001) Plano de Acção para a Redução da Pobreza Absoluta 2001–5 (PARPA). Technical report, Maputo, Mozambique.

—— (2002a) Lei 15/2002 (Introdução dos Novos Impostos sobre o Rendimento), *Boletim da República*, No. 26, Série I, 26 June, and Decreto 20/2002 (Código do Imposto sobre o Rendimento das Pessoas Singulares (IRPS)), Decreto 21/2002 (Código do Imposto sobre o Rendimento das Pessoas Colectivas), *Boletim da República*, No. 30, Série I, 30 July 2003.

—— (2002b) Decreto 16/2002 (Código dos Benifícios Fiscais), *Boletim da República*, 27 June.

—— (2003a) Diploma Ministerial 99/2003 (Regulamento do Regime Aduaneiro para a Indústria Transformadora), *Boletim da República*, No. 33, Série I, 13 August.

—— (2003b) Decreto 52/2003 (Regulemento do Número Único de Indentificação Tributária (NUIT)), *Boletim da República*, No. 52, Série I, 24 December.

—— (2004) Decreto no 55/2004, *Boletim da República*, No. 48, Série I: 528, 10 December.

—— (2005a) Plano de Acção para a Redução da Pobreza Absoluta 2006–9 (PARPA II) (Poverty Reduction Action Plan 2006–9), Versão Preliminar.

—— (2005b) Programa Quinquenal do Governo Para 2005–9 (Government Five-year programme for 2005–9).

—— (2006) Plano de Acção para a Redução da Pobreza Absoluta 2006–9 (PARPA II), Technical Report, Maputo, Mozambique.

Gordon, R. and Li, W. (2005) 'Puzzling tax structures in developing countries: a comparison of two alternative explanations', NBER Working Paper 11661, National Bureau of Economic Research, Inc.

Greene, W.H. (2003) *Econometric Analysis*, 5th edn, Upper Saddle River, NJ: Prentice-Hall, Inc.

Grinblatt, M. and Titman, S. (1998) *Financial Markets and Corporate Strategy*, Singapore: Irwin/McGraw-Hill.

Grobbelaar, N. (2004) 'Every continent needs an America: the experience of South African firms doing business in Mozambique', Business in Africa Research Project, South African Institute of International Affairs.

GTAP (2005) 'Elasticity data for version 6.0, Global Trade Analysis Project', Center for Global Trade Analysis, Department of Agricultural Economics, Purdue University. Online. Available at http://www.gtap.org (accessed 29 May 2008).

Hadi, A.S. (1992) 'A new measure of overall potential influence in linear regression,' *Computational Statistics and Data Analysis*, 14: 1–27.

Hansen, B.E. (1992) 'Testing for parameter instability in linear models', *Journal of Policy Modelling*, 12(4): 517–33.

Haskel, J. and Wolf, H. (2001) 'The law of one price – a case study,' *Scandinavian Journal of Economics*, 103(4): 545–58.

Haughton, J., Quan, N.T. and Bao, H.N. (2006) 'Tax incidence in Vietnam', *Asian Economic Journal*, 20(2): 217–39.

Hausman, J.A. (1978) 'Specification tests in econometrics', *Econometrica*, 46(6): 1251–71.

Heady, C. (2001) 'Taxation policy in low-income countries', Discussion Paper 2001/81, World Institute for Development Economics Research (WIDER).

Hellerstein, R. (2004) 'Who bears the cost of a change in the exchange rate? The case of imported beer', Staff Reports 179 (February), Federal Reserve Bank of New York.

Heltberg, R., Simler, K and Tarp, F. (2001) 'Public spending and poverty in Mozambique', Discussion Paper 2001/63, World Institute for Development Economics Research (WIDER).

Hendry, D.F. and Clements, M.P. (2001) 'Economic forecasting: some lessons from recent research', Working Paper 78, Department of Economics, Oxford University.

Hendry, D.F. and Ericsson, N.R. (2001) *Understanding Economic Forecasts*, Cambridge, Mass.: MIT Press.

Hodges, A. and Souto, M. (2003) 'Study on the organizational structure and human resources of the DNPO', Technical Report, National Directorate of Planning and Budget (DNPO), Ministry of Planning and Finance, Mozambique.

Holden, K. and Peel, D. (1990) 'On testing for unbiasedness and efficiency of forecasts', *Manchester School of Economic and Social Studies*, 58: 120–7.

Hors, I. (2001) 'Fighting corruption in customs administration: what can we learn from recent experiences?', OECD Development Centre Working Paper 175, Organisation for Economic Co-operation and Development.

Houerou, P.L. and Taliercio, R. (2002) 'Medium term expenditure frameworks: from concept to practice – preliminary lessons from Africa', World Bank Africa Region Working Paper Series, 28.

Hsieh, C.-T. and Parker, J. (2006) 'Taxes and growth in a financially underdeveloped country: evidence from the Chilean investment boom', NBER Working Paper 12104, National Bureau of Economic Research, Inc.

Hubbard, M., Delay, S. and Devas, N. (1999) 'Complex management contracts: the case of customs administration in Mozambique', *Public Administration and Development*, 19: 153–63.

Hyndman, R.J. and Koehler, A.B. (2005) 'Another look at measures of forecast accuracy', Monash Econometrics and Business Statistics Working Paper 13/05, Monash University, Department of Econometrics and Business Statistics.

IAF (2002–3) 'Inquérito aos Agregados Familiares Sobre Orçamento Familiar', Household Survey, Instituto Nacional de Estatística, Maputo, Mozambique. Online. Available at http://surveynetwork.org/home/?lvl1 = activities&lvl2 = catalog&lvl3 = surveys&ihsn = 508-2002-002 (accessed 12 May 2008).

Ianchovichina, E. (2005) 'Duty drawbacks, competitiveness, and growth: are duty drawbacks worth the hazzle?', Policy Research Working Paper 3498, World Bank.

IEA (2006) *Energy Prices and Taxes*, Paris: International Energy Agency.

IFC (2003) *Mozambique Industrial Performance and Investment Climate 2003*, Pilot Investment Climate Assessment, International Finance Corporation, World Bank.

IMF (2001a) 'Republic of Mozambique: selected issues and statistical appendices', IMF Country Report, 01/25, International Monetary Fund.

—— (2001b) *Code of Good Practices on Fiscal Transparency*, International Monetary Fund. Online. Available at http://www.imf.org/external/np/fad/trans/code.htm#code (accessed 12 May 2008).

—— (2004a) 'Ex post assessment of Mozambique's performance under fund-supported programmes', IMF Country Report, 04/53, International Monetary Fund.

—— (2004b) 'Policy formulation, analytical frameworks, and program design', Technical Report, Policy Development and Review Department, International Monetary Fund.

—— (2004c) 'Republic of Mozambique: financial system stability assessment', IMF Country Report, 04/52, International Monetary Fund.

—— (2005a) 'Reaping the full benefits of tax reform in Mozambique', *IMF Survey*, 34(19): 308–9, International Monetary Fund.

—— (2005b) 'Republic of Mozambique: selected issues and statistical appendix', IMF Country Report, 05/311, International Monetary Fund.

—— (2006) 'Republic of Mozambique: third review under the three-year arrangement under the Poverty Reduction and Growth Facility and request for modification of performance criteria', IMF Country Report, 06/46, International Monetary Fund.

INE (2004) *CEMPRE: Censo das Empresas*, National Enterprise Census Data, Instituto Nacional de Estatísticas, Mozambique.

Jensen, H.T. and Tarp, F. (2002) 'CGE modelling and trade policy: reassessing the agricultural bias', *Journal of Agricultural Economics*, 53(2): 383–405.

Johnson, S., Kauffman, D., McMillan, J. and Woodruff, C. (2000) 'Why do firms hide? Bribes and unofficial activity after communism', *Journal of Public Economics*, 76: 495–520.

Jones, S. (2006) 'Growth accounting for Mozambique: 1980–2004', DNEAP Discussion Paper 22E, National Directorate of Economic Studies and Policy Analysis, Ministry of Planning and Development, Mozambique.

Kaplow, L. (2006) 'Taxation', NBER Working Paper 12061, National Bureau of Economic Research, Inc.

Keen, M. and Ligthart, J. (2001) 'Coordinating tariff reform and tax reductions', *Journal of International Economics*, 56: 407–25.

Khan, M., Montiel, P. and Haque, N.U. (1990) 'Adjustment with growth: relating the analytical approaches of the IMF and the World Bank', *Journal of Development Economics*, 32: 155–79.

Khandelwal, P. (2004) 'COMESA and SADC: prospects and challenges for regional trade integration', IMF Working Paper 04/227, International Monetary Fund.

King, M. (1974) 'Taxation and the cost of capital', *Review of Economic Studies*, 41 (1): 21–35.

Kirk, R. and Stern, M. (2005) 'The New Southern African Customs Union Agreement', *The World Economy*, 28(2): 169–90.

KPMG (2004) *100 Maiores Empresas de Moçambique – Top 100 Companies in Mozambique*, 2004 edn, Maputo: Imagem Global.

—— (2005) *100 Maiores Empresas de Moçambique – Top 100 Companies in Mozambique*, 2005 edn, Maputo: Imagem Global.

—— (2006a) *100 Maiores Empresas de Moçambique – Top 100 Companies in Mozambique*, 2006 edn, Maputo: Imagem Global.

—— (2006b) 'Corporate tax rate survey: an international analysis of corporate tax rates from 1993 to 2006'. Online. Available at http://www.kpmg.com/NR/exeres/EC5931FC-261B-4D7D-80DF-9E5C49C6F2F8.htm (accessed 9 May 2008).

Krueger, A.O. (1974) 'The political economy of the rent-seeking society', *American Economic Review*, 64(3): 291–303.

Krugman, P.R. (1986) 'Pricing to market when the exchange rate changes', NBER Working Paper 1926, National Bureau of Economic Research, Inc.

Löfgren, H., Harris, R.L. and Robinson, S. with the assistance of M. El-Said and M. Thomas (2002) *Microcomputers in Policy Research, 5: A Standard Computable General Equilibrium (CGE) Model in GAMS*, Washington, DC: IFPRI.

Lopes, P.S. and Sacerdoti, E. (1991) 'Mozambique: economic rehabilitation and the poor', IMF Working Paper 91/101, International Monetary Fund.

Macamo, J.L. (1998) 'Estimates of unrecorded cross-border trade between Mozambique and her neighbors: implications for food security', World Vision International, Mozambique.

—— (2002) 'Barrieras administrativas ao investimento em Moçambique: lições aprendidas da experiencia de investidores recentes', in C. Rolim, A.S. Francisco, B. Bolnick and P.-Å. Anderson (eds), *A Economia Moçambicana Contemporanea: Ensaios*, Maputo: Gabinete de Estudos, Ministry of Planning and Finance.

McCarten, W. 'Large taxpayer units and the VAT,' paper presented at the conference 'The Challenges of Tax Reform in a Global Economy', Georgia State University, May 2004. Online. Available at http://isp-aysps.gsu.edu/academics/conferences/conf2004/McCarten.pdf (accessed 22 July 2008).

MacKellar, L., Woergoetter, A. and Woerz, J. (2000) 'Economic development problems of landlocked countries', Transition Economics Series, 14, Institute for Advanced Studies.

McKenzie, K. and Thompson, A. (1996) 'The economic effects of dividend taxation', Working Paper 96–97, prepared for the Technical Committee on Business Taxation, Department of Finance, Ottawa, Government of Canada.

McLaren, J. (1996) 'Corruption, black markets, and the fiscal problem in LDCS: some recent findings', *Eastern Economic Journal*, 22: 491–503.

—— (1998) 'Black markets and optimal evadable taxation', *Economic Journal*, 108 (448): 665–79.

McMillan, M.S., Welch, K.H. and Rodrik, D. (2003) 'When economic reform goes wrong: cashews in Mozambique', Brookings Trade Forum, The Brookings Institution. Online. Available at http://muse.jhu.edu/journals/brookings_trade_forum/v2003/2003.1mcmillan.html#tab03 (accessed 14 May 2008).

McPherson, M.A. (1996) 'Growth of micro and small enterprises in Southern Africa', *Journal of Development Economics*, 48: 253–77.

Makanza, M. and Munyaradzi, R. (2004) 'Impact evaluation on implementation of the WTO valuation agreement for Mozambique', Technical Report, submitted to Regional Centre for Southern Africa, USAID.

Milner, C., Morrissey, O. and McKay, A. (2005) 'Some simple analytics of the trade and welfare effects of Economic Partnership Agreements', *Journal of African Economies*, 14(3): 327–58.

Ministry of Agriculture and Rural Development (2002) 'Trabalho de Inquérito Agrícola: Valor de produção de culturas alimentares em pequenas, médias e grandes explorações por província', Maputo, Mozambique.

Ministry of Energy (2007a) *Estatística de Energia 2000–2005*, Maputo: Ministério da Energia.

—— (2007b) *Estatística de Energia 2006*, Maputo: Ministério da Energia.

Moss, T., Pettersson, G. and van de Walle, N. (2006) 'An aid-institutions paradox? A review essay on aid dependency and state building in sub-Saharan Africa', Working Paper No. 74, Centre for Global Development.

Mozal (2006) *Annual Report 2006*, Maputo: Mozal.

MPD (2005) 'Quadro-Macroeconomico', Macro-economic Framework, National Directorate of Budget and Planning, Ministry of Planning and Development (formerly part of Ministry of Planning and Finance).

MPF (2002) Pauta aduaneira Dec. no 39/2002, Ministry of Planning and Finance, Maputo, Mozambique. Import taxes available online at http://www.alfandegas.gov. mz/pauta_ad.htm (accessed 29 May 2008).

—— (2004) Data from Direcção Nacional de Impostos e Auditoria (DNIA) and Direcção Geral das Alfandegas (DGA), including customs exemptions and government payment of customs duties, Ministry of Planning and Finance, Maputo, Mozambique.

MPF, IFPRI and Purdue University (2005) 'Poverty and well-being in Mozambique: the second National Assessment (2002–3)', Technical Report, National Directorate of Planning and Budget, Ministry of Planning and Finance, Mozambique, Economic Research Bureau, IFPRI and Purdue University.

Muñoz, S. and Cho, S.S.-W. (2003) 'Social impact of a tax reform: the case of Ethiopia', IMF Working Paper 03/232, International Monetary Fund.

Musgrave, R.A. (1969) *Fiscal Systems*, New Haven, CT: Yale University Press.

Nathan Associates (2004) 'Tax reform and the business environment in Mozambique: a review of private sector reforms', Technical Report, Nathan Associates.

NER (2004) *National Integrated Resource Plan 2, South Africa*, Pretoria: National Electricity Regulator.

Nordhaus, W.D. (1987) 'Forecasting efficiency: concepts and applications', *Review of Economics and Statistics*, 69(4): 667–74.

Obstfeld, M. and Taylor, A.M. (1997) 'Non-linear aspects of goods-market arbitrage and adjustment: Heckscher's commodity points revisited', *Journal of the Japanese and International Economies*, 11(4): 441–79.

OECD (2005) 'Trade facilitation reforms in the service of development', Trade Policy Working Paper 12, OECD Trade Committee, Organisation for Economic Co-operation and Development.

Ogley, A. (2006) 'Study to develop draft guidelines for the application and treatment of tax incentives and a tax expenditure budgeting template in SADC', unpublished study, PMTC International Limited.

Oyugi, L.N. (2005) 'The budget process and economic governance in Kenya', NEPRU Working Paper 98, Namibian Economic Policy Research Unit.

Panagariya, A. (2000) 'Preferential trade liberalization: the traditional theory and new developments,' *Journal of Economic Literature* 38: 287–331.

Phillips, S. and Musso, A. (2002) 'Comparing projections and outcomes of IMF-supported programs', IMF Working Paper 01/45, International Monetary Fund.

Pike, T. and Savage, D. (1998) 'Forecasting the public finances in the Treasury', *Fiscal Studies*, 19(1): 49–62.

Pitt, M.M. (1981) 'Smuggling and price disparity', *Journal of International Economics*, 11: 447–58.

Polak, J.J. (1997) 'The IMF Monetary Model at forty', IMF Working Paper 97/49, International Monetary Fund.

Pollard, P.S. and Coughlin, C.C. (2004) 'Size matters: asymmetric exchange rate pass-through at the industry level', University of Nottingham Research Paper 2004/13, University of Nottingham.

Poterba, J. and Summers, L. (1985) 'The economic effects of dividend taxation', NBER Working Paper 1353, National Bureau of Economic Research, Inc.

Pritchett, L. and Sethi, G. (1994) 'Tariff rates, tariff revenue, and tariff reform: some new facts', *World Bank Economic Review*, 8(1): 1–16.

Rajemison, H., Haggblade, S. and Younger, S.D. (2003) *Indirect Tax Incidence in Madagascar: Updated Estimates Using the Input–Output Table*, Cornell University Food and Nutrition Policy Program. Online. Available at http://www.ilo.cornell.edu/images/wp147.pdf (accessed 29 May 2008).

Reinhart, C. (1995) 'Devaluation, relative prices, and international trade', *IMF Staff Papers*, 42(2): 290–312.

Robinson, S. and Thierfelder, K. (1999) *Note on Taxes, Prices, Wages, and Welfare in General Equilibrium Models*, Trade and Macroeconomics Discussion Paper 39, International Food Policy Research Institute, Washington, DC, USA.

Rodrik, D., Subramanian, A. and Trebbi, F. (2004) 'Institutions rule: the primacy of institutions over geography and integration in economic development', *Journal of Economic Growth*, 9(2): 131–65.

Roodman, D. (2004) 'ABAR: stata module to perform Arellano–Bond test for autocorrelation', Statistical Software Components, Boston College Department of Economics.

Rossi-Hansberg, E. and Wright, M.L.J. (2004) 'Firm size dynamics in the aggregate economy', NBER Working Paper 11261, National Bureau of Economic Research, Inc.

Royston, P. and Altman, D.G. (1997) 'Approximating statistical functions by using fractional polynomial regression', *Journal of the Royal Statistical Society: Series D* (The Statistician), 46(3): 411–22.

Rutherford, T.F. (1995) 'Extension of GAMS for complementarity problems arising in applied economic analysis', *Journal of Economic Dynamics and Control*, 19(8): 1299–324.

SADC (2002) *Memorandum of Understanding on Co-operation in Taxation and Related Matters*, Southern African Development Community. Online. Available at http://www.sadc.int/key_documents/memoranda/taxation.php (accessed 14 May 2008).

Sahn, D.E. and Younger, S.D. (2003) 'Estimating the incidence of indirect taxes', in F. Bourguignon and L.A.P. da Silva (eds) *The Impact of Economic Policies on Poverty and Income Distributions*, New York: World Bank and Oxford University Press.

Salanié, B. (2003) *The Economics of Taxation*, Cambrige, MA, and London: MIT Press.

Sandmo, A. (2004) 'The theory of tax evasion: a retrospective view', Discussion Paper 31/04, Norwegian School of Economics and Business Administration, Oslo, Norway.

SAPP (2005) *SAPP Statistics 2005*, Harare, Zimbabwe: South African Power Pool.

Savana Noticias (2005) Pesquisa sobre Governação e Corrupção divulgada, 5 August.

Schiavo-Campo, S. and Tommasi, D. (1999) 'Managing government expenditure', Asian Development Bank, Manila, Philippines.

Schuh, S. (2001) 'An evaluation of recent macroeconomic forecast errors', *New England Economic Review*, 1: 35–56.

Shah, S.M. and Toye, J. (1978) 'Fiscal incentives for firms in some developing countries: survey and critique', in J. Toye (ed.) *Taxation and Economic Development*, London: Fran Cass.

Siegel, S. (1956) *Non-parametric Statistics for the Behavioural Sciences*, New York: McGraw-Hill.

Skinner, J. (1987) 'Taxation and output growth: evidence from African countries', NBER Working Paper 2335, National Bureau of Economic Research, Inc.

Slemrod, J. (1991) 'Optimal taxation and optimal tax systems', NBER Working Paper 3038, National Bureau of Economic Research, Inc.

Slemrod, J. and Yitzhaki, S. (2000) 'Tax avoidance, evasion and administration', NBER Working Paper 7473, National Bureau of Economic Research, Inc.

Smulders, S. and Vollebergh, H.R.J. (2001) 'Green taxes and administrative costs: the case of carbon taxation', in C. Carraro and G. Metcalf (eds) *Distributional and Behavioral Effects of Environmental Policy*, Chicago, IL: Chicago University Press.

Soludo, C.C. (2002) 'Macroeconomic modelling and economic policy making: a survey of experience in Africa', Research Paper 201, African Economic Research Consortium.

Stern, R., Francis, J. and Schumacher, B. (1976) *Price Elasticities in International Trade: An Annotated Bibliography*, London: Macmillan.

Stotsky, J.G. and WoldeMariam, A. (1997) 'Tax effort in sub-Saharan Africa', IMF Working Paper 97/107, International Monetary Fund.

Sulemane, J. (2001) GDP Deflators 1975–92 in 'Economic decline: a case study of Mozambique', PhD thesis, Notre Dame University, USA.

Tanzi, V. (2004) 'Fiscal policy: when theory collides with reality', paper presented at the Congress of the International Institute of Public Finance, Bocconi University, Milan, 25 August.

Tanzi, V. and Zee, H.H. (2000) 'Tax policy for emerging markets: developing countries', IMF Working Paper 00/35, International Monetary Fund.

Tarp, F. (1993) *Stabilization and Structural Adjustment: Macroeconomic Frameworks for Analysing the Crisis in Sub-Saharan Africa*, London: Routledge.

Tarp, F., Arndt, C., Jensen, H.T., Robinson, S. and Heltberg, R. (2002) *Facing the Development Challenge in Mozambique: An Economy-wide Perspective*, Research Report 126, International Food Policy Research Institute, Washington, DC.

Teera, J.M. and Hudson, J. (2004) 'Tax performance: a comparative study', *Journal of International Development*, 16(6): 785–802.

Timmermann, A. (2006) 'An evaluation of the World Economic Outlook forecasts', IMF Working Paper 06/59, International Monetary Fund.

Tirole, J. (1986) 'Hierarchies and bureaucracies: on the role of collusion in organizations', *Journal of Law, Economics and Organization*, 2: 181–214.

Tsikata, Y.M. (1999) 'Southern Africa: trade, liberalization, and implications for a free trade area', Trade and Industrial Policy Secretariat (TIPS) Annual Forum, Muldersdrif, South Africa, September.

Turnovsky, S.J. (1996) 'Optimal tax, debt, and expenditure policies in a growing economy', *Journal of Public Economics*, 60: 21–44.

UNDP (2004) *Human Development Report 2004: Cultural Liberty in Today's Diverse World*, Human Development Indicators, New York: United Nations Development Programme.

—— (2006) *Human Development Report 2006: Beyond Scarcity: Power, Poverty and the Global Water Crisis*, United Nations Development Programme, New York: Palgrave Macmillan.

Van Dunem, J. (2005a) 'Research for the tax project in Mozambique: preliminary findings in the analysis of customs tax revenue, 2002–4', mimeo, Maputo, Mozambique.

—— (2005b) 'A few preliminary findings in the analysis of Customs Tax Revenue (2002–4)', unpublished document, Tax Incidence Project, Ministry of Planning and Development, Mozambique.

Van Dunem, J. and Arndt, C. (2005) 'Confronting the issue of the elasticity of customs evasion in Mozambique: an empirical study', paper presented at GTAP Conference on Global Economic Analysis, Addis Ababa, Ethiopia, June.

Varian, H.R. (1992) *Microeconomic Analysis*, 3rd edn, New York: W.W. Norton and Company, Inc.

Varsano, R., de Oliveira, M.O., Villela, R. and Yackovlev, I. (2006) 'Mozambique: post-reform evaluation of the tax system', unpublished report, Fiscal Affairs Department, International Monetary Fund.

Verbeek, J. (1999) 'The World Bank's Unified Survey projections: how accurate are they? An ex-post evaluation of US91–US97', Policy Research Working Paper 2071, World Bank.

Vuchelen, J. and Gutierrez, M.-I. (2005) 'Do the OECD 24 month horizon growth forecasts for the G7-countries contain information?', *Applied Economics*, 37(8): 855–62.

Winters, L.A. (2004) 'Trade liberalisation and economic performance: an overview', *Economic Journal*, 114 (February): F4–F21.

Winters, L.A. and Hertel, T. (eds) (2005) *Poverty and the WTO: Impacts of the Doha Development Agenda*, New York and Washington, DC: Palgrave Macmillan and World Bank.

Wooldridge, J.M. (2003) *Econometric Analysis of Cross Section and Panel Data*, Cambridge, MA: MIT Press.

World Bank (1988) *Opportunities and Risks in Managing the World Economy: Public Finance in Development*, World Development Report 1988, World Bank.

—— (1995) 'Mozambique: impediments to industrial sector recovery', Report 13752-MZ, Macro, Industry and Finance Division, Southern Africa Department, World Bank.

—— (2003) 'Mozambique industrial performance and investment climate 2003', World Bank. Online. Available at http://siteresources.worldbank.org/EXTAFRSU MAFTPS/Resources/ICA006.pdf (accessed 29 May 2008).

—— (2005a) *World Development Indicators 2005*, CD-ROM, International Bank for Reconstruction and Development and World Bank.

—— (2005b) 'Mozambique country economic memorandum: sustaining growth and reducing poverty', Report 32615-MZ, World Bank.

—— (2006a) *Doing Business in 2006: Sub-Saharan Africa Region*. Online. Available at http://www.doingbusiness.org/documents/2006-Sub_Saharan.pdf (accessed 14 May 2008).

—— (2006b) *Where is the Wealth of Nations? Measuring Capital for the XXI Century*, International Bank for Reconstruction and Development and World Bank.

—— (2006c) *World Development Indicators 2006*, CD-ROM, International Bank for Reconstruction and Development and World Bank.

—— (2007) *Doing Business 2008: Mozambique*, data, World Bank. Online. Available at www.doingbusiness.org/Documents/CountryProfiles/MOZ.pdf (accessed 14 May 2008).

WTO (2003) 'SACU Trade Policy Review 2003', World Trade Organization. Online. Available at http://www.wto.org/english/tratop_e/tpr_e/tp213_e.htm (accessed 14 May 2008).

Yager, T.R. (2005) *The Mineral Industry in Mozambique*, US Geological Survey Minerals Yearbook 2004, US Geological Survey.

Ylönen, A. (2005) 'Institutions and instability in Africa: Nigeria, Sudan, and reflections from Mises's nation, state and economy', *New Perspectives on Political Economy*, 1(1): 38–60.

Younger, S.D., Sahn, D.E., Haggblade, S. and Dorosh, P.A. (1999) 'Tax incidence in Madagascar: an analysis using household data', *World Bank Economic Review*, 13 (2): 303–31.

Zee, H.H., Stotsky, J.G. and Ley, E. (2002) 'Tax incentives for business investment: a primer for policy makers in developing countries', *World Development*, 30(9): 1497–516.

Zellner, A. (1962) 'An efficient method of estimating seemingly unrelated regression equations and tests for aggregation bias', *Journal of the American Statistical Association*, 57: 348–68.

Zellner, A., Keuzenkamp, H.A. and McAleer, M. (eds) (2001) *Simplicity, Inference and Modelling: Keeping It Sophisticatedly Simple*, Cambridge: Cambridge University Press.

Index

For Product Safety Concerns and Information please contact our EU
representative GPSR@taylorandfrancis.com
Taylor & Francis Verlag GmbH, Kaufingerstraße 24, 80331 München, Germany

www.ingramcontent.com/pod-product-compliance
Lightning Source LLC
Chambersburg PA
CBHW070715280326
41926CB00087B/2135

9 780415 746526